# UNDERSTANDING PUBLIC POLICY

# UNDERSTANDING PUBLIC POLICY

## fourth edition

**THOMAS R. DYE**

*Florida State University*

PRENTICE-HALL, INC., ENGLEWOOD CLIFFS, N.J. 07632

*Library of Congress Cataloging in Publication Data*

Dye, Thomas **R**
    Understanding public policy.

    Includes bibliographies and index.
    1. United States—Social policy. 2. United States
—Social conditions—1960–  1. Title.
HN65.D9  1981      361.6'1'0973      80-36883
ISBN 0-13-936260-6

361.61
D995
1981

Printed in the United States of America

10  9  8  7  6  5  4  3  2  1

Editorial/production supervision and interior design by Marina Harrison
Cover design by Judith A. Matz
Manufacturing buyer: Edmund W. Leone

PRENTICE-HALL INTERNATIONAL, INC., *London*
PRENTICE-HALL OF AUSTRALIA PTY. LIMITED, *Sydney*
PRENTICE-HALL OF CANADA, LTD., *Toronto*
PRENTICE-HALL OF INDIA PRIVATE LIMITED, *New Delhi*
PRENTICE-HALL OF JAPAN, INC., *Tokyo*
PRENTICE-HALL OF SOUTHEAST ASIA PTE. LTD., *Singapore*
WHITEHALL BOOKS LIMITED, *Wellington, New Zealand*

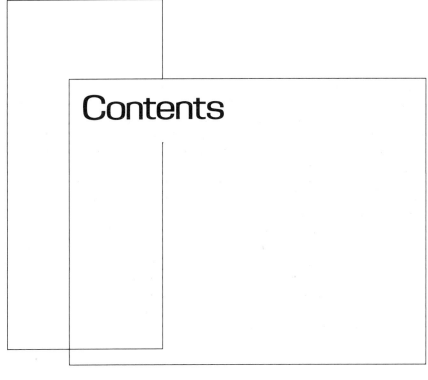

# Contents

# 12 DEFENSE POLICY

# 13 INPUTS, OUTPUTS, AND BLACK BOXES

# 14 THE POLICY-MAKING PROCESS

# 15 POLICY EVALUATION

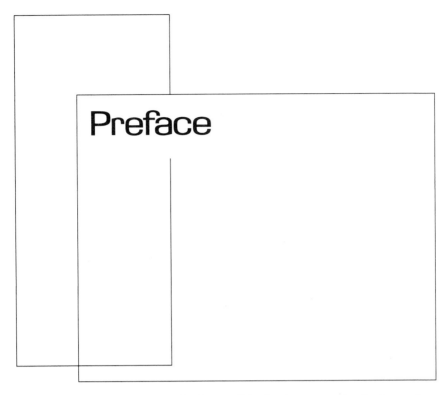

# Preface

If this book has a thesis, it is that political science can be "relevant" to public policy questions without abandoning its commitment to scientific inquiry; that social relevance does not require us to reject systematic analysis in favor of rhetoric, polemics, or activism.

This volume is concerned with "who gets what" in American politics and, more important, "why" and "what difference it makes." We are concerned not only with *what* policies governments pursue but also *why* governments pursue the policies they do, and *what* the consequences of these policies are.

Political science, like other scientific disciplines, has developed a number of concepts and models to help describe and explain political life. These models are not really competitive in the sense that any one could be judged "best." Each focuses on separate elements of politics and each helps us to understand different things about political life.

We begin with a brief description of eight analytic models in political science and the potential contribution of each of them to the study of public policy. They are:

an institutional model     a rational model
a process model            an incremental model

a group model              a game theory model
an elite model             a systems model

We then attempt to describe and explain public policy by the use of these various analytic models. Readers are not only informed about public policy in a variety of key domestic policy areas but, more important, they are encouraged to utilize these conceptual models in political science to explain the causes and consequences of public policies in these areas. The policy areas studied are:

civil rights                          urban affairs and housing
crime, violence, and repression       government spending
welfare and social security           taxation
health                                national defense
education                             state and local spending and services
energy and the environment

Most public policies are a combination of rational planning, incrementalism, competition among groups, elite preferences, systematic forces, political processes, and institutional influences. Throughout this volume we employ these models, both singly and in combination, to describe and explain public policy. However, certain chapters rely more on one model than another.

Any of these policy areas might be studied by employing more than one model. Frequently our selection of a particular analytic model to study a specific policy area was based as much upon pedagogical considerations as anything else. We simply wanted to demonstrate how political scientists employ analytical models. Once readers are familiarized with the nature and uses of analytic models in political science, they may find it interesting to explore the utility of models other than the ones selected by the author in the explanation of particular policy outcomes. For example, we use an elitist model to discuss civil rights policy, but the reader may wish to view civil rights policy from the perspective of group theory. We employ the language of game theory to discuss national defense policy, but the reader might enjoy reinterpreting defense policy in a systems model.

Each chapter concludes with a series of propositions, which are derived from one or more analytic models, and which attempt to summarize the policies discussed. The purposes of these summaries are to suggest the kinds of policy explanations that can be derived from analytic models and to tie the policy material back to one or another of our models.

In short, this volume is not only an introduction to the study of public policy, but also an introduction to the models political scientists use to describe and explain political life.

THOMAS R. DYE
*Florida State University*

A demonstration against reinstituting the draft. *Wide World Photos*.

# Policy Analysis

## the thinking man's response to demands for relevance

1

### Policy Analysis in Political Science

This book is about public policy. It is concerned with what governments do, why they do it, and what difference it makes. It is also about
political science and the ability of this academic discipline to describe,
analyze, and explain public policy.

Public policy is whatever governments choose to do or not to do.[1]

---

DEFINING PUBLIC POLICY:
PLAYING WORD GAMES

This book discourages elaborate academic discussions of the definition of
public policy—we say simply that public policy is whatever governments
choose to do or not to do. Books, essays, and discussions of a "proper"
definition of public policy have proven futile, even exasperating, and they
often divert attention from the study of public policy itself. Moreover, even
the most elaborate definitions of public policy, upon close examination, seem
to boil down to the same thing. For example, political scientist David Easton
defines public policy as "the authoritative allocation of values for the whole

---

[1]See insert, "Defining Public Policy: Playing Word Games."

1

society"—but it turns out that only the government can "authoritatively" act on the "whole" society, and everything the government chooses to do or not to do results in the "allocation of values."

Political scientist Harold Lasswell and philosopher Abraham Kaplan define policy as "a projected program of goals, values, and practices," and political scientist Carl Friedrick says, "It is essential for the policy concept that there be a goal, objective, or purpose." These definitions imply a difference between specific governmental actions and an overall program of action toward a given goal. The problem, however, in insisting that government actions must have *goals* in order to be labled "policy" is that we can never be sure whether or not a particular action has a goal, or if it does, what that goal is. We generally assume that if a government chooses to do something there must be a goal, objective, or purpose, but all we can really observe is what governments choose to do or not to do. Realistically, our notion of public policy must include *all* actions of government and not just stated intentions of governments or government officials.

Still another approach to defining public policy is to break down this general notion into various component parts. Political scientist Charles O. Jones asks that we consider the distinction among various proposals (specified means for achieving goals); programs (authorized means for achieving goals); decisions (specific actions taken to implement programs); and effects (the measurable impacts of programs). But again we have the problem of *assuming* that decisions, programs, goals, and effects are linked. Certainly in many policy areas—welfare and energy, for example—we will see that the decisions of government have little to do with announced "programs," and neither are connected with national "goals." It may be unfortunate that our government does not function neatly to link goals, programs, decisions, and effects, but as a matter of fact, it does not.

Political scientist Heinz Eulau and Kenneth Prewitt supply still another definition of public policy: "Policy is defined as a 'standing decision' characterized by behavioral consistency and repetitiveness on the part of both those who make it and those who abide by it." Now certainly it would be a wonderful thing if government activities were characterized by "consistency and repetitiveness"; but it is doubtful that we would ever find "public policy" in government if we insist on these criteria. Much of what government does is inconsistent and nonrepetitive.

Another ingenious approach is simply to define public policy as whatever the "analyst" identifies as public policy. According to political scientist Hugh Heclo: "A policy may usefully be considered as a course of action or inaction rather than specific decisions or actions, and such a course has to be perceived and identified by the analyst in question." In other words, if you think you know what government is really trying to do, then you can define that as public policy. Of course, the problem here is that what one "analyst" may perceive as public policy, another "analyst" may not. Moreover, it is doubtful that such a definition is really useful—at the extreme, it simply says "public policy is what I say it is."

So we shall stick by our simple definition: *public policy is whatever governments choose to do or not to do.* Note that we are focusing not only on government action, but also on government inaction, that is, what government chooses *not* to do. We contend that government *in*action can have just as great an impact on society as government action.

See David Easton, *The Political System* (New York: Knopf, 1953), p. 129; Harold D. Lasswell and Abraham Kaplan, *Power and Society* (New Haven: Yale University Press, 1970), p. 71; Carl J. Friedrich, *Man and His Government* (New York: McGraw-Hill, 1963), p. 70; Charles O. Jones, *An Introduction to the Study of Public Policy* (Boston: Duxbury, 1977); p. 4; Heinz Eulau and Kenneth Prewitt, *Labyrinths of Democracy* (Indianapolis: Bobbs-Merrill, 1973), p. 465; and Hugh Heclo, "Policy Analysis," *British Journal of Political Science*, 2 (January 1972), 85.

Governments do many things. They regulate conflict within society; they organize society to carry on conflict with other societies; they distribute a great variety of symbolic rewards and material services to members of the society; and they extract money from society, most often in the form of taxes. Thus, public policies may regulate behavior, organize bureaucracies, distribute benefits, or extract taxes—or all these things at once.

Public policy directly allocates about 35 percent of the Gross National Product, the sum of all of the goods and services produced in the nation each year. Government spending—the combined expenditures of *all* 18,000 federal, state, and local governments—comprises 35 percent of the GNP, and government employment comprises 16 percent of the nation's workforce.

Public policies may deal with a wide variety of substantive areas—defense, energy, environment, foreign affairs, education, welfare, police, highways, taxation, housing, social security, health, economic opportunity, urban development, inflation and recession, and so on. They may range from the vital to the trivial—from the allocation of tens of billions of dollars for a mobile missile system to the designation of an official national bird.

Public policy is not a new concern of political science: the earliest writings of political philosophers reveal an interest in the policies pursued by governments, the forces shaping these policies, and the impact of these policies on society. Yet the major focus of attention of political science has never really been on policies themselves, but rather on the institutions and structures of government and on the political behaviors and processes associated with policy making.

*"Traditional"* political science focused its attention primarily on the institutional structure and philosophical justification of government. This involved the study of constitutional arrangements, such as federalism, separation of power, and judicial review; powers and du-

ties of official bodies, such as Congress, president, and courts; intergovernmental relations; and the organization and operation of legislative, executive, and judicial agencies. Traditional studies described the *institutions* in which public policy was formulated. But unfortunately the linkages between important institutional arrangements and the content of public policy were largely unexplored.

Modern *"behavioral"* political science focused its attention primarily on the processes and behaviors associated with government. This involved the study of the sociological and psychological bases of individual and group behavior; the determinants of voting and other political activities; the functioning of interest groups and political parties; and the description of various processes and behaviors in the legislative, executive, and judicial arenas. Although this approach described the *processes* by which public policy was determined, it did not deal directly with the linkages between various processes and behaviors and the content of public policy.

Today many political scientists are shifting their focus to *public policy*—to the *description and explanation of the causes and consequences of government activity*. This may involve a description of the content of public policy; an analysis of the impact of social, economic, and political forces on the content of public policy; an inquiry of the effect of various institutional arrangements and political processes on public policy; and an evaluation of the consequences of public policies on society, in terms of both expected and unexpected consequences. For example: What is the impact of war and depression on the growth of government activity? What are the real priorities among defense and domestic policy needs, and what forces affect the determination of priorities? Can aggression be deterred by threat of nuclear retaliation? Do arms limitations agreements make the world a safer or more dangerous place to live? What is the best mix of conventional and nuclear weapons in America's defense strategy? What forces operate to maintain the status quo in government's programs and policies, and what forces operate to induce change? What is the impact of racial and religious group activity on the allocation of public monies to schools and colleges? Can the criminal justice system be constructed to deter crime? Does greater party competition and increased voter participation bring about more liberal policies in welfare, health, or education? Will a guaranteed minimum income for all American families reduce or increase joblessness and social dependency? Can black students in ghetto schools receive a quality education through improvements in their neighborhood schools, or must they be bused out of the ghetto environment for an equal educational opportunity? Who gains and who loses from the present distribution of tax burdens and "tax loopholes"? Do environmental protection laws increase our dependence on foreign sources of energy? Does it make any differences in the content of public policy whether Democrats or Republicans win control of government? These are the *kinds* of questions that are dealt with in policy analysis.

## Why Study Public Policy?

Traditionally, Americans have assumed that once they *passed a law, created a department,* and *spent money,* the purposes of the law, the department, and the expenditure would be achieved. They assumed that when Congress adopted a policy and appropriated money for it, and when the Executive Branch organized a program, hired people, spent money, and carried out the activities designed to implement the policy, the effects of the policy would be felt by society and the effects would be those intended by the policy. Traditionally, Americans have been optimistic about what public policy can achieve: they believed that governments could eliminate poverty, end racism, insure peace, prevent crime, restore cities, clean the air and water, and so on, if only they would adopt the right policies. But now there is a growing uneasiness among policy makers and scholars about the effectiveness of governments. The national experiences with the Vietnam War, the poverty programs, public housing, public assistance, the energy shortage, and many other public programs indicate the need for a careful appraisal of the real impact of public policy. We have learned from these experiences that America's problems cannot always be resolved by passing a law, creating a new bureaucracy, and throwing a few billion dollars in the general direction of the problem in the hope that it will go away. The result has been an awakening of interest in policy studies over the last decade.[2]

Why should political scientists devote greater attention to the study of public policy? First of all, public policy can be studied for purely *scientific reasons:* understanding the causes and consequences of policy decisions improves our knowledge about society. Public policy can be viewed as a *dependent variable,* and we can ask what socioeconomic forces and political system characteristics operate to shape the content of policy. Or public policy can be viewed as an *independent var-*

[2]See the "Policy Analysis Explosion" Symposium in *Society,* Vol. 16 (September 1979).

*iable,* and we can ask what impact public policy has on society and its political system. By asking such questions we can improve our understanding of the linkages between socioeconomic forces, political processes, and public policy. An understanding of these linkages contributes to the breadth, significance, reliability, and theoretical development of social science.

Public policy can also be studied for *professional reasons:* understanding the causes and consequences of public policy permits us to apply social science knowledge to the solution of practical problems. Factual knowledge is a prerequisite to prescribing for the ills of society. If certain ends are desired, then the question of what policies would best implement these ends is a factual question requiring scientific study. In other words, policy studies can produce professional advice, in terms of "if . . . then . . ." statements, about how to achieve desired goals.

Finally, public policy can be studied for *political purposes:* to insure that the nation adopts the "right" policies to achieve the "right" goals. It is frequently argued that political science cannot be silent or impotent in the face of great social and political crises, and that political scientists have a moral obligation to advance specific public policies. An exclusive focus on institutions, processes, or behaviors is frequently looked upon as "dry," "irrelevant," and "amoral," because it does not direct attention to the really important policy questions facing American society. Policy studies can be undertaken not only for scientific and professional purposes but also to inform political discussion, advance the level of political awareness, and improve the quality of public policy. Of course, these are very subjective purposes—Americans do not always agree on what constitutes the "right" policies or the "right" goals—but we will assume that knowledge is preferable to ignorance, even in politics.

## Policy Analysis and Policy Advocacy

Whether one chooses to study public policy for scientific, professional, or political reasons, it is important to distinguish *policy analysis* from *policy advocacy. Explaining* the causes and consequences of various policies is not equivalent to prescribing what policies governments *ought* to pursue. Learning *why* governments do what they do and what the consequences of their actions are is not the same as saying what governments *ought* to do, or bringing about changes in what they do. Policy advocacy requires the skills of rhetoric, persuasion, organization, and activism. Policy analysis encourages scholars and students to attack critical policy issues with the tools of systematic inquiry. There is an implied assumption in policy analysis that developing scientific knowledge about the forces shaping public policy and the consequences of public policy is itself a socially relevant activity, and that such analysis is a prerequisite to prescription, advocacy, and activism. In short, policy analysis might be labeled the "thinking man's response" to demands that social science become more "relevant" to the problems of society.

Specifically, *public analysis* involves:

1. *A primary concern with explanation rather than prescription.* Policy recommendations—if they are made at all—are subordinate to description and explanation. There is an implicit judgment that understanding is a prerequisite to prescription, and that understanding is best achieved through careful analysis rather than rhetoric or polemics.

2. *A rigorous search for the causes and consequences of public policies.* This search involves the use of scientific standards of inference. Sophisticated quantitative techniques may be helpful in establishing valid inferences about causes and consequences, but they are not really essential.

3. *An effort to develop and test general propositions about the causes and consequences of public policy and to accumulate reliable research findings of general relevance.* The object is to develop general theories about public policy that are reliable and that apply to different governmental agencies and different policy areas. Policy analysts clearly prefer to develop explanations that fit more than one policy decision or case study—explanations that stand up over time in a variety of settings.

Policy analysis contrasts with many of the currently popular approaches to policy questions—rhetoric, dialogue, confrontation, or direct action. Policy analysis offers the serious student an approach to society's problems that is both scientific and relevant. The insistence on explanation as a prerequisite to prescription, the use of scientific standards of inference, and the search for reliability and generality of knowledge can hardly be judged "irrelevant" when these ideas are applied to important policy questions.

## Policy Analysis in Action—Social Scientists and the "Busing" Issue

One of the more interesting examples of policy analysis in recent years is the social science research on equal educational opportunity and how to achieve it. The first influential report on American education was James S. Coleman's *Equality of Educational Opportunity,* frequently referred to as the "Coleman Report."[3] The Coleman Report dealt primarily with the *consequences* of educational policy—specifically, the impact of schools on the aspiration and achievement levels of pupils. Although Coleman's study was not without its critics,[4] it was nonetheless the most comprehensive analysis of the American public school system ever made. The Coleman Report included data on 600,000 children, 60,000 teachers, and 4,000 schools. This report, and the reaction to it, can help us to understand both the problems and possibilities of systematic policy analysis.

The results of Coleman's study undermined much of the conventional wisdom about the impact of public educational policies on student learning and achievement. Prior to the study, legislators, teachers, school administrators, school board members, and the general public assumed that factors such as the number of pupils in the classroom, the amount of money spent on each pupil, library and laboratory facilities, teachers' salaries, the quality of the curriculum, and other characteristics of the school affected the quality of education and educational opportunity. But systematic analysis revealed that these factors had *no* significant effect on student learning or achievement. "Differences in school facilities and curriculum . . . are so little related to differences in achievement levels of students that, with few exceptions, their effects fail to appear even in a survey of this magnitude." Moreover, learning was found to be unaffected by the presence or absence of a "track system," ability grouping, guidance counseling, or other standard educational programs. Even the size of the class was found to be unrelated to learning, although educators had asserted the importance of this factor for decades. Finally, the Coleman study reported that the quality of teaching was not a very significant factor in student achievement compared to family and peer-group influences. In short, the things that "everybody knew" about education turned out not to be so!

The only factors that were found to affect a student's learning to any significant degree were (1) family background, and (2) the family background of classmates. Family background affected the child's ver-

---

[3]James S. Coleman, *Equality of Educational Opportunity* (Washington, D.C.: Government Printing Office, 1966).

[4]For reviews of the Coleman Report, see Robert A. Dentler, "Equality of Educational Opportunity: A Special Review," *The Urban Review* (December 1966); Christopher Jenks, "Education: The Racial Gap," *The New Republic* (October 1, 1966); James K. Kent, "The Coleman Report: Opening Pandora's Box," *Phi Delta Kappan* (January 1968); James S. Coleman, "Educational Dilemmas: Equal Schools or Equal Students," *The Public Interest* (Summer 1966); James S. Coleman, "Toward Open Schools," *The Public Interest* (Fall 1967); and a special issue devoted to educational opportunity of *Harvard Educational Review*, vol. 38 (Winter 1968).

bal abilities and attitudes toward education, and these factors correlated very closely with scholastic achievement. Of secondary but considerable significance were the verbal abilities and attitudes toward education of the child's classmates. Peer-group influence had its greatest impact on children from lower-class families. Teaching excellence mattered very little to children from upper- and middle-class backgrounds; they learned well despite mediocre or poor teaching. Children from lower-class families were slightly more affected by teacher quality.

Coleman also found that schools serving black pupils in this nation were *not* physically inferior to schools serving predominantly white student bodies. In the South, in fact, black schools were somewhat newer than white schools. Black teachers had about the same education and teaching experiences as white teachers, and their pay was equal. Black teachers, however, scored lower than white teachers on verbal tests, and their morale was reported to be lower than that of white teachers.

Reanalyzing Coleman's data for the U.S. Civil Rights Commission, Thomas F. Pettigrew and others found that black students attending predominantly black schools had lower achievement scores and lower levels of aspiration than black students *with comparable family backgrounds* who attended predominantly white schools.[5] When black students attending predominantly white schools were compared with black students attending predominantly black schools, the average difference in levels of achievement amounted to more than *two grade levels*. On the other hand, achievement levels of white students in classes nearly half black in composition were *not* any lower than those of white students in all-white schools. Finally, special programs to raise achievement levels in predominantly black schools were found to have no lasting effect.

The Coleman Report made no policy recommendations. But, like a great deal of policy research, policy recommendations can easily be inferred from its conclusions. First of all, if the Coleman Report is correct, it seems pointless to simply pour more money into the present system of public education—raising per pupil expenditures, increasing teachers' salaries, lowering the number of pupils per classroom, providing better libraries and laboratories, adding educational frills, or adopting any specific curricula innovations. These policies were found to have no significant impact on learning.

The findings of the Coleman Report are particularly important

---

[5]U.S. Commission on Civil Rights, *Racial Isolation in the Public Schools*, 2 vols. (Washington, D.C.: Government Printing Office, 1967).

for Title I of the Elementary and Secondary Education Act (see Chapter 7). This piece of Congressional legislation authorizes large amounts of federal assistance each year for "poverty impacted" schools. The purpose of this program is to remedy learning problems of disadvantaged children by increasing spending for special remedial programs. But the Coleman Report implies that compensatory programs have little educational value. They may have symbolic value for ghetto residents, or political value for officeholders who seek to establish an image of concern for the underprivileged, but they are of little educational value for children.

The U.S. Commission on Civil Rights used the Coleman Report to buttress its policy proposals to end racial imbalance in public schools in both the North and the South. Inasmuch as money, facilities, and compensatory programs have little effect on student learning, and inasmuch as the socioeconomic background of the student's *classmates* does affect his learning, it seemed reasonable to argue that the assignment of lower-class black students to predominantly middle-class white schools would be the only way to improve educational opportunities for ghetto children. Moreover, because the findings indicated that the achievement levels of middle-class white students were unaffected by blacks in the classroom (as long as blacks were less than a majority), the Commission concluded that assigning ghetto blacks to predominantly white schools would not adversely affect the learning of white pupils. Hence, the Commission called for an end to neighborhood schools and for the *busing* of black and white children to racially balanced schools.

The reaction of professional educators was largely one of silence. Perhaps they hoped the Coleman Report would disappear into history without significantly affecting the longstanding assumptions about the importance of money, facilities, classroom size, teacher training, and curricula. Perhaps they hoped that subsequent research would refute Coleman's findings. Daniel Moynihan writes:

> The whole rationale of American public education came very near to crashing down, and would have done so had there not been a seemingly general agreement to act as if the report had not occurred. But it had, and public education will not now be the same. The relations between resource input and educational output, which all school systems, all legislatures, all executives have accepted as given, appear not to be given at all. At very least what has heretofore been taken for granted must henceforth be proved. Without in any way purporting to tell mothers, school teachers, school board superintendents what *will* change educational outcomes, social science has raised profoundly important questions as to what does not.[6]

[6]Daniel P. Moynihan, *Maximum Feasible Misunderstanding* (New York: Free Press, 1969), p. 195.

The reactions of black leaders were mixed.[7] Some blacks were strongly offended by the Report and its implications for public policy. The findings regarding compensatory education efforts were said to deal a "death blow to all black children" in the ghetto. They reasoned that integrated education is a physical impossibility in many big-city school systems with few white pupils, and it is a political impossibility in many other cities. Hence, to discredit compensatory education is to threaten the only hope for improvement in ghetto education. A more emotional reaction was the attack on the Report as "racist" because it implied that ghetto black children could only learn by contact with middle-class white children. One commentator exclaimed: "I don't subscribe to the view that a black kid must sit next to a white kid to learn. The report is based on the myth of white supremacy."

Since its publication, the Coleman Report has been frequently cited by proponents of busing—those urging deliberate government action to achieve racial balance in public schools. Courts and school officials in northern and southern cities have cited the Coleman Report as evidence that racial imbalance denies equality of educational opportunity to black children, and as evidence that deliberate racial balancing in the schools, or busing, is required to achieve equal protection of laws guaranteed by the Fourteenth Amendment.

But in 1972, Harvard sociologist David Armor shocked the academic world with a careful review of the available evidence of the effect of busing on the achievement levels of black students.[8] His conclusions: black students bused out of their neighborhoods to predominantly white schools do not improve their performance relative to white students, even after three or four years of integrated education. His interpretation of the impact of busing on the achievement levels of black students indicated that black students were not being helped "in any significant way" by busing, and her urged consideration of the question of whether psychological harm was being done to black students by placing them in a situation where the achievement gap was so great. Note that Armor was not contradicting the Coleman Report. Coleman was observing black children who were attending predominantly white schools not as a result of deliberate government action, but rather within the previously existing pattern of "neighborhood schools." In contrast, Armor was observing black children who had been deliberately reassigned to integrated schools by government action.

The policy implications of Armor's work appear to support op-

[7]See Kent, "The Coleman Report: Opening Pandora's Box," 244–45.
[8]David J. Armor, "The Evidence on Busing," *The Public Interest,* no. 28 (Summer 1972), 90–126.

ponents of government-mandated racial balancing. Other social scientists have disputed Armor's review of the relevant research findings, including Thomas F. Pettigrew who originally used the Coleman data in support of busing.[9] They contend that Armor's work undermines progress toward an integrated society and reinforces racism. But Armor replies that social science findings cannot be used only when they fit the political beliefs of social scientists, and ignored when their policy implications are painful.[10]

Coleman himself reentered the fray in 1975 with the publication of a new report *Trends in School Desegregation.*[11] This "Second Coleman Report" appeared to counter earlier implications about busing as a means to achieve equality of educational opportunity. In examining changes in segregation over time in twenty-two large cities and forty-six medium-sized cities, Coleman found that an increase in desegregation was associated with a loss of white pupils—"white flight." This white response to desegregation was greatest in large cities with large proportions of black school pupils, which were surrounded by predominately white, independent, suburban school districts. The long-run effect of white-pupil loss in these cities was predicted to offset government efforts to desegregate public schools and contribute to *greater* rather than less racial isolation. As Coleman explained:

> There are numerous examples of government policy in which the result of the interaction between policy and response is precisely the opposite of the result intended by those who initiated the policy. It is especially important in the case of school desegregation to examine this interaction, because many of the actions taken by

---

[9]Thomas F. Pettigrew et al., "Busing: A Review of 'The Evidence,' " *The Public Interest,* no. 31 (Spring 1973), 88–113.

[10]David J. Armor, "The Double Double Standard," *The Public Interest,* no. 31 (Spring 1973), 119–31. Still another reaction to the Coleman Report is found in the work of Harvard educator Christopher Jenks, *Inequality: A Reassessment of the Effect of Family and Schooling in America* (New York: Basic Books, 1972). Jenks reanalyzed Coleman's data and conducted additional research on the impact of schooling on economic success. He found that school quality has little effect on an individual's subsequent success in earning income. He concluded, therefore, that no amount of educational reform would ever bring about economic equality. Jenks assumed that *absolute equality* of income is the goal of society, not merely *equality of opportunity* to achieve economic success. Because the schools cannot insure that everyone ends up with the same income, Jenks concludes that nothing short of a radical redistribution of income (steeply progressive taxes and laws preventing individuals from earning more than others) will bring about true equality in America. Attempts to improve the educational system, therefore, are a waste of time and effort. Thus, the Coleman findings have been used to buttress *radical* arguments about the ineffectiveness of *liberal* reforms.

[11]James S. Coleman et al., *Trends in School Desegregation 1968–1973* (Washington, D.C.: Urban Institute, 1975).

individuals, and some of those taken by their local government bodies, have precisely the opposite effect to that intended by the federal government. The most obvious such individual action, of course, is a move of residences to flee school integration.[12]

The point of this brief discussion is that policy analysis sometimes produces unexpected and even embarrassing findings, that public policies do not always "work" as intended, and that different political interests will interpret the findings of policy research differently—accepting, rejecting, or using these findings as they fit their own purposes.

## Policy Analysis and the Quest for "Solutions" to America's Problems

It is questionable that policy analysis can ever provide "solutions" to America's problems. War, ignorance, crime, poor health, poverty, racial cleavage, inequality, poor housing, pollution, congestion, and unhappy lives have afflicted men and societies for a long time. Of course, this is no excuse for failing to work toward a society free of these maladies. But our striving for a better society should be tempered with the realization that "solutions" to these problems may be very difficult to find. There are many reasons for tempering our enthusiasm for policy analysis, some of which are illustrated in the battle over the Coleman Report.

First of all, it is easy to exaggerate the importance, both for good and for ill, of the policies of governments. It is not clear that government policies, however ingenious, could cure all or even most of society's ills. Governments are constrained by many powerful environmental forces—wealth, technology, population growth, patterns of family life, class structure, child-rearing practices, religious beliefs, and so on. These forces are not easily managed by governments, nor could they be controlled even if it seemed desirable to do so. In the final chapter of this volume we will examine policy impacts, but it is safe to say here that some of society's problems are very intractable. For example, it may be that the *only* way to insure equality of opportunity is to remove children from disadvantaged family backgrounds at a very early age, perhaps before they are six months old. The weight of social science evidence suggests that the potential for achievement may be determined at a very young age. However, a policy of removing children

[12]Ibid., p. 2.

from their family environment at such an early age runs contrary to our deepest feelings about family attachments. The forcible removal of children from their mothers is "unthinkable" as a governmental policy. So it may turn out that we never really provide equality of opportunity because cultural forces prevent us from pursuing an effective policy.

Second, policy analysis cannot offer "solutions" to problems when there isn't general agreement on what the problems are. The Coleman Report assumed that raising achievement levels (measures of verbal and quantitative abilities) and raising aspiration levels (the desire to achieve by society's standards) were the "problems" to which our efforts should be directed. But others have contended that such achievement and aspiration levels are really middle- or upper-class white norms, and that the education of black ghetto children should be adapted toward totally different goals. Some have argued that the educational system should *not* be organized to facilitate the entry of children into middle-class society; instead they have urged that the policies of ghetto schools be to prepare children for life in the ghetto. In other words, there is no real agreement on what societal values should be implemented in educational policy. Policy analysis is not capable of resolving value conflicts. At best it can advise on how to achieve a certain set of end values; it cannot determine what those end values should be.

Third, policy analysis deals with very "subjective" topics and must rely upon "interpretation" of results. Professional researchers frequently interpret the results of their analyses differently. Social science research cannot be "value-free." Even the selection of the topic for research is affected by one's values about what is "important" in society and worthy of attention. As Louis Wirth explained,

> The distinctive character of social science discourse is to be sought in the fact that every assertion, no matter how objective it may be, has ramifications extending beyond the limits of science itself. Since every assertion of a "fact" and the social world touches the interests of some individual or group, one cannot even call attention to the existence of certain "facts" without courting the objections of those whose very raison d'être in society rests upon a divergent interpretation of the "factual" situation.[13]

Another set of problems in systematic policy analysis centers around inherent limitations in the design of social science research. It is not really possible to conduct some forms of controlled experiments on human beings. For example, the researchers cannot order middle-

---

[13]Louis Wirth, Preface to Karl Mannheim, *Ideology and Utopia: An Introduction to the Sociology of Knowledge* (New York: Harcourt Brace Jovanovich, 1936).

class white children to go to ghetto schools for several years just to see if it had an adverse impact on their achievement levels. Instead, social researchers must find situations in which educational deprivation has been produced "naturally" in order to make the necessary observations about the causes of such deprivation. Because we cannot control all the factors that go into a real-world situation, it is difficult to pinpoint precisely what it is that causes educational achievement or nonachievement. Moreover, even where some experimentation is permitted, human beings frequently modify their behavior simply because they know they are being observed in an experimental situation. For example, in educational research it frequently turns out that children perform well under *any* new teaching method or curricula innovation. It is difficult to know whether the improvements observed are a product of the new teaching method or curricula improvement or merely a product of the experimental situation. Finally, it should be noted that the people doing policy research are frequently program administrators who are interested in proving the positive "results" of their programs. It is important to separate research from policy implementation, but this is a difficult thing to do.

Perhaps the most serious reservation about policy analysis is the fact that social problems are so complex that social scientists are unable to make accurate predictions about the impact of proposed policies. *Social scientists simply do not know enough about individual and group behavior to be able to give reliable advice to policy makers.* Occasionally policy makers turn to social scientists for "solutions," but social scientists do not have any "solutions." Most of society's problems are shaped by so many variables that a simple explanation of them, or remedy for them, is rarely possible. A detailed understanding of such a complex system as human society is beyond our present capabilities. The fact that social scientists give so many contradictory recommendations is an indication of the absence of reliable scientific knowledge about social problems. Although some scholars argue that no advice is better than contradictory or inaccurate advice, policy makers still must make decisions, and it is probably better that they act in the light of whatever little knowledge social science can provide than that they act in the absence of any knowledge at all. Even if social scientists cannot predict the impact of future policies, they can at least attempt to measure the impact of current and past public policies and make this knowledge available to decision makers.

Understanding public policy is both an "art" and a "craft." It is an art because it requires insight, creativity, and imagination in identifying societal problems and describing them, in devising public policies which might alleviate them, and then, in finding out whether these policies end up making things better or worse. It is a craft because these tasks usually require some knowledge of economics, political science, public administration, sociology, law, and statistics. Policy analysis is really an applied subfield of all these traditional academic disciplines.

It is sometimes argued that a single "model of choice" can be applied to all kinds of problems—large and small, public and private.[14] (The "model of choice" is similar to the "rational model" described in Chapter 2 of this book.) But we doubt that there is any "model of choice" in policy analysis—that is, a single model or method which is preferable to all others and which consistently renders the best solutions to public problems.

Instead, we are in agreement with political scientist Aaron Wildavsky, who wrote:

> Policy analysis is one activity for which there can be no fixed program, for policy analysis is synonymous with creativity, which may be stimulated by theory and sharpened by practice, which can be learned but not taught.[15]

Wildavsky goes on to warn students that "solutions" to great public questions are not to be expected.

> In large part, it must be admitted, knowledge is negative. It tells us what we cannot do, where we cannot go, wherein we have been wrong, but not necessarily how to correct these errors. After all, if current efforts were judged wholly satisfactory, there would be little need for analysis and less analysts.[16]

There is no one model of choice to be found in this book, but if anyone wants to begin a debate about different ways of understanding public policy, this book is a good place to begin.

## Bibliography

DROR, YEHEZKEL, *Public Policy-Making Re-examined.* San Francisco: Chandler, 1968.

LERNER, DANIEL, and LASSWELL, HAROLD D. (eds.), *The Policy Sciences.* Stanford: Stanford University Press, 1960.

RANNEY, AUSTIN (ed.) *Political Science and Public Policy.* Chicago: Markham, 1968.

[14]See Edith Stokey and Richard Zeckhauser, *A Primer for Policy Analysis* (New York: Norton, 1978), p. 1, 23.
[15]Aaron Wildavsky *Speaking Truth To Power* (New York: Wiley, 1979), p. 3.
[16]Ibid, p. 401.

STOKEY, EDITH, and ZECKHAUSER, RICHARD, *A Primer for Policy Analysis.* New York: Norton, 1978.

SHARKANSKY, IRA (ed.) *Policy Analysis in Political Science.* Chicago: Markham, 1970.

WILDAVSKY, AARON, *Speaking Truth To Power.* New York: Wiley, 1979.

Models of politics: symbols of America. *Irene Springer*.

# Models of Politics

## some help in thinking about public policy

# 2

## Models For Policy Analysis

A model is a simplified representation of some aspect of the real world. It may be an actual physical representation—a model airplane, for example, or the table-top buildings that urban planners use to show how things will look when proposed projects are completed. Or a model may be a diagram—a road map, for example, or a flow chart that political scientists use to show how "a bill becomes a law."

The models we shall use in studying public policy are *conceptual models*. These are word models which try to

1. simplify and clarify our thinking about politics and public policy;

2. identify important aspects of policy problems;

3. help us to communicate with each other by focusing on essential features of political life;

4. direct our efforts to better understand public policy by suggesting what is important and what is unimportant; and

5. suggest explanations for public policy and predict its consequences.

Over the years, political science, like other scientific disciplines, has developed a number of models to help us understand political life. Throughout this volume we will try to see whether these models have any utility in the study of public policy. Specifically we want to examine public policy from the perspective of the following models:

institutional model
process model
group model
elite model
rational model
incremental model
theory model
systems model

Each of these terms identifies a major conceptual model which can be found in the literature of political science. None of these models was derived especially to study public policy, yet each offers a separate way of thinking about policy and even suggests some of the general causes and consequences of public policy.

These models are not competitive in the sense that any one of them could be judged "best." Each one provides a separate focus on political life, and each can help to understand different things about public policy. Although some policies appear at first glance to lend themselves to explanation by one particular model, most policies are a combination of rational planning, incrementalism, interest group activity, elite preferences, systemic forces, game-playing, political processes, and institutional influences. In later chapters these models will be employed, singularly and in combination, to describe and explain specific policies. Following is a brief description of each model, with particular attention to the separate ways in which public policy can be viewed.

## Institutionalism: Policy As Institutional Output

Governmental structures and institutions have long been a central focus of political science. Traditionally, political science has been defined as the study of governmental institutions. Political activities generally center around particular government institutions—Congress, the presidency, courts, states, municipalities, political parties, etc. Public policy is authoritatively determined, implemented, and enforced by governmental institutions.

The relationship between public policy and governmental institutions is very close. Strictly speaking, a policy does not become a *public* policy until it is adopted, implemented, and enforced by some governmental institution. Governmental institutions give public policy three distinctive characteristics. First of all, government lends *legitimacy* to

policies. Governmental policies are generally regarded as legal obligations which command the loyalty of citizens. People may regard the
policies of other groups and associations in society—corporations,
churches, professional organizations, civic associations, etc.—as important and even binding. But only government policies involve legal obligations. Second, government policies involve *universality*. Only government policies extend to all people in a society; the policies of other
groups or organizations only reach a part of the society. Finally, government monopolizes *coercion* in society—only government can legiti-
mately imprison violators of its policies. The sanctions that can be imposed by other groups or organizations in society are more limited. It
is precisely this ability of government to command the loyalty of all its
citizens, to enact policies governing the whole society, and to monopo-
lize the legitimate use of force that encourages individuals and groups
to work for enactment of their preferences into policy.

Traditionally, the institutional approach in political science did
*not* devote much attention to the linkages between the structure of governmental institutions and the content of public policy. Instead, institutional studies usually described specific governmental institutions—
their structures, organization, duties, and functions—without systematically inquiring about the impact of institutional characteristics on
policy outputs. Constitutional and legal arrangements were described
in detail, as were the myriad government offices and agencies at the
federal, state, and local level. (See Figure 2.1 for an organizational description of the federal government.) Public policies were sometimes
described, but seldom analyzed. The linkage between structure and
policy remained largely unexamined.

Despite the narrow focus of early institutional studies in political
science, the structural approach is not necessarily an unproductive one.
Governmental institutions are really structured patterns of behavior of
individuals and groups. By "structured" we mean that these patterns
of behavior tend to persist over time. These stable patterns of individual and group behavior may affect the content of public policy. Institutions may be so structured as to facilitate certain policy outcomes and
to obstruct other policy outcomes. They may give advantage to certain
interests in society and withhold advantage from other interests. Certain individuals and groups may enjoy greater access to government
power under one set of structural characteristics than under another
set. In short, the structure of governmental institutions may have important policy consequences.

The institutional approach need not be narrow or descriptive. We
can ask what relationships exist between institutional arrangements
and the content of public policy, and we can investigate these relationships in a comparative, systematic fashion. For example, in the area of

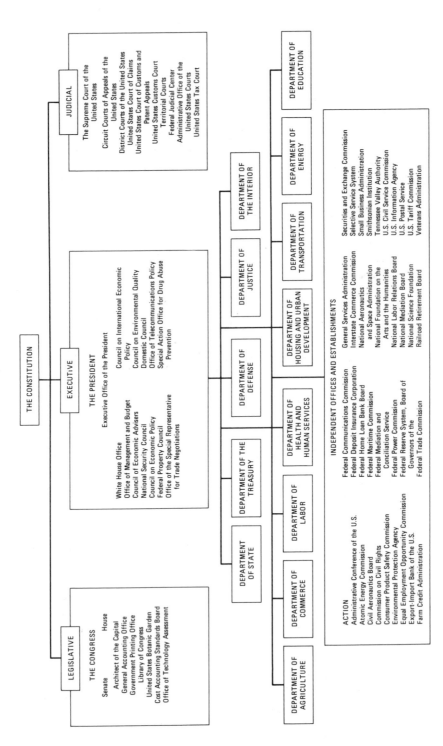

**FIG. 2-1** An institutional model: The organization of the United States Government

*Source: U.S. Government Organizations Manual, 1975–1976, p. 21.*

urban affairs we can ask: Are the policies of federal agencies (Congress, President, Department of Housing and Urban Development, etc.) more responsive to urban problems than are the policies of state or local governments? How does the division of responsibility for urban services among federal, state, and local governments affect the content of urban policy? These policy questions can be dealt with systematically and involve a focus on institutional arrangements.

---

### INSTITUTIONALISM: APPLYING THE MODEL

Governmental institutions and organizations are mentioned throughout this book. But in Chapter 9, "Urban Affairs," particular attention is given to the organizational problems in federal urban policy, and in Chapter 10 "Priorities and Price Tags," we shall examine some of the problems of American federalism—the distribution of money and power between federal, state, and local governments.

---

It is important to remember that the impact of institutional arrangements on public policy is an empirical question that deserves investigation. Too frequently, enthusiastic reformers have asserted that a particular change in institutional structure would bring about changes in public policy without investigating the true relationship between structure and policy; they have fallen into the trap of *assuming* on the basis of a priori logic that institutional changes will bring about policy changes. We must be cautious in our assessment of the impact of structure on policy. We may discover that both structure and policy are largely determined by environmental forces, and that tinkering with institutional arrangements will have little independent impact on public policy if underlying environmental forces—social, economic, and political—remain constant.

## Processes: Policy As Political Activity

Political processes and behaviors have been a central focus of political science for several decades. Modern "behavioral" political science since World War II has studied the activities of voters, interest groups, legislators, presidents, bureaucrats, judges, and other political actors. One of the main purposes has been to discover identifiable patterns of activities—or "processes." Recently some political scientists have tried to group various activities according to their relationship with public policy. The result is a set of *policy processes* which usually follow this general outline:

| Identifying Problems | (Demands for government action) |
| Formulating Policy Proposals | (Initiation and development public program proposals) |
| Legitimating Policies | (Selecting a proposal, building political support for it, and enacting it as law) |
| Implementing Policies | (Organizing bureaucracies, providing payments or services, levying taxes) |
| Evaluating Policies | (Studying programs, evaluating outputs and impacts, suggesting changes and adjustments) |

In short, one can view the policy process as a series of political activities—problem identification, formulation, legitimation, implementation, and evaluation. A popular example of the process approach is shown in Table 2.1

It has been argued that *political scientists* must limit their studies of public policy to these processes, and only these processes. According to political scientist Charles O. Jones:

> I maintain that the special purview of the political scientist is the political process and how it works. His or her interest in the substance of problems and policies, therefore, is in how it interacts with process, not necessarily in the substance itself this also suggests that my remedies for the social system tend to be of the proc-

**TABLE 2–1**  The Policy Process—A Framework for Analysis

| Functional Activities | Categorized in Government | and as Systems | with Output |
|---|---|---|---|
| Perception Definition Aggregation Organization Representation | Problems to Government | Problem Identification | Problem to Demand |
| Formulation Legitimation Appropriation | Action in Government | Program Development | Proposal to Budgeted Program |
| Organization Interpretation Application | Government to Problem | Program Implementation | Varies (Service, payments, facilities, controls, etc.) |
| Specification Measurement Analysis | Program to Government | Program Evaluation | Varies (Justification, recommendation, etc.) |
| Resolution/ Termination | Problem resolution or change | Program Termination | Solution or change |

*Source:* Charles O. Jones, *An Introduction to the Study of Public Policy,* 2nd ed. (Boston: Duxbury, 1977), p. 12.

ess variety—more access for more interest, providing for criticism and opposition, publicizing decisions, and how they are made.[1]

This argument allows the students of political science to study *how* decisions are made, and perhaps even how they *should* be made. But it does not permit students of political science to comment on the substance of public policy—who gets what and why. Books organized around the process theme have sections on identifying problems, formulating proposals, legitimating policies, etc.; but they seldom have sections on abortion, affirmative action, the death penalty, national health insurance, public housing, nuclear energy, SALT II, the tax revolt, etc. It is not the *content* of public policy that is to be studied, but rather the *processes* by which public policy is developed, implemented, and changed.

Despite the narrow focus of the process model, it is still useful in helping us to understand the various activities involved in policy making. We want to keep in mind that *policy making* involves agenda setting (capturing the attention of policy makers); formulating proposals (devising and selecting policy options); legitimating policy (developing political support, winning congressional, presidential, or court approval); implementing policy (creating bureaucracies, spending money, enforcing laws); and evaluating policy (finding out whether policies work, whether they are popular).

Indeed, it may even be the case that the way policies are made affects the content of public policy and vice versa. At least this is a question that deserves attention. For example, it may turn out that the way television networks present the "news" determines what the policy agenda will be; if groups other than television networks could set the agenda of national decision making, different decisions would be made. It may turn out that the way the President formulates energy policy—whether the President tries to balance the views of scores of different groups, from oil producers and utility companies to conservationists and environmentalists, or whether he chooses to develop a single, rational, integrated plan recommended by energy experts—will affect the content of energy policy. It may turn out that the way Congress "legitimizes" a new national military draft may affect whether the nation accepts registration as necessary or clings to the All-Volunteer Army. It may turn out that the way the Department of Education and the Equal Employment Opportunity Commission implement the Civil Rights Acts through "affirmative action" guidelines helps determine the success or failure of blacks and women to advance in education and employment.

[1]Charles O. Jones *An Introduction to the Study of Public Policy* (Boston: Duxbury, 1978), p. 6.

In short, many policies may be directly affected by the process by which they came into being. But again, just as we warned readers in our discussion of the institutional model: we do not want to fall into the trap of *assuming* that a change in the process of policy making will always bring about changes in the content of policy. It may turn out that social, economic, or technological constraints on policy makers are so great that it makes little or no difference in the content of policy whether the process of policy making is open or closed, competitive or noncompetitive, pluralist or elitist, or whatever. Political scientists are fond of discussing "how a bill becomes a law," and even how various interests succeed in winning battles over policy questions. But changing either the formal or informal processes of decision making may or may not change the content of public policy.

We all may prefer to live in a political system where everyone has an equal voice in policy making, where many separate interests put forward solutions to public problems, where discussion, debate, and decision are open and accessible to all, where policy choices are made democratically, where implementation is reasonable, fair, and compassionate. But merely because we prefer such a political system does not necessarily mean that such a system would produce significantly different policies in national defense, energy, urban affairs, education, welfare, health, or criminal justice. The linkages between *process* and *content* must still be investigated.

---

### PROCESSES: APPLYING THE MODEL

Political processes and behaviors are considered in each of the policy areas studied in this book, and most chapters have separate "Evaluation" sections. Additional commentary on the impact of political activity on public policy is found in Chapter 14, "The Policy-Making Process."

---

## Group Theory: Policy As Group Equilibrium

Group theory begins with the proposition that interaction among groups is the central fact of politics.[2] Individuals with common interests band together formally or informally to press their demands upon government. According to political scientist David Truman, an interest group is "a shared-attitude group that makes certain claims upon other groups in the society"; such a group becomes political "if and when it makes a claim through or upon any of the institutions of govern-

---

[2]Group theory is explained at length in David B. Truman, *The Governmental Process* (New York: Knopf, 1951).

ment."[3] Individuals are important in politics only when they act as part of, or on behalf of, group interests. The group becomes the essential bridge between the individual and his government. Politics is really the struggle among groups to influence public policy. The task of the political system is to *manage group conflict* by (1) establishing rules of the game in the group struggle, (2) arranging compromises and balancing interests, (3) enacting compromises in the form of public policy, and (4) enforcing these compromises.

According to group theorists, public policy at any given time is the equilibrium reached in the group struggle (see Figure 2–2). This equilibrium is determined by the relative influence of interest groups. Changes in the relative influence of any interest groups can be expected to result in changes in public policy; policy will move in the direction desired by the groups gaining in influence and away from the desires of groups losing influence. Political scientist Earl Latham described public policy from the group theory viewpoint as follows:

> What may be called public policy is actually the equilibrium reached in the group struggle at any given moment, and it represents a balance which the contending factions or groups constantly strive to tip in their favor. . . .The legislature referees the group struggle, ratifies the victories of the successful coalition, and records the terms of the surrenders, compromises, and conquests in the form of statutes.[4]

The influence of groups is determined by their numbers, wealth, organizational strength, leadership, access to decision makers, and internal cohesion.

Group theory purports to describe all meaningful political activity in terms of the group struggle. Policy makers are viewed as constantly

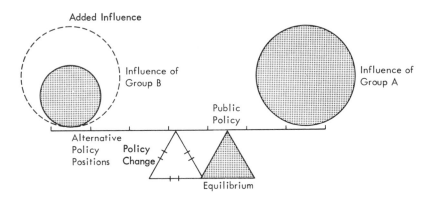

FIG. 2–2  The group model

[3]Ibid., p. 37.

[4]Earl Latham, "The Group Basis of Politics," in Heinz Eulau, Samuel J. Eldersveld, and Morris Janowitz, eds., *Political Behavior* (New York: Free Press, 1956), p. 239.

responding to group pressures—bargaining, negotiating, and compromising among competing demands of influential groups. Politicians attempt to form a majority coalition of groups. In so doing, they have some latitude in determining what groups are to be included in the majority coalition. The larger the constituency of the politician, the greater the number of diverse interests, and the greater his latitude in selecting the groups to form a majority coalition. Thus, congressmen have less flexibility than senators who have larger and generally more diverse constituencies; and the president has more flexibility than congressmen and senators. Executive agencies are also understood in terms of their group constituencies.

Parties are viewed as coalitions of groups. The Democratic party coalition from the Roosevelt era until recently was composed of labor, central-city dwellers, ethnic groups, Catholics, the poor, liberal intellectuals, blacks, and Southerners. The difficulties of the Democratic party today can be traced largely to the weakening of this group coalition— the disaffection of the South and the group conflict between white labor and ethnic groups and blacks. The Republican coalition has consisted of rural and small-town residents, the middle class, whites, Protestants, white-collar workers, and suburbanites.

The whole interest group system—the political system itself—is held together in equilibrium by several forces. First of all, there is a large, nearly universal, *latent group* in American society which supports the constitutional system and prevailing "rules of the game." This group is not always visible but can be activated to administer overwhelming rebuke to any group that attacks the system and threatens to destroy the equilibrium.

Second, *overlapping group membership* helps to maintain the equilibrium by preventing any one group from moving too far from prevailing values. Individuals who belong to any one group also belong to other groups, and this fact moderates the demands of groups who must avoid offending their members who have other group affiliations.

Finally, the *checking and balancing resulting from group competition* also helps to maintain equilibrium in the system. No single group con-

---

GROUP THEORY: APPLYING THE MODEL

Throughout this volume we will describe struggles over public policy. In Chapter 7, "Education," we will examine group conflict over public policy in our discussion of federal aid to education and other school issues. In Chapter 8, "Energy and the Environment," we will observe the unhappy results of the failure of competing interests to reach *any* compromise.

stitutes a majority in American society. The power of each group is checked by the power of competing groups. "Countervailing" centers of power function to check the influence of any single group and protect the individual from exploitation.

## Elite Theory: Policy As Elite Preference

Public policy may also be viewed as the preferences and values of a governing elite.[5] Although we often assert that public policy reflects the demands of "the people," this may express the myth rather than the reality of American democracy. Elite theory suggests that "the people" are apathetic and ill-informed about public policy, that elites actually shape mass opinion on policy questions more than masses shape elite opinion. Thus, public policy really turns out to be the preferences of elites. Public officials and administrators merely carry out the policies decided upon by the elite. Policies flow "downward" from elites to masses; they do not arise from mass demands. (See Figure 2–3.)

Elite theory can be summarized briefly as follows:

1. Society is divided into the few who have power and the many who do not. Only a small number of persons allocate values for society; the masses do not decide public policy.

2. The few who govern are not typical of the masses who are governed

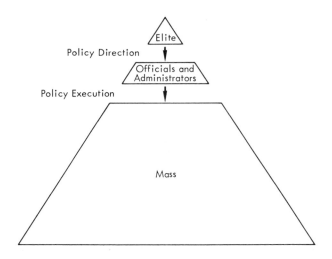

FIG. 2–3  The elite model

[5]Elite theory is explained at length in Thomas R. Dye and Harmon Zeigler, *The Irony of Democracy,* 5th ed. (Belmont, Calif.: Wadsworth, 1981).

Elites are drawn disproportionately from the upper socioeconomic strata of society.

3. The movement of nonelites to elite positions must be slow and continuous to maintain stability and avoid revolution. Only nonelites who have accepted the basic elite consensus can be admitted to governing circles.

4. Elites share consensus in behalf of the basic values of the social system and the preservation of the system. In America, the bases of elite consensus are the sanctity of private property, limited government, and individual liberty.

5. Public policy does not reflect demands of masses but rather the prevailing values of the elite. Changes in public policy will be incremental rather than revolutionary.

6. Active elites are subject to relatively little direct influence from apathetic masses. Elites influence masses more than masses influence elites.

What are the implications of elite theory for policy analysis? First of all, elitism implies that public policy does not reflect demands of "the people" so much as it does the interests and values of elites. Therefore, change and innovations in public policy come about as a result of redefinitions by elites of their own values. Because of the general conservatism of elites—that is, their interest in preserving the system—change in public policy will be incremental rather than revolutionary. Public policies are frequently modified but seldom replaced. Changes in the nature of the political system occur when events threaten the system, and elites, acting on the basis of enlightened self-interest, institute reforms to preserve the system and their place in it. The values of elites may be very "public-regarding." A sense of *noblesse oblige* may permeate elite values, and the welfare of the masses may be an important element in elite decision making. Elitism does not mean that public policy will be against mass welfare, but only that the responsibility for mass welfare rests upon the shoulders of elites, not masses.

Second, elitism views the masses as largely passive, apathetic, and ill-informed; mass sentiments are more often manipulated by elites, rather than elite values being influenced by the sentiments of masses; and for the most part, communication between elites and masses flows downward. Therefore, popular elections and party competition do not enable the masses to govern. Policy questions are seldom decided by the people through elections or through the presentation of policy alternatives by political parties. For the most part these "democratic" institutions—elections and parties—are important only for their symbolic value. They help tie the masses to the political system by giving them a role to play on election day and a political party with which they can identify. Elitism contends that the masses have at best only an indirect influence over the decision-making behavior of elites.

Elitism also asserts that elites share in a consensus about fundamental norms underlying the social system, that elites agree on the basic "rules of the game," as well as the continuation of the social system itself. The stability of the system, and even its survival, depends upon elite consensus in behalf of the fundamental values of the system, and only policy alternatives that fall within the shared consensus will be given serious consideration. Of course, elitism does not mean that elite members never disagree or never compete with each other for preeminence. It is unlikely that there ever was a society in which there was no competition among elites. But elitism implies that competition centers around a very narrow range of issues and that elites agree on more matters than they disagree.

In America elite consensus includes constitutional government, democratic procedures, majority rule, freedom of speech and press, freedom to form opposition parties and run for public office, equality of opportunity in all segments of life, the sanctity of private property, the importance of individual initiative and reward, and the legitimacy of the free enterprise, capitalist, economic system. Masses may give superficial support to democratic symbols, but they are not as consistent or reliable in their support for these values as elites.

---

ELITE THEORY: APPLYING THE MODEL

In Chapter 3 "Civil Rights," we will portray the civil rights movement as an effort by established national elites to extend equality of opportunity to blacks. Opposition to civil rights policies is centered among white masses in the states. In Chapter 4 "Criminal Justice," we will observe how elites try to deal with violations of established "rules of game."

---

## Rationalism: Policy As Efficient Goal Achievement

A rational policy is one that is correctly designed to maximize "net value achievement."[6] By "net value achievement" we mean that all relevant values of a society are known, and that any sacrifice in one or more values that is required by a policy is more than compensated for by the attainment of other values. This definition of rationality is interchangeable with the concept of efficiency. We can say that a policy is

[6]See Robert Henry Haveman, *The Economics of the Public Sector* (New York: John Wiley, 1970).

rational when it is most *efficient*—that is, if the ratio between the values it achieves and the values it sacrifices is positive and higher than any other policy alternative. One should *not* view efficiency in a narrow dollars-and-cents framework in which basic social values are sacrificed for dollar savings. Our idea of efficiency involves the calculation of *all* social, political, and economic values sacrificed or achieved by a public policy, not just those that can be measured in dollars.

To select a rational policy, policy makers must (1) know all the society's value preferences and their relative weights; (2) know all the policy alternatives available; (3) know all the consequences of each policy alternative; (4) calculate the ratio of achieved to sacrificed societal values for each policy alternative; (5) select the most efficient policy alternative.[7] This rationality assumes that the value preferences of *society as a whole* can be known and weighted. It is not enough to know and weight the values of *some* groups and not others. There must be a complete understanding of *societal* values. Rational policy making also requires *information* about alternative policies, the *predictive capacity* to foresee accurately the consequences of alternate policies, and the *intelligence* to calculate correctly the ratio of costs to benefits. Finally, rational policy making requires a *decision-making system* that facilitates rationality in policy formation. A diagram of such a system is shown in Figure 2–4.

Many types of rational decision models are found in the literature of economics, political science, management, administrative science, and budgeting.[8] An example of a rational approach to resource allocation policy is portrayed in Figure 2–5. This model assumes that a society has an "indifference curve" which represents the combination of values to which society is indifferent. The indifference curve slopes in a convex fashion from the upper left (a high return of Value A at the expense of lower returns on other values) to the lower right (a lower return on Value A in exchange for higher returns of other values). Any point on the curve is assumed to be equally satisfactory to society. Of course, all combinations on a higher indifference curve are preferable to those on a lower indifference curve. But we can assume that society does not have sufficient resources to achieve high levels of Value A *and* high levels of all other values. We can plot this assumption with a "value achievement curve" which represents the combination of values which it is possible for government to produce given the limitations of resources. The value achievement curve always slopes in a concave fashion from upper left (a high achievement of Value A at the

---

[7]See Yehezkel Dror, *Public Policy-Making Re-examined,* Part IV, "An Optional Model of Public Policy-Making" (San Francisco: Chandler, 1968).

[8]L. L. Wade and R. L. Curry, Jr., *A Logic of Public Policy: Aspects of Political Economy* (Belmont, Calif.: Wadsworth, 1970).

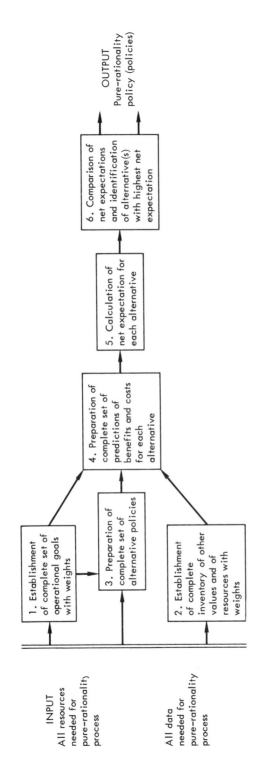

FIG. 2-4  A rational model of a decision system

INPUT
All resources
needed for
pure-rationality
process

All data
needed for
pure-rationality
process

1. Establishment
of complete set of
operational goals
with weights

2. Establishment
of complete
inventory of other
values and of
resources with
weights

3. Preparation of
complete set of
alternative policies

4. Preparation of
complete set of
predictions of
benefits and costs
for each
alternative

5. Calculation of
net expectation for
each alternative

6. Comparison of
net expectations
and identification
of alternative(s)
with highest net
expectation

OUTPUT
Pure-rationality
policy (policies)

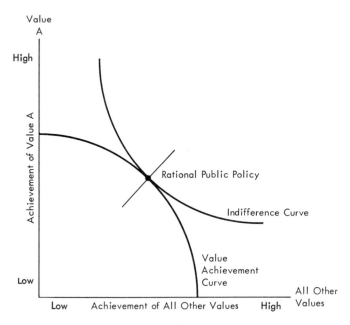

FIG. 2–5   A rational resource-allocation model

sacrifice of other values) to lower right (a lower achievement of Value A but a higher achievement of other values). Any point on the curve is possible for society to achieve. A rational public policy would be determined by the intersection of society's indifference curve and its value achievement curve. This point represents the highest level of indifference (satisfaction) allowable within society's resources.

There are many barriers to such rational decision making.[9] In fact, there are so many barriers to rational decision making that it rarely takes place at all in government. Yet the model remains important for analytic purposes because it helps to identify barriers to rationality. It assists in posing the question: Why is policy making not a more rational process? At the outset we can hypothesize several important obstacles to rational policy making:

1. There are no *societal* values that are usually agreed upon, but only the values of specific groups and individuals, many of which are conflicting.

2. The many conflicting values cannot be compared or weighted; for

[9]See Charles E. Lindblom, "The Science of Muddling Through," *Public Administration Review,* 19 (Spring 1959), 79–88; David Braybrooke and Charles E. Lindblom, *A Strategy of Decision* (New York: Free Press, 1963); Aaron Wildavsky, *The Politics of the Budgetary Process* (Boston: Little, Brown, 1964).

example, it is impossible to compare or weigh the value of individual dignity against a tax increase.

3. The environment of policy makers, particularly the power and influence system, renders it impossible for them to see or accurately weigh many societal values, particularly those values which have no active or powerful proponents.

4. Policy makers are not motivated to make decisions on the basis of societal goals, but instead try to maximize their own rewards—power, status, reelection, money, etc.

5. Policy makers are not motivated to *maximize* net goal achievement, but merely to *satisfy* demands for progress; they do not search until they find "the one best way" but halt their search when they find an alternative that "will work."

6. Large investments in existing programs and policies ("sunk costs") prevent policy makers from reconsidering alternatives foreclosed by previous decisions.

7. There are innumerable barriers to collecting all the information required to know all possible policy alternatives and the consequences of each alternative, including the cost of information gathering, the availability of the information, and the time involved in its collection.

8. Neither the predictive capacities of the social and behavioral sciences nor the predictive capacities of the physical and biological sciences are sufficiently advanced to enable policy makers to understand the full range of consequences of each policy alternative.

9. Policy makers, even with the most advanced computerized analytical techniques, do not have sufficient intelligence to calculate accurately cost-benefits ratios when a large number of diverse political, social, economic, and cultural values are at stake.

10. Policy makers have personal needs, inhibitions, and inadequacies which prevent them from performing in a highly rational manner.

11. Uncertainty about the consequences of various policy alternatives compels policy makers to stick as closely as possible to previous policies to reduce the likelihood of disturbing, unanticipated consequences.

12. The segmentalized nature of policy making in large bureaucracies makes it difficult to coordinate decision making so that the input of all the various specialists is brought to bear at the point of decision.

### RATIONALISM: APPLYING THE MODEL

The problems of achieving rationality in public policy are discussed in Chapter 5 "Poverty and Welfare," and in Chapter 6 "Health." We will describe the general design of alternative strategies in dealing with poverty, health, and welfare. We will observe how these strategies are implemented in public policy, and we will analyze some of the obstacles to the achievement of rationality in public policy.

## Incrementalism: Policy As Variations On The Past

Incrementalism views public policy as a continuation of past government activities with only incremental modifications. Political scientist Charles E. Lindblom first presented the incremental model in the course of a critique of the traditional rational model of decision making.[10] According to Lindblom, decision makers do *not* annually review the whole range of existing and proposed policies, identify societal goals, research the benefits and costs of alternative policies in achieving these goals, rank-order preferences for each policy alternative in terms of the ratio of benefits to costs, and then make a selection on the basis of all relevant information. On the contrary, constraints of time, intelligence, and cost prevent policy makers from identifying the full range of policy alternatives and their consequences. Constraints of politics prevent the establishment of clear-cut societal goals and the accurate calculation of cost-benefit ratios. The incremental model recognizes the impractical nature of "rational-comprehensive" policy making, and describes a more conservative process of decision making.

Incrementalism is conservative in that existing programs, policies, and expenditures are considered as a base, and attention is concentrated on new programs and policies and on increases, decreases, or modifications of current programs. (See Figure 2–6) Policy makers generally accept the legitimacy of established programs and tacitly agree to continue previous policies.

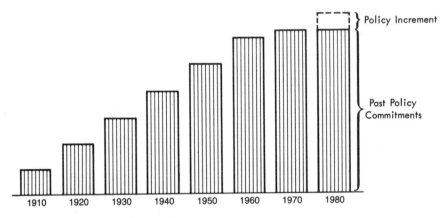

FIG. 2–6  The incremental model

10Lindblom, "The Science of Muddling Through," 79–88.

They do this, first of all, because they do not have the time, intelligence, or money to investigate all the alternatives to existing policy. The cost of collecting all this information is too great. Policy makers do not have sufficient predictive capacities, even in the age of computers, to know what all the consequences of each alternative will be. Nor are they able to calculate cost-benefit ratios for alternative policies when many diverse political, social, economic, and cultural values are at stake. Thus completely "rational" policy may turn out to be "inefficient" (despite the contradiction in terms) if the time, intelligence, and cost of developing a rational policy are excessive.

Second, policy makers accept the legitimacy of previous policies because of the uncertainty about the consequences of completely new or different policies. It is safer to stick with known programs when the consequences of new programs cannot be predicted. Under conditions of uncertainty, policy makers continue past policies or programs whether or not they have proven effective.

Third, there may be heavy investments in existing programs ("sunk costs" again) which preclude any really radical change. These investments may be in money, buildings, or other hard items, or they may be in psychological dispositions, administrative practices, or organizational structure. It is accepted wisdom, for example, that organizations tend to persist over time regardless of their utility, that they develop routines that are difficult to alter, and that individuals develop a personal stake in the continuation of organizations and practices, which makes radical change very difficult. Hence, not all policy alternatives can be seriously considered, but only those which cause little physical, economic, organizational, and administrative dislocation.

Fourth, incrementalism is politically expedient. Agreement comes easier in policy making when the items in dispute are only increases or decreases in budgets, or modifications to existing programs. Conflict is heightened when decision making focuses on major policy shifts involving great gains or losses, or "all or nothing," "yes or no" policy decisions. Because the political tension involved in getting new programs or policies passed *every* year would be very great, past policy victories are continued into future years unless there is a substantial political realignment. Thus incrementalism is important in reducing conflict, maintaining stability, and preserving the political system itself.

The characteristics of policy makers themselves also recommend the incremental model. Rarely do human beings act to maximize all their values; more often they act to satisfy particular demands. People are pragmatic: they seldom search for the "one best way" but instead end their search when they find "a way that will work." This search usually begins with the familiar—that is, with policy alternatives close to current policies. Only if these alternatives appear to be unsatisfactory will the policy maker venture out toward more radical policy innovation. In most cases modification of existing programs will satisfy particular demands, and the major policy shifts required to maximize values are overlooked.

Finally, in the absence of any agreed-upon societal goals or values, it is easier for the government of a pluralist society to continue existing programs rather than to engage in overall policy planning toward specific societal goals.

---

INCREMENTALISM: APPLYING THE MODEL

We will give special attention to incrementalism in our discussion of government spending in Chapter 10 "Priorities and Price Tags" and in our discussion in Chapter 11 of "Tax Policy."

---

## Game Theory: Policy As Rational Choice in Competitive Situations

Game theory is the study of rational decisions in situations in which two or more participants have choices to make and the outcome depends on the choices made by each of them. It is applied to policy making where there is no *independently* "best" choice that one can make—where the "best" outcomes depend upon what others do.

The idea of a "game" is that decision makers are involved in choices that are interdependent. Each "player" must adjust his conduct to reflect not only his own desires and abilities but also his expectations about what others will do. Perhaps the connotation of a "game" is unfortunate, suggesting that game theory is not really appropriate for *serious* conflict situations. But just the opposite is true: game theory can be applied to decisions about war and peace, the use of nuclear weapons, international diplomacy, bargaining and coalition building in Congress or the United Nations, and a variety of other important political situations. A "player" may be an individual, a group, or a national government—indeed, anybody with well-defined goals that is capable of rational action.

Game theory is an abstract and deductive model of policy making. It does not describe how people actually make decisions, but rather how they would go about making decisions in competitive situations if they were completely rational. Thus, game theory is a form of rationalism, but it is applied in *competitive* situations where the outcome depends on what two or more participants do.

The *rules of the game* describe the choices that are available to all the players. The choices are frequently portrayed in a "matrix"—a diagram which presents the alternative choices of each player and all the possible outcomes of the game. A two-by-two matrix is the simplest; there are only two players and each player has only two alternatives to choose from:

PLAYER A

|  |  | Alternative $A_1$ | Alternative $A_2$ |
|---|---|---|---|
| PLAYER B | Alternative $B_1$ | outcome | outcome |
|  | Alternative $B_2$ | outcome | outcome |

There are four possible outcomes to this simple game, each represented by a cell in the matrix. The actual outcome depends upon the choices of both Player A and Player B.

In game theory, payoff refers to the values that each player receives as a result of his choices and those of his opponent. Payoffs are frequently represented by numerical values placed on each outcome; these numerical values are placed inside each cell of the matrix and presumably correspond to the values each player places on each outcome. Because players value different outcomes differently, there are two numerical values inside each cell—one for each player.

Consider the game of "chicken." Two adolescents drive their cars toward each other at high speed, each with one set of wheels on the center line of the highway. If neither veers off course they will crash. Whoever veers is "chicken." Both drivers prefer to avoid death but they also want to avoid the "dishonor" of being "chicken." The outcome depends on what both drivers do, and each driver must try to predict how the other will behave. This form of "brinkmanship" is common in international relations (see Figure 2–7).

Inspection of the payoff matrix suggests that it would be better for both drivers to veer in order to minimize the possibility of a great loss ($-10$). But the matrix is too simple. One or both players may place a different value on the outcomes than is suggested by the numbers. For example, one player may prefer death to dishonor in the game. Each player must try to calculate the values of the other and neither has complete information about the values of his opponent. Moreover, bluffing or the deliberate misrepresentation of one's values or re-

DRIVER A

| | | Stay on course | Veer |
|---|---|---|---|
| DRIVER B | Stay on Course | A: −10<br>B: −10 | A: −5<br>B: +5 |
| | Veer | A: +5<br>B: −5 | A: −1<br>B: −1 |

FIG. 2–7  A game-theoretic matrix for the game of "chicken"
The game theorist himself supplies the numerical values to the payoffs. If Driver
A chooses to stay on course and Driver B chooses to stay on course also, the
result might be scored as −10 for both players. But if Driver A chooses to stay
on course and Driver B veers, then Driver A might get +5 ("Courage") and
Driver B −5 ("Dishonor"). If Driver A veers but Driver B stays on course, the
results would be reversed. If both veer, each is dishonored slightly (−1) but
not as much as when one or the other stayed on course.

sources to an opponent is always a possibility. For example, a possible
strategy in the game of chicken is to allow your opponent to see you
drink heavily before the game, stumble drunkenly toward your car,
and mumble something about having lived long enough in this rotten
world. The effect of this communication on your opponent may increase his estimate of your likelihood of staying on course, and hence
provide incentive for him to veer and allow you to win.

A key concept in game theory is *strategy*. Strategy refers to rational decision making in which a set of moves is designed to achieve
optimum payoff even after consideration of all of the opponent's possible moves. Game theorists employ the term "minimax" to refer to the
rational strategy that either *minimizes the maximum loss or maximizes the
minimum gain* for a player, regardless of what his opponent does. The
minimax strategy is designed to protect a player against his opponent's
best play. It might be viewed as a conservative strategy in that it is designed to reduce losses and insure minimum gains rather than to seek
maximum gains at the risk of great losses. But most game theorists
view minimax as the best rational strategy. (The rational player in the
game of chicken will veer, because this choice minimizes his maximum
loss.)

It should be clear from this discussion that game theory embraces
both very complex and very simple ideas. The crucial question is
whether any of these game theory ideas is really useful in studying
public policy.

Game theory is more frequently proposed as an *analytic* tool by
social scientists than as a practical guide to policy making by government officials. The conditions of game theory are seldom approxi-

mated in real life. Seldom do policy alternatives present themselves neatly in a matrix. More importantly, seldom can policy makers know the real payoff values for themselves or their opponents of various policy alternatives. Finally, as we have already indicated, there are many obstacles to rational policy making by governments.

Yet game theory provides an interesting way of thinking clearly about policy choices in conflict situations. Perhaps the real utility of game theory in policy analysis at the present time is in suggesting interesting questions and providing a vocabulary to deal with policy making in conflict situations.

---

### GAME THEORY: APPLYING THE MODEL

Game theory is frequently applied in international conflict situations. We will explore the utility of game theory in our own efforts to describe and explain *Defense Policy* in Chapter 12.

---

## Systems Theory: Policy As System Output

Another way to conceive of public policy is to think of it as a response of a political system to forces brought to bear upon it from the environment.[11] Forces generated in the environment which affect the political system are viewed as *inputs*. The *environment* is any condition or circumstance defined as external to the boundaries of the political system. The political *system* is that group of interrelated structures and processes which functions authoritatively to allocate values for a society. *Outputs* of the political system are authoritative value allocations of the system, and these allocations constitute *public policy*.

This conceptualization of political activity and public policy can be diagramed as in Figure 2–8. This diagram is a simplified version of the idea of the political system described at great length by political scientist David Easton. The notion of a political system has been employed, either implicitly or explicitly, by many scholars who have sought to analyze the causes and consequences of public policy.

Systems theory portrays public policy as an output of the political *system*. The concept of "system" implies an identifiable set of institutions and activities in society that function to transform demands into authoritative decisions requiring the support of the whole society. The

[11]This conceptualization is based upon David Easton, "An Approach to the Analysis of Political Systems," *World Politics*, 9 (1957), 383–400; and Easton, *A Framework for Political Analysis* (Englewood Cliffs, N.J.: Prentice-Hall, 1965).

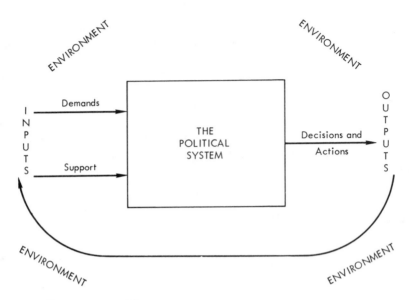

FIG. 2–8   The systems model

concept of "system" also implies that elements of the system are inter-related, that the system can respond to forces in its environment, and that it will do so in order to preserve itself. Inputs are received into the political system in the form of both demands and support. Demands occur when individuals or groups, in response to real or perceived environmental conditions, act to affect public policy. Support is rendered when individuals or groups accept the outcome of elections, obey the laws, pay their taxes, and generally conform to policy decisions. Any system absorbs a variety of demands, some of which conflict with each other. In order to transform these demands into outputs (public policies), it must arrange settlements and enforce these settlements upon the parties concerned. It is recognized that outputs (public policies) may have a modifying effect on the environment and the demands arising from it, and may also have an effect upon the character of the political system. The system preserves itself by (1) producing reasonably satisfying outputs, (2) relying upon deeply rooted attachments to the system itself, and (3) using, or threatening to use, force.

The value of the systems model to policy analysis lies in the questions that it poses:

1. What are the significant dimensions of the environment that generate demands upon the political system?

2. What are the significant characteristics of the political system that enable it to transform demands into public policy and to preserve itself over time?

3. How do environmental inputs affect the character of the political system?

4. How do characteristics of the political system affect the content of public policy?

5. How do environmental inputs affect the content of public policy?

6. How does public policy affect, through feedback, the environment and the character of the political system?

---

### SYSTEMS THEORY: APPLYING THE MODEL

The systems model is particularly helpful in Chapter 13 "Inputs, Outputs, and Black Boxes" in examining public policies in the American States. By *comparing* states, we will assess the impact of various environmental conditions—particularly wealth, urbanization, and education—on levels of spending, benefits, and services in education, welfare, highways, police, corrections, and finance. We will see how federal policy sometimes tries to offset the impact of environmental variables on domestic policy in the states. We will examine the impact of political system characteristics—particularly competition and participation—on levels of taxing, spending, benefits, and service, and attempt to compare the impact of these system characteristics on public policy with the impact of environmental conditions.

---

## Models: How To Tell If They Are Helping Or Not

A model is merely an abstraction or representation of political life. When we think of political "systems" or "elites" or "groups" or "rational decision making" or "incrementalism" or "games" we are abstracting from the real world in an attempt to simplify, clarify, and understand what is really important about politics. Before we begin our study of public policy, let us set forth some general criteria for evaluating the usefulness of concepts and models.

1. Certainly the utility of a model lies in its ability to *order and simplify* political life so that we can think about it more clearly and understand the relationships we find in the real world. Yet too much simplification can lead to inaccuracies in our thinking about reality. If a concept is too narrow or identifies only superficial phenomena, we may not be able to use it to explain public policy. On the other hand, if a concept is too broad, and suggests overly complex relationships, it may

become so complicated and unmanageable that it is not really an aid to understanding. In other words, some theories of politics may be too complex to be helpful, while others may be too simplistic.

2. A model should also *identify* the really significant aspects of public policy. It should direct attention away from irrelevant variables or circumstances, and focus upon the "real" causes and "significant" consequences of public policy. Of course, what is "real," "relevant," "significant" is to some extent a function of an individual's personal values. But we can all agree that the utility of a concept is related to its ability to identify what it is that is really important about politics.

3. Generally, a model should be *congruent with reality*—that is, it ought to have real empirical referents. We would expect to have difficulty with a concept that identifies a process that does not really occur, or symbolizes phenomena that do not exist in the real world. On the other hand, we must not be too quick to dismiss "unrealistic" concepts *if* they succeed in directing our attention to why they are unrealistic. For example, no one contends that government decision making is completely rational—public officials do not always act to maximize societal values and minimize societal costs. Yet the concept of "rational decision making" may be still useful, albeit "unrealistic," if it makes us realize how irrational government decision making really is and prompts us to inquire about why it is irrational.

4. A concept or model should also *communicate* something meaningful. If too many people disagree over the meaning of a concept, its utility in communication is diminished. For example, if no one really agrees on what constitutes an "elite," then the concept of an elite does not mean the same thing to everyone. If one defines an "elite" as democratically elected public officials who are representative of the general public, then he is communicating a different idea in using the term than one who defines an elite as an unrepresentative minority that makes decisions for society based on its own interests.

5. A model should help to *direct inquiry and research* into public policy. A concept should be operational—that is, it should refer directly to real-world phenomena that can be observed, measured, and verified. A concept, or a series of interrelated concepts (which we refer to as a "model"), should suggest relationships in the real world that can be tested and verified. If there is no way to prove or disprove the ideas suggested by a concept, then the concept is not really useful in developing a science of politics.

6. Finally, a model approach should *suggest an explanation* of public policy. It should suggest hypotheses about the causes and consequences of public policy—hypotheses that can be tested against real-world data. A concept that merely *describes* public policy is not as useful

as a concept that *explains* public policy, or at least suggests some possible explanations.

## Bibliography

DYE, THOMAS R., and HARMON ZEIGLER, *The Irony of Democracy*. Belmont, Calif.: Wadsworth, 1970.

EASTON, DAVID, *A Framework for Political Analysis*. Englewood Cliffs, N.J.: Prentice-Hall, 1965.

JONES, CHARLES O., *An Introduction to the Study of Public Policy*. Boston: Duxbury, 1977.

TRUMAN, DAVID B., *The Governmental Process*. New York: Knopf, 1971.

WADE, L. L., and R. L. CURRY, JR., *A Logic of Public Policy: Aspects of Political Economy*. Belmont, Calif.: Wadsworth, 1970.

WILDAVSKY, AARON, *The Politics of the Budgetary Process*. Boston: Little, Brown, 1964.

Busing: the constitutional question. *Stan Wakefield*.

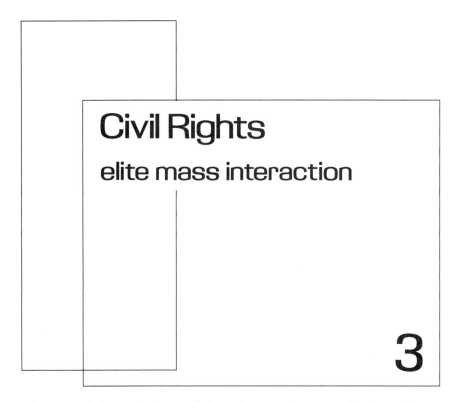

# Civil Rights
## elite mass interaction

**3**

The central domestic issue of American politics over the long history of the nation has been the place of blacks in American society. In describing this issue we have relied heavily on the elite model—because elite and mass attitudes toward civil rights differ a great deal, and public policy appears to reflect the attitudes of *elites* rather than masses. Civil rights policy is a response of a national elite to conditions affecting a minority of Americans, rather than a response of national leaders to majority sentiments. Policies of the national elite in civil rights have met with varying degrees of resistance from states and communities. We will contend that national policy has shaped mass opinion more than mass opinion has shaped national policy.

## Elite Mass Attitudes and Civil Rights

White America has long harbored an ambivalence toward black America—a recognition of the evils of inequality but a reluctance to take steps to eliminate it. Gunnar Myrdal, writing in 1944, captured the essence of the American racial dilemma:

> The "American dilemma" . . . is the ever-raging conflict between, on the one hand, the valuations preserved on the general plane which we shall call the "American

**47**

creed," where the American thinks, talks, and acts under the influence of high national and Christian precepts, and, on the other hand, the evaluation on specific planes of individual and group living, where personal and local interests; economic, and social, and sexual jealousies; considerations of community prestige and conformity; group prejudices against particular persons or types of people; all sorts of miscellaneous wants, impulses, and habits dominate his outlook.[1]

The attitudes of white masses toward blacks in America are ambivalent. Most whites believe that blacks suffer injustices and that discrimination is wrong. Yet even though they admit the injustices of discrimination, an overwhelming majority of whites believe that blacks are moving "too fast." In general, whites are willing to support laws eliminating discrimination and guaranteeing equality of opportunity. But what about compensatory efforts to overcome the effects of past discrimination and uplift the black community? Here the evidence is that most whites are not prepared to make any special effort to change the conditions of blacks.

For example a Gallup Poll reports that the overwhelming majority of white Americans, and even a majority of black Americans, *oppose* affirmative action programs.[2]

QUESTION:  Some people say that to make up for past discrimination, women and members of minority groups should be given preferential treatment in getting jobs and places in colleges. Others say that ability, as determined by test scores, should be the main consideration. Which point of view comes closest to how you feel on this matter?

|  | Give Preference | Ability Main Consideration | No Opinion |
|---|---|---|---|
| Total | 11% | 81% | 8% |
| Male | 10 | 82 | 8 |
| Female | 12 | 80 | 8 |
| White | 9 | 84 | 7 |
| Nonwhite | 30 | 55 | 15 |

In general, white Americans are much more sympathetic toward black rights today than they were in years past. A national sample of white Americans was asked the question, "Do you think white students and Negro students should go to the same schools or separate schools?" in 1942, 1956, 1963, 1966, and 1973 (see Table 3–1). In 1942, not one American white in three approved of integrated schools.

[1]Gunnar Myrdal, *An American Dilemma: The Negro Problem and Modern Democracy*, vol. I (New York: McGraw-Hill, 1944), p. xxi.
[2]*Gallup Opinion Index* (February 1978), p. 8.

**TABLE 3-1**  Attitude Change among Whites: White and Negro Students Should Attend the Same Schools, 1942–1973

| | Percentage Yes | | | | |
|---|---|---|---|---|---|
| | *1942* | *1956* | *1963* | *1966* | *1973* |
| Total whites | 30 | 49 | 62 | 67 | 82 |
| Northern whites | 40 | 61 | 73 | 78 | 84 |
| Southern whites | 2 | 15 | 31 | 36 | 65 |

*Source:* Paul B. Sheatsley, "White Attitudes Toward the Negro," *Daedalus,* 95, no. 1 (Winter 1966). Reprinted by permission of *Daedalus,* Journal of the American Academy of Arts and Sciences, Boston, Mass., Winter 1966, *The Negro American*—2. Updating from *Gallup Opinion Index* (October 1973).

Even in the North, a majority was opposed to school integration, while in the South only two whites in a hundred supported integration. In 1956, two years after the historic *Brown* v. *Topeka,* white attitudes had shifted markedly. Nationwide support for integration characterized about half of the white population; in the North it was the majority view, and in the South the proportion supporting integration had risen to one in seven. By 1963, two out of every three whites believed in integrated schools, and, even more noteworthy, one out of three Southern whites believed in integration. Since 1963 there has been a continuation of the upward trend in the proportion of white Americans who favor school integration. Additional survey information suggest that whites are becoming increasingly accommodating toward equal rights for blacks over time in other areas as well. But it should be noted that white opinion generally *follows* public policy, rather than leading it.

There is a wide gap between the attitudes of masses and elites on the subject of the black revolution. The most hostile attitudes toward blacks are found among the less privileged, less educated whites. Low-income whites are much less willing to have contact with blacks than high-income whites, whether it is a matter of using the same public restrooms, or going to a movie or restaurant, or living next door. It is the affluent, well-educated American who is most concerned with discrimination against blacks and who is most willing to have contact with them.

The political implication of this finding is obvious: opposition to civil rights legislation and to black advancement in education, jobs, income, housing, and so on is likely to be strongest among low-income whites. Within the white community, support for civil rights will continue to come from the educated, affluent American.

The black revolution has deeply divided *white* America. Although it is true that there is a wide gulf between blacks and whites in terms of the speed of progress, the tactics of the revolution, and perhaps even the ultimate objective of the revolution, there is also a wide gulf between poor and affluent whites in their response to the black struggle. The better educated, more privileged whites are much more sympathetic toward black aspirations than are poorly educated, low-income whites. Less privileged whites do not agree that the condition of blacks in America is worse than the condition of whites, or that blacks are discriminated against. As Louis Harris notes: "If there are two races in this country poles apart on the race issue, then it is equally true there are two white societies just as far apart."[3]

## The Development of Civil Rights Policy

The initial goal in the struggle for equality in America was the elimination of discrimination and segregation practiced *by governments*, particularly in voting and public education. Later, discrimination in both public *and private* life—in transportation, theaters, parks, stores, restaurants, businesses, employment, and housing—came under legal attack.

At the outset it is important to realize that the elimination of discrimination does not in itself ensure equality. The civil rights policies of the national government do not affect the conditions of equality in America as directly as we might suppose. Civil rights laws have not dramatically affected the living conditions of the masses of blacks in either the North or the South. The problem of racial inequality—inequality between blacks and whites in income, health, housing, employment, education, and so on—is more than a problem of direct legal discrimination. However, the movement to end direct discrimination laid the foundation for the politics of equality today.

The Fourteenth Amendment declares:

> All persons born or naturalized in the United States, and subject to the Jurisdiction thereof, are citizens of the United States and of the State wherein they reside. No State shall make or enforce any law which shall abridge the privileges or immunities of citizens of the United States; nor shall any State deprive any person of life, liberty, or property, without due process of law; nor deny to any person within its jurisdiction the equal protection of the laws.

The language of the Fourteenth Amendment and its historical context leaves little doubt that its original purpose was to achieve the full measure of citizenship and equality for black Americans. Some radical Republicans were prepared in 1867 to carry out in Southern society the revolution this amendment implied. But by 1877, it was

[3]Louis Harris, *Black and White* (New York: Simon & Schuster, 1967), p. 137.

clear that Reconstruction had failed; the national government was not prepared to carry out the long, difficult, and disagreeable task of really reconstructing society in the eleven states of the former Confederacy. In the Compromise of 1877, the national government agreed to end military occupation of the South, give up its efforts to rearrange Southern society, and lend tacit approval to white supremacy in that region. In return, the Southern states pledged their support of the Union, accepted national supremacy, and, of course, agreed to permit the Republican candidate, Rutherford B. Hayes, to assume the presidency, even though his Democratic opponent, Samuel J. Tilden, had won more popular votes in the disputed election of 1876.

The Supreme Court agreed to the terms of the compromise. The result was a complete inversion of the meaning of the Fourteenth Amendment so that it became a bulwark of segregation. State laws segregating the races were upheld as long as persons in each of the separated races were protected equally. The constitutional argument in behalf of segregation under the Fourteenth Amendment was that the phrase "equal protection of the laws" did not prevent state-enforced separation of the races. Schools and other public facilities that were "separate but equal" won constitutional approval. This separate but equal doctrine became the Supreme Court's interpretation of the Equal Protection Clause of the Fourteenth Amendment in *Plessy* v. *Ferguson:*

> The object of the [14th] Amendment was undoubtedly to enforce the absolute equality of the two races before the law, but in the nature of things it could not have been intended to abolish distinctions based upon color, or to enforce social, as distinguished from political, equality, or a commingling of the two races upon terms unsatisfactory to either. Laws permitting, and even requiring, their separation in places where they are liable to be brought into contact do not necessarily imply the inferiority of either race to the other, and have been generally, if not universally recognized as within the competency of the state legislatures in the exercise of their police power. The most common instance of this is connected with the establishment of separate schools for white and colored children, which has been held to be a valid exercise of the legislative power. . . .[4]

However, segregated facilities, including public schools, were seldom if ever equal, even with respect to physical conditions. In practice, the doctrine of segregation was "separate and *un*equal." The Supreme Court began to take notice of this after World War II. Although it declined to overrule the segregationist interpretation of the Fourteenth Amendment, it began to order the admission of individual blacks to white public universities where evidence indicated that separate black institutions were inferior or nonexistent.[5]

[4]*Plessy* v. *Ferguson,* 163 U.S. 537 (1896).
[5]*Sweatt* v. *Painter,* 339 U.S. 629 (1950).

Leaders of the newly emerging civil rights movement in the 1940s and 1950s were not satisfied with court decisions that examined the circumstances in each case to determine if separate school facilities were really equal. Led by Roy Wilkins, executive director of the National Association for the Advancement of Colored People, and Thurgood Marshall, chief counsel for the NAACP, the civil rights movement pressed for a court decision that segregation itself meant inequality within the meaning of the Fourteenth Amendment, whether or not facilities were equal in all tangible respects. In short, they wanted a complete reversal of the "separate but equal" interpretation of the Fourteenth Amendment, and a ruling that laws *separating* the races were unconstitutional.

The civil rights groups chose to bring suit for desegregation in Topeka, Kansas, where segregated black and white schools were equal with respect to buildings, curricula, qualifications and salaries of teachers, and other tangible factors. The object was to prevent the Court from ordering the admission of blacks because *tangible* facilities were not equal, and to force the Court to review the doctrine of segregation itself.

The Court rendered its historic decision in *Brown* v. *Board of Education of Topeka, Kansas* on May 17, 1954:

> Segregation of white and colored children in public schools has a detrimental effect upon the colored children. The impact is greater when it has the sanction of law, for the policy of separating the races is usually interpreted as denoting the inferiority of the Negro group. A form of inferiority affects the motivation of a child to learn. Segregation with the sanction of law, therefore, has a tendency to retard the educational and mental development of Negro children and to deprive them of some of the benefits they would receive in a racially integrated school system.
>
> Whatever may have been the extent of psychological knowledge of the time of *Plessy* v. *Ferguson*, this finding is amply supported by modern authority. Any language in *Plessy* v. *Ferguson* contrary to this source is rejected.[6]

The original *Brown* v. *Topeka* decision was symbolically very important. Although it would be many years before any significant number of black children would attend formerly segregated white schools, the decision by the nation's highest court undoubtedly stimulated black hopes and expectations. Black sociologist Kenneth Clark writes:

> This [civil rights] movement would probably not have existed at all were it not for the 1954 Supreme Court school desegregation decision which provided a tremendous boost to the morale of Negroes by its *clear* affirmation that color is irrelevant to the rights of American citizens. Until this time the Southern Negro generally had accommodated to the separation of the black from the white society.[7]

[6]*Brown* v. *Board of Education of Topeka, Kansas*, 347 U.S. 483 (1954).
[7]Kenneth B. Clark, *Dark Ghetto* (New York: Harper & Row, 1965), pp. 77–78.

Note that this first great step toward racial justice in the twentieth century was taken by the *nonelective* branch of the federal government. Nine men, secure in their positions with lifetime appointments, responded to the legal arguments of highly educated black leaders, one of whom—Thurgood Marshall—would later become a Supreme Court Justice himself. The decision was made by a judicial elite, not by "the people" or their elected representatives.

## Mass Resistance to Civil Rights Policy

Although the Supreme Court had spoken forcefully in the Brown case in declaring segregation unconstitutional, from a *political* viewpoint, the battle over segregation was just beginning. Segregation would remain a part of American life, regardless of its constitutionality, until effective elite power was brought to bear to end it. The Supreme Court, by virtue of the American system of federalism and separation of powers, has little formal power at its disposal. Congress, the president, state governors and legislatures, and the people have more power at their disposal than the federal judiciary. The Supreme Court must rely largely on the other branches of the federal government, on the states, and on private individuals and organizations to effectuate the law of the land.

Yet in 1954 the practice of segregation was widespread and deeply ingrained in American life. Seventeen states *required* the segregation of the races in public schools.:

| | |
|---|---|
| Alabama | Texas |
| Arkansas | Virginia |
| Florida | Delaware |
| Georgia | Kentucky |
| Louisiana | Maryland |
| Mississippi | Missouri |
| North Carolina | Oklahoma |
| South Carolina | West Virginia |
| Tennessee | |

The Congress of the United States *required* the segregation of the races in the public schools of the District of Columbia. Four additional states—Arizona, Kansas, New Mexico, and Wyoming—*authorized* segregation upon the option of local school boards. (See Figure 3–1.)

Thus, in deciding *Brown* v. *Topeka*, the Supreme Court struck down the laws of twenty-one states and the District of Columbia in a single opinion. Such a far-reaching decision was bound to meet with difficulties in implementation. In an opinion delivered the following

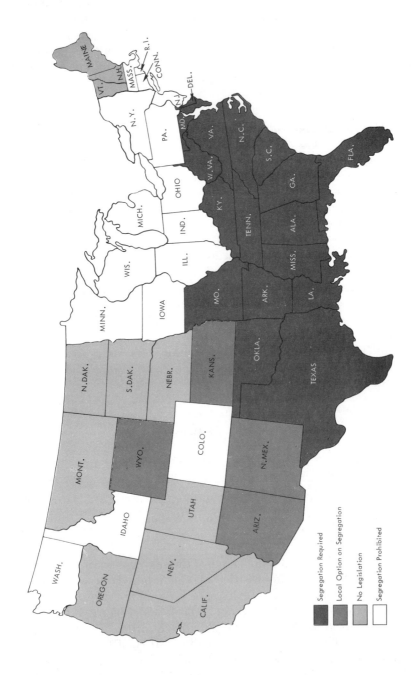

FIG. 3–1    Segregation laws in the United States in 1954

Segregation Required
Local Option on Segregation
No Legislation
Segregation Prohibited

year, the Supreme Court declined to order immediate nationwide desegregation, but instead turned over the responsibility for desegregation to state and local authorities under the supervision of federal district courts. The way was open for extensive litigation, obstruction, and delay by states that chose to resist desegregation.

The six border states with segregated school systems—Delaware, Kentucky, Maryland, Missouri, Oklahoma, West Virginia—together with the school districts in Kansas, Arizona, and New Mexico that had operated segregated schools, chose not to resist desegregation formally. The District of Columbia also desegregated its public schools the year following the Supreme Court's decision.

However, resistance to school integration was the policy choice of the eleven states of the Old Confederacy. Refusal of a school district to desegregate until it was faced with a federal court injunction was the most common form of delay. Segregationists also pressed for state laws that would create an endless chain of litigation in each of the nearly 3,000 school districts in the South in the hope that these integration efforts would drown in a sea of protracted court controversy. State laws that were obviously designed to evade constitutional responsibilities to end segregation were struck down in federal courts; but court suits and delays slowed progress toward integration. Of all delaying tactics, the most successful was the pupil placement law. Under this law each child was guaranteed "freedom of choice" in the selection of his school. School authorities relied on the fact that most blacks and most whites selected the schools they had previously attended—that is, segregated schools. Eventually, federal courts struck down these laws when it became clear that they perpetuated segregation. Yet, on the whole, those states that chose to resist desegregation were quite successful in doing so from 1954 to 1964. In late 1964, ten years after the *Brown* decision, only about two percent of the black school children in the eleven southern states were attending integrated schools!

Finally Congress entered the civil rights field in support of court efforts to achieve desegregation. The Civil Rights Act of 1964, Title VI, provided that every federal department and agency must take action to end segregation in all programs or activities receiving federal financial assistance. It was specified that this action was to include termination of financial assistance if states and communities receiving federal funds refused to comply with federal desegregation orders. Thus, in addition to *court orders* requiring desegregation, states and communities faced *administrative orders* or "guidelines" from federal executive agencies, particularly the U.S. Office of Education, threatening loss of federal funds for noncompliance. Acting under the authority of Title VI, the U.S. Office of Education required all school districts in the seventeen formerly segregated states to submit desegregation plans as a condition of federal assistance. "Guidelines" governing the acceptability of these plans were frequently unclear, often contradictory, and always changing, yet progress toward desegregation was speeded up.

The last legal excuse for delay in implementing school desegregation collapsed in 1969 when the Supreme Court rejected a request by Mississippi school officials for a delay in implementing school desegregation in that state. School officials contended that immediate desegregation in several southern Mississippi counties would encounter "administrative and legislative difficulties." The Supreme Court stated that no delay could be granted. The court declared that every school district was obligated to end dual school systems "at once" and "now and hereafter" to operate only unitary schools.[8] The effect of the decision, fifteen years after the original Brown case, was to eliminate any further legal justification for the continuation of segregation in public schools.

Southern school desegregation has now progressed to the point where more black pupils are attending integrated schools in the South than in the North. The percentage of black pupils in the North attending schools which are predominantly black (95 to 100 percent black) is over 50 percent, compared to only 19 percent of black pupils in the South attending such schools.[9] This is an important comparison between the diminishing impact of segregation *by law* in the South, and the continuing impact of *de facto* segregation in the North. If the issue is posed as one of "racial isolation," it turns out that the efforts of federal courts and executive agencies in eliminating segregation by law has reduced racial isolation in the South to the point that it is less than racial isolation in the North.

### "De Facto" School Segregation and Busing

In *Brown* v. *Board of Education of Topeka,* the Supreme Court quoted approvingly the view that segregation had "a tendency to retard the educational and mental development of Negro children and to deprive them of some of the benefits they would receive in a racially integrated school system." The U.S. Commission on Civil Rights reported that even when the segregation was *de facto*—that is, the product of segregated housing patterns and neighborhood schools rather than direct discrimination—the adverse effects on black students were still significant.[10] Black students attending predominantly black schools had lower achievement scores and lower levels of aspiration than blacks with com-

---

[8]*Alexander* v. *Holmes County Board of Education,* 396 U.S. 19 (1969).

[9]*Statistical Abstract of the United States, 1977,* p. 145.

[10]U.S. Commission on Civil Rights, *Racial Isolation in the Public Schools* (Washington, D.C.: Government Printing Office, 1966).

parable socioeconomic backgrounds who attended predominantly white schools. When a group of black students attending school with a majority of advantaged whites was compared to a group of blacks attending school with a majority of disadvantaged blacks, the average difference in levels of achievement amounted to more than two grade levels. On the other hand, the Commission found that the achievement levels of white students in classes roughly half white in composition were not substantially different from those of white students in all-white schools. This finding comprises perhaps the best single argument for ending *de facto* segregation in Northern urban systems.

Racial isolation of public school pupils is widespread throughout the nation. The U.S. Commission on Civil Rights reported that 75 percent of the black elementary school pupils in 75 large cities attended predominantly black schools (those with 95 to 100 percent black enrollment).

Ending racial isolation in the public schools frequently involves busing school children into and out of segregated neighborhoods ("ghettos"). The objective is to achieve a racial "balance" in each public school, so that each has roughly the same percentage of blacks and whites as are found in the total population of the entire school district. Indeed, in some large cities where blacks comprise the overwhelming majority of public school students, desegregation may require city students to be bused to the suburbs and suburban students to be bused to the core city.

The argument *for* busing is that it is the most effective and efficient method of providing minority groups with equal opportunities in education. Currently, black ghetto schools do not provide the same educational opportunities that are provided in predominantly white outer-city and suburban schools. As a black city councilman in Detroit put it:

> It's pragmatic. We don't have any desire to be close to white people just for the sake of being close to white people. We want the same thing everyone else wants so we can have the same opportunities for our kids to learn and grow.[11]

Blacks have a constitutional right to equal educational opportunities. Busing is an inconvenience, but it certainly is a minor inconvenience compared with the value of equal educational opportunity. Moreover, many supporters of busing argue that *de facto* segregation has indeed been abetted by government policies—for example, federal housing programs that build low-income public housing in central cities and promote middle-class home ownership in suburbs; transportation policies that make it easier for affluent white middle-class residents to

[11]*Time*, November 15, 1971, p. 64.

leave the central city for homes in the suburbs while retaining their jobs in the cities—and therefore governments have a clear responsibility to take affirmative steps, including busing, to integrate public schools. Suburban residents contributed to *de facto* segregation in the central city when they moved to the suburbs, and now it is only fair that their children be bused back and forth between the suburbs and the ghettos in order to rectify the resulting racial imbalance.

The argument against busing is not necessarily "racist." Many middle-class parents feel that busing their children to ghetto schools will expose them to the social problems of ghettos—crimes, drugs, and violence. White parents fear that their children will be exposed to what blacks themselves are trying to escape—the rapes, ripoffs, robberies, and drug abuse that have turned many inner-city schools into blackboard jungles. Middle-class whites who have moved to a suburb for the sake of its school system resent the fact that courts will order their children to be bused back to the poorer quality city schools. A Michigan mother argues: "I don't see any reason why they've got a right to come in here and tell me my kids can't use the school I bought and paid for."[12] Ending *de facto* segregation requires drastic changes in the prevailing concept of "neighborhood schools." Schools would no longer be a part of the neighborhood or the local community but rather part of a large citywide or areawide school system. Finally, the ending of *de facto* segregation would require school districts to classify students on the basis of race and use racial categories as a basis for school placement. Although this would supposedly be a benign form of racial classification, nevertheless it would represent a return to both government-sponsored racial classification and the differential application of laws to the separate races (in contrast to the notion that the law should be "colorblind").

The greatest opposition to busing comes when white middle-class children are ordered to attend ghetto schools. Opposition is greatly reduced when ghetto children are ordered to attend predominantly white middle-class schools (see Table 3–2). Most whites do not believe in sending youngsters from a good school to a bad school in order to achieve racial integration. Busing also destroys the concept of a neighborhood school, where children are educated near their homes under the guidance of their parents. Neighborhood schools are said to stimulate community involvement in the educational process, bringing teachers, parents, and students together more frequently. In addition, busing involves educational time wasted in riding buses, educational funds spent on buses rather than learning materials, and an unnecessary increase in the risk of accidents to many children. Proponents of

[12]Ibid., p. 57.

**TABLE 3–2**  Mass Opinion on School Integration

QUESTION: Would you, yourself, have any objection to sending your children to a school where a few of the children are Negroes? Where half are Negroes? Where more than half are Negroes?

| | Percentage Objecting | |
| --- | --- | --- |
| | Northern White Parents | Southern White Parents |
| Where a few are Negroes? | | |
| 1963 | 10% | 61% |
| 1970 | 6 | 16 |
| 1973 | 6 | 16 |
| Where half are Negroes? | | |
| 1963 | 33% | 78% |
| 1970 | 24 | 43 |
| 1973 | 23 | 36 |
| Where more than half are Negroes? | | |
| 1963 | 53% | 86% |
| 1970 | 51 | 69 |
| 1973 | 63 | 69 |

Source: Data derived from Gallup Opinion Index (October 1973), p. 14.

busing argue that it brings children of different cultures together and teaches them to live, work, and play with others who are different from themselves. But opponents of busing cite the record of racial violence in mixed schools. Besides, racial balancing does not always result in genuine integration; as one Pennsylvania high-school student remarked after a citywide busing program: "I thought the purpose of busing was to integrate the schools, but in the long run, the white kids sit in one part of the bus and the black kids in another part."[13]

## Busing: The Constitutional Question

The question of equality in public education, however, is a constitutional question to be resolved by federal courts rather than public opinion. The Fourteenth Amendment guarantees "equal protection of the laws." If the Supreme Court requires busing and racial balancing in all public schools in order to fulfill the constitutional mandate of the Fourteenth Amendment, then only another amendment to the Constitution specifically prohibiting busing and racial balancing could overturn that decision.

Where racial imbalance and *de facto* segregation are a product of

[13]Ibid., p. 63.

past discriminatory practices by states or school districts, the Supreme Court has held that school officials have a duty to eliminate all vestiges of segregation, and this responsibility may entail busing and deliberate racial balancing to achieve integration in education. In the important case of *Swann* v. *Charlotte-Mecklenburg Board of Education* (1971),[14] the Supreme Court held that the racial composition of the school in a southern district that had previously been segregated by law could be used as evidence of violation of constitutional rights, and busing to achieve racial balance could be imposed as a means of ending all traces of dualism in the schools. The Supreme Court was careful to say, however, that racial imbalance in school is not itself grounds for ordering busing unless it is also shown that some present or past government action has contributed to that imbalance. Thus, the impact of the Swann decision falls largely on *southern* schools.

The constitutional question in *northern* cities is somewhat different from that in southern cities. In *Milliken* v. *Bradly* (1974), the Supreme Court decided by a 5-to-4 vote that the Fourteenth Amendment does *not* require busing across city-suburban school district boundaries to achieve integration.[15] Where central-city schools are predominantly black, and suburban schools are predominantly white, *cross-district* busing is not required, unless it is shown that some official action brought about this segregation. The Supreme Court threw out a lower federal court order for massive busing of students between Detroit and fifty-two suburban school districts. Although Detroit city schools were 70 percent black, none of the Detroit area school districts segregated students within their own boundaries.

Chief Justice Burger, writing for the majority, said:

> The constitutional right of the Negro respondents residing in Detroit is to attend a unitary school system in that district. Unless petitioners drew the district lines in a discriminatory fashion, or arranged for the white students residing in the Detroit district to attend schools in Oakland or Macomb counties, they were under no constitutional duty to make provisions for Negro students to do so.

In a strong dissent, Justice Thurgood Marshall wrote:

> In the short run it may seem to be the easiest course to allow our great metropolitan areas to be divided up each into cities—one white, the other black—but it is a course, I predict, our people will ultimately regret.

This important decision means that largely black central cities, surrounded by largely white suburbs, will remain *de facto* segregated

[14]*Swann* v. *Charlotte-Mecklenburg Board of Education,* 402 U.S. 1 (1971).
[15]*Milliken* v. *Bradly,* 418 U.S. 717 (1974).

because there are not enough white students living within the city to achieve integration.

Note that this decision applies only to city-suburban cross-district busing. If a federal district court judge in any city, North or South, finds that any actions by governments or school officials have contributed to racial imbalances (for example, drawing school district attendance lines), the judge may still order busing within the city to overcome any racial imbalances produced by official action. In recent years, an increasing number of northern cities has come under federal district court orders to improve racial balances in their schools through busing.

The city of Chicago was ordered by a federal court in 1979 to "desegregate" its city schools, even though only 19 percent of the city's public school pupils were white. Nonetheless, the court ordered the busing of hundreds of thousands of pupils on one-way trips of up to forty minutes just to insure that every school had approximately 19 percent white enrollment. White children are bused far from home to be part of a 19 percent minority at a distant school; and black children are bused far from home to schools where they will still be part of a black majority—just so they can have a few whites in their classrooms. "Desegregation" programs such as these raise the question of the effectiveness of busing in achieving equality of educational opportunity.

## Busing: An Evaluation

Desegregation has *not* come to mean the elimination of racial imbalance in the public schools. Indeed, there is some evidence that government efforts to "desegregate" city schools in both the North and the South have resulted in *greater* racial imbalances. The reason, of course, is that many white parents confronted with busing and racial integration chose to move out of the city or to enroll their children in private schools. The result is the withdrawal of whites from city public schools and "resegregation" when black pupil percentages climb to 50, 75, or 95 percent of total public school enrollment. Thus, racial isolation in American schools remains quite high.

The most influential evidence of the failure of busing to achieve integration is sociologist James S. Coleman's *Trends in School Desegregation,* a 1975 study sometimes called the "Second Coleman Report," by the same scholar who provided the original evidence that racial imbalance lowers the scores of black school children. In this study, however, Coleman is concerned with whether court-ordered busing produces its intended effects, that is, improved racial balance—or whether it merely stimulates white flight and makes matters worse. In observing *all* U.S. cities, Coleman concludes that racial imbalance is decreasing, particularly in the South. However, among the largest metropolitan areas (1) there is a "sizable loss of whites" when government desegregation programs go into effect, and (2) white loss is greatest with larger black populations and surrounding white suburban rings.

Blacks now comprise the overwhelming majority of public school pupils in Detroit, Philadelphia, Boston, Atlanta, Chicago, Baltimore, Cleveland, Gary, Memphis, New Orleans, Newark, Richmond, St. Louis, and almost all the public school pupils in Washington, D.C.

Critics of the notion of "white flight" argue that there are many other reasons besides desegregation which encourage white migration out of the city. For example, a family that flees the city of Detroit may be reacting to the city's income tax, or its 1967 racial riot, or its black mayor, or the massive housing abandonment, or the loss of jobs in the city, or its severe financial difficulties, etc. School desegregation may only be the final factor that leads the family move *now*, but the general condition of the city virtually guarantees that the family would move eventually. Critics also point to some big-city school districts which have *not* experienced white flight, despite large-scale, court-ordered desegregation plans involving busing.

## Black Activism and the Civil Rights of 1964

The first goal of the civil rights movement in America was to prevent discrimination and segregation by governments, particularly states, municipalities, and school districts. But even while important victories for the civil rights movement were being recorded in the prevention of discrimination by governments, particularly in the Brown case, the movement began to broaden its objectives to include the elimination of discrimination in *all* segments of American life, private as well as public. Governments should not only cease discriminatory practices of their own, they should also act to halt discrimination by private organizations and individuals.

The goal of eliminating discrimination in private life creates a positive obligation of government to act forcefully in public accommodations, employment, housing, and many other sectors of society. When the civil rights movement turned to combating private discrimination, it had to carry its fight into the legislative branch of government. The federal courts could help restrict discrimination by state and local governments and school authorities, but only Congress, state legislatures, and city councils could restrict discrimination practiced by private owners of restaurants, hotels and motels, private employers, and other individuals who were not government officials.

The leadership in the struggle to eliminate discrimination and segregation from private life was provided by a young black minister, Martin Luther King, Jr. King's father was the pastor of one of the South's largest and most influential congregations, the Ebenezer Baptist Church in Atlanta, Georgia. Martin Luther King, Jr., received his doctorate from Boston College and began his ministry in Montgomery, Alabama. In 1955 the black community of Montgomery began a year-long boycott with frequent demonstrations against the Montgomery city buses over segregated seating practices. The dramatic appeal and the eventual success of the boycott in Montgomery brought nationwide attention to its leader, and led to the creation in 1957 of the Southern Christian Leadership Conference.

Under King's leadership the civil rights movement developed and refined political techniques for minorities in American politics including "nonviolent direct action." Nonviolent direct action is a form of protest which involves breaking "unjust" law in an open, "loving," nonviolent fashion. The general notion of civil disobedience is not new; it has played an important role in American history from the Boston Tea Party to the abolitionists who illegally hid runaway slaves, to the suffragettes who demonstrated for women's voting rights, to the labor organizers who formed the nation's major industrial unions, to the civil rights workers of the early 1960s who deliberately violated segregation laws. The purpose of nonviolent direct action is to call attention, or to "bear witness" to, the existence of injustice. In the words of Martin Luther King, Jr., civil disobedience "seeks to dramatize the issue so that it can no longer be ignored."[16]

There should be no violence in true civil disobedience, and only "unjust" laws are broken. Moreover, the law is broken "openly, lovingly" with a willingness to accept the penalty. Punishment is actively sought rather than avoided, since punishment will help to emphasize the injustice of the law. The object is to stir the conscience of an elite, and win support for measures which will eliminate the injustices. By willingly accepting punishment for the violation of an unjust law, one demonstrates the strength of his convictions. The dramatization of injustice makes news; the public's sympathy is won when injustices are spotlighted; and the willingness of demonstrators to accept punishment is visible evidence of their sincerity. Cruelty or violence directed

---

[16]For an inspiring essay on "nonviolent direct action" and civil disobedience in a modern context, read Martin Luther King, Jr., "Letter from Birmingham City Jail," April 16, 1963, reprinted in Thomas R. Dye and Brett W. Hawkins, eds., *Politics in the Metropolis* (Columbus: Charles E. Merrill, 1967).

against the demonstrators by police or others play into the hands of the protesters by further emphasizing the injustices they are experiencing.[17]

In 1963 a group of Alabama clergymen petitioned Martin Luther King, Jr., to call off mass demonstrations in Birmingham. King, who had been arrested in the demonstrations, replied in his famous "Letter from Birmingham Jail":

> In no sense do I advocate evading or defying the law as the rabid segregationist would do. This would lead to anarchy. One who breaks an unjust law must do it *openly, lovingly* (not hatefully as the white mothers did in New Orleans when they were seen on television screaming "nigger, nigger, nigger") and with a willingness to accept the penalty. I submit that an individual who breaks a law that conscience tells him is unjust, and willingly accepts the penalty by staying in jail to arouse the conscience of the community over its injustice, is in reality expressing the very highest respect for law.

It is important to note that King's tactics relied primarily on an appeal to the conscience of white elites. The purpose of demonstrations was to call attention to injustice and stimulate established elites to remedy the injustice by lawful means. The purpose of civil disobedience was to dramatize injustice; only *unjust* laws were to be broken "openly and lovingly," and punishment was accepted to demonstrate sincerity. King did *not* urge black masses to remedy injustice themselves by any means necessary; and he did *not* urge the overthrow of established elites.

In 1964, Martin Luther King, Jr., received the Nobel Peace Prize in recognition of his unique contributions to the development of non-violent methods of social change.

Perhaps the most dramatic confrontation between the civil rights movement and southern segregationists occurred in Birmingham, Alabama, in the spring of 1963. In support of a request for desegregation of downtown eating places and the formation of a biracial committee to work out the integration of public schools, Martin Luther King, Jr., led several thousand Birmingham blacks in a series of orderly street marches. The demonstrators were met with strong police action, including fire hoses, police dogs, and electric cattle prods. Newspaper pictures of blacks being attacked by police and bitten by dogs were flashed all over the world. More than 25,000 demonstrators, including Dr. King, were jailed.

The year 1963 was probably the most important for nonviolent

[17]For more detailed examinations of the purposes, functions, and rationale of civil disobedience, see Paul F. Power, "Civil Disobedience as Functional Opposition," *Journal of Politics*, 34 (February 1972), 37–55; and "On Civil Disobedience in Recent American Thought," *American Political Science Review*, 64 (March 1970), 35–47.

direct action. The Birmingham action set off demonstrations in many parts of the country; the theme remained one of nonviolence, and it was usually whites rather than blacks who resorted to violence in these demonstrations. Responsible black elites remained in control of the movement and won widespread support from the white liberal community. The culmination of the nonviolent philosophy was a giant, yet orderly march on Washington, held on August 28, 1963. More than 200,000 blacks and whites participated in the march, which was endorsed by many labor leaders, religious groups, and political figures. It was in response to this march that President Kennedy sent a strong civil rights bill to Congress which was passed after his death—the famous Civil Rights Act of 1964.

The Civil Rights Act of 1964 passed both houses of Congress by better than a two-thirds favorable vote; it won the overwhelming support of both Republican and Democratic Congressmen. It was signed into law on July 4, 1964. It ranks with the Emancipation Proclamation, the Fourteenth Amendment, and *Brown* v. *Topeka* as one of the most important steps toward full equality for blacks in America.

The Civil Rights Act of 1964 provides that:

1. It is unlawful to apply unequal standards in voter registration procedures, or to deny registration for irrelevant errors or omissions on records or applications.

2. It is unlawful to discriminate or segregate persons on the grounds of race, color, religion, or national origin in any public accommodation, including hotels, motels, restaurants, movies, theaters, sports arenas, entertainment houses, and other places that offer to serve the public. This prohibition extends to all establishments whose operations affect interstate commerce or whose discriminatory practices are supported by state action.

3. The attorney general shall undertake civil action on behalf of any person denied equal access to a public accommodation to obtain a federal district court order to secure compliance with the act. If the owner or manager of a public accommodation should continue to discriminate, he would be in contempt of court and subject to peremptory fines and imprisonment without trial by jury. (This mode of enforcement gave establishments a chance to mend their ways without punishment, and it also avoided the possibility that southern juries would refuse to convict persons for violations of the act.)

4. The attorney general shall undertake civil actions on behalf of persons attempting orderly desegregation of public schools.

5. The Commission on Civil Rights, first established in the Civil Rights Act of 1957, shall be empowered to investigate deprivations of the right to vote, study, and collect information regarding the discrimination in America, and make reports to the President and Congress.

6. Each federal department and agency shall take action to end discrimination in all programs or activities receiving federal financial assistance in any form. This action shall include termination of financial assistance.

7. It shall be unlawful for any employer or labor union to discriminate against any individual in any fashion in employment, because of his race, color, religion, sex, or national origin, and that an Equal Employment Opportunity Commission shall be established to enforce this provision by investigation, conference, conciliation, persuasion, and if need be, civil action in federal court.

For many years "fair housing" had been considered the most sensitive area of civil rights legislation. Discrimination in the sale and rental of housing was the last major civil rights problem on which Congress took action. Discrimination in housing had not been mentioned in any previous legislation—not even in the comprehensive Civil Rights Act of 1964. Prohibiting discrimination in the sale or rental of housing affected the constituencies of northern members of Congress more than any of the earlier southern-oriented legislation.

The prospects for a fair housing law were not very good at the beginning of 1968. However, when Martin Luther King, Jr., was assassinated on April 4 the mood of Congress changed dramatically and many leaders felt that Congress should pass a fair housing law as tribute to the slain civil rights leader.

The Civil Rights Act of 1968 prohibited the following forms of discrimination:

Refusal to sell or rent a dwelling to any person because of his race, color, religion, or national origin.

Discrimination against a person in the terms, conditions, or privileges of the sale or rental of a dwelling.

Advertising the sale or rental of a dwelling indicating a preference or discrimination based on race, color, religion, or national origin.

Inducing persons to sell or rent a dwelling by referring to the entry into the neighborhood of persons of a particular race, religion, or national origin (the "blockbusting" technique of real estate selling).

But despite a "fair housing" legislation, America is becoming *more* segregated over time, as black populations of large, central cities increase and white populations flee to surrounding suburbs. Black majorities will soon be found in more than a dozen of the nation's large cities: Washington, Atlanta, Newark, Detroit, Baltimore, St. Louis, New Orleans, Oakland, Cleveland, Gary. This suggests a developing pattern of predominantly black core cities, surrounded by nearly all-white suburbs. Even if direct discrimination is ended by "fair housing" laws, economic forces will continue to separate most black and white housing.

## Public Policy and Affirmative Action

Although the gains of the civil rights movement were immensely important, it must be recognized that they were *symbolic* rather than *actual* changes in the conditions under which most blacks live in America. Racial politics today center around the actual inequalities between blacks and whites in incomes, jobs, housing, health, education, and other conditions of life.

The problem of inequality is usually posed as differences in the "life chances" of blacks and whites. Figures can reveal only the bare outline of the black's "life chances" in American society (see Table 3–3). The average income of a black family is only 57 percent of the average white family's income. Nearly one-third of all black families are below the recognized poverty line, while less than 10 percent of white families live in poverty. The black unemployment rate is almost twice as high as the white unemployment rate. Blacks are less likely to hold prestigious white-collar jobs in professional, managerial, clerical, or sales work. They do not hold many skilled craft jobs in industry, but are concentrated in operative, service, and laboring positions. The civil rights movement opened up new opportunities for black Americans. But equality of *opportunity* is not the same as *absolute* equality.

What public policies should be pursued to achieve equality in America? Is it sufficient that government eliminate discrimination, guarantee "equality of opportunity," and apply "colorblind" standards to both blacks and whites? Or should government take "affirmative action" to overcome the results of past unequal treatment of blacks—preferential or compensatory treatment that will favor black applicants for university admissions and scholarships, job hiring and promotion, and other opportunities for advancement in life?

The earlier emphasis of government policy, of course, was nondiscrimination, or *equal employment opportunity.* Equal employment opportunity ". . . was not a program to offer special privilege to any one group of persons because of their particular, race, religion, sex, or national origin."[18] This appeared to conform to the original nondiscrimination approach of executive orders, beginning with President Harry Truman's decision to desegregate the armed forces in 1946, and

[18]See David H. Rosenbloom, "The Civil Service Commission's Decision to Authorize the Use of Goals and Timetables in Federal Equal Employment Opportunity Programs," *Western Political Quarterly,* 26 (June 1973), 236–51.

**TABLE 3–3**  Change in Black-White Life Chances

### Median Income of Families

|  | 1947 | 1960 | 1968 | 1970 | 1972 | 1974 | 1978 |
|---|---|---|---|---|---|---|---|
| White | $4,916 | $6,857 | $8,937 | $10,236 | $11,549 | $13,356 | $16,782 |
| Black | $2,514 | $3,794 | $5,590 | $ 6,516 | $ 6,864 | $ 7,808 | $ 9,485 |

### Median Income of Families of Black and Other Races as a Percent of White Family Income

| 1950 | | 54 | 1964 | | 56 | 1972 | | 62 |
|---|---|---|---|---|---|---|---|---|
| 1955 | | 55 | 1966 | | 60 | 1974 | | 58 |
| 1959 | | 52 | 1968 | | 63 | 1978 | | 57 |
| 1960 | | 55 | 1970 | | 64 | | | |

### Persons Below Poverty Level

|  | Millions | | Percent of Total | |
|---|---|---|---|---|
|  | Black | White | Black | White |
| 1959 | 11.0 | 28.5 | 56 | 18 |
| 1965 | 10.7 | 22.5 | 47 | 13 |
| 1969 | 7.6 | 16.7 | 31 | 10 |
| 1974 | 7.5 | 16.3 | 31 | 9 |
| 1978 | 8.3 | 16.4 | 29 | 9 |

### Occupation: Blacks and Other Races as Percent of All Workers in Selected Occupations

|  | 1960 | 1970 | 1974 | 1978 |
|---|---|---|---|---|
| Professional | 4 | 6 | 7 | 8 |
| Medical | 4 | 8 | 8 | 8 |
| Teachers | 7 | 10 | 9 | 9 |
| Managers | 2 | 3 | 4 | 5 |
| Clerical | 5 | 8 | 9 | 10 |
| Sales | 3 | 4 | 4 | 5 |
| Craftsmen | 5 | 7 | 7 | 7 |
| Operatives | 12 | 14 | 13 | 14 |
| Nonfarm laborers | 27 | 24 | 20 | 18 |
| Private household | 46 | 44 | 41 | 36 |
| Other service | 20 | 19 | 19 | 18 |
| Farm | 16 | 11 | 9 | 9 |

### Percent of Persons 25 to 29 Years Old Who Completed 4 Years of High School or More

|  | Male | | Female | |
|---|---|---|---|---|
|  | Black | White | Black | White |
| 1960 | 37 | 64 | 42 | 66 |
| 1968 | 55 | 78 | 58 | 77 |
| 1971 | 59 | 81 | 63 | 80 |
| 1978 | 74 | 87 | 74 | 86 |

*Source:* Bureau of the Census, "The Social and Economic Status of the Black Population in the United States," Current Population Reports, Series No. 23; U.S. Commission on Civil Rights, *Social Indicators of Equality for Minorities and Women* (Washington: Government Printing Office, 1978).

carrying through Title VI and Title VII of the Civil Rights Act of 1964 to eliminate discrimination in federally aided projects and private employment. Before 1970 there were no quota systems for black applicants which might result in lower-qualified blacks being selected over higher-qualified whites for schools, jobs, or promotions.

Increasingly, however, the goal of the civil rights movement shifted from the traditional aim of equality of opportunity through nondiscrimination alone, to affirmative action to establish "goals and timetables" to achieve absolute equality between blacks and whites. While usually avoiding the term "quota," the notion of affirmative action tests the success of equal employment opportunity by observing whether blacks achieve admissions, jobs, and promotions in proportion to their numbers in the population.

Affirmative action programs are products of the federal bureaucracy. These programs were not enacted by Congress. Instead, these programs were developed by the federal executive agencies which were authorized by the Civil Rights Act of 1964 to develop "rules and regulations" for desegregating activities receiving federal funds (Title VI) and private employment (Title VII). One of the first applications of affirmative action occurred in 1967 when the U.S. Office of Federal Contract Compliance issued the "Philadelphia Plan," which required contractors bidding on federal projects to submit affirmative action plans including specific percentage goals for the employment of minorities. At first the U.S. Civil Service Commission resisted the imposition of "goals" in federal employment.[19] But as pressure developed for greater minority representation, the Civil Service Commission relented and distinguished between "quotas" and "goals": "While quotas are not permissible, federal agencies may use numerical guidelines to assess progress toward equal employment opportunity and as one means of deterring the need for additional affirmative action regarding minority employment."[20] In 1972 the U.S. Office of Education issued guidelines which mandated "goals" for university admissions and faculty hiring of blacks and women. The Equal Employment Opportunity Commission established by the Civil Rights Act of 1964 (Title VII) to eliminate discrimination in private employment has carried the notion of affirmative action beyond federal contractors and recipients of federal aid into all sectors of private employment.

Federal officials generally measure "progress" in "affirmative action" in terms of the number of blacks admitted, employed, or promoted. The pressure to show "progress" and retain federal financial

---

[19]Letter from Civil Service Commission, July 24, 1970; cited ibid., p. 247.
[20]Letter from Civil Service Commission, February 3, 1971; cited ibid., p. 247.

support can result in preferential treatment of blacks and discrimination against whites with equal or better qualifications. It also puts pressure on traditional measures of qualifications—test scores and educational achievement. Blacks argue that these are not good predictors of performance on the job or in school and that these measures are biased in favor of white culture. State and local governments, schools, colleges and universities, and private employers are under pressure to drop these standards.[21] But how far can any school, agency, or employer go in dropping traditional standards? It is not difficult to drop educational requirements for sanitation workers, but what about for physicians, surgeons, attorneys, pilots, and others whose skills directly affect health and safety?

The question becomes even more complex if we try to weigh the costs of some "reverse discrimination" against the value of achieving greater representation of blacks in all echelons of society. Perhaps it is better for society as a whole to make some sacrifices to bring black Americans into the mainstream of economic life—to give them a "stake in society," and hence to sew up the worn fabric of the social system. But who must make these sacrifices? It is not the established white upper classes, but the sons and daughters of white middle- and working-class families who are in direct competition with upwardly mobile blacks. Must the price of past discrimination against blacks now fall on these young whites? Another problem: can preferential treatment eventually create new injustices for blacks who have been recipients of such treatment? Will it create a facade of equality and representation, while actually patronizing black recipients? Does preferential treatment imply that blacks cannot "make it" without such treatment? Clearly there are sensitive moral and ethical questions surrounding this area of public policy, as well as the constitutional question of equal protection of the laws.

## Affirmative Action: Bakke and Weber

The constitutional question posed by "affirmative action" programs is whether or not they discriminate against whites in violation of the Equal Protection Clause of the Fourteenth Amendment. A related question is whether or not affirmative action programs discriminate against whites in violation of the Civil Rights Act of 1964, which prohibits discrimination "on account of race," not just discrimination

---

[21]See Frank J. Thompson, "Bureaucratic Responsiveness in the Cities: The Problem of Minority Hiring," *Urban Affairs Quarterly*, 10 (September 1974), 40–68.

against blacks. Clearly, these are questions for the Supreme Court to resolve, but unfortunately the Court has failed to develop clear-cut answers.

In *Regents of the University of California* v. *Bakke* (1978), the Supreme Court struck down a special admissions program for minorities at a state medical school on the grounds that it excluded a white applicant because of his race and violated his rights under the Equal Protection Clause. Allan Bakke applied to the University of California Davis Medical School two consecutive years and was rejected; in both years black applicants with significantly lower grade point averages and medical aptitude test scores were accepted through a special admissions program which reserved sixteen minority places in a class of one hundred.[22] The University of California did not deny that its admission decisions were based on race. Instead, it argued that its racial classification was "benign," that is, designed to assist minorities, not to hinder them. The special admissions program was designed (1) to "reduce the historical deficit of traditionally disfavored minorities in medical schools and the medical profession," (2) "to counter the effects of societal discrimination," (3) to "increase the number of physicians who will practice in communities currently underserved," and (4) to "obtain the educational benefits that flow from an ethnically diverse student body."

The Court held that these objectives were legitimate and that race and ethnic origin *may* be considered in reviewing applications to a state school without violating the Equal Protection Clause. However, the Court also held that a *separate* admissions program for minorities with a specified quota of openings which were unavailable to white applicants violated the Equal Protection Clause. "The guarantee of equal protection cannot mean one thing when applied to one individual and something else when applied to another. If both are not accorded the same protection, then it is not equal."

The Court ordered Bakke admitted to medical school and the elimination of the special admissions program. It recommended that California consider an admission program developed at Harvard that considered disadvantaged racial or ethnic background as a "plus" in an overall evaluation of an applicant, but did not set numerical quotas or exclude any persons from competing for all positions.

Reaction to the decision was predictable: supporters of affirmative action, particularly government officials from affirmative action

[22]Bakke's grade point average was 3.51; his MCAT scores were: verbal—96, quantitative—94, science—97, general information—72. The average for the special admissions students were: grade point average—2.62, MCAT verbal—34, quantitative—30, science—37, general information—18.

programs, emphasized the Supreme Court's willingness to allow minority status to be considered a positive factor; opponents emphasized the Supreme Court's unwillingness to allow quotas which excluded whites from competing for a certain number of positions. Since Bakke had "won" the case, most observers felt that the Supreme Court was not going to permit discriminatory quota systems.

However, in *United Steelworkers of America* v. *Weber* (1979), the Supreme Court approved a plan developed by a private employer and a union to reserve 50 percent of higher paying, skilled jobs for minorities. Kaiser Aluminum Corporation and the United Steelworkers Union, under federal government pressure, had established a program to get more blacks into skilled technical jobs; only 2 percent of the skilled jobs were held by blacks in the plant where Weber worked, while 39 percent of the local workforce was black. When Weber was excluded from the training program, and blacks with less seniority and fewer qualifications were accepted, Weber filed suit in federal court claiming that he had been discriminated against because of his race in violation of Title VII of the Civil Rights Act of 1964. (Weber could not claim that his rights under the Fourteenth Amendment's Equal Protection Clause had been violated, because this clause applies only to the "state," that is governmental discrimination, and not to private employers.) Title VII prevents *all* discrimination in employment on the basis of race; it does not specify only discrimination against blacks or minorities.

The Supreme Court held that Title VII of the Civil Rights Act of 1964 "left employers and unions in the private sector free to take such race-conscious steps to eliminate manifest racial imbalances in traditionally segregated job categories. We hold that Title VII does not prohibit such . . . affirmative action plans." Weber's reliance on the clear language of Title VII was "misplaced." According to the Court, it would be "ironic indeed" if the Civil Rights Act were used to prohibit "all voluntary private race-conscious efforts to traditional patterns" of discrimination.

The Weber ruling was applauded by the U.S. Equal Employment Opportunity Commission, as well as by various civil rights organizations, who hoped to use the decision to step up affirmative action plans in industry and government. The decision does not directly affect women, but it may be used as a precedent to strengthen affirmative action programs for them.

How can the Bakke and Weber decisions be reconciled into a coherent policy on affirmative action? They probably *cannot* be reconciled. It is true that the Bakke case struck down a quota system established by a *state* agency under the Equal Protection Clause, while the Weber case upheld a quota system voluntarily established by a *private* employer under Title VII of the Civil Rights Act of 1964. But it is unlikely the Supreme Court will continue to differentiate between state agencies and private employers. Rather than search for consistency in the law, perhaps we should resign ourselves to some uncertainties about how far "affirmative action" programs can go without becoming "reverse discrimination." Perhaps each program will have to be judged separately, and no clear-cut national policy will emerge.

## Equality of Opportunity: An Evaluation

Occasionally, the rhetoric of politics suggests that the conditions of blacks in America are worsening, that America is hopelessly racist, and that there is no possibility of real progress. This is not true. Blacks have made great progress over the last decade in income, jobs, education, housing, and other conditions of life.

Perhaps the best way to evaluate progress in equality is to observe long-term changes in "social indicators"—measures of well-being in society. For example, the proportion of blacks living below the recognized poverty line has fallen from 56 percent of all blacks to 29 percent (see Table 3–3). Blacks have increased their percentage of professional, managerial, sales, clerical, and other white-collar jobs, and reduced their percentage of laborers, service workers, and farmers. The proportion of blacks living in substandard housing has fallen from nearly one-half to less than one-quarter. Blacks also have narrowed the gap in education; the percentage of black college graduates has doubled.

There is some disturbing evidence, however, that suggests a recent slowdown in progress toward equality. For example, median black family income, which had risen from 54 to 64 percent of median white family income between 1950 and 1970, has slipped back in recent years to 57 percent. Blacks have not kept up with inflationary pressures in the economy as well as whites have. Nevertheless, black educational progress has continued, and so has black movement into professional and managerial positions. Thus, despite long-term progress in narrowing black-white "life chances" in America, there is no justification for complacency. Continued progress will require a healthy economy and conscious efforts by blacks and whites to insure equality of opportunity.

It is important that we do not mistake failure to progress fast enough with failure to progress at all. Of course whites have made progress too, and in every measure of "life chances" blacks remain below average white levels. Doubtlessly, the progress made by blacks in recent years has been long overdue, and no rate of progress can be considered fast enough. But progress has been impressive.

## Sexual Equality and Public Policy

Women constitute slightly over 50 percent of the American population, but few women have entered the ranks of the nation's governing elite. There have never been more than nineteen women among the 535 members of Congress. And many of these women gained their seats through widowhood, having been appointed or elected to fill the term of a deceased husband. No woman has yet served on the Supreme Court; and even though women have headed governments of other nations (Golda Meier of Israel, Margaret Thatcher of Great Britain, Indira Gandhi of India), no women have ever been seriously considered for the American presidency. Only four women have ever served as governors, and only two of these, Ella Grasso of Connecticut and Dixie Lee Ray of Washington, did not serve in the shadow of a husband. Women are also seriously underrepresented in top positions in corporations, banks, universities, foundations, and the mass media.[23]

The earliest active "feminist" organizations grew out of the pre-Civil War antislavery movement. The first generation of feminists included Lucretia Mott, Elizabeth Cady Stanton, Lucy Stone, and Susan B. Anthony. They learned to organize, hold public meetings, and conduct petition campaigns as abolitionists. After the Civil War, women were successful in changing many state laws which abridged the property rights of married women and otherwise treated them as "chattel" (property) of their husbands. Women were also prominent in the Anti-Saloon League, which succeeded in outlawing prostitution and gambling in every state (except Nevada) and providing a major source of support for the Eighteenth Amendment (Prohibition). In the early twentieth century the feminist movement concentrated on women's suffrage—the drive to guarantee women the right to vote. The early suffragettes employed mass demonstrations, parades, picketing, and occasional disruption and civil disobedience—tactics similar to those of the civil rights movement of the 1960s. The culmination of the early feminist movement was the passage in 1920 of the Nineteenth Amend-

[23]See Thomas R. Dye, *Who's Running America?* 2nd ed. (Englewood Cliffs, N.J.: Prentice-Hall, 1979).

| Would you vote for a woman presidential candidate if she were qualified for the job? | | | |
|---|---|---|---|
| | Yes | No | No Opinion |
| 1976 | 73 | 23 | 4 |
| 1971 | 66 | 29 | 5 |
| 1969 | 54 | 39 | 7 |
| 1967 | 57 | 39 | 4 |
| 1955 | 52 | 44 | 4 |
| 1949 | 48 | 48 | 4 |
| 1937 | 31 | 65 | 4 |

Source: Gallup Opinion Index (March 1976), p. 4.

ment to the Constitution: "The right of citizens of the United States to vote shall not be denied or abridged by the United States or by any state on account of sex." The more moderate wing of the American suffrage movement became the League of Women Voters; in addition to women's vote, they sought protection of women in industry, child welfare laws, and honest election practices.

Renewed interest in feminist politics came after the civil rights movement of the 1960s. The women's liberation movement of recent years has worked in the states and in Congress on behalf of a wide range of reforms—the Twenty-Seventh (Equal Rights) Amendment to the Constitution, equal employment opportunities for women, reform of marriage and divorce laws, more convictions in rape cases, and liberalization of abortion laws. New organizations have sprung up to compete with the conventional activities of the League of Women Voters by presenting a more militant and activist stance toward women's liberation. The largest of these new organizations is the National Organization of Women (NOW) founded in 1966, which promises to change "the false image of women now prevalent in the mass media and in the texts, ceremonies, laws and practices of our major social institutions" which "perpetuate contempt for women by society and by women for themselves."[24]

### Employment

The federal Civil Rights Act of 1964, Title VII, prevents sexual (as well as racial) discrimination in hiring, pay, and promotions. The

[24]Congressional Quarterly, *The Women's Movement* (Washington, D.C.: Congressional Quarterly Inc., 1973), p. 14.

Equal Employment Opportunity Commission (EEOC), which is the federal agency charged with eliminating discrimination in employment, has established guidelines barring stereotyped classifications of "men's jobs" and "women's jobs." State laws and employer practices which differentiate between men and women in hours, pay, retirement age, etc., have been struck down. Under active lobbying from feminist organizations, federal agencies, including the U.S. Office of Education and the Office of Federal Contract Compliance, have established affirmative action guidelines for government agencies, universities, and private businesses doing work for the government; these guidelines set goals and timetables for employers to alter their workforce to achieve higher female percentages at all levels.

### Credit

The Federal Equal Credit Opportunity Act of 1974 prohibits sex discrimination in *credit* transactions. Most states now have similar laws. Both federal and state laws prevent banks, credit unions, savings and loan associations, retail stores, and credit card companies from denying credit because of sex or marital status. However, these businesses may still deny credit for a poor or nonexistent credit rating, and some women who have always maintained accounts in their husband's name may still face credit problems if they apply in their own name.

### Education

In recent years, the states, particularly state colleges and universities, have been trying to comply with Title IX of the federal Education Amendment of 1972 dealing with sex discrimination in *education*. This federal law bars discrimination in admissions, housing, rules, financial aid, faculty and staff recruitment and pay, and—most troublesome of all—athletics. The latter problem has proven very difficult because men's football and basketball programs have traditionally brought in the money to finance all other sports, and men's football and basketball have received the largest share of school athletic budgets. To divide athletic budgets equally between men's and women's sports might threaten the financial base of all school athletics. Currently, many schools are striving to upgrade women's sports and provide equal funding *per participant*. But it is not clear whether this satisfies the requirement of Title IX.

At the center of feminist activity in recent years has been the Equal Rights Amendment to the Constitution. The ERA would strike down all existing legal inequalities in state and federal laws between men and women. The amendment states simply: "Equality of rights under the law shall not be denied or abridged by the United States or by any state on account of sex." The ERA passed the Congress easily in 1972 and was sent to the states for necessary ratification of three-fourths (38) of them. The amendment won quick ratification by half the states, but a developing "Stop ERA" movement slowed progress and threatened to defeat the amendment itself.[25] In 1979, the original seven-year time period for ratification—the period customarily set by Congress for ratification of constitutional amendments—expired. However, proponents of ERA persuaded Congress to extend the ratification period for three more years, to 1982.

Proponents of ERA have argued in the state legislatures that most of the progress woman have made toward equality in marriage, property, employment, credit, education, and so on, depends upon states and federal *law*. The guarantee of equality of the sexes would be much more secure if this guarantee were made part of the U.S. Constitution. Moreover, ERA would eliminate the need to pass separate laws on a wide variety of fields to insure sexual equality. ERA, as a permanent part of the U.S. Constitution, would provide a sweeping guarantee of equality, directly enforceable by court action. Finally, ERA has taken on a great deal of symbolic meaning; even if federal and state laws prohibit sexual discrimination now, it is nonetheless important to many to see ERA as part of the U.S. Constitution—"the supreme law of the land."

Opponents of ERA have suggested that it may eliminate many legal protections for women, such as financial support by husbands, an interest in the husband's property, exemption from military service, and so forth. In addition to these specific objections, opposition to "women's liberation" in general has charged that the movement weakens the family institution and demoralizes women who wish to devote their lives to their family, husbands, and children. Finally, some state

---

[25]By 1980, thirty-four states had ratified ERA. Three of them—Idaho, Nebraska, and Tennessee—subsequently voted to "rescind" their ratifications; but the U.S. Constitution does not mention "rescinding" votes. The states which had not ratified by 1980 were Nevada, Utah, Arizona, Oklahoma, Illinois, Indiana, Missouri, Arkansas, Louisiana, Mississippi, Alabama, Georgia, Florida, North Carolina, South Carolina, and Virginia.

legislators have observed that the very vague wording of ERA will greatly increase the power of the federal courts and Congress to intervene in the affairs of states, communities, and private citizens.

## Abortion and the Right to Life

Potentially the most important and far-reaching decision in the recent history of the Supreme Court is its action in the legalization of abortion.[26] Historically, abortions for any purpose other than saving the life of the mother were criminal offenses under state law. About a dozen states acted in the late 1960s to permit abortions in cases of rape or incest, or to protect the physical health of the mother, and in some cases her mental health as well. Relatively few abortions were performed under these laws, however, because of the red tape involved—review of each case by several concurring physicians, approval of a hospital board, and so forth. Then in 1970, New York, Alaska, Hawaii, and Washington enacted laws that in effect permitted abortion at the request of the woman involved and concurrence of a physician.

Abortion is a highly sensitive issue. It is not an issue that can easily be compromised. The arguments touch on fundamental moral and religious principles. Proponents of liberal abortion laws argue that a woman should be permitted to control her own body and should not be forced by law to have unwanted children. They cite the heavy toll in lives lost in criminal abortions and the psychological and emotional pain of an unwanted pregnancy. Opponents of abortion generally base their belief on the sanctity of life, including the life of the unborn child, which they believe deserves the protection of law—the right to life. Many believe that the killing of an unborn child for any reason other than the preservation of the life of the mother is murder.

The movement for liberal abortion laws in America began with a struggle for the liberalization of state laws. It won a national victory when the Supreme Court ruled that the constitutional guarantee of personal liberty in the First and Fourteenth Amendments included a woman's decision to bear or not to bear a child. In the *Roe* v. *Wade* and *Doe* v. *Bolton* decisions, the Supreme Court ruled that the word "person" in the Constitution did not include the unborn child. Therefore the Fifth and Fourteenth Amendments to the Constitution, guaranteeing all persons "life, liberty, and property," did not protect the "life" of the fetus. The court also ruled that a state's power to protect the health

[26]*Roe* v. *Wade*, 410 U.S. 113 (1973); *Doe* v. *Bolton* 410 U.S. 179 (1973).

and safety of the mother could not justify any restriction on abortion in the first three months of pregnancy. Between the third and sixth months of pregnancy, the state could set standards for how and when abortions can be performed in order to protect the health of the mother; but the state cannot prohibit abortions in this period. Only in the final three months of pregnancy, the Supreme Court said, can a state ban all abortions to safeguard the life and health of the mother.

Nonetheless, there are still many unresolved policy issues in abortion laws. Right-to-life groups have sprung up in many states to continue the fight against legalized abortion, as well as to push for a constitutional amendment to define the fetus as a person. Some states have passed legislation protecting doctors and nurses from loss of jobs or other penalties for refusing to carry out abortions because of their moral and religious convictions.[27] State laws are ambiguous about efforts to save aborted fetuses which emerge alive. Some state laws are still very restrictive in their definition of an "approved facility" for an abortion. Congress has spent many hours debating whether or not Medicaid funds for the poor should be used to pay for abortions. Currently, federal law allows the use of public funds for abortions only if the health of the mother is threatened. Some have argued that the "right" to an abortion should include public funds to pay for abortions for the poor. In summary, abortion legislation is still an important item on the agenda of Congress and state legislatures.

## Summary

Let us try to set forth some propositions that are consistent with elite theory and assist in describing the development of civil rights policy.

1. Elites and masses in America differ in their attitudes toward blacks. Support for civil rights legislation has come from educated, affluent whites in leadership positions.

2. Mass opinion toward civil rights has generally *followed* public policy, and not led it. Mass opinion did not oppose legally segregated schools until after elites had declared national policy in *Brown* v. *Topeka*.

3. The greatest impetus to the advancement of civil rights policy in this century was the U.S. Supreme Court's decision in *Brown* v. *To-*

---

[27]However, in *Planned Parenthood of Central Missouri* v. *Danforth* (1976), the Supreme Court struck down state laws requiring a husband's consent for his wife's abortion, and also struck down state laws requiring parental consent for a child's (under 18) abortion.

*peka.* Thus, it was the Supreme Court, nonelected and enjoying life terms in office, which assumed the initiative in civil rights policy. Congress did not take significant action until ten years later.

4. Resistance to the implementation of *Brown* v. *Topeka* was centered in states and communities that had the *largest* black population percentages. Resistance to national policy was remarkably effective for over a decade; blacks were not admitted to white schools in the South in large numbers until all segments of the national elite—Congress and the executive branch, as well as the judicial branch—acted in support of desegregation.

5. The elimination of legal discrimination and the guarantee of equality of opportunity in the Civil Rights Act of 1964 were achieved largely through the dramatic appeals of middle-class black leaders to consciences of white elites. Black leaders did not attempt to overthrow the established order, but to open opportunities for blacks to achieve success within the American system.

6. National elites legally guaranteed nondiscrimination in the sale or rental of housing in 1968, an action that was clearly at variance with the preferences of white masses at the time.

7. Elite support for equality of opportunity does not satisfy the demands of black masses for absolute equality. Inequalities between blacks and whites in life changes—income, education, employment, health—persist, although the gap may be narrowing over the long run.

8. Affirmative action programs are pressed upon governments, universities, and private employers by federal agencies seeking to reduce inequalities. But white masses generally reject the notion of compensatory actions which they believe to disadvantage working-class and middle-class white males.

9. Although women compose slightly more than half the population, few women have ever served in top leadership positions. From its earliest beginnings, the feminist movement has frequently relied on the tactics of minorities—demonstrations, parades, and occasional civil disobedience—to convince governing elites to recognize women's rights. However the Equal Rights Amendment, easily passed by Congress, has run up against serious opposition in the states.

10. Abortion was prohibited by most of the states until the Supreme Court decided in *Roe* v. *Wade* and *Doe* v. *Bolton* in 1973 that women had a constitutional right under the Fifth and Fourteenth Amendments to terminate pregnancies. Thus, the Supreme Court established as a constitutional right what proabortion forces had failed to gain through political processes at the state level.

## Bibliography

BERMAN, DANIEL M., *It Is So Ordered.* New York: Norton, 1966.

CARMICHAEL, STOKELY, and CHARLES V. HAMILTON, *Black Power.* New York: Random House, 1968.

CLARK, KENNETH B., *Dark Ghetto.* New York: Harper & Row, 1965.

DYE, THOMAS R., *The Politics of Equality.* New York: Bobbs-Merrill, 1971.

PARSONS, TALCOTT, and KENNETH B. CLARK, eds., *The Negro American.* Boston: Beacon Press, 1965.

WALTON, HANES, JR., *Black Politics.* Philadelphia: Lippincott, 1972.

"The Women's Movement." *Congressional Quarterly.* Washington D.C.: Congressional Quarterly, 1973.

Police action and activity. *Sybil Shelton*.

# Criminal Justice
## elite response
## to crime and disorder

# 4

Crime, violence, and disorder are central problems confronting any society. So also is the problem of government repression. For thousands of years, men have wrestled with the question of balancing governmental power against individual freedom. How far can individual freedom be carried without undermining the stability of society, threatening the safety of others, and risking anarchy? The early English political philosopher, Thomas Hobbes (1588–1679), believed that society must establish a powerful "Leviathan"—the state—in order to curb the savage instincts in men.[1] He believed that a powerful authority in society was needed to prevent men from attacking each other for personal gain— "a war of every man against every man" where "notions of right and wrong, justice and injustice, have no place." According to Hobbes, without law and order there is no real freedom—the fear of death and destruction permeates every act of life: "every man is enemy to every man"; "force and fraud are the two cardinal virtues"; and "the life of man is solitary, poor, nasty, brutish, and short." It is clear, then, that freedom is *not* the absence of law and order. On the contrary, law and order are required if there is to be any freedom in society at all.

But what happens when a government becomes too strong for the liberties of its citizens? Men agree to abide by law and accept restric-

---

[1]Thomas Hobbes, *Leviathan,* Collier Classics Edition (New York: Macmillan, 1967).

tions on their personal freedom in order to secure peace and self-pres-ervation; but how much liberty must be surrendered in order to secure an orderly society? This is the classic dilemma of free government: men must create laws and governments to protect freedom; the laws and governments themselves restrict freedom.

## The Problem of Crime

It is not an easy task to learn exactly how much crime occurs in society. The *official* crime rates are based upon the Federal Bureau of Investi-gations' *Uniform Crime Reports,* but the FBI reports are based on figures supplied by state and local police agencies (see Table 4–1). The FBI has established a uniform classification of the number of serious crimes per 100,000 people that are reported to the police—murder and non-negligent manslaughter, forcible rape, robbery, aggravated assault, burglary, larceny, and theft, including auto theft. But one should be cautious in interpreting official crime rates. They are really a function of several factors: (1) the diligence of police in detecting crime, (2) the adequacy of the reporting system tabulating crime, and (3) the amount of crime itself.

Between 1960 and 1975 the crime rate in America rose very rap-idly. Every category of crime more than doubled, including the mur-der rate. However, in recent years, the crime rate has continued to in-crease, although not quite as rapidly as a few years ago. We can only speculate about possible reasons for this modest success: (1) police are becoming more effective with training and equipment provided by the

**TABLE 4–1** Crime Rates in the United States; Offenses Known to the Police (Rates per 100,000 Population)

|  | 1960 | 1965 | 1970 | 1972 | 1975 | 1978 |
|---|---|---|---|---|---|---|
| Murder and nonnegligent manslaughter | 5 | 5 | 8 | 9 | 10 | 9 |
| Forcible rape | 9 | 12 | 18 | 22 | 26 | 31 |
| Robbery | 52 | 61 | 172 | 180 | 209 | 191 |
| Aggravated assault | 82 | 107 | 162 | 187 | 214 | 256 |
| Burglary | 465 | 605 | 1,068 | 1,126 | 1,429 | 1,424 |
| Larceny and theft | 1,028 | 1,521 | 2,066 | 1,980 | 2,473 | 2,744 |
| Auto theft | 179 | 251 | 454 | 423 | 461 | 455 |
| Total crimes against person | 148 | 185 | 360 | 398 | 459 | 487 |
| Total crimes against property | 1,672 | 2,177 | 3,588 | 3,529 | 4,363 | 4,622 |

*Source:* FBI, *Uniform Crime Reports,* in *Statistical Abstract of the United States 1979* (pub-lished annually by U.S. Bureau of the Census), p. 291.

federal government, (2) business and industry are installing protective technology (steering locks on autos, for example), and they are hiring more private security guards, or more likely (3) the most "crime-prone" age group, persons fifteen to twenty-four years old, is no longer increasing as a percentage of the population.

We know that the FBI's official crime rates vastly understate the real amount of crime. Citizens do not report many crimes to police. The National Opinion Research Center of the University of Chicago asked a national sample of individuals whether they or any member of their household had been a victim of crime during the past year. This survey revealed that the "victimization rate" is several times greater than the crime rate reported by the FBI. There are more than twice as many crimes committed as reported to the police. The number of forcible rapes was more than three and one-half times the number reported, burglaries three times, aggravated assaults and larcenies more than double, and robbery 50 percent greater than the reported rate. Only auto theft statistics were reasonably accurate, indicating that most people call the police when their cars are stolen.[2]

Why do people fail to report crime to the police? The most common reason given by interviewers was the feeling that police could not be effective in dealing with the crime. This is a serious comment about police protection in America today. Other reasons included the feeling that the crime was "a private matter" or that the victim did not want to harm the offender. Fear of reprisal was mentioned much less frequently, usually in cases of assaults and family crimes.

The current system of criminal justice is certainly no serious deterrent to crime. The best available estimates of the ratio between crime and punishment suggest that the likelihood of an individual being jailed for a serious crime is less than two in one hundred (see Figure 4–1). Police are successful in clearing only about one in five *reported* crimes by arresting the offender. The judicial system only convicts about one in four of the persons arrested and charged; others are not prosecuted, are handled as juveniles, are found not guilty, or are permitted to plead guilty to a lesser charge and released. Only about half of all convicted felons are given prison sentences.

## Police and Law Enforcement

At least three important functions in society are performed by police—law enforcement, keeping the peace, and furnishing services. Actually,

---

[2]See Wesley G. Skogan, "The Validity of Official Crime Statistics: An Empirical Investigation," *Social Science Quarterly*, 55 (June 1974), 25–38.

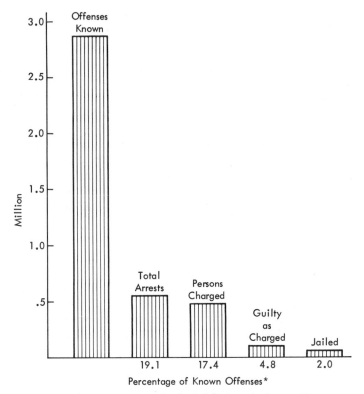

*Actual crime is estimated to be 2-1/2 times the known offenses.
If the base is actual crime, these percentages would be less than
half of those appearing in the figure. Thus, persons jailed as a
percentage of actual crime is less than 1 percent.

FIG. 4–1   Law enforcement in relation to crime
*Source: Statistical Abstract of the United States, 1975* (Washington, D.C.: U.S. Government
Printing Office), p. 157.

law enforcement may take up only a small portion of a policeman's
daily activity, perhaps only 10 percent.[3] The service function is far
more common—attending accidents, directing traffic, escorting crowds,
assisting stranded motorists, handling drunks, and so on (see Table
4–2). The function of peace-keeping is also very common—breaking
up fights, quieting noisy parties, handling domestic or neighborhood
quarrels, and the like. It is in this function that police exercise the
greatest discretion in the application of the law. In most of these inci-

[3]James Q. Wilson, *Varieties of Police Behavior* (Cambridge: Harvard University
Press, 1968), p. 18; Arthur Niederhoffer, *Behind the Shield* (New York: Doubleday,
1967), p. 71.

**TABLE 4–2**  Citizen Complaints Radioed to Police Vehicles

| Calls | Number in Sample | Percentage |
|---|---|---|
| *Information Gathering* | 69 | 22.1 |
| Book and check | 2 | |
| Get a report | 67 | |
| | | |
| *Service* | 117 | 37.5 |
| Accidents, illnesses, ambulance calls | 42 | |
| Animals | 8 | |
| Assist a person | 1 | |
| Drunk person | 8 | |
| Escort vehicle | 3 | |
| Fire, power line or tree down | 26 | |
| Property damage | 6 | |
| | | |
| *Maintenance of Order* | 94 | 30.1 |
| Gang disturbance | 50 | |
| Family trouble | 23 | |
| Assault, fight | 9 | |
| Investigation | 8 | |
| Neighbor trouble | 4 | |
| | | |
| *Law Enforcement* | 32 | 10.3 |
| Burglary in progress | 9 | |
| Check a car | 5 | |
| Open a door or window | 8 | |
| Prowler | 6 | |
| Make an arrest | 4 | |
| TOTALS | 312 | 100.0 |

*Source:* James Q. Wilson, *Varieties of Police Behavior* (Cambridge: Harvard University Press, 1968), p. 18.

dents, it is difficult to determine blame. Participants are reluctant to file charges and police must use personal discretion in handling each case.

Police are on the front line of society's efforts to resolve conflict. Indeed, instead of a legal or law enforcement role, the police are more likely to adopt a peace-keeping role. Police are generally lenient in their arrests practices; that is, they use their arrest practice less often than the law allows.[4] Rather than arresting people, the police prefer first to reestablish order. Of course, the decision to be more or less lenient in enforcing the law gives the police a great deal of discretion—the police exercise decision-making powers on the streets.

What factors influence police decision making? Probably the first factor to influence police behavior is the attitude of the other people involved in police encounters. If a person adopts an acquiescent role,

[4]See Donald J. Black, "Social Organization of Arrest," in *The Criminal Justice Process*, eds. William B. Sanders and Howard C. Davidstel (New York: Praeger, 1976).

displays deference and respect for the police, and conforms to police expectations, he is much less likely to be arrested than a person who shows disrespect or uses abusive language toward police.[5] This is not just an arbitrary response of police. They learned through training and experience the importance of establishing their authority on the streets. One study neatly summarizes "police culture" in terms of attitudes that police bring to the streets.[6]

1. People cannot be trusted; they are dangerous.
2. Experience is better than abstract rules.
3. You must make people respect you.
4. Everyone hates a cop.
5. Police make better decisions about guilt or innocence than courts.
6. People who are not controlled will break laws.
7. Police must appear respectable.
8. Police can accurately identify criminals.
9. The major job of police is to prevent crime.
10. Stronger punishment will deter crime.

The tasks assigned to police in an urban society would confound highly trained social scientists. Yet police are generally recruited from working-class families; only a handful come from middle-class backgrounds, and only a few have more than a high-school education. Generally, the segment of the population from which police are recruited is less tolerant of unpopular views and more rigid in its ideas of family and social life. Formal police training emphasizes self-control and caution in dealing with the public, but on-the-job experiences probably reinforce predispositions toward distrust of others. The element of danger in the policeman's job makes him naturally suspicious of others. Policemen see much of the "worst kind" of people, and they see even the "best kind" at their worst.

Police forces are semimilitary organizations engaged in rule enforcement. Police must be concerned with authority themselves, and they expect others to respect authority. It is often difficult for even the most well-meaning police officer to develop respect or sympathy for ghetto residents. One policeman described this problem as follows:

The police have to associate with lower-class people, slobs, drunks, criminals, riff-raff of the worst sort. Most of these . . . are Negroes. The police officers see these

[5]Stuart A. Sheingold, "Cultural Cleavage and Criminal Justice," *Journal of Politics,* 40, 865–97.
[6]Peter Manning, "The Police," in *Criminal Justice in America,* ed. Richard Quinney (Boston: Little, Brown, 1974).

people through middle-class or lower-middle-class eyeballs. But even if he saw them through highly sophisticated eyeballs he can't go in the street and take this night after night. When some Negro criminal says to you a few times, "you white mother-fucker, take that badge off and I'll shove it up your ass," well, it's bound to affect you after a while. Pretty soon you decide they're all just niggers and they'll never be anything but niggers. It would take not just an average man to resist this feeling, it would take an extraordinary man to resist it, and there are very few ways by which the police department can attract extraordinary men to join them.[7]

The policeman's attitude toward ghetto residents is often affected by the high crime rates in ghetto areas. The policeman is suspicious of ghetto residents because crime rates tell him that his suspicions are often justified.

One commentator described the dilemma of police-ghetto relations as follows:

First, the police department recruits from a population (the working class) whose numbers are more likely than the average population to hold anti-Negro attitudes; second, the recruits are given a basic classroom training program that is unlikely to change the anti-Negro sentiments; third, the recruit goes out on the street as a patrolman and is more likely than not to have his anti-Negro attitudes reinforced and hardened by the older officer; fourth, in the best departments, the most able officers are soon transferred to specialized administrative duties in training, recruitment, juvenile work, etc., or are promoted after three to five years to supervisory positions; fifth, after five years the patrolman on street duty significantly increases in levels of cynicism, authoritarianism, and generalized hostility to the nonpolice world. Finally, it is highly likely that the worst of the patrolmen will wind up patrolling the ghetto because that tends to be the least wanted assignment.

If this is an accurate description of the urban police system (and my personal observations over the past five years tell me this is so), then the reason is clear why every poll of black citizens shows the same high level of distrust and hostility against policemen.[8]

Out on the city streets, police do not have the time or inclination to dwell on the social conditions associated with crime—poverty, racism, unemployment, undereducation, high-density living, and so forth. Instead, most police adopt a working attitude which Jerome Skolnik refers to as the "rotten-apple" view of man: crime is attributable to the intentions of bad individuals. Skolnik cites one policeman's simple summary: "Poverty doesn't cause crime; people do."[9] This attitude leads the wary police to quickly categorize persons on the street who are likely to be dangerous as "suspicious-looking persons"; emaciated

[7]Wilson, *Varieties of Police Behavior*, p. 43.

[8]Burton Levy, "Cops in the Ghetto," in *Riots and Rebellion*, eds. Louis Masoti and Donald Bowen (New York: Sage Publications, 1968), p. 353.

[9]Jerome H. Skolnik, *The Politics of Protest* (New York: Ballantine Books, 1969), p. 259.

persons who appear to avoid an officer or who are visibly "rattled" by an officer's presence; loiterers near restrooms, playgrounds, shopping centers, etc.

If police are overly suspicious of blacks, the attitudes of many ghetto blacks toward police are equally hostile. Black novelist James Baldwin writes of police in the ghetto:

> Their very presence is an insult, and it would be, even if they spent their entire day feeding gumdrops to children. They represent the force of the white world, and that world's real intentions are simply, to keep the black man corralled up here, in his place. The badge, the gun and the holster and the swinging club make vivid what will happen should his rebellion become overt. . . .
>
> He has never himself done anything for which to be hated—which of us has? And yet he is facing, daily and nightly, people who would gladly see him dead, and he knows it.[10]

Does increased police protection significantly reduce crime? The common assumption is that increased police manpower and increased police expenditures can significantly reduce crime in cities. But, unfortunately, it is very difficult to produce firm evidence to support this assumption. E. Terrance Jones studied crime rates in relation to police manpower and expenditure in 155 cities from 1958 through 1970 and failed to find any evidence to support the more-police-activity-equals-less-crime theory.[11] So many other factors may affect crime rates in cities—size, density, youth, unemployment, race, poverty, etc.—that police activity appears insignificant. Or an increase in police activity may result in increased crime reporting, which tends to obscure any actual reduction in crime in official statistics. Whatever the explanation, the reduction of crime in America appears to be a very elusive goal.

## Crime and the Courts

Chief Justice Warren E. Burger has argued persuasively that rising crime in America is partly due to inadequacies in our system of criminal justice. "The present system of criminal justice does not deter criminal conduct," he said in a special State of the Federal Judiciary Message. "Whatever deterrent effect may have existed in the past has now virtually vanished."[12] He urged major reforms in law enforcement, courts, prisons, probation, and parole.

[10]James Baldwin, *Nobody Knows My Name* (New York: Dell, 1962), pp. 61–62.
[11]E. Terrance Jones, "Evaluating Everyday Policies: Police Activity and Crime Incidence," *Urban Affairs Quarterly*, 8 (March 1973), 267–79.
[12]Chief Justice Warren Burger, Address on the State of the Federal Judiciary to the American Bar Association, August 10, 1970.

A major stumbling block to effective law enforcement is the current plight of America's judicial machinery.

Major congestion on court dockets that delays the hearing of cases months or even years. Moreover, actual trials now average twice as long as ten years ago.

Failure of courts to adopt modern management and administrative practice to speed and improve justice.

Increased litigation in the courts. Not only are more Americans aware of their rights, but more are using every avenue of appeal. Seldom do appeals concern the guilt or innocence of the defendant; they usually focus on procedural matters.

Excessive delays in trials. According to Burger, "Defendants, whether guilty or innocent, are human; they love freedom and hate punishment. With a lawyer provided to secure release without the need for a conventional bail bond, most defendants, except in capital cases, are released pending trial. We should not be surprised that a defendant on bail exerts a heavy pressure on his court-appointed lawyer to postpone the trial as long as possible so as to remain free. These postponements—and sometimes there are a dozen or more—consume the time of judges and court staffs as well as of lawyers. Cases are calendared and reset time after time while witnesses and jurors spend hours just waiting."

Excessive delays in appeals. "We should not be surprised at delay when more and more defendants demand their undoubtedly constitutional right to trial by jury because we have provided them with lawyers and other needs at public expense; nor should we be surprised that most convicted persons seek a new trial when the appeal costs them nothing and when failure to take the appeal will cost them freedom. Being human, a defendant plays out the line which society has cast him. Lawyers are competitive creatures and the adversary system encourages contention and often rewards delay; no lawyers want to be called upon to defend the client's charge of incompetence for having failed to exploit all the procedural techniques which we have deliberately made available."

Excessive variation in sentencing. Some judges let defendants off on probation for crimes that would draw five- or ten-year sentences by other judges. Although flexibility in sentencing is essential in dealing justly with individuals, perceived inconsistencies damage the image of the courts in the public mind.

Excessive "plea bargaining" between the prosecution and the defendant's attorney in which the defendant agrees to plead guilty to a lesser offense if the prosecutor will drop more serious charges.

The Warren Court—the Supreme Court of the 1950s and 1960s, under the guidance of Chief Justice Earl Warren—greatly strengthened the rights of accused persons in criminal cases. Several key decisions were made by a split vote on the Court, and drew heavy criticism from law enforcement officers and others as hamstringing police in their struggle with lawlessness. These decisions included the following:

> *Mapp* v. *Ohio* (1961)—Barring the use of illegally seized evidence in criminal cases by applying the Fourth Amendment guarantee against unreasonable searches and seizures. Even if the evidence seized proves the guilt of the accused, the accused goes free because the police committed a procedural error.
>
> *Gideon* v. *Wainwright* (1963)—Ruling that equal protection under the Fourteenth Amendment requires that free legal counsel be appointed for all indigent defendants in all criminal cases.
>
> *Escobedo* v. *Illinois* (1964)—Ruling that a suspect is entitled to confer with counsel as soon as police investigation focuses on him, or once "the process shifts from investigatory to accusatory."
>
> *Miranda* v. *Arizona* (1966)—Requiring that police, before questioning a suspect, must inform him of all his constitutional rights including the right to counsel, appointed free if necessary, and the right to remain silent. Although the suspect may knowingly waive these rights, the police cannot question anyone who at any point asks for a lawyer or indicates "in any manner" that he does not wish to be questioned. If the police commit an error if these procedures, the accused goes free, regardless of the evidence of guilt.

It is very difficult to ascertain to what extent these decisions have really hampered efforts to halt the rise in crime in America. The Supreme Court under Chief Justice Burger has not reversed any of these important decisions. So whatever progress is made in law enforcement will have to be made within the current definition of the rights of defendants. It is important to note that Chief Justice Burger's recommendations for judicial reform center on the speedy administration of justice and not on changes in the rights of defendants.

## Evaluation:
## Deterrence and Criminal Justice

Does the criminal justice system deter crime? This is a difficult question to answer. First we must distinguish between deterrence and incapacity. *Incapacity* can be imposed by long terms of imprisonment, particularly for habitual offenders; the policy of "keeping criminals off the streets" does indeed protect the public for a period of time, although it is done at a considerable cost ($15,000 to $25,000 per year per prisoner). The object of *deterrence* is to make the certainty and severity of punishment so great as to inhibit potential criminals from committing crimes.

For many years sociologists scorned the notion of deterrence, arguing that many crimes were committed without any consideration of consequences—particularly "crimes of passion." They also argued that urbanization, density, poverty, age, race, and other demographic factors had more effect on crime rates than did the characteristics of the legal system. However, recent systematic studies have challenged this view. Sociologist Jack P. Gibbs studied criminal homicide rates and related them to the *certainty* and *severity* of imprisonment in the states.[13] The certainty of imprisonment for criminal homicides (the percentage of persons sent to prison divided by the number of homicides) ranged from 21 percent in South Carolina and South Dakota to 87 percent in Utah. The severity of imprisonment (the average number of months served for a criminal homicide) ranged from a low of 24 in Nevada to a high of 132 in North Dakota. Gibbs was able to analyze statistically these measures of certainty and severity in relation to homicide rates in the states. His conclusions:

1. States above the median-certainty and median-severity rates have lower homicide rates than states below both medians. Indeed, the homicide rate for low-certainty-rate and low-severity-rate states was three times greater than the average rate for high-certainty and high-severity states.

2. Certainty of imprisonment may be more important than severity of punishment in determining homicide rates, but there is conflicting evidence on which of these variables is more influential.

3. Both certainty and severity reduce homicide rates even after controlling for all other demographic variables.

Economists have generally confirmed these findings.[14] Their general premise, of course, is that if you increase the cost of something (crime), less of it will be consumed (there will be fewer crimes). Their own studies confirm the deterrent effect of both the certainty and severity of punishment. Economist Gordon Tullock dismisses the notion that "crimes of passion" cannot be reduced by increasing the certainty and severity of punishment.

> The prisoners in Nazi concentration camps must frequently have been in a state of well-justified rage against some of their guards; yet this almost never led to their using violence against the guards, because punishment—which if they were lucky, would mean instant death, but was more likely to be death by torture—was so obvious and certain.[15]

[13]See Maynard L. Erickson and Jack P. Gibbs, "The Deterrence Question," *Social Science Quarterly*, 54 (December 1973), 534–51; and Jack P. Gibbs, "Crime, Punishment, and Deterrence," *Social Science Quarterly*, 48 (March 1968), 515–30.

[14]See Gordon Tullock, "Does Punishment Deter Crime?" *The Public Interest* (Summer 1974), pp. 103–11.

[15]Ibid., p. 108.

Tullock argues that to increase the deterrent effect of punishment, potential criminals must be given information about it. Indeed, he suggests, governments might even lie—that is, pretend that punishment is more certain and severe than it really is—in order to reduce crime.

## Prisons and Correctional Policies

At least four separate theories of crime and punishment compete for preeminence in guiding correctional policies.[16] First, there is the ancient Judeo-Christian idea of holding the individual responsible for his guilty acts and compelling him to pay a debt to society. Another philosophy argues that punishment should be sure, speedy, commensurate with the crime, and sufficiently conspicuous to deter others from committing crime. Still another consideration in correctional policy is that of protecting the public from lawbreakers or habitual criminals by segregating these people behind prison walls. Finally, there is the theory that criminals are partly or entirely victims of social circumstances beyond their control and that society owes them comprehensive treatment in the form of rehabilitation.

Over two million Americans each year are prisoners in a jail, police station, juvenile home, or penitentiary. The vast majority are released within one year. There are, however, about a quarter of a million inmates in state and federal prisons in the United States. These prisoners are serving time for serious offenses: 90 percent had a record of crime before they committed the act that led to their current imprisonment.

If correctional systems could be made to work—that is, actually to rehabilitate persons as useful, law-abiding citizens—the benefits to the nation would be enormous. The Law Enforcement Assistance Administration estimates that 80 percent of all felonies are committed by repeaters—individuals who have had prior contact with the criminal justice system and were not corrected by it.[17] Penologists generally recommend more education and job training, more and better facilities, smaller prisons, halfway houses where offenders can adjust to civilian life before parole, more parole officers, and greater contact between prisoners and their families and friends. But as Daniel Glaser points out: "Unfortunately there is no convincing evidence that this investment reduces what criminologists call 'recidivism,' the offender's return to crime."[18] In short, there is no evidence that people can be

[16]See Daniel Glaser, *The Effectiveness of a Prison and Parole System* (Indianapolis and New York: Bobbs-Merrill, 1964).
[17]See *Crime and the Law* (Washington, D.C.: Congressional Quarterly, 1971), p. 11.
[18]Glaser, *The Effectiveness of a Prison and Parole System*, p. 4.

"rehabilitated" no matter what is done! But prison policies now combine conflicting philosophies in a way that accomplishes *none* of society's goals. They do not effectively punish or deter individuals from crime. They do not succeed in rehabilitating the criminal. They do not even protect the public by keeping criminals off the streets; nineteen out of every twenty persons sent to prison will eventually return to society. Even the maintenance of order *within* prisons and the protection of the lives of guards and inmates have become a serious national problem. The deaths of forty-three prisoners and guards in Attica State Prison in New York in a bloody riot in 1971 directed public attention to the serious dilemmas of state correctional policy.

Over two-thirds of all prisoner releases come about by means of parole. Modern penology, with its concern for reform and rehabilitation, appears to favor parole releases rather than unconditional releases. The function of parole and postrelease supervision is (1) to procure information on the parolees' postprison conduct, and (2) to facilitate and graduate the transition between the prison and complete freedom. These functions are presumably oriented toward protecting the public and rehabilitating the offender. But states differ substantially in their use of parole: in some states, 90 percent of all releases come about because of parole, while in other states, parole is granted to less than 30 percent of all prisoners. Generally, urban industrial states with higher income and educational levels release a higher proportion of prisoners on parole than rural farm states with lower income and educational characteristics.

What is the effect of correctional expenditures, sentencing policies, and parole systems on *recidivism*—the percentage of released prisoners who return to prison for new crime? Unfortunately, the weight of evidence suggests *no* relationship between any specific means of handling prisoners and successful rehabilitation. For example, a ten-year study in Georgia comparing inmates released under parole (carefully selected, counseled, and supervised) with inmates released without parole showed no difference in the two groups in recidivism.[19] The parole system appears to be worthless. Similarly disappointing results were obtained in a California study comparing parolees given close supervision to those given little supervision; both groups committed the same number of new felonies. Finally, a comparative analysis of expenditures and manpower for corrections, parole, and probation in all fifty states revealed "the almost total absence of linkage between correction variables and recidivism."[20] In summary, prisons do not rehabilitate. If rehabilitation is set as the goal, prisons are bound to be judged as failures.

[19]See Frank K. Gibson et al., "A Path Analytic Treatment of Corrections Output," *Social Science Quarterly*, 54 (September 1973), 281–91.
[20]Ibid., p. 291.

## Capital Punishment: The Constitutional Issues

Perhaps the most heated debate in criminal justice policy today concerns capital punishment. Opponents of the death penalty argue that it is "cruel and unusual punishment" in violation of the Eighth Amendment of the Constitution. They also argue that the death penalty is applied unequally. A large proportion of those executed have been poor, uneducated, and nonwhite. In contrast, there is a strong sense of justice among many Americans that demands retribution for heinous crimes—a life for a life. A mere jail sentence for a multiple murderer or rapist murderer seems unjust compared with the damage inflicted upon society and the victims. In most cases, a life sentence means less than ten years in prison under the current parole and probation policies of many states. Convicted murderers have been set free, and some have killed again. Moreover, prison guards and other inmates are exposed to convicted murderers who have "a license to kill," because they are already serving life sentences and have nothing to lose by killing again.

Prior to 1972, the death penalty was officially sanctioned by about half of the states. Federal law also retained the death penalty. However, no one had actually suffered the death penalty since 1967 because of numerous legal tangles and direct challenges to the constitutionality of capital punishment.

In *Furman* v. *Georgia* (1972), the Supreme Court ruled that capital punishment as then imposed violated the Eighth and Fourteenth Amendment prohibitions against cruel and unusual punishment and due process of law. The reasoning in the case is very complex. Only two justices, Brennan and Marshall, declared that capital punishment itself is cruel and unusual. The other justices in the majority felt that death sentences had been applied unfairly: a few individuals were receiving the death penalty for crimes for which many others were receiving much lighter sentences. These justices left open the possibility that capital punishment would be constitutional, if it was specified for certain kinds of crime and applied uniformly.

After this decision, a majority of states rewrote their death penalty laws to try to insure fairness and uniformity of application. Generally, these laws mandate the death penalty for murders committed during rape, robbery, hijacking, or kidnapping; murders of prison guards, murder with torture; and multiple murders. Two trials would be held—one to determine guilt or innocence and another to determine the penalty. At the second trial, evidence of "aggravating" and "mitigating" factors would be presented; if there were aggravating factors but no mitigating factors, the death penalty would be mandatory.

In a series of cases in 1976 *(Gregg* v. *Georgia, Profitt* v. *Florida, Jurek* v. *Texas)* the Supreme Court finally held that "the punishment of death does *not* invariably violate the Constitution." The court upheld the death penalty, employing the following rationale: The men who drafted the Bill of Rights accepted death as a common sanction for crime. It is true that the Eighth Amendment prohibition against cruel and unusual punishments must be interpreted in a dynamic fashion, reflecting changing moral values. But the decisions of more than half of the nation's state legislatures to reenact the death penalty since 1972 and the decision of juries to impose the death penalty on more than 450 persons under these new laws, is evidence that "a large proportion of American society continues to regard it as an appropriate and necessary criminal sanction." Moreover, said the Court, the social purposes of retribution and deterrence justify the use of the death penalty. This ultimate sanction is "an expression of society's moral outrage at particularly offensive conduct." The Court reaffirmed that *Furman* v. *Georgia* (1972) only struck down the death penalty where it was inflicted in "an arbitrary and capricious manner." The Court upheld the death penalty in states where the trial was a two-part proceeding, and during the second part the judge or jury was provided with relevant information and standards in deciding whether to impose the death penalty. The Court approved the consideration of "aggravating and mitigating circumstances." The Court also approved of automatic review of all death sentences by state Supreme Courts to insure that the sentence was not imposed under the influence of passion or prejudice, that aggravating factors were supported by the evidence, and that the sentence was not disproportionate to the crime. However, the Court disapproved of state laws making the death penalty mandatory in first degree murder cases holding that such laws were "unduly harsh and unworkably rigid."

## Capital Punishment: An Evaluation

Is the death penalty a deterrent to murder? Does capital punishment save lives because it prevents killings through the threat of execution? This is, indeed, a question of life or death, and it is a question which social science should be able to answer. Unfortunately, however, it is difficult to measure the deterrent effect of the death penalty because we cannot directly observe nonbehavior. We can never know for certain whether the fear of capital punishment was the reason why someone refrained from killing another person. All we can do is compare homicide rates in states which have used the death penalty over time with those states which have not; and in comparing states over time, we must remember that there are many other factors besides capital punishment which can raise or lower the homicide rate: age, race, poverty, gun ownership, and so on.

Perhaps the most controversial study in recent years is economist Isaac Ehrlich's analysis of the death penalty's use in forty-eight states between 1933 and 1969.[21] He studied execution rates and murder rates, controlling for many other variables, and concluded that the tradeoff between executions of convicted murderers and the reduction of killings was approximately one for eight. In other words, each execution was associated with saving the lives of eight potential victims. Let us assume his calculations are correct: we know that when capital punishment was in frequent use, there were four executions for every 100 convicted murderers. Today, with over 8,000 convictions for murder each year, using the earlier ratio would result in about 320 executions per year; these executions would save about 2,500 innocent lives.

However, other researchers, using similar methods, have *not* reported the same dramatic findings about the deterrent effects of capital punishment. Indeed, some social scientists specifically deny that the death penalty has any deterrent effect.[22] They attribute increases in the murder rate during the years and in the states which the death penalty was not used to a wide range of factors, including the increased ownership of handguns.[23]

Much of the debate in the states over the death penalty, however, has not centered on the crucial question of deterrence. Unfortunately, rhetoric has substituted for research and slogans have substituted for study. Opponents of the death penalty call it "murder" and contend that it is morally indefensible for the state to take away life. Proponents of the death penalty say that the unwillingness of the state to impose capital punishment implies that little value is placed upon the lives of innocent victims. In short, contemporary discussions of the death penalty are largely emotional, and social science research is generally left out of these discussions. Public opinion now favors the death penalty by almost three to one. Only for a few years during the mid-1960s did public opinion oppose the death penalty, and then only by a small margin. With increases in the crime rate in the late 1960s and 1970s, heavy majorities have swung back in favor of capital punishment.

[21]Isaac Ehrlich, "The Deterrent Effect of Capital Punishment: A Question of Life or Death," *American Economic Review*, 65 (June 1975), 397–414.

[22]Hugo Adam Bedau, *The Death Penalty in America* (New York: Doubleday, 1967); Peter Passell, "The Deterrent Effect of the Death Penalty," *Standard Law Review*, 28 (November 1975), 61–80.

[23]Gary Kleck, "Capital Punishment, Gun Ownership, and Homicide," *American Journal of Sociology*, 84 (January 1979), 882–910.

## Violence in Black Ghettos

Civil disorder and violence are not new on the American scene. The nation itself was founded in armed revolution. And violence as a form of political protest has continued intermittently in America to the present day. Yet even though domestic violence has played a prominent role in America's history, the ghetto riots of the 1960s shocked the nation with massive and widespread civil disorders. All these riots involved black attacks on established authority—policemen, firemen, National Guardsmen, whites in general, and property owned by whites. Three of these riots—Watts, California, in 1965, and Newark and Detroit in 1967—amounted to major civil disorders. Detroit was the scene of the bloodiest racial violence of the twentieth century. A week of rioting in Detroit, July 23–28, 1967, left forty-three dead and more than 1,000 injured. Whole sections of the city were reduced to charred, smoky ruins. Firemen who tried to fight fires were stoned and occasionally shot by ghetto residents. Over 1,300 buildings were totally demolished and 2,700 businesses sacked.

Detroit's upheaval began when police raided an after-hours club and arrested the bartender and several customers for selling and consuming alcoholic beverages after authorized closing hours. A force of 15,000 city and state police, National Guardsmen, and finally, federal troops fought to quell the violence. Most of the looted retail businesses were liquor stores, groceries, and furniture stores. Many black merchants scrawled "Soul Brother" on their windows in an attempt to escape the wrath of the black mobs.

In the end, homes and shops covering a total area of fourteen square miles were gutted by fire. Of the forty-three persons killed during the riot, thirty-three were black and ten were white. Among the dead were one National Guardsman, one fireman, one policeman, and

Michigan national guardsmen in Detroit's riot-torn West Side, July 1967. UPI Photo

one black private guard. Both the violence and the pathos of the ghetto riots were reflected in the following report from Detroit:

> A Negro plain clothes officer was standing in an intersection when a man threw a Molotov cocktail into a business establishment on the corner. In the heat of the afternoon, fanned by the 20–25 miles per hour winds of both Sunday and Monday, the fire reached the home next door within minutes. As its residents uselessly sprayed the flames with garden hoses, the fire jumped from roof to roof of adjacent two- and three-story buildings. Within the hour the entire block was in flames. The ninth house in the burning row belonged to the arsonist who had thrown the Molotov cocktail. . . .
>
> Employed as a private guard, fifty-five-year-old Julius L. Dorsey, a Negro, was standing in front of a market, when accosted by two Negro men and a woman. They demanded he permit them to loot the market. He ignored their demands. They began to berate him. He asked a neighbor to call the police. As the argument grew more heated, Dorsey fired three shots from his pistol in the air.
>
> The police radio reported: "Looters, they have rifles." A patrol car driven by a police officer and carrying three National Guardsmen arrive. As the looters fled, the law enforcement personnel opened fire. When the firing ceased, one person lay dead. He was Julius L. Dorsey. . . .[24]

## The National Advisory Commission on Civil Disorders concluded:

1. No civil disorder was "typical" in all respects. . . .

2. While civil disorders of 1967 were racial in character, they were not *inter*racial. The 1967 disorders, as well as earlier disorders of the recent period, involved action within Negro neighborhoods against symbols of white American society—authority and property—rather than against white persons.

3. Despite extremist rhetoric there was no attempt to subvert the social order of the United States. Instead, most of those who attacked white authority and property seemed to be demanding fuller participation in the social order and the material benefits enjoyed by the vast majority of American citizens.

4. Disorder did not typically erupt without pre-existing causes, as a result of a single "triggering" or "precipitating" incident. Instead, it developed out of an increasingly social atmosphere, in which typically a series of tension-heightening incidents over a period of weeks or months became linked in the minds of many in the Negro community with a shared network of underlying grievances.

5. There was, typically, a complex relationship between the series of incidents, and the underlying grievances. For example, grievances about allegedly abusive police practices . . . were often aggravated in the minds of many Negroes by incidents involving the police, or the inaction of municipal authorities on Negro complaints about police action.

[24]National Advisory Commission on Civil Disorders, *Report* (Washington, D.C.: Government Printing Office, 1968), p. 4.

6. Many grievances in the Negro community resulted from discrimination, prejudice, and powerlessness which Negroes often experience. . . .

7. Characteristically the typical rioter was not a hoodlum, habitual criminal, or riff-raff. . . . Instead, he was a teenager or young adult, a life-long resident of the city in which he rioted, high school drop-out—but somewhat better than his Negro neighbor—and almost invariably under-employed or employed in a menial job. He was proud of his race, extremely hostile to both whites and middle class negroes and, though informed about politics, highly distrustful of the political system and of political leaders.

8. Numerous Negro counter-rioters walked the street, urging the rioters to "cool it. . . ."

9. Negotiation between Negro and white officials occurred during virtually all of this disorder. . . .

10. . . . Some rioters may have shared neither the conditions nor the grievance of their Negro neighbors; some may have coolly and deliberately exploited the chaos created by others; some may have been drawn into the melee merely because they identified with, or wished to emulate, others.

11. The background of disorder in the riot cities was typically characterized by severely disadvantaged conditions for Negroes, especially as compared with those of whites. . . .

12. In the immediate aftermath of disorder, the status quo of daily life before the disorder generally was quickly restored. Yet despite some notable public and private efforts, little basic change took place in the conditions underlying the disorder. In some cases, the result was increased dislike between blacks and whites, diminished inter-racial communication, and the growth of Negro and white extremist groups.[25]

## Assessing the Causes of Riots

One explanation of urban violence is that it is a product of the "relative deprivation" of ghetto residents.[26] "Relative deprivation" is the discrepancy between people's expectations about the goods and conditions of life to which they are justifiably entitled and what they perceive to be their *chances* for getting and keeping what they feel they deserve. Relative deprivation is not just a complicated way of saying that people are

[25]Ibid., pp. 110–12.
[26]For a full discussion of the "relative deprivation" explanation as well as alternative explanations, see Dan R. Bowen and Louis H. Masotti, "Civil Violence: A Theoretical Overview," in Masotti and Bowen, eds., *Riots and Rebellion* (Beverly Hills, Calif.: Sage Publications, 1968). See also James C. Davies, "Toward a Theory of Revolution," *American Sociological Review*, 27 (February 1962), 6; and Ted Gurr, *Why Men Rebel* (Princeton, N.J.: Princeton University Press, 1970).

deprived and therefore angry because they have less than what they want; it is more complex than that. Relative deprivation focuses on (1) what people think they *deserve,* not just what they want in an ideal sense, and (2) what they think they have a *chance of getting,* not just what they have.

Relative deprivation differs considerably from the "absolute deprivation" hypothesis. The absolute deprivation idea suggests that the individuals who are most deprived are most likely to rise up. Of course, it is true that conditions in America's ghettos provide the necessary environment for violence. Racial imbalance, *de facto* segregation, slum housing, discrimination, unemployment, poor schools, and poverty all provide excellent kindling for the flames of violence. But these underlying conditions for violence existed for decades in America, and the nation never experienced simultaneous violent uprisings in nearly all its major cities before the 1960s. This suggests the deprivation itself is not a sufficient condition for violence. Some new ingredients were added to the incendiary conditions in American cities that touched off the violence of the 1960s.

Relative deprivation focuses on the distance between one's current status and his expectation level. According to this hypothesis, it is neither the wholly downtrodden—who have no aspirations—nor the very well off—who can satisfy theirs—who represent a threat to civil order. The threat is posed by those whose expectations about what they deserve outdistance the capacity of the political system to satisfy them. Often rapid increases in expectations are a product of minor or symbolic improvements in conditions. This leads to the apparent paradox of violence and disorder occurring at the very time that improvements in the conditions of blacks are being made. It is hope, not despair, that generates civil violence and disorder. Masotti and Bowen remark: "The reason why black Americans riot is because there has been just enough improvement in their condition to generate hopes, expectations, or aspirations beyond the capacities of the system to meet them."[27]

Once racial violence has broken out anywhere in the nation, the mass media play an important role in disseminating images of violence as well as the symbols and rationalizations of the rioters. Television offers the rioter a mass audience. Moreover, television images may reinforce predispositions to participate and to give legitimacy to participation. Television enables blacks in one ghetto to see what blacks in another ghetto are doing, and explains simultaneous rioting in ghettos across the nation.

There is little likelihood that violence will produce the attitude

---

[27]Masotti and Bowen, *Riots and Rebellion,* pp. 24–25.

change among white elites necessary for progress in the struggle for equality. On the contrary, violence has resulted in a negative reaction among whites. It has served to reinforce prejudice and to justify antagonisms against blacks rather than to effect any attitude changes. Violence in the urban ghettos in the 1960s failed to shock white Americans into action in behalf of equality or even to scare them into such action. Instead, the urban violence led to a strong "law and order" movement which was reflected in local, state, and national politics. The violence provided white masses with an opportunity to express hostile stereotypes about blacks, e.g., that the riots were "mainly a way of looting and things like that." The riots also gave white elites a new political theme—"law and order"—which played a major role in the 1968 presidential election.

The reaction of most government officials was negative. Both the president and Congress pointedly ignored the recommendations of the Advisory Commission on Civil Disorders for more jobs, housing, and educational programs in the ghettos. There was substantial fear that new public programs might appear to "reward violence." No more money was poured into the ghettos. Both Congress and the president became disenchanted with the Poverty Program. The rhetoric of government officials emphasized "law and order" rather than massive programs aimed at equalizing black and white living standards.

## Federal Law Enforcement Policy

Historically, the principal responsibility for law enforcement in America has rested with state and local governments. The Federal Bureau of Investigation (FBI) in the Department of Justice was created in the 1920s and charged with the responsibility of enforcing only federal laws. Today, the role of the federal government in law enforcement is growing, but state and local governments continue to carry the major burdens of police protection, judicial systems, and prison and parole programs. The federal government employs less than 50,000 persons in all law enforcement activities, compared with over one-half million state and local government law enforcement personnel. Federal prisons contain about 25,000 inmates, compared with about 200,000 in state prisons.

One product of the "law and order" movement of the late 1960s was the Federal Crime Control and Safe Streets Act of 1968. This act created the Law Enforcement Assistance Administration (LEAA) in the Department of Justice to channel federal funds to states and communities to help them upgrade law enforcement programs. Most of these funds come to the states as "bloc grants" to be employed as state and local officials see fit in improving law enforcement. Each state creates a state planning agency responsible for preparing a comprehensive law enforcement and criminal justice plan. Federal funds may be spent on court reform and correctional programs as well as police protection.

Early critics of LEAA argued that not enough money was channeled to the highest crime areas and too much money was spent on "hardware"—special equipment for public forces. In response, LEAA has tried to stress the entire "criminal justice system"—police, prosecution, courts, prison, and parole.

## Summary

In this chapter we have examined crime and disorder, and have looked at government policies designed to cope with these ills. We have examined the conflict between our desire to retain individual freedoms and our desire to insure the safety of our people.

1. Crime rates rose steadily between 1960 and 1975; only recently have crime rates begun to level off. This leveling off is more likely to be a product of the relative decline of youth in the population than the crime deterrence policies of government. The "victimization rate" is several times greater than the reported crime rate. These statistics suggest that the current system of criminal justice is not a serious deterrent to crime.

2. Established elites, notably the Supreme Court, have strengthened the rights of accused persons in criminal cases. The Court has maintained that efforts to reduce crime must not infringe upon the rights of defendants.

3. Social scientists, who once believed that punishment had little effect on the incidence of crime, are now reconsidering the possibility of legal deterrence. The *certainty* and *severity* of punishment appear to operate together to reduce crime rates, but to date, the criminal justice system does not insure certain and secure punishment for crimes.

4. Elites have failed to settle upon a consistent theory of correctional policy. For years the notion of "rehabilitation" dominated prison and parole programs; but there is no evidence that *any* correctional system can successfully "rehabilitate" people. Thus, newer approaches to correctional policy have emphasized deterrence and the separation of criminals from the general population.

5. Elites have struggled over the issue of capital punishment. The movement to abolish the death penalty was very strong in the 1960s, but rising crime rates and terrorism appear to have reinforced public support for capital punishment. In response, the Supreme Court has

upheld the death penalty as long as it is imposed fairly and uniformly, with many procedural safeguards.

6. Civil disorder and violence have occurred frequently in America's history. Aspiration levels of black masses increased rapidly in the 1960s, but actual conditions of life in the ghettos did not change much. The result was frustration, bitterness, and civil disorder.

7. White elites responded to this mass violence with a strong "law and order" movement. Congress and the president wished to avoid urban programs which would appear to "reward" violence. Instead, the Crime Control and Safe Streets Act of 1968 created a federal Law Enforcement Assistance Administration (LEAA) with the task of strengthening local law enforcement.

## Bibliography

GURR, TED, *Why Men Rebel.* Princeton, N.J.: Princeton University Press, 1970.

MASOTTI, LOUIS H., and DON R. BOWEN, eds., *Riots and Rebellion.* Beverly Hills, Calif.: Sage Publications, 1970.

National Advisory Commission on Civil Disorders, *Report.* Washington, D.C.: Government Printing Office, 1968.

WILSON, JAMES Q., *Varieties of Police Behavior.* Cambridge, Mass.: Harvard University Press, 1968.

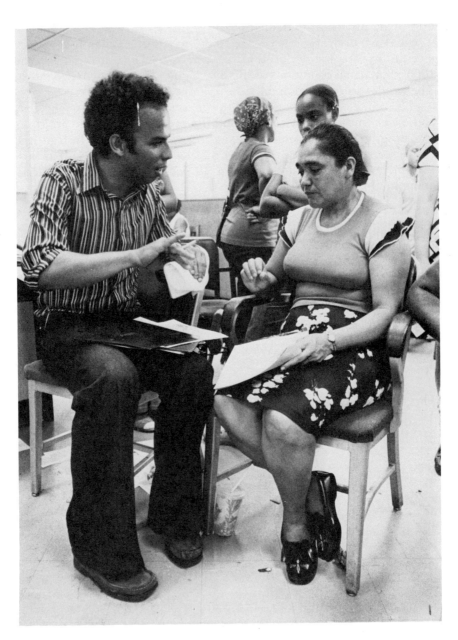

Caseworker with welfare recipient. *Wide World Photos*.

# Poverty and Welfare

## the search for
## a rational strategy

5

## Poverty in America

The first obstacle to a rational approach to poverty lies in conflict over the definition of the problem. Measuring the extent of poverty in America is itself a political activity. Proponents of programs for the poor frequently make high estimates of the number of poor. They view the problem of poverty as a persistent one, even in an affluent society; they contend that many millions of people suffer from hunger, exposure, and remedial illness, and that some of them even starve to death. Their definition of the problem practically mandates immediate and massive public programs.

In contrast, others minimize the number of poor in America. They see poverty diminishing over time without major public programs; they view the poor in America as considerably better off than the middle class of fifty years ago and even wealthy by the standards of most other societies in the world; and they deny that anyone needs to suffer from hunger, exposure, remedial illness, or starvation if they make use of the services and facilities available to them. This definition of the problem minimizes demands for public programs to fight poverty.

According to the U.S. Social Security Administration there are about 24 million poor people in the United States. This is approximately 12 percent of the population. This *official* definition of poverty is estimated to include all those Americans whose annual cash income falls below that which is required to maintain a decent standard of living. This definition of the poverty line by the Social Security Administration is derived by careful calculation of costs of food, housing, clothing, and other items for rural and urban families of different sizes. The dollar amounts on these lines are flexible to take into account the effect of inflation; these amounts rise each year with the rate of inflation. In 1980 the poverty line for an urban family of four was approximately $7,500 per year.

There are several problems in this definition of poverty. First of all, it does not take into account regional differences in the costs of living, climate, or accepted styles of living. Second, it does not account for family assets; for example, a family that owns its own home does not usually devote as much income to housing as a family that rents. Third, there are many families and individuals whose particular circumstances may place them officially among the poor but who do not think of themselves as "poor people,"—students, for example. Doubtless there are others whose income is above the poverty line but who have special problems—such as serious or chronic sickness—which leave them impoverished. Fourth, the official definition of poverty does not recognize the problems of those who spend their incomes unwisely. If money goes for liquor, drugs, or expensive cars, or if money is siphoned off by loan sharks, impoverished relatives and friends, or high prices charged by ghetto storeowners, then even a reasonably high income family can live in poverty. Finally, the official definition of poverty excludes "in kind" (nonmonetary) benefits given to the poor by governments. These benefits include, for example, free medical care, public housing, food stamps, free school lunches, etc. If these benefits were "costed out" (calculated as monetary income), there may be only half as many poor people as shown in official statistics. Yet despite these problems, the Social Security Administration's definition has provided the best available estimate of poverty in America.

How poor is "poor"? There is reason to believe that the 24 million Americans living in official poverty do not all suffer hardship and deprivation.[1] About 45 percent own cars, 42 percent own their own homes, and more than half have some savings. Nearly 80 percent of the poor have television sets and 75 percent have refrigerators or freezers. Over three-quarters have hot water, access to a telephone for receiving calls, kitchen with cooking equipment, a flush toilet, and a bath. Yet the diets of the poor are nutritionally bad, whether from ignorance or poverty.

[1]Herman P. Miller, "The Dimensions of Poverty," in *Poverty as a Public Issue*, ed. Ben B. Seligman (New York: Free Press, 1965).

How persistent is poverty? Researchers from the Survey Research Center, University of Michigan, tracked 5,000 American families for ten years and found that only *3 percent* were persistently poor, that is, they were poor throughout the entire period. This is a much smaller figure than 12 percent reported as poor at any one time. This means that people slip into, and out of, the poverty category over time. People lose their jobs, retire, divorce or separate, become ill, etc., and then later they find new jobs, remarry, get well, etc., and their financial condition changes.

Who are the poor? Poverty occurs in many different kinds of families and in all environmental settings. However, the incidence of poverty varies sharply among groups living under different circumstances, and several groups experience poverty in greater proportions than the national average. First of all, the likelihood of blacks experiencing poverty is three times greater than whites; the percentage of the black population of the United States falling under the poverty line is 31.3 compared to 8.9 percent for the white population. (See Table 5–1.) Second, female-headed families experience poverty far more frequently than do male-headed families; 32.8 percent of all female-headed families live below the poverty line. Third, the young and the aged experience more poverty than persons of working age; 14.1 percent of the population over sixty-five lives below the poverty line. Al-

**TABLE 5–1**  Percentage of Population, by Categories, with Income Below Poverty Level

|  | Percent of Total in Category |
|---|---|
| Total | 11.6 |
| White population | 8.9 |
| Black population | 31.3 |
| Those living in central cities | 15.4 |
| Those living in suburbs | 6.8 |
| Those living in rural areas | 13.9 |
| Under age 25 | 16.1 |
| Ages 25–65 | 8.5 |
| Over age 65 | 14.1 |
| Families with male head | 6.9 |
| Families with female head | 32.8 |
| Less than eight years school | 22.6 |
| Eight years school | 12.9 |
| High-school graduate | 6.9 |
| College graduate | 3.2 |

*Source:* U.S. Bureau of the Census, Characteristics of the Low-Income Population Series P–60, (Washington, D.C.: Government Printing Office, 1979).

though we think of poverty as a characteristic of persons living in large, central-city ghettos, rural families also experience considerable poverty. On the other hand, central cities have more poverty than their surrounding suburbs. The poorly educated suffer a great deal more poverty than the well-educated; 22.6 percent of the population with less than eight years of school lives in poverty.

Are the poor disappearing? In Franklin D. Roosevelt's second inaugural address in 1937 he said, "I see one-third of a nation ill-housed, ill-clad, ill-nourished." Since that time the American political and economic system has succeeded in reducing the proportion of poor to less than 12 percent. If current rates in the reduction of poverty in America continue in the future, there will be virtually no poverty remaining in 25 to 50 years.

Figure 5–1 allows us to observe the change in the number and percentage of poor since 1947. All these figures account for the effect of inflation, so there is no question that the number and percentage of the population living in poverty has declined despite increases in the population. Both white and black poverty is declining, although the rate of decline among blacks has not been as great as the rate of decline among whites. However, in the last decade the number and percentage of the poor has not changed much. The percentage of the population living below the poverty line has remained relatively constant around 12 percent.

## Poverty as Inequality

Poverty can also be defined as "a state of mind"—some people think they have less income or material possessions than most Americans, and they believe they are entitled to more. Their sense of deprivation is not tied to any *absolute* level of income. Instead, their sense of deprivation is *relative* to what most Americans have, and what they, therefore, feel they are entitled to. Even fairly substantial incomes may result in a sense of "relative deprivation" in a very affluent society when commercial advertising and the mass media portray the "average American" as having a high level of consumption and material well-being.

Today the poor are not any more deprived, relative to the nonpoor, than in the past. However, they *feel* more deprived—they perceive the gap to be wider, and they no longer accept the gap as legitimate. Blacks are overrepresented among the poor; the civil rights movement made blacks acutely aware of their position in American society relative to whites. Thus, the black revolution contributed to a new

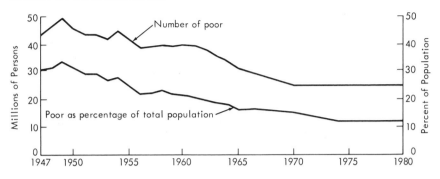

**FIG. 5–1** Poverty in the United States

*Source:* Redrawn after G. Bach, *Economics,* 7th Ed. (Englewood Cliffs, N.J.: Prentice-Hall, Inc., © 1971), Fig. 37–1, p. 535. Data from Council of Economic Advisers and Social Security Administration.

awareness of the problem of poverty in terms of relative differences in income and conditions of life.

Defining poverty as "relative deprivation" really defines it as *inequality* in society. As Victor Fuchs explains:

> By the standards that have prevailed over most of history, and still prevail over large areas of the world, there are very few poor in the United States today. Nevertheless, there are millions of American families who, both in their own eyes and in those of others, are poor. As our nation prospers, our judgment as to what constitutes poverty will inevitably change. When we talk about poverty in America, we are talking about families and individuals who have much less income than most of us. When we talk about reducing or eliminating poverty, we are really talking about changing the distribution of income.[2]

Thus, eliminating poverty, if it is defined as relative deprivation, would mean achieving absolute equality of incomes and material possessions in America.

Let us try systematically to examine poverty as relative deprivation. Table 5–2 divides all American families into five groups—from the lowest one-fifth, in personal income, to the highest one-fifth—and shows the percentage of total family personal income received by each of these groups over the years. (If perfect income equality existed, each fifth of American families would receive 20 percent of all family personal income, and it would not even be possible to rank fifths from highest to lowest.) The poorest one-fifth received 5 percent of all fam-

[2]Victor R. Fuchs, "Redefining Poverty and Redistributing Income," *The Public Interest* (Summer 1967), 91.

**TABLE 5–2** Percent Distribution of Family Personal Income[1] by Quintiles and Top 5 Percent of Consumer Units,[2] Selected Years, 1947–1978

| Quintiles | 1947 | 1950 | 1951 | 1954 | 1956 | 1959 | 1962 | 1968 | 1972 | 1975 | 1978 |
|---|---|---|---|---|---|---|---|---|---|---|---|
| Lowest | 5.0 | 4.8 | 5.0 | 4.8 | 4.8 | 4.6 | 4.6 | 5.7 | 5.5 | 5.4 | 5.2 |
| Second | 11.0 | 10.9 | 11.3 | 11.1 | 11.3 | 10.9 | 10.9 | 12.4 | 12.0 | 12.0 | 11.6 |
| Third | 16.0 | 16.1 | 16.5 | 16.4 | 16.3 | 16.3 | 16.3 | 17.7 | 17.4 | 17.6 | 17.5 |
| Fourth | 22.0 | 22.1 | 22.3 | 22.5 | 22.3 | 22.6 | 22.7 | 23.7 | 23.5 | 24.1 | 24.2 |
| Highest | 46.0 | 46.1 | 44.9 | 45.2 | 45.3 | 45.6 | 45.5 | 40.6 | 41.6 | 41.0 | 41.5 |
| Total | 100.0 | 100.0 | 100.0 | 100.0 | 100.0 | 100.0 | 100.0 | 100.0 | 100.0 | 100.0 | 100.0 |
| Top 5 percent | 20.9 | 21.4 | 20.7 | 20.3 | 20.2 | 20.2 | 19.6 | 14.0 | 14.4 | 15.3 | 15.7 |

[1]Family personal income includes wage and salary receipts (net of social insurance contributions), other labor income, proprietors' and rental income, dividends, personal interest income, and transfer payments. In addition to monetary income flows, it includes certain nonmonetary or imputed income such as wages in kind, the value of food and fuel produced and consumed on farms, net imputed value of owner-occupied homes, and imputed interest. Personal income differs from national income in that it excludes corporate profits taxes, corporate saving (inclusive of inventory valuation adjustment), and social security contributions of employers and employees, and includes transfer payments (mostly governmental) and interest on consumer and government debt.

[2]Consumer units include farm operator and nonfarm families and unattached individuals. A family is defined as a group of two or more persons related by blood, marriage, or adoption, and residing together.

*Source:* U.S. Bureau of the Census, *Current Population Reports,* Series P–60, No. 118.

ily personal income in 1947; in 1978, this group was still only receiving 5.2 percent of family personal income. The highest one-fifth of American families in personal income received 46 percent of all family personal income in 1947; in 1978, this percentage had declined to 41.5. This was the only income group to lose in relation to other income groups. The middle classes improved their relative income position more than the poor. Another measure of income equalization over time is the decline in the percentage of income received by the top 5 percent in America. The top 5 percent received 21 percent of all family personal incomes in 1947, but only 15.7 percent in 1978.

Although the income of the lowest fifth of the population appears small (5.2 percent) in comparison to the income of higher fifths, some of the hardships of this lowest fifth are reduced by government services—benefits which are not counted as income. These "in-kind" benefits include food stamps, public housing, medicare and medicaid, school lunches, and similar programs. Indeed, one economist estimates that if these benefits are included, the "adjusted income distribution" of the lowest fifth would be raised to 12 percent.[3] Moreover, with the

[3]Edgar K. Browning, "How Much More Equality Can We Afford," *The Public Interest* (Spring 1976), 90–110. The Congressional Budget Office estimates that if "in-kind" benefits are considered, the proportion of the U.S. population below the poverty level declines from 12 to 7 percent. Congressional Quarterly, *Weekly Report,* January 22, 1977, p. 131.

expansion of these benefit programs for the poor in recent years, the percentage of "adjusted income" received by the poor is increasing rapidly.

It is unlikely that income differences will ever disappear completely from a society that rewards skill, talent, risk taking, and ingenuity. If the problem of poverty is defined as relative deprivation—that is, *inequality*—then the problem is not really capable of solution. Regardless of how well-off the poor may be in absolute terms, there will always be a lowest one-fifth of the population receiving something less than 20 percent of all income. Income differences may decline over time, but *some* differences will remain, and even minor differences can acquire great importance and hence pose a "problem."

In describing federal antipoverty programs, we will be dealing with policies that were designed primarily to raise the poor above the poverty line. Policies dealing with income redistribution through taxation are discussed in Chapter 11.

## Rationality and Irrationality in Welfare Policy

Approximately 7 percent of the nation's population—16 million people—receive welfare payments. This is nearly twice the number of people on welfare rolls a few years ago (see Figure 5–2). The costs of welfare and the growth of social dependency outrage many working, taxpaying Americans. But their outrage is matched by that of the recipients themselves who claim that the payments are inadequate to maintain a decent standard of living. Nationwide, welfare payments are well below poverty levels established by the Social Security Administration. The welfare bureaucracy is a nightmare—long lines, endless forms, insensitive officials, and pointless regulations. No one is more bitter about the welfare system in America than the recipients themselves. Even the welfare officials who operate the system are offended by it. Turnover among caseworkers is high. Caseworkers are assigned so many cases that they can rarely be of direct assistance to families. All they can do is process forms and send checks. Finally, the greatest inequity in the welfare system is its total exclusion of the *working* poor—those millions of American families who live in poverty but cannot receive government assistance because one member of the family is working.

Racial antagonisms are another part of the welfare dilemma. About 25 percent of the nation's black population receives public assistance of one kind or another; only about 4 percent of the white population is on welfare. In the nation's large cities the welfare rolls are overwhelmingly black. Hence, conflict over welfare is closely related to racial problems.

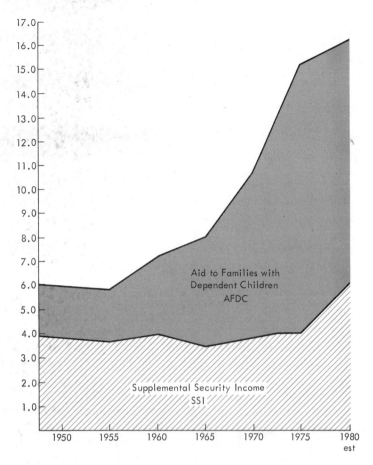

FIG. 5–2 The welfare explosion

Incredibly enough, today's welfare dilemma is the product of more than forty years of rational planning. Social security, unemployment compensation, public assistance, Medicaid and Medicare, food stamps, manpower training, the "war on poverty," and a variety of other programs and policies were initially presented to the nation as rational approaches to the problems of the poor. Yet none of these programs has succeeded in eliminating poverty or even reducing public demands that "something be done" about "the welfare mess." All of these programs have produced serious, unanticipated consequences.

It is not really possible in this chapter to describe all the problems of the poor in America or to describe all the difficulties in developing rational health and welfare policies. But it is possible to describe the general design of alternative strategies to deal with poverty in America,

Welfare lines, New York City. UPI Photo

to observe how these strategies have been implemented in public policy, and to outline some of the obstacles to a rational approach to the problems of the poor.

## The Punitive Strategy—Early Welfare Policy

Public welfare has been a recognized responsibility of governments in English-speaking nations for almost 400 years. Prior to the 1930s, care of the poor in the United States resembled the early patterns of poor relief established as far back as the Poor Relief Act of 1601 by the English Parliament. Early "Elizabethan" welfare policy was a combination of punitive as well as alleviative strategies that discouraged all but the most desperately poor from seeking aid, and provided only minimal assistance to those persons clearly unable to care for themselves. The "able-bodied poor," those we call the unemployed, were sent to county workhouses; the "worthy poor"—widows, aged, orphans, and handicapped—were sent to poorhouses. Indigent persons who were mentally or physically ill were often kept in the same institutions. Destitute children were kept in county orphanages or sent to foster homes. Thus, public welfare was limited almost exclusively to institutional care; the distribution of food or clothing or other aid to homes of the poor was left to private charities. Whatever relief was provided by the public could never exceed the value of the income of the lowest-paid person in the community who was not on relief. Poor rolls were made public, and relief was forthcoming only if there were no living relatives who could be legally required to support a destitute member of their family.

Under Elizabethan law, the care of the poor was the responsibility of the local governments rather than the state and local governments. The parish in England, and the city or county in the United States, had to care for their poor out of their general tax funds. Because local governments wished to make certain that they were not caring for the poor of other communities, residence requirements were established for welfare care, and communities generally limited their support to those who had been born in the area or who had lived there for some time.

The rationale behind Elizabethan policy—a rationale that has not altogether disappeared from the welfare scene today—was that poverty was a product of moral or character deficiencies in the individual. Only a punitive strategy would dissuade people from indolence and keep poverty to a minimum.

During the period of rapid industrialization and heavy immigration in America (roughly 1870 to 1920) private charities, churches, and big city political "machines" and "bosses" assisted the impoverished.

The political machine operated as a large, although inefficient, brokerage organization. It traded off baskets of food, bushels of coal, minor patronage, and petty favors in exchange for the votes of the poor. To get funds to pay for this primitive welfare assistance, it traded off city contracts, protection, and privileges to business interests who paid off in cash. The machine was not very efficient as a welfare organization, because a great many middlemen came between the cash paid for a business franchise and the Christmas turkey sent to Widow O'Leary. But it worked. Recipients of such assistance were spared much of the red tape and delays experienced by recipients of public assistance today. More importantly, the aid was provided in a very personal fashion without making the recipient feel inferior or dependent. They were trading something valuable—their votes—for the assistance they received.

The Depression brought about significant changes in attitudes toward public welfare and in the policies and administration of welfare programs. Millions who had previously considered welfare recipients to be unworthy of public concern now joined in the breadlines themselves. One out of four Americans was unemployed and one out of six was receiving some sort of welfare care. No longer were many people willing to believe that poverty was a product of the individual's moral or character faults. This widespread experience with poverty changed public attitudes toward welfare and led to a change away from Elizabethan policy.

## The Preventative Strategy—Social Security

The administration of President Franklin D. Roosevelt lent legitimacy to the concept of national planning. In the broadest sense national planning meant attempts by the federal government to develop rational programs to achieve societal goals. Roosevelt himself was a master at articulating broad national purposes that could enlist the support of a large cross section of the national public. However, Roosevelt was something less than a master in devising specific rational policy alternatives to achieve these purposes. Despite a great deal of New Deal rhetoric implying rationality and consistency in solving national problems, the actual record of the Roosevelt Administration indicated pragmatism, experimentalism, and improvisation. According to Roosevelt, the times required

> full, persistent experimentation. If it fails, admit it frankly and try something else. But above all, try something. The millions who are in want will not stand by silently forever until the things to satisfy their needs are within easy reach.[4]

[4]Richard Hofstadter, *American Political Tradition* (New York: Knopf, 1948), p. 316.

Yet there was an underlying logic to the most important piece of legislation of the New Deal—the Social Security Act of 1935. In this act, the federal government undertook to establish the basic framework for welfare policies at the federal, state, and local level and, more importantly, to set forth a new approach to the problem of poverty. The Depression convinced the national leadership and a great many citizens that indigency could result from forces over which the individual had no control—loss of his job, old age, death of the family breadwinner, or physical disability. The solution was to require individuals to purchase insurance against their own indigency resulting from any of these misfortunes.

The *social insurance* concept devised by the New Deal planners was designed to prevent poverty resulting from uncontrollable forces. Social insurance was based on the same notion as private insurance—the sharing of risks and the setting aside of money for a rainy day. Social insurance was not to be charity or public assistance; it was to be preventative. It relied upon the individual's (compulsory) contribution to his own protection. In contrast, public assistance is only alleviative, and relies upon general tax revenues from all taxpayers. Indeed, when the Roosevelt Administration presented the social insurance plan to Congress in the Social Security Act of 1935, it was contended that it would eventually abolish the need for any public assistance program, because individuals would be compelled to protect themselves against poverty!

The distinction between a *social insurance* program and a *public assistance* program is an important one, and has on occasion been a major political issue. If the beneficiaries of a government program are required to make contributions to it before claiming any of its benefits, and if they are entitled to the benefits regardless of their personal wealth, then the program is said to be financed on the *social insurance* principle. On the other hand, if a program is financed out of general tax revenues, and if the recipients are required to show they are poor before claiming its benefits, then the program is said to be financed on the *public assistance* principle.

One of the key features of the Social Security Act of 1935 is the Old Age Survivor's Disability and Health Insurance (OASDHI) program. This is a compulsory social insurance program financed by regular deductions from earnings which gives individuals a legal right to benefits in the event of certain occurrences that cause a reduction of their income: old age, death of the head of household, illness in old age, or permanent disability.[5] OASDHI is based on the same principle

---

[5]The original Social Security Act of 1935 did not include disability insurance; this was added by amendment in 1950. Health insurance for the aged—Medicare—was added by amendment in 1965; this is discussed in the next chapter.

as private insurance—sharing the risk of the loss of income—except that it is a government program and it is compulsory for all workers. OASDHI is not public *charity*, but a way of compelling people to provide *insurance* against a loss of income. OASDHI now covers about nine out of every ten workers in the United States. Both employees and employers must pay equal amounts toward the employees' OASDHI insurance. Upon retirement, an insured worker is entitled to monthly benefit payments based upon age at retirement and the amount earned during working years. However, average monthly payments are really quite modest: the average monthly amount for a retired worker, aged 65, with a spouse, is less than $450. So OASDHI has not eliminated poverty from the ranks of the retired in America.

OASDHI also insures benefit payments to survivors of an insured worker, including a spouse if there are dependent children. But if there are no dependent children, benefits will not begin until the spouse reaches retirement age. OASDHI insures benefit payments to persons who suffer permanent and total disabilities that prevent them from working for more than one year. However, on the whole, payments to survivors and disabled workers are just as modest as those provided retired workers. Finally, OASDHI provides prepaid health insurance for the aged under Medicare, which we will examine more closely later in the next chapter.

OASDHI is a completely federal program administered by the Social Security Administration in the Department of Health and Human Services. But it has an important indirect effect on state and local welfare programs: by compelling people to insure themselves against the possibility of their own poverty, social security has doubtlessly reduced the welfare problems that state and local governments would otherwise face. The growth of OASDHI in numbers of recipients (beneficiaries), average monthly payments, and percentage of the federal government's budget is shown in Table 5–3.

Social security benefits are specifically exempted from federal income taxes. Persons over sixty-five also receive a double personal exemption on their federal income taxes.

The second feature of the Social Security Act of 1935 was that it induced states to enact unemployment compensation programs through the imposition of the payroll tax on all employers. A federal unemployment tax is levied on the payroll of employers of four or more workers, but employers paying into state insurance programs that meet federal standards may use these state payments to offset most of their federal unemployment tax. In other words, the federal government threatens to undertake an unemployment compensation program and tax, if the states do not do so themselves. This federal program succeeded in inducing all fifty states to establish unemployment compensation programs. However, the federal standards are flexible and the

**TABLE 5–3**  Social Security, 1940–1978

|  | 1940 | 1950 | 1960 | 1965 | 1970 | 1972 | 1975 | 1978 |
|---|---|---|---|---|---|---|---|---|
| Numbers of beneficiaries (in thousands) | 222 | 3,477 | 14,845 | 20,867 | 25,312 | 30,556 | 31,598 | 34,083 |
| Average monthly benefit, retired worker | $23 | $44 | $74 | $84 | $100 | $117 | $183 | $243 |
| Social insurance receipts as percent of all federal receipts |  |  | 15.9 | 19.1 | 22.5 | 24.0 | 29.0 | 31.0 |
| Medicare expenditures (in millions) | 0 | 0 | 0 | 0 | $6,800 | $8,819 | $14,191 | $27,582 |

Source: *The Budget of the United States Government, 1980* (Washington, D.C.: Government Printing Office, 1979), and past issues of U.S. Bureau of the Census, *Statistical Abstract of the United States.*

states have considerable freedom in shaping their own unemployment programs. In all cases, unemployed workers must report in person and show that they are willing and able to work in order to receive unemployment compensation benefits. States cannot deny workers benefits for refusing to work as strike-breakers or refusing to work for rates lower than prevailing rates. But basic decisions concerning the amount of benefits, eligibility, and the length of time that benefits can be drawn are largely left to the states.

### Evaluation: Intended and Unintended Consequences of Social Security

The framers of the Social Security Act of 1935 created an OASDHI trust fund with the expectation that a reserve would be built up from social insurance premiums from working persons. The reserve would earn interest, and the interest and principle would be used in later years to pay benefits. Benefits for an individual would be in proportion to his contributions. General tax revenues would not be used at all. It was intended that the system would resemble the financing of private insurance. But it turned out not to work that way at all.

The social insurance system is now financed on a pay-as-you-go, rather than a reserve, system. Political pressure to raise benefit levels while keeping payments low reduced the reserve to a very minor role in social security finance. Today, the income from all social insurance programs—over $160 billion—matches the outgo in social security benefits. Today, this generation of workers is paying for the benefits of the last generation, and it is expected that this generation's benefits will be financed by the next generation of workers. Social security trust fund revenues are now lumped together with general tax revenues in the federal budget.

Since current workers must pay for the benefits of current retirees and other beneficiaries, the "dependency ratio" becomes an important component of evaluating the future of social security. The "dependency ratio" for social security is the number of recipients as a percentage of the number of contributing workers. At present, each one hundred workers support about 29 beneficiaries. But as the U.S. population grows older—due to lower birth rates and longer life span—we can expect 44 beneficiaries for each one hundred workers after the year 2000. This will result in additional pressures on the system for financial support. If the system cannot finance promised benefits, Congress will be forced to use general tax revenues to make benefit payments.

Congress has gradually increased the social security payroll tax from 3 percent combined employee and employer contributions on the first $3,000 of wages to 13.4 percent combined contribution of the first $31,800. To keep up with the generous benefits which Congress finds politically expedient to vote year after year, the social security tax is now *the second largest source of federal revenue*. More important, it is also *the fastest growing source of federal revenue*. Social insurance and welfare payments are now *the largest expenditure of the federal government*, surpassing expenditures for national defense.

The decline of the insurance concept began in the very first years of the program when FDR's planners quickly realized that building a reserve was taking money from the economy and adding to the Depression. The plan to build a large self-financing reserve fund was abandoned in 1939. Now Congress regularly alters the levels of benefits and the formula for the computation, a practice very much at variance with sound insurance practices. More and more groups of workers have been given coverage under social security. Benefits are no longer really proportionate to contributions; they are figured more generously for those whose wages were low than for those whose wages were high. The only remaining aspect of an insurance program is that individuals must have paid into the system to receive its benefits, and beneficiaries are not required to prove they are needy. Most Americans view their benefits as a right.

The social security tax is regressive. It takes a much larger share of the income of middle- and low-income workers than wealthy investors and others whose income is from sources other than wages. This was not a serious factor when the payments amounted to very little, but today the size of social security revenues—fully one-quarter of the federal government's income—has an important impact on the total revenue structure. The tax is only on *wages*, not total *income*. And wages above certain levels ($31,800 in 1982) are completely untaxed.

Despite rises in benefit levels, the average monthly payment for a retired couple remains below $450. Without additional retirement or investment income, all social security recipients would live in poverty, and a significant proportion of them have no such additional income. Although there is no question that social security has reduced the amount of poverty that would exist in the absence of the program, it has failed to eliminate poverty.

## The Alleviative Strategy—Public Assistance

The Social Security and Unemployment Compensation programs were based upon the insurance strategy for preventing indigency, but the federal government also undertook in the Social Security Act of 1935 to help the states in providing public assistance payments to certain needy persons. This strategy was designed to alleviate the conditions of poverty; there was no effort to attack the causes of poverty. The notion was to provide a minimum level of subsistence to certain categories of needy adults—the aged, blind, and disabled—and to provide for the care of dependent children. This was to be done by providing small amounts of cash in monthly payments through state-administered welfare programs. The federal grant-in-aid device was employed because welfare functions traditionally had been the responsibility of state and local governments. The entire federal effort in public assistance was supposed to be temporary in duration, declining in importance as social insurance took over the burden of assuring security.

Today the federal government directly aids three categories of welfare recipients—the aged, the blind, and the disabled—under the Supplemental Security Income program (SSI). The federal government also provides grants to the states to assist the fourth and largest category—families with dependent children. Within broad outlines of the federal policy, states retain considerable discretion in the Aid to Families with Dependent Children (AFDC) program in terms of the amounts of money appropriated, benefits to be paid to recipients, rules of eligibility, and rules of the programs. Each state may choose to grant assistance beyond the amounts supported by the national government. Each state establishes its own standards to determine "need." As a result, there is a great deal of variation among the states in ease of access to welfare rolls and in the size of welfare benefits.

It is important to note that the federal government aids only four category—families with dependent children. Within broad outlines of who are aged, blind, or disabled fall within the categories of recipients eligible for federal support. Aid to persons who do not fall into any of these categories but who, for one reason or another, are "needy," is referred to as "general assistance." General assistance programs are entirely state-financed and state-administered. Without federal participation, these programs differ radically from state to state in terms of the persons aided, the criteria for eligibility, the amount and nature of benefits, and administration of financing. Many of these programs continue to resemble Elizabethan welfare policy. The average general assistance payment is lower than comparable payments in federally supported programs.

States also continue to maintain institutions to care for those individuals who are so destitute, alone, or ill that money payments cannot meet their needs. These institutions include state orphanages, homes for the aged, and homes for the ill. They are, for the most part, state-financed as well as state-administered. However, persons living in these tax-supported institutions may be eligible for federal assistance— social security, SSI, and Medicare, for example.

Federal standards for state AFDC programs, which are established as a prerequisite to receiving federal aid, allow considerable flexibility in state programs. Federal law requires the states to make financial contributions to their public assistance programs and to supervise these programs either directly or through local agencies. Whatever standards a state adopts must be applicable throughout the state, and there must be no discrimination in these welfare programs. The Social Security Administration demands periodic reporting from the states, insists that states administer federally supported programs under a merit personnel system, and prevents the states from imposing unreasonable residence requirements on recipients. But in important questions of administration, standards of eligibility, residence, types of assistance, and amounts of payments, the states are free to determine their own welfare programs. Beginning in 1972, the federal government required "employable" welfare recipients to register for the Work Incentive (WIN) Program; individuals prepared for work are referred to jobs while others are enrolled in training or job experience programs. But the definition of "employable" generally excludes the aged, the ill, and mothers of preschool children; indeed, only a tiny fraction of all welfare recipients have participated in the WIN program.

The *Food Stamp Program,* administered by the Department of Agriculture, now distributes nearly $7 billion in federal monies to improve food and nutrition among the poor. Eligible persons may obtain food stamps, generally from county welfare departments. The stamps may then be used to purchase food at supermarkets. This program has mushroomed very rapidly since 1972, with expansions in eligible population and increases in the cost of food. Eligibility for food stamps now extends to many low-income persons who are not poor enough to qualify for cash public assistance payments. Of course, food stamps are also made available to public assistance recipients. Federal expenditures for food stamps are rapidly approaching federal expenditures for the AFDC program, making food stamps a major subsidy for low-income families.

Public assistance recipients are generally eligible for participation in a variety of social service programs. These include Medicaid, public housing, school lunch and milk, manpower training, Office of Economic Opportunity antipoverty programs, various educational and child-care programs and services, and the food stamp program. Some of the programs are described elsewhere in this volume (public housing, Chapter 9; educational programs, Chapter 7).

The effect of these multiple social service programs on the alleviation of poverty is considerable. Indeed, it is difficult to determine just how "poor" the poor really are because it is difficult to add up the dollar value of the many separate programs serving the poor. (See Table 5–4.)

## Evaluation: The Welfare Mess

Public assistance turned out to be politically one of the most unpopular programs ever adopted by Congress. It is disliked by national, state, and local legislators who must vote the skyrocketing appropriations for it; it is resented by the taxpayers who must bear the ever-increasing burdens of it; it is denounced by the officials and caseworkers who must administer it; and it is accepted with bitterness by those who were intended to benefit from it.

Certainly our public assistance programs have not succeeded in reducing dependency. Since 1965 the number of welfare recipients has more than doubled, and public assistance costs have more than quadrupled (see Figure 5–2). Interestingly, it has not been programs for the aged, blind, or disabled, or even the general assistance programs that have incurred the greatest burdens. It is the Aid to Families with Dependent Children (AFDC) and Food Stamp programs that are the largest, most expensive, and most rapidly growing of all welfare programs, and the most controversial.

This growth in welfare rolls has occurred during a period of relatively high employment; it cannot be attributed to economic depression. The acceleration has occurred because more people are applying for public assistance. They have been aided by the activities of civil rights and welfare rights organizations, community action agencies,

**TABLE 5–4** Federal Income Security Programs

| | Estimated costs (Billions $) | | |
|---|---|---|---|
| | 1978 | 1980 | 1982 |
| Social Insurance | | | |
| Social Security (OASDHI) | 87.9 | 115.7 | 150.0 |
| Medicare | 27.6 | 35.8 | 52.3 |
| Railroad Retirement | 3.8 | 4.3 | 4.8 |
| Disabled Coal Miners | 1.0 | 1.6 | 1.4 |
| Federal Employee Retirement | 14.7 | 15.7 | 14.0 |
| Public Assistance | | | |
| SSI | 5.2 | 6.4 | 7.2 |
| AFDC | 6.3 | 7.0 | 7.5 |
| Food Stamps | 5.6 | 6.9 | 7.3 |
| School Lunch | 3.4 | 4.5 | 5.0 |
| Housing Assistance | 32.3 | 27.5 | 28.0 |
| Medicaid | 10.7 | 12.7 | 15.2 |
| Other Health Sources | 3.5 | 3.9 | 4.1 |
| Total | 202.0 | 240.0 | 296.8 |
| Percent of Total Federal Budget | 45.6 | 45.1 | 48.3 |

Source: Budget of the United States Government 1980 (Washington: Government Printing Office, 1979).

and comparable groups, which have informed eligible persons of the law and encouraged them to apply for assistance. Increases in assistance levels, relaxation of eligibility requirements, and a more sympathetic attitude on the part of welfare administrators have also contributed to the increase in welfare rolls. So also has the movement of persons from Southern and rural areas, where welfare administration is tighter, to Northern urban areas, where access to welfare rolls is less restricted.

Despite increased dependency upon welfare and the growing burden of welfare costs, many of the nation's poor do *not* receive public assistance. There were 24 million poor people in America in 1978, yet only about 16 million persons on welfare rolls. Most of the nation's poor are *working poor*, who are ineligible for welfare assistance because they hold jobs, even though these jobs pay very little.

State administration of welfare has resulted in wide disparities among the states in eligibility requirements and benefits levels. For example, in 1978 average AFDC monthly payments ranged from a high of $371 per family in New York to a low of $47 per family in Mississippi. A state's income is the single most important variable determining the level of welfare benefits. In terms of welfare payments, it is far better to be poor in a wealthy state than in a poor one.

Operating policies and administration of welfare have produced a whole series of problems, including disincentives to family life and work. Until recently, many states denied AFDC benefits if a man was living with his family, even though he had no work. This denial was based on the assumption that an employable man in the household meant that children were no longer "dependent" upon the state. Thus, if a man lived with his family, he could watch them go hungry; if he abandoned them, public assistance would enable them to eat. Moreover, an unmarried mother could get on welfare rolls more easily than a married mother (who had to prove she was not receiving support from her husband). These rules have been relaxed in recent years, but it is still more difficult for whole families to get on public assistance than for fatherless families.

In most states, if a recipient of assistance takes a full-time job, assistance checks are reduced or stopped. If the recipient is then laid off, it may take some time to get back on the welfare roll. In other words, employment is uncertain, while assistance is not. More importantly, the jobs available to most recipients are very low-paying jobs which do not produce much more income than does assistance, particularly when transportation, child care, and other costs of working are considered. All these facts discourage people from looking for work.

The merits of cash versus goods and services as a form of public assistance have long been debated. It is frequently argued that cash payments are ineffective in alleviating poverty because recipients are often unable to manage household money. They fall prey to advertising which encourages them to spend money for nonessential items and to overlook the food and clothing needs of themselves and their children. Assistance in the form of goods (for example, food stamps which can only be used to purchase basic food items) and services (for example, health care, day care for children, home management counseling) might represent a more effective approach. However, recipients themselves resent the goods and services approach, charging that it is paternalistic, that it curtails flexibility in family spending, and that it implies irresponsibility on the part of the recipient. Today most caseworkers argue for joint provision of cash and goods and services; they contend that cash is more effective when accompanied by services, and services are more effective when accompanied by cash.

Welfare administration is made difficult by the heavy load assigned to caseworkers, many of whom are recent college graduates. They spend much of their time determining eligibility, computing payments, and filling out an avalanche of proper forms. With caseloads averaging up to 100 or 200 families, their contacts with recipients must be hurried, infrequent, and impersonal. Caseworkers are unable to develop any close bonds of friendship or rapport with persons in need of

Photo by Fred W. McDarrah

help. Recipients often come to view caseworkers with distrust or worse. The strain on caseworkers is very great; big-city welfare departments report high turnover among caseworkers.

Fraudulent welfare claims are a source of concern for federal and state administrators. The U.S. Office of Management and Budget cites survey studies which indicate that 40 percent of all welfare claims under the AFDC program are inaccurate.[6] About 10 percent of AFDC recipients are not eligible for any payment, 23 percent are receiving greater payments than they should, and another 8 percent are underpaid. The Food Stamp program experiences about the same proportion of ineligibles and overpayments as the AFDC program. Most of these inaccuracies are technical errors rather than outright fraud. It is estimated that about 10 percent of Medicaid payments are also fraudulent. The recipients of fraudulent income under Medicaid are unethical doctors, clinics, and laboratories who charge Medicaid for services not actually provided to poor patients.

Social dependency and disincentives to work are magnified by the "pyramiding effect" of separate public assistance and social service programs. A family on the welfare rolls is generally entitled to participate in the Food Stamp program, to receive health care through Medicaid, to gain access to free or low-rent public housing, to receive free lunches in public schools, and to receive a variety of other social and educational benefits at little or no cost to themselves. These benefits and services available to the poor are not counted as income, yet the nonpoor must pay for similar services out of their own earnings. If a family head on welfare takes a job, he or she not only loses welfare assistance, but, more importantly perhaps, becomes ineligible for food stamps, Medicaid, public housing, and many other social services.

Various studies have reported that an urban family would have to earn more than $10,000 to $15,000 per year to live as well as a family receiving just four basic social benefits—public assistance, food stamps, school lunches, and Medicaid.[7] These reports argue that the level of benefits from multiple social programs discourages work unless the anticipated earnings are very high. These studies have also reported that female-headed families are far better off than male-headed (or "intact") families because of eligibility rules for various social programs. Thus, only a fairly well-paying job would justify going off the welfare rolls.

[6]*The Budget of the United States Government, 1975* (Washington, D.C.: Government Printing Office, 1974), pp. 128–29.

[7]Report prepared for the Joint Economic Subcommittee on Fiscal Policy released July 8, 1973, reported in Congressional Quarterly, *The Future of Social Programs* (Washington, D.C.: Congressional Quarterly, 1973), p. 87.

Do current welfare programs destroy the work ethic and increase social dependency? At first glance it would appear that social science could help answer such a question and truly contribute to the development of rational public policy. Indeed, the now defunct Office of Economic Opportunity once employed social scientists to conduct large-scale experiments on the effect of a guaranteed annual income on the work incentives of the poor (see Chapter 15). But as we shall observe later, attempts to assess systematically the impact of welfare policies on the poor have proven very difficult. We have not yet rationalized welfare policy.

## New Strategies for Income Maintenance

There is fairly wide agreement on the goals of welfare reform: to raise the income of the poor, to narrow disparities among states in benefit levels, to assist the working as well as the nonworking poor, to increase incentives to work, to keep families together, to prevent fraud, and to reduce bureaucratization and impersonality in welfare administration. We might expect this general agreement on goals to facilitate a rational approach to devising a new income maintenance program. However, reform has proven a very difficult task.

Perhaps the most common reform proposal is to "federalize" all welfare programs giving the federal government full responsibility for financing and administering all public assistance programs, including AFDC. This would eliminate differences in eligibility requirements and benefit levels among the states. It would also relieve states and cities from the burden of cost sharing in welfare care. Mayors and governors (who frequently complain about federal intervention in other fields) have generally supported the notion of a federal takeover of welfare responsibilities. The president and Congress have been reluctant to assume these increased costs into the federal budget, but "federalizing" welfare is a likely possibility in the near future.

A different basic approach to reform is set forth by advocates of the "negative income tax" or "guaranteed annual income." This group argues that reforming welfare is hopeless—welfare payments will always mean punitive rules, meddling social workers, and humiliation of the poor. They propose scrapping the welfare system altogether in favor of a general system of income payments entirely separate from any other kind of social service. The negative income tax would guarantee everyone a minimum income, and it would encourage recipients to work by allowing them to keep a proportion of their earnings without deducting them from the minimum guarantee. For example, a guarantee might be set at $4,000 for a family of four with an earnings deduction of 50 percent. Under such a system a family with no earnings would receive a payment of $4,000; a family with $4,000 in earnings would receive a payment of $2,000 for a total income of $6,000; and a family earning $8,000, the break-even point, would receive no government benefit. The proposal seems like a logical extension of the progressive income tax. Everyone would file a declaration of income as they do now; most would pay taxes as they do now, but those at the low end of the income scale would receive payments (negative taxes). Checks would be issued directly from the Treasury Department with little or no participation by federal or state welfare bureaucracies.

The long-run impact of such a policy reform is difficult to predict. The first problem is cost: a negative income tax or guaranteed annual income plan would double the cost of welfare over the current system and might run three to four times greater. There is no reliable information on the number of working poor who would apply for assistance. Moreover, Congress would be under constant pressure to raise the minimum income for each year.

It is not certain whether this expansion of welfare assistance to many working families would increase or reduce economic dependency in America. It is conceivable that such an expansion in welfare assistance would destroy the "work ethic" and encourage dependency by making the acceptance of such assistance a common family practice, extending well up into the middle class. Certainly the percentage of the population receiving some form of public assistance would be greatly increased; it is conceivable that 20 percent of the population would eventually gain access to welfare rolls under a guaranteed annual income program. (Social science research on the effect of guaranteed income on the working behavior of the poor is discussed in Chapter 15.)

A guaranteed annual income does not necessarily tackle the problem of pyramiding welfare programs. Even if the prospect of keeping fifty cents on each dollar earned proved to be an incentive, benefits under multiple income test programs might be lost—notably, food stamps, child care, Medicaid, and public housing—again leaving the working poor worse off than the nonworking poor. Moreover, earnings would also be reduced by the costs of working—transportation, clothing, etc.—and social security contributions. If working provides little improvement in the lives of the poor, we can hardly expect them to join the labor force.

There is widespread agreement that the nation's welfare system is in urgent need of reform. But there is little agreement on the direction of reform. The problems of welfare reform illustrate again the political obstacles to rational policy making.

## The Curative Strategy—
## Federal Employment and Training Programs

Another general approach to poverty is one of applying a "curative strategy" to the problems of the poor. In contrast to the alleviative strategy of public assistance or the preventative strategy of social security, the curative strategy tries to help the poor and unemployed become self-supporting by bringing about changes in the individuals themselves.[8] For example, the federal government has undertaken a variety of employment training programs. These programs are designed to increase the skills and employment opportunities of the poor to enable them to become productive members of the nation's workforce. The programs provide skill training, transitional employment experience, job placement assistance, and even related child-care, social, and health services.

This approach to poverty began with the Manpower Development and Training Act of 1962, which authorized federal grants to state employment agencies and private enterprise for on-the-job training programs to help workers acquire new job skills. Additional manpower training programs were authorized under the Economic Opportunity Act of 1964 and directed at persons living below the poverty line. In 1973 all manpower programs were brought together under the Comprehensive Employment and Training Act (CETA).

Federal manpower programs under CETA provide for both institutional (classroom) and on-the-job training. On-the-job training is provided by private and governmental employers who recruit and train low-skilled persons to fill regular job vacancies. The employers are reimbursed for the costs of training, remedial education, counseling, and supportive services. More than half the costs of the program have been for enrollee allowances—payments to participants during their training period. In the past the CETA program concentrated on retraining technologically displaced workers, but in recent years it has also attempted to teach skills to unemployed persons with little or no work experience.

The Job Corps is a specialized program for disadvantaged youth. It provides education, vocational training, and work experience in rural conservation camps for unemployable youth between the ages of

---

[8]The rationale for a "curative strategy" was described in an influential book: John K. Galbraith, *The Affluent Society* (Boston: Houghton-Mifflin, 1958). This strategy was the favored approach to poverty in the administrations of Presidents John F. Kennedy and Lyndon B. Johnson. It is represented in the Economic Development Act of 1965; the Appalachian Regional Development Act of 1965; the Comprehensive Employment and Training Act of 1973 (originally the Manpower Development and Training Act of 1962); and the Economic Opportunity Act of 1964. These latter two efforts are described in the pages that follow.

sixteen and twenty-one. It is not a simple manpower training effort; Job Corps enrollees are considered to lack the attitudes and basic education required to gain and hold a job. Reading and basic arithmetic are taught, as well as auto mechanics, clerical work, and the use of tools. Health care and personal guidance and counseling are also provided. Removing the enrollees from their home environment is considered helpful in breaking habits and associations that are obstacles to useful employment. It is very difficult to measure the effectiveness of the program; its dropout rate is very high; the cost of the program per enrollee is very high; and there is no solid evidence that Job Corps alumni do better in the labor market than they would have done without Job Corps experience. The Job Corps was begun as part of the 1964 Economic Opportunity Act "war on poverty," but it is now operated by the Department of Labor under CETA.

Federal Work-Study programs help students from low-income families remain in school by giving them federally paid part-time employment with cooperating public or private agencies. Many universities and colleges are participants in this program; they benefit from the federally paid labor and students benefit from the part-time jobs created.

The Work Incentive Program (WIN) is designed specifically to deal with disadvantaged adults. The WIN program was mandated for all employable welfare recipients in 1972. Participants in this program are poor; they generally have few skills and little or no work experience. It is very difficult to evaluate WIN's success. Numerically, very few individuals have escaped poverty and found rewarding jobs as a direct result of it. However, programs like this have tried to assist long-term public assistance recipients, habitual offenders, narcotic addicts, and alcoholics, and the very difficulty of the task precludes a high success rate.

In addition to the programs mentioned above, the Department of Health and Human Services provides federal grants to states to undertake vocational rehabilitation programs for physically or mentally handicapped persons, and the Veterans Administration operates a vocational rehabilitation program for disabled veterans.

The federal government also funds the Federal-State Employment Service with its network of 2,300 local offices providing job-placement services for nearly 10 million persons per year. Although these placement services are available to everyone, special efforts are given to placing disadvantaged persons.

"Public service employment" (PSE) is a new federal program which is modeled after an old New Deal strategy for combating poverty—the creation of "public service jobs" to put the unemployed to work on government projects. A "temporary" public service jobs program was enacted during the 1973–1975 recession, after compromise between a Democratic Congress and the Republican Administration of President Gerald Ford. But under the leadership of Senator Hubert H. Humphrey (D., Minn.) in the years immediately prior to his death, Congress gradually expanded the public service employment concept.

The Humphrey-Hawkins Act in 1978 attempted to "guarantee" jobs to every "able and willing" adult American. The federal government was to be viewed as "the employer of last resort" for individuals unable to find employment in the private sector. Lowering the unemployment rate to 3 percent was to be a "national goal." Despite the ambitious language in the act, to date implementation has been modest. The federal government has subsidized PSE jobs in state and local government and some nonprofit agencies. The Carter Administration has tied the number of PSE jobs and total federal funds for this purpose to the condition of the economy. We can expect PSE to increase during recessions and retrench during periods of relatively full employment.

One major problem in dealing with unemployment is accurately assessing the meaning of the U.S. Labor Department's official "unemployment rate." A national unemployment rate of 3 percent appears unrealistic; except in wartime, the unemployment rate has never been this low. (Five to six percent unemployment appears "normal" in a flourishing economy; unemployment in the 1973–1975 recession reached nearly 9 percent.) Today's officially unemployed include teenagers, second and third wage earners in the same household, and individuals who sign up for jobs at the U.S. Employment Service because doing so is a requirement to receive certain welfare benefits. Years ago, the officially unemployed were almost exclusively heads of households with no other source of income. Hence, "unemployment" today is not the equivalent of "unemployment" a few decades ago.

## Evaluation: Why We Lost the "War on Poverty"

President Lyndon B. Johnson launched a massive "war on poverty" in the 1960s. The most important legislation in the "war on poverty" was the Economic Opportunity Act of 1964.[9] This act established the Office of Economic Opportunity (OEO) directly under the president with authority to support varied and highly experimental techniques for combating poverty at the community level. However, most key features of this war on poverty were abandoned in the 1970s (by Democrats as well as Republicans). The Office of Economic Opportunity was abol-

[9]For a description of the programs under the Economic Opportunity Act, see Joseph A. Kershaw, *Government against Poverty* (Chicago: Markham, 1970).

ished in 1975. There are many important lessons that can be learned about public policy by studying how we lost this "war on poverty."

The objective of the ill-fated Economic Opportunity Act was to help the poor and unemployed become self-supporting and capable of earning adequate incomes, by bringing about changes in the individuals themselves or in their environments. The strategy was one of "rehabilitation, not relief." OEO had no authority to make direct grants to the poor as relief or public assistance. All its programs were aimed, whether accurately or inaccurately, at curing the causes of poverty rather than alleviating its symptoms.

The core of the Economic Opportunity Act was a grassroots Community Action Program to be carried on at the local level with federal financial assistance, by public or private nonprofit agencies. Communities were urged to form a "community action agency," composed of representatives of government, private organizations, and, most importantly, the poor themselves. It was originally intended that OEO would *support antipoverty programs* devised by the local community action agency. Projects might include (but were not limited to) literacy training, health services, homemaker services, legal aid for the poor, neighborhood service centers, manpower vocational training, and childhood development activities. The act also envisioned that a community action agency would help *organize the poor* so that they could become participating members of the community and avail themselves of the many public programs designed to serve the poor. Finally, the act attempted to *coordinate federal and state programs for the poor* in each community.

Community action was to be "developed, conducted, and administered with the maximum feasible participation of the residents of the areas and members of the groups served." This was one of the more controversial phrases in the act itself. Militants within the OEO administration frequently cited this phrase as authority to "mobilize" the poor "to have immediate and irreversible impact on the communities." This language implied that the poor were to be organized as a political force, by federal antipoverty warriors using federal funds. Needless to say, neither Congress nor the Democratic administration of President Lyndon Johnson intended to create rival political organizations in communities that would compete for power with local governments. But some OEO administrators thought that the language of the act gave them this authority.

Community action agencies were expected to devise specific antipoverty projects for submission to Washington offices of OEO for funding. The most popular of these projects was Operation Head Start—usually a cooperative program between the community action agency and the local school district for six to eight weeks of special summer preparation before entering kindergarten or first grade.

But there was never any clear evidence that Head Start actually helped remedy learning problems. Studies comparing poor children who had attended Head Start with poor children who had not showed that differences in achievement levels disappeared after one or two years. (However, Head Start remained popular among parents even if it had no lasting effect on children.)

Another popular antipoverty project was the Legal Services Program. Many community action agencies established free legal services to the poor to assist them in rent disputes, contracts, welfare rules, minor police action, housing regulations, and so on. But arming the poor with lawyers frequently antagonized local and state government agencies—welfare, housing, health, schools, etc.—who were providing benefits and services to the poor and did not enjoy defending themselves in court against publicly financed poverty lawyers. Other kinds of antipoverty projects funded by OEO included family planning programs—the provision of advice and devices to facilitate family planning by the poor; homemaker services—advice to poor families on how to stretch low family budgets; manpower training—special outreach efforts to bring hardcore unemployed into more established manpower programs; "Follow Through"—to remedy the recognized failures of Head Start and continue special educational experiences for poor children after they enter school; "Upward Bound"—educational counseling for poor children, and so forth. But again there was little evidence that the "hardcore" poor were helped by these programs. Indeed, the greatest beneficiaries seemed to be black and white middle-class officials who were hired with poverty funds to administer these programs.

The typical Community Action Agency was governed by a board consisting of public officials (perhaps the mayor, a county commissioner, a school board member, public health officer, etc.), prominent public citizens (from business, labor, civil rights, religious, and civic affairs organizations), and representatives of the poor (in some cases elected in agency-sponsored elections but more often handpicked by ministers, social workers, civil rights leaders, etc.). A staff was hired, including a full-time director. A target area was defined—generally it was the low-income area of the county or the ghetto of a city. Neighborhood centers were established in the target area, perhaps with general counselors, employment assistance, a recreation hall, a child-care center, and some sort of health clinic. These centers assisted the poor in contacting the school system, the welfare department, employment agencies, the public housing authority, and so on. Frequently, the centers and the antipoverty workers who manned them acted as intermediaries between the poor and public agencies. The jargon describing this activity was "outreach."

Even before President Johnson left office in 1969, the war on poverty had become another unpopular war. The Nixon Administration "reorganized" OEO in 1973, turning over some programs like Head Start to other agencies. In 1975, the Ford Administration and Congress abolished OEO altogether. The reasons for the failure of the war on poverty are complex.

The Office of Economic Opportunity was always the scene of great confusion. New and untried programs were organized at breakneck speed. There was a high turnover in personnel. There was delay and confusion in releasing funds to local community action agencies. There was scandal and corruption, particularly at the local level. Community action agencies with young and inexperienced personnel frequently offended experienced governmental administrators as well as local political figures. Congressional action was uncertain, the project's life was extended for a year at a time, and appropriations were often delayed. But most damaging of all, even though programs were put in operation, there was little concrete evidence that these programs were successful in their objectives, that is, in eliminating the causes of poverty.

The demise of the economic opportunity programs cannot be attributed to political partisanship. Daniel P. Moynihan summarized the community action experiences as follows:

> Over and again the attempts by official and quasi-official agencies (such as the Ford Foundation) to organize poor communities led first to the radicalization of the middle-class persons who began the effort; next to a certain amount of stirring among the poor, but accompanied by heightened radical antagonism *on the part of the poor* if they happened to be black; next to retaliation from the larger white community; whereupon it would emerge that the community action agency, which had talked so much, been so much in the headlines, promised so much in the way of change in the fundamentals of things, was powerless. A creature of a Washington bureaucracy, subject to discontinuation without notice. Finally, much bitterness all around.[10]

And in obvious reference to public policies affecting the poor and the black in America, Aaron Wildavsky wrote:

> A recipe for violence: Promise a lot; deliver a little. Lead people to believe they will be much better off, but let there be no dramatic improvement. Try a variety of small programs, each interesting but marginal in impact and severely underfinanced. Avoid any attempted solution remotely comparable in size to the dimensions of the

[10]Daniel P. Moynihan, *Maximum Feasible Misunderstanding: Community Action in the War on Poverty* (New York: The Free Press, 1969), pp. 134–35.

problem you are trying to solve. Have middle-class civil servants hire upper-class student radicals to use lower-class Negroes as a battering ram against the existing local political systems; then complain that people are going around disrupting things and chastise local politicians for not cooperating with those out to do them in. Get some poor people involved in local decision-making, only to discover that there is not enough at stake to be worth bothering about. Feel guilty about what has happened to black people; tell them you are surprised they have not revolted before; express shock and dismay when they follow your advice. Go in for a little force, just enough to anger, not enough to discourage. Feel guilty again; say you are surprised that worse has not happened. Alternate with a little suppression. Mix well, apply a match, and run. . . ."[11]

## Summary

The difficulties of rational policy making are evidenced in policies and programs dealing with the poor.

1. Contrasting definitions of the problem of poverty constitute an obstacle to national policy making. Official government sources define poverty in terms of minimum dollar amounts required for food, housing, clothing, and other necessary items. Poverty, by this definition, is declining over time.

2. If poverty is defined in relative terms, then the problem of poverty is nearly insoluble. Income inequality is slowly decreasing over time. However, unless all incomes in America are equalized among all persons, there will always be some individuals who fall below average income levels. Even if the differences in incomes are substantially narrowed, small differences may come to have great symbolic value and the problem of "poverty" will remain.

3. The strategy of early welfare policy was to discourage poverty by providing only minimal assistance, generally in institutions, to the most destitute in society. Heavy reliance was placed on local governments and upon private charity. Poverty was viewed as a product of moral deficiency in the individual, and it was reasoned that only a punitive strategy would dissuade people from indolence.

4. The social insurance concept was designed as a preventive strategy to insure persons against indigency arising from old age, death of a family breadwinner, or physical disability. It was hoped that social security would eventually abolish the need for public welfare, because individuals would be insured against poverty.

5. Despite the fact that social insurance is now the largest expenditure item of the federal government, welfare rolls are still high. Average monthly payments under social security fall below recognized

[11]Aaron Wildavsky, "The Empty-Headed Blues: Black Rebellion and White Reaction," *The Public Interest* (Spring 1968), 3.

poverty levels. The trust fund concept has been abandoned. The tax itself is highly regressive.

6. The federal government also undertook an alleviative strategy in helping the states provide public assistance payments to certain categories of needy persons—aged, blind, disabled, and dependent children. Federal grants-in-aid to the states assisted them in providing monthly cash payments to the needy.

7. Dependence upon public assistance in America continues to grow, despite a reasonably healthy economy. Aid to families with dependent children is the largest, most expensive, and most rapidly growing of all welfare programs. Yet many of the nation's poor do not receive welfare payments, notably the working poor. Welfare benefits are uneven among the states. Program policies include disincentives to both family life and work. Caseworkers are too overloaded for effective counseling, and administration is heavy with red tape. Multiplication of programs serving the poor mask the real income of the poor, and there is a pyramiding of disincentives to work.

8. The "war on poverty" was designed as a curative strategy to help the poor become self-supporting. But the "community action" programs of the old Economic Opportunity Act of 1964 lost political support over the years; the Office of Economic Opportunity was abolished in 1973. These programs promised the poor a great deal but failed to bring about any significant change in their condition. Frustration and bitterness were frequent products of antipoverty efforts.

9. Welfare reform—in terms of a guaranteed annual income or negative income tax—is another attempt at rationalizing welfare policy. It is designed to assist the working as well as the nonworking poor, to provide a federally guaranteed floor on minimum incomes, and to reduce dependency by work incentives. However, the outcomes are difficult to predict; the number of participants and future costs are difficult to estimate; the impact on social dependency is difficult to foresee; and the work incentives may turn out to be inappropriate or ineffective.

## Bibliography

AARON, HENRY J., *Politics and the Professors: The Great Society in Perspective.* Washington: Brookings Institution, 1978.

BUDD, EDWARD C., *Inequality and Poverty.* New York: Norton, 1967.

GALBRAITH, JOHN K., *The Affluent Society.* Boston: Houghton-Mifflin, 1958.

HARRINGTON, MICHAEL, *The Other America: Poverty in the United States.* New York: Macmillan, 1962.

HAVEMAN, ROBERT H., ed., *A Decade of Federal Antipoverty Programs*. New York: Academic Press, 1976.

KERSHAW, JOSEPH A., *Government Against Poverty*. Chicago: Markham, 1970.

LEVINE, ROBERT A., *The Poor Ye Need Not Have With You*. Cambridge: M.I.T. Press, 1970.

LEVITAN, SAR A., *The Great Society's Poor Law*. Baltimore: Johns Hopkins Press, 1969.

MARMOR, THEODORE R., ed., *Poverty Policy*. Chicago: Aldine-Atherton, 1971.

MOYNIHAN, DANIEL P., *Maximum Feasible Misunderstanding: Community Action and the War on Poverty*. New York: Free Press, 1969.

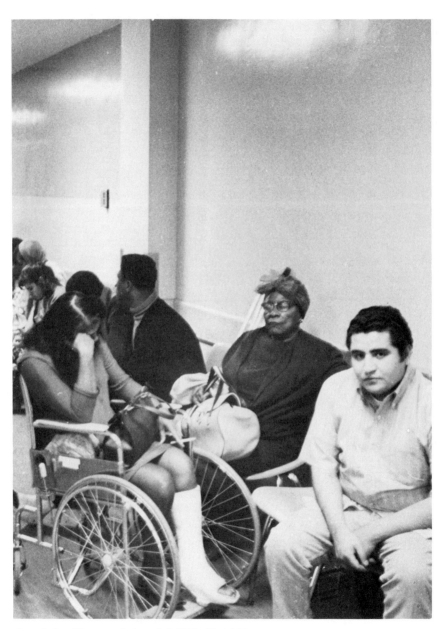

Crowded waiting room in hospital. *Wide World Photos*.

# Health
## the pathology
## of rational policy

# 6

## Health or Medical Care?

There is no better illustration of the dilemmas of rational policy making in America than in the field of health. Again, the first obstacle to rationalism is in defining the problem. Is our goal to be *good health*—that is, whether we live at all (infant mortality), how well we live (days lost to sickness), and how long we live (life spans and adult mortality)? Or is our goal to be *good medical care*—frequent and inexpensive visits to the doctor, well-equipped and accessible hospitals, and equal access to medical care by rich and poor alike?

Perhaps the first lesson in health policy is understanding that good medical care does *not* necessarily mean good health. Good health correlates best with factors over which doctors and hospitals have no control: heredity, lifestyle (smoking, eating, drinking, exercise, worry), and the physical environment (sewage disposal, water quality, conditions of work, etc.). Most of the bad things that happen to people's health are beyond the reach of doctors and hospitals.

Of course, doctors can set broken bones, stop infections with drugs, and remove swollen appendixes. And if you happen to be suffering from these or similar problems you want the careful attention of a skilled physician. But in the long run, infant mortality, sickness and disease, and life span are affected very little by the quality of medical care.[1] If you want a long healthy life, choose parents who have lived a long healthy life, and then do all the things your mother always told you to do: don't smoke, don't drink, get lots of exercise and rest, don't overeat, relax, and don't worry. You can spend millions on medical care, and you will not enjoy the same good health as you will by following these traditional guidelines.

Historically, most of the reductions in infant and adult death rates have resulted from public health and sanitation including immunization against smallpox, clean public water supply, sanitary sewage disposal, improved diets, and increased standards of living. Many of the leading causes of death today (see Table 6–1) including heart disease, stroke, cirrhosis of the liver, accidents, and suicides are closely linked to personal habits and lifestyles and beyond the reach of medicine. Other leading causes of death, including increasing deaths due to cancer and emphysema, may be related to environmental health hazards. Thus, the greatest contribution to better health is likely to be found in altered personal habits and lifestyles, and improved environmental conditions, rather than in more medical care.

Nonetheless, health policy in America is largely centered around the questionable notion that better medical care means better health.

## Health Care for the Poor

A liberal society feels a special responsibility for providing health care to the poor. The "right to life" must include the right to survive and to live in dignity. No one should be denied medical care for lack of money; no one should suffer or die for lack of financial resources to obtain adequate food; nor should anyone suffer desperation or pain for the lack of medical care that money can buy. We can find general agreement on these broad ethical principles. The tough questions arise when we try to find a way of implementing these principles.

It is not difficult to demonstrate that the poor and the black in America have higher mortality rates than the affluent and the white. For example, the infant mortality rate is believed to be especially sensitive to the adequacy of medical care; it is used frequently as a general indicator of the adequacy of health care. Infant mortality rates have been consistently higher for blacks than for whites. (See Table 6–2.) Infant mortality rates have declined for both races since 1950, but

[1]The literature on this point is extensive. See, for example, Victor R. Fuchs, *Who Shall Live? Health, Economics, and Social Choice* (New York: Basic Books, 1974); Nathan Glazer, "Paradoxes of Health Care," *The Public Interest* (Winter 1971), 62–77, Leon R. Kass, "Regarding the End of Medicine and the Pursuit of Health," *The Public Interest* (Summer 1975), 11–42.

**TABLE 6–1**  Death Rates From Leading Causes of Death, 1950–1975

|  | 1950 | 1965 | 1975 | Percent Change |
|---|---|---|---|---|
| All Causes | 841.5 | 741.8 | 666.2 | − 20.8 |
| Leading Causes |  |  |  |  |
| Heart disease | 307.6 | 275.6 | 232.7 | − 24.3 |
| Cancer | 125.4 | 127.9 | 131.8 | + 5.1 |
| Stroke | 88.8 | 73.1 | 59.9 | − 32.5 |
| Accidents | 57.5 | 53.4 | 46.0 | − 20.0 |
| Infant mortality | 40.5 | 28.6 | 13.6 | − 66.4 |
| Pneumonia | 26.2 | 23.4 | 16.9 | − 35.5 |
| Cirrhosis | 8.5 | 12.1 | 14.8 | + 74.1 |
| Suicide | 11.0 | 11.4 | 112.2 | + 10.9 |
| Homicide | 5.4 | 6.2 | 10.8 | +100.0 |
| Diabetes | 14.3 | 13.5 | 12.5 | + 12.6 |
| Arteriosclerosis | 16.2 | 12.0 | 7.6 | − 53.1 |
| Emphysema, Asthma | 3.7 | 11.6 | 9.2 | +148.6 |

*Source:* U.S. Department of Health, Education and Welfare, Division of Vital Statistics, *Mortality Trends 1950–1975* (Washington: Government Printing Office, 1977).

black infant deaths have continued to be significantly higher than white infant deaths. These and other figures clearly suggest that the poor do not enjoy the same good health as the affluent. *But* is this a product of inadequate medical care, or is it a product of nutrition, lifestyle, environment, and other nonmedical factors?

Contrary to popular stereotypes, the poor in America see doctors *more often* than the nonpoor. This situation has come about since 1965 with the beginning of the Medicaid program for the poor and Medicare for the aged. Indeed, the poor see their doctors about 20 percent more often than the nonpoor. Periodic examinations by physicians are considered good medical practice. We must therefore assume that the poor are receiving more, if not better, medical care than the nonpoor. Yet despite the increase in medical care for the poor, the health of the poor remains below the health of the nonpoor.

What has been accomplished for the poor? The health of the poor, relative to the nonpoor, does not increase with new government policies and programs. However, *access to medical care* for the poor has indeed improved with new government policies and programs. The

**TABLE 6–2**  Infant Mortality Rates by Race, 1950–1975

|  | 1950 | 1975 | Percent Change |
|---|---|---|---|
| White | 26.8 | 14.8 | − 44.8 |
| Nonwhite | 44.5 | 24.9 | − 44.0 |
| Total | 29.2 | 16.7 | − 42.8 |

*Source:* U.S. Department of Health, Education and Welfare, Division of Vital Statistics, *Mortality Trends 1950–1975* (Washington: Government Printing Office, 1977).

poor see doctors more often than the affluent, but this is largely irrelevant to health.

## Medicaid: Health Care as Welfare

Medicaid is the federal government's largest single welfare program for the poor. The costs of Medicaid now exceed the costs of all traditional welfare programs—including AFDC, SSI, and the Food Stamp program. Medicaid was begun in 1965 and grew quickly into the nation's largest welfare program.

Medicaid is a combined federal and state program. The states exercise fairly broad administrative powers and carry almost half of the financial burden. Medicaid is a welfare program designed for needy persons: no prior contributions are required, monies come from general tax revenues, and most recipients are already on welfare rolls. Although states differ in their eligibility requirements for Medicaid, states must cover all AFDC families and most states also cover SSI recipients. In addition, a majority of states extend coverage to other "medically needy"—individuals who do not qualify for public assistance but whose incomes are low enough to qualify as needy. About half of the states extend Medicaid to families whose head is receiving unemployment compensation.

Approximately 25 million people per year will receive Medicaid payments—a figure roughly comparable to the poverty figure for the nation. However, because of the tangle of separate state eligibility requirements, we cannot be sure that all of the poor are receiving Medicaid, or that many nonpoor are not receiving Medicaid.

States also help set benefits under Medicaid. All states are required by the federal government to provide inpatient and outpatient hospital care, physicians' services, family planning, laboratory and X-ray, and nursing and home health care. States must also develop an early and periodic screening, diagnosis, and treatment (EPSDT) program for all children under Medicaid. However, states themselves generally decide upon the rate of reimbursement to hospitals and physicians. Low rates can discourage hospitals and physicians from providing good care under Medicaid. To make up for low payments hospitals and doctors may schedule too many patients in too short a span of time or prescribe unnecessary tests and procedures designed to make treatment more expensive.

The costs of Medicaid have far exceeded original estimates. The rapid rise in welfare rolls in the late 1960s accounted for a large proportion of the increased costs of Medicaid. Another factor has been the high rate of inflation in medical care prices. Hospital costs and physicians' fees have raced ahead of even the high inflation rate affecting all segments of the economy. Ironically, part of the medical inflation has been produced by the Medicaid and Medicare programs themselves, which have created heavier demands for medical care. Finally, over one-third of all Medicaid payments go to nursing homes for the aged. The availability of Medicaid payments for nursing home care has spawned a large number of nursing homes and resulted in larger numbers of aged people being placed in nursing homes. Thus, Medicaid costs have run up due to (1) increase in welfare rolls, (2) inflation in medical costs, and (3) increased use of nursing homes.

## Medicare: Health Care as Social Insurance

Medicare, like Medicaid, was enacted in 1965 as an amendment to the nation's basic Social Security Act. Medicare provides prepaid hospital insurance for the aged under social security and low-cost voluntary medical insurance for the aged, directly under federal administration. Medicare includes (1) HI—a compulsory basic health insurance plan covering hospital costs for the aged, which is financed out of payroll taxes which are collected under the social security system; and (2) SMI—a voluntary, supplemental medical insurance program that will pay doctor's bills and additional medical expenses, financed in part by contributions from the aged and in part by general tax revenues.

Only *aged* persons are covered by Medicare provisions. Eligibility is *not* dependent on income; *all* aged persons eligible for social security are also eligible for Medicare. Medicare is a part of the social security system—OASDHI: Old Age Survivor's Disability and Health Insurance—which compels employers and employees to pay into the program during their working years in order to enjoy the benefits, including health insurance, after retirement. Benefits include hospital insurance (HI) which covers a broad range of hospital services (after the first day of care which must be paid by the beneficiary) as well as nursing home care following hospital treatment. Benefits also include supplemental medical insurance (SMI) which covers physicians' services, outpatient hospital care, and other medical services. SMI is voluntary and open to all individuals over sixty-five, whether they are eligible for social security or not. No physical examination is required and preexisting conditions are covered. The costs of SMI are so low to the beneficiaries—approximately one hundred dollars per year—that participation by the elderly is almost universal. SMI insurance payments can be deducted automatically from social security payments.

Beneficiaries of SMI must pay the first $60 of physicians' services themselves, after which SMI pays 80 percent of allowed charges for medical services.

Note that both the HI and SMI provisions of Medicare require patients to pay a small *initial* charge. The purpose is to discourage unnecessary hospital or Medicare care. HI generally pays the full hospital charge, but many doctors charge higher rates than allowable under SMI. Indeed, it is estimated that only about half of the doctors in the nation accept SMI allowable payments as payment in full. Many doctors bill Medicare patients for charges above the allowable SMI payments. Medicare does *not* pay for prescription drugs, eyeglasses, or hearing aids.

## Evaluation: Health Care for the Poor and Aged

There is no doubt that Medicaid and Medicare have *improved access* to medicine by the poor and the aged. Both the poor and the aged now see physicians more often than the nonpoor and the nonaged. There are no clear indications, however, that Medicaid or Medicare has improved the health of the poor or the aged.

The nation's health, as measured by infant mortality rates, death rates due to specific causes, and average life spans, is improving over time. *But there is no indication that Medicaid or Medicare has been mainly or even partly responsible for these improvements.* Indeed, declines in the leading causes of death (shown in Table 6–1) were just as great *prior to* the enactment of Medicaid and Medicare (1950–1965) as they have been after the enactment of these programs. As Aaron Wildavsky observes:

> If the question is, "Does health increase with government expenditure on medicine?" the answer is likely to be "No." Just alter the question: "Has access to medicine been improved by government programs?" and the answer is most certainly with a little qualification, "Yes."[2]

No system of health care can provide as much as people will use. Each individual, believing his health and life are at stake, will want the most thorough diagnostic testing, the most constant care, the most advanced treatment. And doctors have no strong incentive to try to save on costs; they want the most advanced diagnostic and treatment facilities available for their patients. Under conditions of uncertainty in a medical situation—and there is always some uncertainty—physicians can always think of one more thing which might be done—one more

[2]Aaron Wildavsky, *Speaking Truth to Power* (Boston: Little, Brown, 1979), p. 286.

consultation, one more test, one more therapeutic approach. The patient wants *the best*, and the doctor wants it too. Any tendency for doctors to limit testing and treatment is countered by the threat of malpractice suits; it is always easier to order one more test or procedure than to risk even the remote chance that the failure to do so will some day be cause for court suit. So both patients and doctors push up the costs of health care, particularly when public or private insurance pays.

Approximately 90 percent of the population is covered by some sort of health insurance—most by private insurance companies providing group insurance through employers, and the rest by Medicaid and Medicare. However, private health insurance often leaves gaps in coverage. For example, many private plans only cover the first thirty or sixty days of hospital care; many plans have an overall dollar limit on payments which will be made to physicians; many plans exclude various diagnostic tests, or outpatient care, or office visits, etc. Private insurance often will not cover individuals initially found to be in poor health.

Perhaps the most serious concern about private insurance is that it frequently fails to cover "catastrophic" medical costs—costs that may run to tens or hundreds of thousands of dollars for serious, long-term illness. Medicaid and Medicare help to minimize the costs of "catastrophic" illness for the poor and the aged. But many nonpoor and nonaged can lose their life savings due to serious illness.

One of the most pronounced effects of Medicaid and Medicare is to contribute to the spiraling inflation in health care costs. The costs of health care in the United States have risen much faster than prices in general. Medical costs have tripled over the last ten years. The nation's total medical bill is approximately $250 billion—over 10 percent of the Gross National Product.

Medicaid and Medicare have added significantly to the demand for medical services and thus contributed to this inflation. But these programs are certainly not the only causes of medical inflation. Another cause has been the rapid growth in *private* insurance plans. It is now estimated that two-thirds of the private costs of medicine are paid by private insurance companies, rather than directly by patients. Private insurance companies have been no more successful in holding down medical costs than government agencies.

Another cause of higher health costs has to do with advances in medical technology that require expensive equipment and highly trained personnel. The typical example is the new CAT scanner (Computerized Axial Tomography), a complex X-ray device that gives excellent diagnostic information, but costs in excess of one-half million dollars. Another cause of higher medical costs is an unnecessary expansion of hospital facilities. Tens of thousands of hospital rooms and beds are empty, yet the overhead costs of maintaining these facilities must be paid.

In short, modern, high technology medical care is expensive. There are few if any cost control elements in the nation's current health care system. Patients and doctors want "the best." Private insurance, Medicaid, and Medicare remove most of the cost constraints from patients and doctors. Threats of malpractice encourage still more expenses, as doctors overtreat their patients to protect themselves from possible legal action.

Health care *cost containment* has become a major new policy concern. It is not clear, however, given the record of Medicaid and Medicare, that the federal government is really capable of holding down medical inflation. One method would be to require all hospitals to keep rate increases under federal guidelines. Federal payments could be denied to hospitals that exceed federal guidelines. But hospital administrators object that such a sweeping measure would hurt the quality of health care and limit the availability of high technology medical diagnostic and treatment facilities. Another method would be to allow the Social Security Administration to enter into specific agreements with hospitals to pay for services at predetermined rates. Indeed, already some states have rate-setting agencies for hospitals.

One approach to cost containment that has already been tried is found in the National Health Planning and Resources Development Act of 1974. The act creates two hundred *health system agencies* (HSAs) across the nation with authority to grant or withhold "certificates of need" for new medical facilities. These HSAs are designed to prevent duplication of facilities, overbuilding, and unnecessary costs. Withholding a "certificate of need" can lead to a withholding of Medicaid and Medicare payments to a hospital. But to date there is little evidence to suggest that HSAs have made any significant contribution to reducing medical inflation.

The federal government has also experimented with health costs and health care delivery by supporting *health maintenance organizations* (HMOs). HMOs are membership organizations which hire doctors and other health professionals at fixed salaries to serve dues-paying members. HMOs typically provide comprehensive health care for enrolled members. The members pay a regular fee and they are entitled to hospital care and physicians' services at no extra cost. Advocates of HMOs say that this is less costly than fee-for-service medical care because doctors have no incentive to overtreat patients. Moreover, HMOs emphasize preventive medicine and therefore minimize serious illnesses. In 1973 Congress endorsed the HMO idea by passing a Health Maintenance Organization Act offering federal assistance to the development of HMOs. Surprisingly, however, there has been no rapid expansion in HMOs. Many of the complaints about HMOs correspond to complaints about service in other bureaucratic settings: patients see different doctors on different days; doctors in HMOs do not work as hard as private physicians; care is "depersonalized"; and so forth.

## National Health Insurance: The Great Debate

When the original Social Security Act of 1935 was passed, efforts were made in Congress to include "a comprehensive national health insurance system with universal and mandatory coverage." But President Franklin D. Roosevelt backed off when he was convinced by representatives of the American Medical Association that the plan would not work without the support of the nation's physicians. President Harry Truman pushed hard for a national health insurance program tied to social security, but again opponents led by the American Medical Association were successful in defeating the proposal. President Lyndon Johnson opted for a somewhat narrower goal—health insurance for the poor and the aged (Medicaid and Medicare)—and he was successful in amending the Social Security Act to achieve these purposes in 1965. But the decades old debate over national health care continues.

Current national health insurance proposals, notably the proposal which has long been recommended by Senator Edward M. Kennedy, call for compulsory national health insurance for *all* Americans. This insurance would be managed by a federal health insurance corporation. Financing would come mainly from payroll taxes paid by both employers and employees; but since the program is expected to cost a great deal, some financing would also come from general federal revenues.

Debate in Congress has centered around benefit levels and costs. Kennedy has pressed for comprehensive benefits covering most hospital, physician, outpatient, office visits, X-ray, drugs, and alcoholism and drug abuse treatment. The costs of such a program are likely to be very high. Indeed, total health care expenditures in the nation now run nearly $250 billion per year, an amount which far exceeds national defense spending. Proponents of comprehensive health insurance, of course, place lower estimates on its costs. On the other hand, opponents contend that virtually free medical care might result in a much higher national medical bill than we have today.

National health insurance would *not* be "socialized medicine," that is, hospitals would not be federally owned and doctors would not be federal employees. Patients would still choose their own doctors and hospitals. However, a major portion of the medical *insurance* business would be government operated. Occasionally references are made in debate over national health insurance to the government owned and operated health care system in Great Britain. But a better analogy would be the national health insurance system in Canada "where the long waits and indifferent service that many complain about in England do not exist."[3]

Financially, the greatest obstacle to comprehensive health insurance for all Americans is the potentially ruinous inflation that might accompany such a program. Medicaid and Medicare turned out to be immensely more expensive than original estimates, and these programs have contributed significantly to medical inflation. Proponents of comprehensive health insurance have promised to tie such a program to strict cost containment efforts—limits on hospital charges and physicians' fees. But such efforts have not been particularly successful in the past in holding down medical inflation.

Politically, the greatest obstacle to comprehensive health insurance for all Americans is the success of Medicare and Medicaid. The existence of these programs for the aged and the poor removes much of the incentive for a comprehensive health insurance program. The programs subtract two important constituencies from a universal mandatory insurance program. Indeed, about 90 percent of all Americans are covered by some kind of medical insurance—private insurance, usually purchased through employers or unions, or Medicaid or Medicare. Half of all medical bills today are paid by "third parties," that is, by government or by private insurance companies.

Proponents of comprehensive health insurance argue that even though most people are covered by existing private and public insurance programs there are still major gaps in coverage. Many "working poor," whose incomes are too high to qualify for welfare or Medicaid, do not purchase insurance at all, or they purchase inadequate coverage—perhaps $20 to $25 per day against $100 or $150 per day hospital room charges. Or private insurance runs out after the first thirty or sixty days of hospital care, and eventually the seriously ill are impoverished by medical bills.

*Catastrophic* health insurance offers an alternative to the more costly *comprehensive* health insurance. Federal catastrophic health insurance would cover medical costs after the first $2,000 per year. Thus, every American would be protected against "catastrophic" health costs, but would be responsible for their own day-to-day (under $2,000) health care. Republican Gerald Ford proposed such a plan in 1975, and Democrat Jimmy Carter endorsed such a plan as a "first step" to-

---

[3]Congressional Quarterly, Inc., *National Health Issues* (Washington: Congressional Quarterly Inc., 1977), p. 19.

ward comprehensive health insurance in 1979. Catastrophic health insurance would be much less expensive than comprehensive health insurance; catastrophic insurance could be paid for with relatively modest increases in social security taxes on employers and employees.

Another unresolved issue in the debate over national health insurance is what role, if any, should be given to private insurance companies. The Kennedy comprehensive health plan envisions a strictly federal program, with no specific provision for private insurance. But other plans have incorporated private insurance programs, for example, by authorizing the federal government to pay part or all of the premium costs for insured persons. Of course, the federal government would have to approve private insurance plans before payments would be made.

Finally, whether or not the nation adopts comprehensive health insurance, or catastrophic health insurance, or continues current reliance on private insurance, Medicaid, and Medicare, the problem of medical inflation persists. Cost containment will be a crucial aspect of any *new* health insurance program, and it will also be considered under existing programs.

## Preventative Strategies: Successes and Failures

Governments have long concerned themselves with the general health and safety of their citizens. Nonetheless, government efforts to reduce deaths due to accident or preventable illness have not always been successful.

Occasionally government actions improve health or safety without setting out specifically to do so. When the United States adopted a national 55-mile-per-hour speed limit *to save gasoline*, the result was a reduction in annual highway accident deaths from over 55,000 per year to 46,000 per year—a saving of 9,000 lives each year. Rarely is *any* public health program so successful. It is ironic that this program was adopted to save gas, rather than to save lives. It is also ironic that no giant Washington bureaucracy was established to implement this particular law, and relatively little federal money was spent to enforce it. Yet no other single action of the federal government has ever been so successful in saving so many lives.

Just the opposite experience occurred with the creation of the Occupational Safety and Health Administration (OSHA) in 1970. OSHA was established as a large Washington bureaucracy with a substantial budget ($200 million in 1980), and a great deal of fanfare a decade ago. Its responsibilities included the tasks of drawing up safety regulations for virtually every type of private employment and then enforcing these regulations with 2,500 inspectors issuing citations against businesses, large or small, found to be in violation of the regulations.

Approximately 14,000 persons die in work-related accidents each year. But there is no indication that OSHA has affected this statistic. The number of work-related deaths declines slightly each year, but the declines were the same both before and after the creation of OSHA.

It turned out that most of OSHA's regulation writers and inspectors had very little experience in the workplace. Their regulations were sometimes farcical: "All toilets must have u-shaped seats." Small businesses were particularly distressed by the new maze of regulations: "How can a small businessman determine whether his wooden ladders are constructed in compliance with 11 pages of fine print on the subject which contains everything from algebraic equations to fibre stress characteristics of more than 50 different types of wood."[4]

OSHA did not make provisions for assistance to business to help bring them into compliance. If a businessman called OSHA to ask for advice on correcting work hazards, OSHA was likely to cite the businessman for violation of its rules rather than to provide consultation and an opportunity to correct the deficiency.

But the greatest problem was the refusal of OSHA to apply a cost-benefit ratio to its rules. In our daily business and private lives, we all take risks—in driving to work, in crossing a street, in climbing stairs, in flying in airplanes. We generally believe that these are "acceptable risks," that is, we know there is a small possibility of injury or death but we believe the benefits of these activities outweigh whatever minor risks are involved. But OSHA has imposed very costly requirements on businesses without regard to their costs, or more specifically, without weighing the benefits against the costs of these regulations.

By 1977, the Carter Administration had decided that OSHA was a political liability and needed a major overhaul. OSHA was instructed to concentrate its attentions on a few of the more dangerous industries (construction, heavy manufacturing, transportation, and petrochemicals) and to drop its more trivial safety rules.

In short, it appears as if the bureaucratic command-control approach to safety and health is frequently ineffective.

In contrast to the government's failure with the bureaucratic approach in occupational health and safety, it is interesting to observe the government's success with the public education approach to smoking and health. The decrease in the percentage of adult smokers in recent years has been substantial. And yet, the federal government has not

[4]Congressional Quarterly, Inc., *National Health Issues* (Washington: Congressional Quarterly Inc., 1977), p. 78.

banned smoking or the manufacturing of cigarettes; no federal bureaucracy has been created specifically to implement antismoking laws; and relatively few tax dollars have been spent to curtail smoking. (On the contrary, the federal government spends millions each year to support the price of tobacco in its agricultural commodity credit program.)

According to the U.S. Public Health Service, the proportion of American adults who smoke decreased from 42.5 percent in 1965 to 33.5 percent in 1975:[5]

|  | *1965* | *1975* |
|---|---|---|
| Men | 52.8% | 39.2% |
| Women | 31.5 | 28.9 |
| Total | 42.5 | 33.5 |

What could account for this significant change in a health-related habit?

In 1962, the American Cancer Society persuaded President John F. Kennedy to establish a special advisory commission to the Surgeon General of the United States to undertake a comprehensive review of all the data relating to smoking and health. The famous "Surgeon General's Report" was published in 1964.[6] It concluded that cigarette smoking was a serious health hazard and that cigarette smoking was causally related to lung cancer. It also reported that cigarette smoking was associated with coronary disase, chronic bronchitis, and emphysema. The tobacco industry vainly tried to discredit the report, but cigarette sales dropped sharply. Although sales recovered after several years, increasing percentages of adults gave up smoking, or never started the habit.

In 1966, the Federal Cigarette Labeling and Advertising Act required all cigarette packages (and later all cigarette advertising) to print the statement: "Caution: Cigarette Smoking May Be Dangerous to Your Health." In 1970, Congress approved legislation banning all cigarette commercials on radio and television. In 1971 the Interstate Commerce Commission restricted smoking to certain sections of buses and trains, and the Civil Aeronautics Board did the same on airlines in 1973.

Note that the federal government's actions in smoking have been largely *educational.* In this case, these efforts have met with significant success. But the federal government's bureaucratic command and control efforts have been much less successful.

[5]Ibid. p. 56.
[6]Report of the Advisory Committee to the Surgeon General of the Public Health Service, *Smoking and Health* (Washington: Government Printing Office, 1964).

## Summary

A "rational" approach to health policy requires a clear definition of objectives, the development of alternative strategies for achieving these objectives, and a careful comparison and weighing of the costs and benefits of each alternative. But again in health, as well as welfare, there are seemingly insurmountable problems in developing a "rational policy":

1. The paramount objective in national health policy has never been clearly defined. Is it *good health,* as defined by lower death rates, less illness, and longer life? Or is it *better medical care,* as defined by easy access to inexpensive hospital and physician care?

2. If good health is the objective, then preventative efforts to change people's personal habits and lifestyles are more likely to improve health than anything else. For example, the 55-mile-per-hour speed limit reduced death rates more than any other recent governmental action. However, relatively little federal money is devoted to preventative measures.

3. Medical care does not contribute directly to good health. However, our ethical commitments require that we insure adequate medical care for all, particularly the poor and the aged.

4. Medicaid is now the nation's largest single welfare program. The poor visit doctors more often and stay in hospitals longer than the nonpoor. But the health of the poor is still not as good as the health of the nonpoor. This suggests that the focus of public policy is an access to medical care rather than good health.

5. Medicare offers prepaid medical insurance for the aged under social security. Prior to the adoption of Medicare in 1965, the aged found it difficult to obtain medical insurance from private firms. Medicare removes the fear of impoverishment through hospital bills, even if it does not increase life span.

6. Both Medicaid for the poor and Medicare for the aged, together with private medical insurance, have contributed to inflation in medical care costs. The *success* of these programs (in terms of numbers of beneficiaries) has led to a new policy problem—medical care cost containment. In other words, solving one policy problem created another.

7. Alternative health care programs for the *entire* population have been proposed in the form of "comprehensive" health insurance and "catastrophic" health insurance. Comprehensive health insurance would commit the federal government to pay a major share of all medical costs in the nation, an alternative that risks increased inflation, heavy taxing and spending, and greater controls over doctors and hospitals. Catastrophic health insurance would commit the federal govern-

ment to pay medical costs over a certain amount, to prevent impoverishment due to extraordinarily heavy medical bills.

8. It is very difficult to predict the success or failure of preventative health programs. The U.S. Public Health Service's educational campaign against smoking has dramatically reduced the percentage of adult smokers. The Occupational Safety and Health Administration's control efforts have not significantly reduced accidents in the workplace.

## Bibliography

DAVIS, KAREN, and CATHY SCHOEN, *Health and the War on Poverty.* Washington: Brookings Institution, 1978.

FUCHS, VICTOR R., *Who Shall Live? Health, Economics and Social Choice.* New York: Basic Books, 1974.

HOLAHAN, JOHN, *Financing Health Care for the Poor: The Medicaid Experience.* Boston: Heath, 1975.

MARMOR, THEODORE R., *The Politics of Medicare.* New York: Aldine, 1973.

Formal and informal structures of education. *Stan Wakefield.*

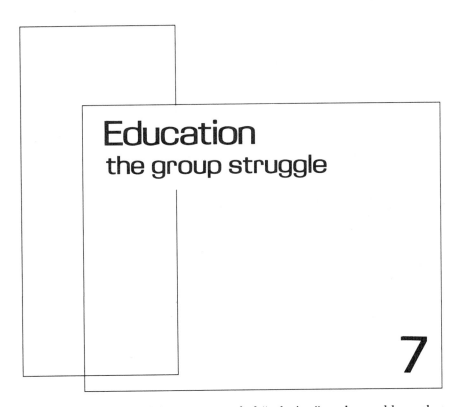

# Education
## the group struggle

7

Perhaps the most widely recommended "solution" to the problems that confront American society is more and better schooling. If there ever was a time when schools were only expected to combat ignorance and illiteracy, that time is far behind us. Today schools are expected to do many things: resolve racial conflict and build an integrated society; inspire patriotism and good citizenship; provide values, aspirations, and a sense of identity to disadvantaged children; offer various forms of recreation and mass entertainment (football games, bands, choruses, majorettes, and the like); reduce conflict in society by teaching children to get along well with others and to adjust to group living; reduce the highway accident toll by teaching students to be good drivers; fight disease and poor health through physical education, health training, and even medical treatment; eliminate unemployment and poverty by teaching job skills; end malnutrition and hunger through school lunch and milk programs; produce scientists and other technicians to continue America's progress in science and technology; fight drug abuse and educate children about sex; and act as custodians for teenagers who have no interest in education but whom we do not permit either to work or to roam the streets unsupervised. In other words, nearly all the nation's problems are reflected in demands placed on the nation's schools. And, of course, these demands are frequently conflicting.

It is important to note at the outset, however, that some of the pressures which have confronted American education are changing as total enrollments decline. Elementary and secondary school enrollments peaked around 1970; since then, declines in the birth rate (which began in the 1960s) have gradually reduced the total number of children in school. Of course, enrollments are uneven across the nation: some school districts still face burgeoning enrollments, while others must close down classrooms and stop hiring new teachers. But overall, the problems confronting the nation's schools do *not* now include increasing enrollments. Even colleges and universities, which still managed small enrollment gains in the 1970s, are expected to see declines in the 1980s as the effect of lower birth rates reaches this educational level. (See Figure 7–1.)

Educational policy affects a wide variety of interests, and stimulates a great deal of interest-group activity. We will describe the major interests involved in federal educational policy and examine the group struggle over federal aid to education. We will examine the constitutional provisions and court policies dealing with religion in the public schools. We will observe how both racial and religious group interests are mobilized in educational policy making, and we will see the impor-

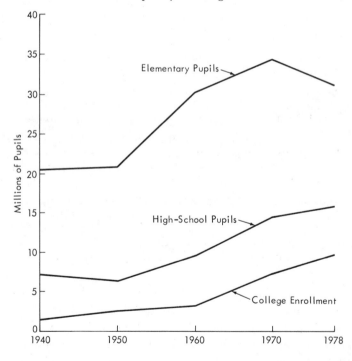

FIG. 7–1   The Leveling Off of School Enrollment in the United States

tance of resolving group conflict in the development of educational policy. We shall also describe the structure of educational decision making and the resulting multiple points of group access in a fragmented federal-state-local educational system. We shall attempt to describe the broad categories of group interests—teachers, taxpayers, school board members, school administrators—involved in educational policy at the local level. Finally, we will examine the governing and financing of public higher education—the nation's increasingly costly investment in state colleges and universities.

## The Federal Role in Education

The federal government's role in education is a longstanding one. In the famous Northwest Ordinance of 1787, Congress offered land grants for public schools in the new territories and gave succeeding generations words to be forever etched on grammar school cornerstones: "Religion, morality, and knowledge, being necessary to good government and the happiness of mankind, schools and the means for education should ever be encouraged." The earliest democrats believed that the safest repository of the ultimate powers of society was the people themselves. If the people made mistakes, the remedy was not to remove power from their hands but to help them in forming their judgment through education. If the common man was to be granted the right to vote, he must be educated to his task. This meant that public education had to be universal, free, and compulsory. Compulsory education began in Massachusetts in 1852 and was eventually adopted by Mississippi in 1918.

In 1862 the Morrill Land Grant Act provided grants of federal land to each state for the establishment of colleges specializing in agricultural and mechanical arts. These became known as "land grant colleges." In 1867 Congress established a U.S. Office of Education; in 1979, a separate, cabinet-level Department of Education was created. The Smith-Hughes Act of 1917 set up the first program of federal grants-in-aid to promote vocational education, enabling schools to provide training in agriculture, home economics, trades, and industries. In the National School Lunch and Milk Programs, begun in 1946, federal grants and commodity donations were made for nonprofit lunches and milk served in public and private schools. In the Federal Impacted Areas Aid Program, begun in 1950, federal aid was authorized for "federally impacted" areas of the nation. These are areas in which federal activities create a substantial increase in school enrollments or a reduction in taxable resources because of a federally owned property.

Federal funds can be used for construction, operation, and maintenance of schools in these public school districts. This program is an
outgrowth of the defense-impacted area aid legislation in World War
II.

In response to the Soviet Union's success in launching the first
satellite into space, Congress became concerned that the American educational system might not be keeping abreast of advances being made
in other nations, particularly in science and technology. The Russian
space shot created an intensive debate over education in America, and
prompted Congress to reexamine the responsibilities of the national
government in public education. "Sputnik" made everyone realize that
education was closely related to national defense. In the National Defense Education Act of 1958, Congress provided financial aid to states
and public school districts to improve instruction in science, mathematics, and foreign languages; to strengthen guidance counseling and
testing; and to improve statistical services. And also to establish a system of loans to undergraduates, fellowships to graduate students, and
funds to colleges—all in an effort to improve the training of teachers
in America.

Despite these many individual federal programs in education,
prior to 1965 the overall contribution of the federal government to education was very small. No general federal aid to education bill was
able to win Congressional approval, for reasons we will explore later.
Federal programs were only peripheral in character and limited in impact. There was some aid to federally impacted areas, some assistance
in school lunch and milk programs, some support for vocational-tech-
nical education, some grants for science, mathematics, and foreign language projects. But there was no real general assistance to public and
private schools in building classrooms or paying teacher salaries.

The Elementary and Secondary Education Act of 1965 marked
the first real breakthrough in large-scale federal aid to education.
ESEA is now the largest federal aid-to-education program. Yet even
ESEA cannot be termed a *general* aid-to-education program that would
assist all public and private schools with costs of school construction
and teachers' salaries. The main thrust of ESEA is in "poverty-impacted" schools, instructional materials, and educational research and
training.

The Elementary and Secondary Education Act provided for the
following:

> Title I: Financial assistance to "local educational agencies serving areas with con-
> centrations of children from low-income families" for programs "which contribute
> particularly to meeting the special needs of educationally deprived children."

Grants would be made on application to the Office of Education on the basis of the number of children from poverty-stricken families.

Title II: Grants to "public and private elementary and secondary schools" for the acquisition of school library resources, textbooks, and other instructional materials.

Title III: Grants for public and private schools for "supplementary educational centers and services" including remedial programs, counseling, adult education, specialized instruction and equipment, etc.

Title IV: Grants to universities, colleges, or other nonprofit organizations for research or demonstration projects in education.

Title V: Grants to stimulate and strengthen state educational agencies.

Note that the Act does include private, church-related schools in some of its benefits, as long as the federal aid money is used for nonreligious purposes within such schools. However, the greatest amounts of money distributed under ESEA has been to public schools in poverty-impacted areas.

## Federal Aid to Education and the Group Struggle

The long struggle for federal aid to education is an excellent example of the power of interest groups in blocking legislation that has wide-spread public support, and the necessity of accommodating specific interest groups and finding workable compromises before a bill can be passed. Every year from 1945 to 1965—a period spanning two decades and the administrations of both Democratic and Republican presidents and both Democratic and Republican Congressional majorities—federal aid-to-education bills were introduced and debated at great length. Yet no general aid-to-education bill passed the Congress in this period. These bills were lost *despite* overwhelming public support for federal aid to education revealed in all national opinion polls during this period, and *despite* announced presidential support for such aid. The failure of federal aid to education under these conditions can be attributed to the conflict between major *racial* and *religious* group interests in America over the character of such aid. Federal aid to education became lost in the major racial and religious controversies in the nation. Not until these issues were resolved, and bargains struck with the influential interest groups involved, was it possible to secure the passage of the Elementary and Secondary Education Act of 1965.[1]

[1]A detailed account of the long struggle leading to the passage of the Elementary and Secondary Education Act of 1965 is found in Eugene Eidenberg and Roy D. Morey, *An Act of Congress* (New York: Norton, 1969).

Leading the fight for federal aid to education was the National Education Association. The NEA represents school administrators, state departments of education, university schools of education, as well as large numbers of dues-paying teachers. Whatever differences existed within these various categories of members, the NEA was united in its support of federal aid to education. The national office of NEA, located in a modern well-equipped office building in Washington, works closely with the Office of Education, located only a few blocks away. The NEA also has affiliates in every one of the fifty states and most local school districts in the nation. Although NEA was a strong advocate of federal aid, it actively opposed public funds for private church-related schools. Other groups supporting federal aid were the AFL-CIO (particularly its constituent union, the American Federation of Teachers, which frequently competes with NEA for the loyalties of classroom teachers), Americans for Democratic Action, National Congress of Parents and Teachers, and other library and professional groups.

The first divisive issue was that of *race*. For many years the question of whether or not the federal government would assist racially segregated Southern schools posed a major obstacle to federal aid to education. Southern Congressmen stood to gain from any federal aid program designed to equalize educational expenditures among the states, because Southern states are among the poorest in the nation. But the prospect of federal aid money being used as leverage to achieve integration was an anathema to this group. On the other hand, the NAACP and many liberal groups opposed any federal aid to schools operated on a racially segregated basis. The 1954 decision (*Brown* v. *Board of Education of Topeka, Kansas*) that racial segregation in public schools was unconstitutional strengthened the resolve of the liberals to deny federal aid to segregated schools. Throughout the 1950s Representative Adam Clayton Powell of Harlem introduced amendments to federal aid-to-education bills barring such aid for segregated schools. The NEA, the AFL-CIO, and other education groups opposed these Powell amendments, believing correctly that such amendments would involve federal school aid in the sensitive segregation issue and thereby lead to its defeat. Once a Powell amendment was part of a bill, the coalition of conservative Republicans and Southern Democrats defeated it.

The Civil Rights Act of 1964 greatly assisted the movement for federal aid to education, even though it made no direct mention of such aid. Title VI of that Act specified that every federal department and agency must take action to end segregation by issuing rules, regulations, and orders (later known as "guidelines"), and withholding federal aid from any programs that have failed to comply with terms.

The Act was supported by large majorities of both Democrats and Republicans in the House and the Senate. The effect of the Act was to resolve the issue raised by Representative Powell and others, and clear the track of at least one obstacle to federal aid to education.

The second divisive issue in federal aid to education was *religion*, i.e., whether or not federal aid should go to private, church-related schools. The Catholic Church operates a very large elementary and secondary school system in the United States. Catholic groups, particularly the National Catholic Welfare Conference, generally refused to support any federal aid bill that did not include aid to parochial schools. Yet many Protestant groups were equally convinced that federal aid to church-related schools would destroy the historic concept of separation of church and state. Many Protestant denominations, as well as the National Council of Churches, went on record against federal aid for parochial schools. The failure of President Kennedy's aid-to-education bill in 1961 is generally attributed to the religious conflict it engendered. In honoring a 1960 campaign pledge to Protestants, the nation's first Catholic president introduced a federal aid-to-education bill which *excluded* parochial schools.[2] To the school aid bill's usual enemies—conservative Republicans wary of federal bureaucracy and Southern Democrats wary of integration efforts—President Kennedy added a substantial bloc of Catholic Congressmen, many of whom had supported aid to education in the past.

By 1965, twenty years of group struggle over federal aid to education convinced proponents of the policy that *compromise between major interest groups* was essential to its adoption.

Congress, particularly members of the House and Senate committees most directly concerned with education legislation, expected the administration to work out the appropriate group compromise before Congress would consider a federal aid bill. In effect, Congress stood ready to legitimatize whatever compromise could be arranged among the major interests. The key to success, then, was working out a compromise acceptable to the NEA and other educational groups, the National Catholic Welfare Conference and other representatives of the Catholic Church, and the National Council of Churches and other Protestant groups.[3]

The Johnson Administration plan was to emphasize "aid to children" rather than aid to schools, and particularly aid to children from low-income families. It was hoped that by placing the emphasis on the

[2]In a speech before the Greater Houston Ministerial Association in 1960 Kennedy stated: "I believe in an America where separation of Church and State is absolute . . . where no church or church school is granted any public funds or political preference."

[3]Eidenberg and Morey, *An Act of Congress*, p. 77.

child, the church-state issue could be submerged. The president identified the program with his "war on poverty" rather than with earlier aid-to-education efforts. The greatest proportion of ESEA funds would be given under Title I to *public* school districts with children from low-income families. But as a concession to Catholic interests, the president's bill allowed parochial schools to receive funds along with public schools under Title II and Title III for libraries, textbooks, and instructional materials, and for supplementary educational centers and services. This money was only for peripheral items—not classroom construction or teachers' salaries—and specifically prohibited the use of federal funds for sectarian instruction or worship.

The NEA accepted the compromise despite its longstanding opposition to giving any public funds to church schools. The National Council of Churches was not really enthusiastic about the Johnson bill; they very much preferred President Kennedy's 1961 bill which would have completely excluded Catholic schools from federal aid programs. Yet responsible spokesmen for Protestant churches in America did not want to be charged with having hurt public education in America or blocked assistance for impoverished school children. Strong Catholic opposition to the bill might have meant failure. Catholic groups were also unenthusiastic about the bill. There was no guarantee that Catholic education would receive proportionately equal funding with public education under the legislation. Public school interests would be administering the grant money. It was not clear whether the bill was a victory for Catholics or whether it merely held out token support to Catholic education. But in the end the Catholic interests withheld their objections.

Once support of the major interests was obtained, Congressional approval of ESEA was practically assured. Congressmen deliberately avoided any amendments that would upset the church-state compromise. The bill was introduced on January 12, 1965, and signed into law by the president on April 11, with very little change in the original wording. Most of the floor debate in the House and the Senate centered around minor variations in the aid formula. The ease and rapidity with which the bill passed Congress was a striking contrast to the bloody battles of earlier years. This turnabout in Congressional behavior would have mystified anyone who was not aware of the interest-group compromise.

## Reading, Writing, and Religion in the Courts

The First Amendment to the Constitution of the United States contains two important guarantees of religious freedom: (1) "Congress shall make no law respecting an establishment of religion . . ." and (2) "or prohibiting the free exercise thereof." The Due Process Clause of the Fourteenth Amendment made these guarantees of religious liberty applicable to the states and their subdivisions as well as to Congress. Most of the debate over religion in the public schools centers around the "no establishment" clause of the First Amendment rather than the "free exercise" clause. However, it was respect for the "free exercise" clause that caused the Supreme Court in 1925 to declare unconstitutional an attempt on the part of a state to prohibit private and parochial schools and to force all children to attend public schools. In the words of the Supreme Court: "The fundamental theory of liberty upon which all governments in this Union repose excludes any general power of the state to standardize its children by forcing them to accept instruction from public teachers only. The child is not the mere creature of the state."[4] It is this decision that protects the entire structure of parochial schools in this nation.

A great deal of religious conflict in America has centered around the meaning of the "no establishment" clause, and the public schools have been the principal scene of this conflict. One interpretation of the clause holds that it does not prevent government from aiding religious schools or encouraging religious beliefs in the public schools, as long as it does not discriminate against any particular religion. Another interpretation of the "no establishment" clause is that it creates a "wall of separation" between church and state in America to prevent government from directly aiding religious schools or encouraging religious beliefs in any way.

Those favoring government aid to parochial schools frequently refer to the language found in several cases decided by the Supreme Court, which appears to support the idea that government can *in a limited fashion* support the activities of church-related schools. In the case of *Pierce* v. *The Society of Sisters* (1925), the Court stated that the right to send one's children to parochial schools was a fundamental liberty guaranteed to all. In *Cochran* v. *the Board of Education* (1930), the Court upheld a state law providing free textbooks for children attending both public and parochial schools on the grounds that this aid benefited the *children* rather than the Catholic Church and hence did not constitute an "establishment" of religion within the meaning of the First Amendment."[5]

In *Everson* v. *Board of Education* (1947), the Supreme Court upheld bus transportation for parochial school children at public expense on the grounds that the "wall of separation between church and state"

[4]*Pierce* v. *The Society of Sisters*, 268 U.S. 510 (1925).
[5]*Cochran* v. *Board of Education*, 281 U.S. 370 (1930).

does not prohibit the state from adopting a general program which helps *all* children.[6] Interestingly, in this case even though the Supreme Court permitted the expenditure of public funds to assist children going to and from parochial schools, the Supreme Court voiced the opinion that the "no establishment" clause of the First Amendment should constitute a wall of separation between church and state. In the words of the Court:

> Neither a state nor the federal government can set up a church. Neither can pass laws which aid one religion, aid all religions, or prefer one religion over another. Neither can force nor influence a person to go to or to remain away from church against his will, or force him to profess a belief or disbelief in any religion. No person can be punished for entertaining or professing religious beliefs or disbeliefs, for church attendance or nonattendance. No tax in any amount, large or small, can be levied to support any religious activities or institutions, whatever they may be called, or whatever form they may adopt to teach or practice religion. Neither a state nor the federal government can, openly or secretly, participate in the affairs of any religious organizations or groups, and vice versa.[7]

So the Everson case can be cited by those interests which support the allocation of public funds for assistance to children in parochial schools, as well as those interests which oppose any public support, direct or indirect, of religion.

The question of how much government aid can go to church schools and for what purposes is still unresolved. Recently, in response to fiscal crises, Catholic church leaders have pressed hard for more aid from the federal government and the states. Many of these states have passed bills giving financial support to nonpublic schools for such purposes as textbooks, bus transportation, and remedial courses. Proponents of public aid for parochial schools argue that these schools render a valuable public service by instructing millions of children who would have to be instructed by the state, at great expense, if the parochial schools closed. There seemed to be many precedents for public support of religious institutions: church property has always been exempt from taxation; church contributions are deductible from federal income taxes; federal funds have been appropriated for the construction of religiously operated hospitals; chaplains are provided in the armed forces as well as in the Congress of the United States; veterans' programs permit veterans to use their educational subsidies to finance college educations in Catholic universities; federal grants and loans for college construction are available to Catholic as well as to public colleges, and so on.

[6]*Everson v. Board of Education*, 330 U.S. 1 (1947).
[7]Ibid.

Opponents of state aid to parochial schools challenge the idea that Catholic parents are being discriminated against when parochial schools are denied tax funds. They argue that free public schools are available to the parents of all children regardless of religious denomination. If Catholic parents are not content with the type of school that the state provides, they should expect to pay for the establishment and operation of special schools. The state is under no obligation to finance the religious preferences in education of Catholics or other religious groups. In fact, they contend that it is unfair to compel taxpayers to support religion directly or indirectly; furthermore, the diversion of any substantial amount of public education funds to parochial schools would weaken the public school system. The public schools bring together children of different religious backgrounds and by so doing supposedly encourage tolerance and understanding. In contrast, church-related schools segregate children of different backgrounds, and it is not in the public interest to encourage such segregation. And so the dispute continues.

One of the most important Supreme Court decisions in the history of church-state relations in America came in 1971 in the case of *Lemon* v. *Kurtzman*.[8] The Supreme Court held that it was unconstitutional for a state (Pennsylvania) to pay the costs of teachers' salaries or instructional materials in parochial schools. The Court acknowledged that it had previously approved the provision of state textbooks and bus transportation directly to parochial school children. But the Court held that state payments to parochial schools involved "excessive entanglement between government and religion" and violated both the establishment and free exercise clauses of the First Amendment. State payments to religious schools, the Court said, would require excessive government controls and surveillance to insure that funds were used only for secular instruction. Moreover, the Court expressed the fear that state aid to parochial schools would create "political divisions along religious lines . . . one of the principal evils against which the First Amendment was intended to protect." However, in *Roemer* v. *Maryland* (1976) the Supreme Court upheld general public grants of money to church-related *colleges:* "Religious institutions need not be quarantined from public benefits which are neutrally available to all."[9]

Religious conflict in public schools also centers around the question of prayer and Bible-reading ceremonies conducted by public schools. A few years ago the practice of opening the school day with prayer and Bible-reading ceremonies was widespread in American

[8]*Lemon* v. *Kurtzman*, 403 U.S. 602 (1971).
[9]*Roemer* v. *Maryland*, 415 U.S. 382 (1976).

public schools. Usually the prayer was a Protestant rendition of the Lord's Prayer and Bible reading was from the King James version. In order to avoid the denominational aspects of these ceremonies, the New York State Board of Regents substituted a nondenominational prayer, which it required to be said aloud in each class in the presence of a teacher at the beginning of each school day.

> Almighty God, we acknowledge our dependence upon Thee, and we beg Thy blessings upon us, our parents, our teachers, and our country.

New York argued that this prayer ceremony did not violate the "no establishment" clause, because the prayer was denominationally neutral and because student participation in the prayer was voluntary. However, in *Engle* v. *Vitale* (1962), the Supreme Court stated that "the constitutional prohibition against laws respecting an establishment of a religion must at least mean in this country it is no part of the business of government to compose official prayers for any group of the American people to recite as part of a religious program carried on by government."[10] The Court pointed out that making prayer voluntary did not free it from the prohibitions of the no establishment clause; that clause prevented the establishment of a religious ceremony by a government agency, regardless of whether the ceremony was voluntary or not:

> Neither the fact that the prayer may be denominationally neutral, nor the fact that its observance on the part of the students is voluntary can serve to free it from the limitations of the establishment clause, as it might from the free exercise clause, of the First Amendment, both of which are operative against the states by virtue of the Fourteenth Amendment. . . . The establishment clause, unlike the free exercise clause, does not depend on any showing of direct governmental compulsion and is violated by the enactment of laws which establish an official religion whether those laws operate directly to coerce nonobserving individuals or not.

One year later in the case of *Abbington Township* v. *Shempp*, the Court considered the constitutionality of Bible-reading ceremonies in the public schools.[11] Here again, even though the children were not required to participate, the Court found that Bible reading as an opening exercise in the schools was a religious ceremony. The Court went to some trouble in its opinion to point out that it was not "throwing the Bible out of the schools," for it specifically stated that the study of the Bible or of religion, when presented objectively as part of a secular program of education, did not violate the First Amendment, but reli-

---

[10]*Engle* v. *Vitale*, 370 U.S. 421 (1962).
[11]*Abbington Township* v. *Schempp*, 374 U.S. 203 (1963).

gious *ceremonies* involving Bible reading or prayer, established by a state or school district, did so.

## The Formal Structure of Educational Decision Making

The formal responsibility for public education in America rests with the fifty state governments. State laws create local school boards and provide a means for choosing their members, usually, but not always, by popular election. State laws authorize boards to lay and collect taxes, to borrow money, to engage in school construction, to hire instructional personnel, and to make certain determinations about local school policy. Yet in every state, the authority of local school districts is severely circumscribed by state legislation. State law determines the types and rates of taxes to be levied, the maximum debt that can be incurred, the number of years of compulsory school attendance, the minimum salaries to be paid to teachers, the types of schools to be operated by the local boards, the number of grades to be taught, the qualifications of teachers, and the general content of curricula. In addition, many states choose the textbooks, establish course outlines, recommend teaching methods, establish statewide examinations, fix minimum teacher-pupil ratios, and stipulate course content in great detail. Some states outlaw the mention of communism or the teaching of evolution in the classroom.

Statewide administrative agencies, sometimes called the state board of education, state department of education, or the superintendent of public instruction, oversee local school districts and ensure implementation of state policies. Although there are some variations among the states in the power vested in these agencies, one trend is common to all the states: state educational agencies are gradually centralizing state control over education. One means of ensuring the implementation of state educational policies is state grants of money to local school districts. Every state provides grants in one form or another to local school districts to supplement locally derived school revenue. In every state, an equalization formula in the distribution of state grants to local districts operates to help equalize educational opportunities in all parts of the state. Equalization formulas differ from state to state as do the amounts of state grants involved, but in every state, poorer school districts receive larger shares of state funds than wealthier districts. This enables the state to guarantee a minimum "foundation" program in education throughout the state. In addition, because state grants to local school districts are administered through state departments of education, state school officials are given an effective tool for implementing state policies—namely, withholding or threatening to withhold state funds from school districts that do not conform to state standards.

One of the most dramatic reorganization and centralization movements in American government in this century has been the successful drive to reduce, through consolidation, the number of local school districts in the United States. Over the last thirty-year period, three out of every four school districts have been eliminated through consolidation. Support for school district consolidation has come from state school officials in every state.

The federal government's share of the costs of education rose significantly after the passage of the Elementary and Secondary Education Act in 1965. (See Table 7–1.) Nonetheless, federal monies account for less than 10 percent of the total educational expenditures in the nation. State and local governments share the largest burdens of school spending; over time state educational burdens are increasing in relation to local burdens.

## The Informal Structure of Educational Groups

The formal structure of local school districts often obscures the realities of educational politics in communities. School politics will differ from one community to another, but it is possible to identify a number of political groups that appear on the scene in school politics in almost every community. There is, first of all, that small band of *voters* who turn out for school elections. It is estimated that, on the average, only about one-third of the eligible voters bother to cast ballots in school elections. Voter turnout at school bond and tax elections shows no groundswell of public interest in school affairs. Perhaps even more interesting is the finding that the larger the voter turnout in a school

**TABLE 7–1**  Federal, State, and Local Contributions to Public Elementary and Secondary Education

| | **Percent of School Revenue Received From:** | | | |
| | *Federal Sources* | *State Sources* | *Local Sources* | *Other* |
| --- | --- | --- | --- | --- |
| 1979 | 8.5 | 40.3 | 40.9 | 0.1 |
| 1975 | 8.3 | 37.7 | 43.9 | 0.1 |
| 1970 | 7.4 | 34.6 | 47.5 | 0.2 |
| 1960 | 3.9 | 31.1 | 52.8 | 0.6 |

*Source:* U.S. Bureau of the Census, *Statistical Abstract of the United States, 1979*, p. 136.

bond referendum, the more likely the defeat of proeducational proposals. In general, the best way to defeat a school bond referendum is
to have a large turnout. Public support for education appears to have
declined over the last decade. The proportion of bond referendums
for financing schools that have won voter approval has declined from
89 percent in the early 1960s to 48 percent in the early 1970s.[12] Proponents of educational expenditures are better advised not to work for
a large turnout, but for a better-informed and more educationally oriented electorate.

*School board members* constitute another important group of actors
in school politics. School board members are generally better educated
than their constituents. They are selected largely from among business
owners, proprietors, and managers. There is some evidence that people who are interested in education and have some knowledge of what
the schools are doing tend to support education more than do the less
informed citizens. However, the occupational background of school
board members suggests that they are sensitive to tax burdens placed
upon businessmen and property owners.

Many *professional educators* are distrustful of the lay people who
compose the school boards; they often feel that educational policy
should be in the hands of professional educators. They may feel that
important decisions about curriculum, facilities, personnel, and finances should be the special province of persons trained in education.
They view the school board's role as one of defending the schools
against public criticism and persuading the community to open its
pocketbook. Professional educators often support the idea that "politics" should be kept out of education; to them, this means that laymen
should not interfere with decisions that professional educators wish to
make for themselves. School boards and voters (those who supply the
money for public schools and therefore feel that it is their legitimate
right to control them) believe that citizen control of education is a vital
safeguard of democracy. But professional educators sometimes feel
that school board members are uninformed about school problems and
unwilling or unable to support the needs of education. As a case in
point, school board members throughout the nation were much less
likely to support federal aid to education than were professional educators. Many school board members felt that the federal government
would strip them of their local power over the schools, while professional educators were less fearful of dictation from Washington.[13]

[12]Congressional Quarterly, *Education for a Nation* (Washington, D.C.: Congressional
Quarterly Inc., 1972), p. 6.
[13]See Harmon Zeigler and M. Kent Jennings, *Governing American Schools* (Boston:
Duxbury Press, 1974).

The professional educators can be divided into at least three distinct groups. Numerically, the largest group (two and one-half million) is the *school teachers*. But perhaps the most powerful group is the professional *school administrators*, particularly the superintendents of schools. A third group consists of the *faculties of teachers colleges* and departments of education at universities. This latter group often has contacts with state departments of education, diffuses educational innovations and ideologies to generations of teachers, and influences requirements for teacher certification within the states.

Democratic theory assumes that schools are public institutions which should be governed by the local citizenry through their elected representatives. This was the original concept in American public education developed in the nineteenth century. But as school issues became more complex, the knowledge of citizen school boards seemed insufficient to cope with the many problems confronting the schools—teaching innovations, curricula changes, multimillion-dollar building programs, special educational programs, and so forth. In the twentieth century, the school superintendent and his administrative assistants came to exercise more and more control over day-to-day operations of the schools. Theoretically, the superintendent only implements the policies of the board, but in practice he has assumed much of the policy making in education. He devotes full time to his job, receives direct advice from attorneys, architects, accountants, and educational consultants, and generally sets the agenda for school board meetings.

The resulting "professionalism" in education tangles directly with the "democratic" notion of control of schools. There are few meetings of local school boards which do not involve at least some tug-of-war between board members and the superintendent. (It is interesting to note that in European countries education has long been under the control of professionals, with little or no direct citizen participation in school governance.) Professional educators are frequently disdainful of the lay people who compose the school board: the professionals must patiently explain matters of curriculum, faculties, personnel, and finance to citizen board members who are untrained in the matters about which they must decide. Professional educators often support the idea that "politics" should be kept out of education; this means that elected school board members should not interfere in educational decisions.

But school board members and interested citizens generally believe that popular control of education is a vital component of democracy. Schools should be "responsive" to community needs and desires. The "new math," the "look-say" method of reading, sex education, the moral quality of reading material, and many other school problems have inspired increased citizen interest in what is happening in "their" schools. Frequently, citizen criticism has focused on the schools' failure to teach basic skills—reading, writing, and arithmetic. (The verbal and mathematical scores on the national College Board test for high-school seniors have dropped each year since 1963.) Another frequent source of citizen concern is the perceived retreat of the schools from traditional moral values. These issues have in turn raised the underlying question—who should govern our schools, professional educators or interested citizens?

The struggle for power over the schools between interested citizens, school board members, and professional educators has now been joined by still another powerful force—the nation's growing new teachers' unions. Most of the nation's two million teachers are organized into either the older, larger National Education Association (NEA), or the smaller but more militant American Federation of Teachers (AFT), an affiliate of the AFL-CIO. Until recently the NEA was considered a "professional" organization of both teachers and administrators. But today state and district chapters of the Classroom Teachers Association formed out of the NEA are demanding collective bargaining rights for their members and even threatening to strike to achieve them. Since its origin, the AFT has espoused the right to organize, bargain collectively, and strike in the fashion of other labor unions. The AFT is small in numbers but its membership is concentrated in the nation's largest cities where it exercises considerable power. Both AFT and NEA chapters have shut down schools to force concessions by superintendents, board members, and taxpayers—not only in salaries and benefits, but also in pupil-teacher ratios, classroom conditions, school discipline, and other educational matters.

## The Challenge of School Finance: Haves and Have-Nots

A central issue in the group struggle over public education is that of distributing the benefits and costs of education in an equitable fashion. Most school revenues are derived from *local* property taxes. In every state except Hawaii, local school boards must raise money from property taxes to finance their schools. This means that communities that do *not* have much taxable property cannot finance their schools as well as communities that are blessed with great wealth. Frequently, wealthy communities can provide better educations for their children at *lower* tax rates than poor communities can provide at *higher* tax rates, simply because of disparities in the value of taxable property from one community to the next.

Representatives of poor, black, and Spanish-speaking groups have charged that reliance on local property taxation for school finance discriminates against poor communities. In an important state decision—*Serrano* v. *Priest*—the California Supreme Court held that the California system of public school finance "with its substantial dependence on local property taxes and resultant wide disparities in school revenue, violates the equal protection clause of the Fourteenth Amendment (of the U.S. Constitution)." The California court cited, for example, disparities of tax rates and tax yields between Beverly Hills and Baldwin Park, two nearby communities in Los Angeles County. Property owners in wealthy Beverly Hills paid only $2.38 per $100 of assessed property value, while in poorer Baldwin Park residents paid $5.48 per $100. Yet Beverly Hills, because of its better tax base, was able to spend $1,232 on each pupil in its schools, compared to only $577 in Baldwin Park. "We have determined," the California court said, "that this funding arrangement discriminates against the poor because it makes the quality of a child's education a function of the wealth of his parents and neighbors." Decisions similar to this California case have been rendered recently in other states. Their effect should be to speed the movement toward *state* funding of the costs of public education. Note that the argument does not attack the use of property taxes, but rather the inequable distribution of property tax revenues from one jurisdiction to another. Presumably, if a *state* would collect all property taxes statewide and then distribute the revenues equally among all communities, there would be little objection from have-not groups.

The Supreme Court of the United States has declined to intervene in this struggle over educational finance. By a 5–4 vote in *Rodriguez* v. *San Antonio Independent School Board* (1973), the Supreme Court ruled that disparities in property values between jurisdictions relying on property taxes to finance education did *not* violate the equal protection clause of the Fourteenth Amendment. The Supreme Court declined to substitute its own judgment about how schools should be financed for the judgments of forty-nine states. Writing for the majority, Justice Lewis F. Powell said:

> We are urged to abrogate systems of financing public education presently in existence in virtually every state . . . . [to declare unconstitutional] what many educators for half a century have thought was an enlightened approach to a problem for which there is no perfect solution. We are unwilling to assume for ourselves a level of wisdom superior to that of legislators, scholars, and educational authorities in 49 states, especially when the alternatives proposed are only recently conceived and nowhere yet tested.[14]

[14]*Rodriguez* v. *San Antonio Independent School Board*, 411 U.S. 1 (1973).

It is likely that the struggle over educational finance will continue.


## Public Policy and Higher Education

State governments have been involved in public higher education since the colonial era. State governments in the Northeast frequently made contributions to support private colleges in their states, a practice that continues today. The first state university to be chartered by a state legislature was the University of Georgia in 1794. Before the Civil War, Northeastern states relied exclusively on private colleges, and the Southern states assumed the leadership in public higher education. The ante-bellum curricula at Southern state universities, however, resembled the rigid classical studies of the early private colleges—Greek and Latin, history, philosophy, and literature.

It was not until the Morrill Land Grant Act of 1862 that public higher education began to make major strides in the American states. Interestingly, the Eastern states were slow to respond to the opportunity afforded by the Morrill Act to develop public universities; Eastern states continued to rely primarily on their private colleges and universities. The Southern states were economically depressed in the post-Civil War period, and leadership in public higher education passed to the Midwestern states. The philosophy of the Morrill Act emphasized agricultural and mechanical studies rather than the classical curricula of Eastern colleges, and the movement for "A and M" education spread rapidly in the agricultural states. The early groups of Midwestern state universities were closely tied to agricultural education, including agricultural extension services. State universities also took over the responsibility for the training of public school teachers in colleges of education. The state universities introduced a broad range of modern subjects in the university curricula—business administration, agriculture, home economics, education, engineering. It was not until the 1960s that the Eastern states began to develop public higher education, notably the huge, multi-campus State University of New York.

Today public higher education enrolls three-quarters of the nation's college and university students. Perhaps more importantly, the nation's leading state universities can challenge the best private institutions in academic excellence. The University of California at Berkeley, the University of Michigan, and the University of Wisconsin are deservedly ranked with Harvard, Yale, Princeton, Stanford, and Chicago.

Federal aid to colleges and universities comes in a variety of forms. Historically, the Morrill Act of 1862 provided the groundwork for federal assistance in higher education. In 1890 Congress activated several federal grants to support the operations of the land-grant colleges, and this aid, although very modest, continues to the present.

The GI Bills following World War II and the Korean War (enacted in 1944 and 1952 respectively) were not, strictly speaking, aid-to-education bills, but rather a form of assistance to veterans to help them adjust to civilian life. Nevertheless, these bills had a great impact on higher education in terms of the millions of veterans who were able to enroll in college. In 1966 Congress finally acted to make veterans' educational benefits a permanent program for "all those who risk their lives in our armed forces," but the benefits were reduced from the World War II and Korean levels.

The National Defense Education Act of 1958 also affected higher education by assisting superior students through loans and grants to continue undergraduate and graduate education, and by directly assisting institutions in which they enroll. Preference was given to undergraduate students intending to teach in elementary or secondary schools, particularly in science, mathematics, and modern foreign languages, and to graduate students preparing to teach in college.

Federal support for scientific research has also had an important impact on higher education. In 1950 Congress established the National Science Foundation to promote scientific research and education. NSF has provided fellowships for graduate education in the sciences, supported the development of science institutes and centers at universities, funded training institutes for science teachers at all levels, supported many specific scientific research projects, and supported other miscel-

**TABLE 7–2**   Higher Education Finance

|  | Sources of Operating Funds in Percent | |
|---|---|---|
|  | Public Institutions % | Private Institutions % |
| Tuition and Student Fees | 11.8 | 34.1 |
| Federal Government | 13.3 | 13.4 |
| State Governments | 40.3 | 1.1 |
| Local Governments | 4.9 | 0.5 |
| Endowment Earnings | 0.4 | 5.1 |
| Private Gifts | 0.4 | 7.8 |
| Other General Revenue | 7.5 | 9.6 |
| Auxiliary Revenue | 13.2 | 15.9 |
| Student Aid Grants | 2.5 | 3.9 |
| Public Service Programs | 5.7 | 8.6 |

*Source: Statistical Abstract of the United States, 1973, p. 135.*

laneous scientific enterprises. In 1965, Congress established a National Endowment for the Arts and Humanities, but funded these fields at only a tiny fraction of the amount given to NSF. In addition to NSF, many other federal agencies—the Department of Defense, Atomic Energy Commission, Office of Education, Public Health Service, and so forth—have granted research contracts to universities for specific projects. Thus, research has become a very big item in university life.

In 1972, Congress established a Basic Educational Opportunity Grant program. The program was intended to offer any college student in good standing a maximum grant of $1,600 per year minus the amount his family would reasonably be expected to contribute to his educational expenses. The program is potentially very costly, but each year Congress and the president have severely limited the funds available. As a result, the number of students aided has been small, and the average grant is closer to $1,000.

Congress also authorized a Student Guaranteed Loan program that seeks to encourage private banks to make low-interest loans to students. The federal government pays the interest charges while the student is in school and guarantees repayment in the event the student defaults on the payment after graduation. However, many banks find the interest rates too low and administrative details too cumbersome; student defaults have run higher than expected; and as a result, the number of student loans has fallen below expectations.

Congress has also authorized a National Direct Student Loan program which allows students to borrow directly from the student aid offices of their own colleges or universities. Again, no interest is charged while the student is in school; repayment is delayed until after the student leaves school.

## Groups in Higher Education

Among the influential groups in public higher education—aside from the governors and legislators who must vote the funds each year—are the boards of trustees (or "regents") that govern public colleges and universities. Their authority varies from state to state. But in nearly every state, they are expected not only to set broad policy directions in higher education but also to insulate higher education from direct political involvement of governors and legislators.

Prominent citizens who are appointed to these boards are expected to champion higher education with the public and the legislature. In the past, there were separate boards for each institution and separate consideration by the governor's office and the legislature of each institution's budgetary request. But the resulting competition has caused state after state to create unified "university system" boards to coordinate higher education. These university system boards consolidate the budget requests for each institution, determine systemwide priorities, and present a single budget for higher education to the governor and the legislature. The stronger and more independent the university system board, the less likely that universities and colleges throughout the state will be distributed to cities and regions in a pork barrel fashion by legislators seeking to enhance their local constituencies.

Another key group in higher education is composed of university and college presidents and their top administrative assistants. Generally, university presidents are the chief spokesmen for higher education, and they must convince the public, the regents, the governor, and the legislature of the value of state colleges and universities. The president's crucial role is one of maintaining support for higher education in the state; he frequently delegates administrative responsibilities for the internal operation of the university to the vice-presidents and deans. Support for higher education among the public and its representatives can be affected by a broad spectrum of university activities, some of which are not directly related to the pursuit of knowledge. A winning football team can stimulate legislative enthusiasm and win appropriations for a new classroom building. University service-oriented research—developing new crops or feeds, assessing the state's mineral resources, advising state and local government agencies on administrative problems, analyzing the state economy, advising local school authorities, and so forth—may help to convince the public of the practical benefits of knowledge. University faculty may be interested in advanced research and the education of future Ph.D.s, but legislators and their constituents are more interested in the quality and effectiveness of undergraduate teaching.

The faculty of the nation's 2,500 colleges and universities—over two and one-half million strong—traditionally identified themselves as professionals with strong attachments to their institutions. The historic pattern of college and university governance included faculty participation in policy making—not only academic requirements but also budgeting, personnel, building programs, etc. But governance by faculty committee has proven cumbersome, unwieldy, and time-consuming in an era of large-scale enrollments, multimillion dollar budgets, and increases in the size and complexity of academic administration. Increasingly, concepts of public "accountability," academic "management," cost control, and centralized budgeting and purchasing have transferred power in colleges and universities from faculty to professional academic administrators.

The traditional organization of faculty has been the American Association of University Professors (AAUP); historically this group has confined itself to publishing data on faculty salaries and officially "censoring" colleges or universities that violated longstanding notions of academic freedom or tenure. (Tenure is the notion that a faculty member who has demonstrated his competence by service in a college or university position for three to seven years cannot thereafter be dismissed except for "cause"—a serious infraction of established rules or dereliction of duty, provable in an open hearing.) In recent years, the American Federation of Teachers (AFT) has succeeded in convincing some faculty that traditional patterns of *individual* bargaining over salaries, teaching load, and working conditions in colleges and universities should be replaced by *collective* bargaining in the style of unionized labor. The AFT is growing in power and membership. (In 1976 the AFT won collective bargaining rights on behalf of all state university faculty in Florida—the first entire state university system to come under AFT control.) The growth of the AFT has spurred the AAUP on many campuses to assume a more militant attitude on behalf of faculty interests. The AAUP remains the largest faculty organization in the nation, but most of the nation's 2.5 million faculty are not affiliated with either the AAUP or the AFT. Faculty collective bargaining is complicated by the fact that faculty continue to play some role in academic governance—choosing deans and department heads, sitting on salary committees, etc.

## Summary

Let us summarize educational policy with particular reference to the group interests involved:

1. Historically, educational policy has been decentralized in America, with states and communities carrying the major responsibility for public elementary and secondary and higher education. However, federal aid to education is nearly as old as the nation itself. Prior to 1865, federal aid was distributed for specific programs and services—vocational education; school lunch and milk; federally impacted schools; science, mathematics, and foreign language; and higher education facilities—rather than general support of education.

2. The Elementary and Secondary Education Act of 1965 was the first large-scale federal aid-to-education program. The long struggle over federal aid to education indicates the power of interest groups in

blocking legislation that has widespread public support, and the necessity of accommodating specific interest groups in policy formation.

3. The difficulty in securing passage of a significant federal aid-to-education bill can be attributed to conflict between major racial and religious group interests over the character of such aid rather than to opposition to the idea of federal aid.

4. For many years the question of whether federal aid should be withheld from racially segregated schools divided proponents of federal aid to education. Only after the passage of the Civil Rights Act of 1965, barring the use of federal funds in *any* segregated program or activity, was this divisive issue removed as a direct obstacle to federal aid to education.

5. Another divisive issue over federal aid to education was that of whether or not such aid should be withheld from private, church-related schools. Catholic interests would not support a bill that excluded such schools from assistance, and Protestant interests, as well as the National Education Association, opposed the idea of federal aid to church schools.

6. Congress stood ready to enact whatever compromise the various religious and educational groups could agree upon. Experience clearly indicated that no policy of federal aid to education was possible without prior group compromise. The final compromise—enacted as the Elementary and Secondary Education Act of 1965—focused on "aid to children" in poverty-impacted areas, and allowed church-related schools to receive federal funds for specific nonreligious educational services and facilities.

7. Although educational decision making is still largely decentralized in America, state education departments are gradually centralizing policy making by means of state grants to local school boards, and gradually reducing by means of consolidation the number of local school boards.

8. Important groups in local school politics include taxpayers who vote in school board elections; school board members who are frequently owners of small businesses in the community; professional school administrators at the local level and from the state departments of education and faculties of teacher colleges; and school teachers. The American Federation of Teachers is a labor union representing many classroom teachers in large cities. The National Education Association, an older and larger "professional group," represents school administrators and teachers; it has become more militant in recent years in protecting teacher interests.

# Bibliography

COLEMAN, JAMES S., *Equality of Educational Opportunity.* Washington, D.C.: Government Printing Office, 1966.

EIDENBERG, EUGENE, and ROY D. MOREY, *An Act of Congress.* New York: Norton, 1969.

GITTELL, MARILYN, and ALAN G. HEVESI, eds., *The Politics of Urban Education.* New York: Praeger, 1969.

ZEIGLER, HARMON, *The Political Life of American Teachers.* Englewood Cliffs, N.J.: Prentice-Hall, 1967.

ZEIGLER, HARMON, and M. KENT JENNINGS, *Governing American Schools.* Boston: Duxbury Press, 1974.

The energy challenge. *Irene Springer.*

# Energy and the Environment
## group stalemate

# 8

## The Energy Challenge

The energy crisis is real. It is not merely speculation about possible future disasters, nor is it a hoax contrived by oil companies to raise prices. The nation's first dramatic realization of the energy crisis occurred in 1973–1974, with gasoline shortages, station closings, long lines, and rapid price increases. A second public shock occurred in 1978–1979 which jarred the nation back to the realization that the energy challenge would not easily go away. Both shocks were created by the same conditions: (1) an interruption in oil supplies from the Middle East (the Yom Kippur War in 1973 and the Iranian Revolution in 1978), and (2) a large increase in prices by the petroleum-exporting countries. Hopefully, the second shock will end American tendencies to pronounce the energy crisis as a thing of the past. Awareness of the crisis must not be allowed to fade away; citizens and politicians must face the difficult decisions required to formulate a national energy policy.

The energy challenge confronting the United States has many causes:

1. Increasing demand for energy, and lifestyles (reliance on auto rather than rail transit, electrical appliances and air conditioning, etc.) that use large amounts of energy.

2. A leveling off of output of domestic fuels, particularly oil and gas, and a decline in coal production.

3. Government regulation of the price of electricity, and government control of the price of oil and natural gas, which encouraged waste and discouraged producers from constructing new plants or expanding exploration and drilling operations.

4. Government red tape at the federal, state, and local levels obstructing the building of new energy projects, particularly nuclear power plants.

5. Environmental regulations which forced the conversion of coal-burning power plants to oil-burning plants to meet clean air standards, and which have slowed or halted strip mining of coal and offshore drilling for oil.

6. The formation of a cartel of oil-producing and exporting countries (OPEC) which forced steep increases in the price of oil and threatened embargoes against nations that opposed the political aims of OPEC member nations.

Americans use almost one-third of the entire world's energy production, and our appetite is growing. Indeed, even if our conservation programs are effective, our energy use will probably increase from 37 mbd (millions of barrels per day of oil equivalent) to 51 mbd in the decade of the 1980s—an increase of 40 percent (see Table 8–1).

Oil currently provides about half of the nation's energy needs; this oil is roughly half domestic and half imported. Natural gas pro-

**TABLE 8–1**  U.S. Energy Supply: Actual and Projected

|  | Actual | | Projected | |
|---|---|---|---|---|
|  | 1979 | | 1989 | |
|  | mbd* | Percent | mbd* | Percent |
| **Domestic** | | | | |
| Oil | 10 | 27 | 10 | 20 |
| Natural Gas | 9 | 24 | 9 | 18 |
| Coal | 7 | 19 | 12 | 24 |
| Nuclear | 1 | 3 | 3 | 6 |
| Hydro, Solar | 1 | 3 | 2 | 4 |
| **Imported** | | | | |
| Oil | 9 | 24 | 14 | 27 |
| Gas | ** | | 1 | 2 |
| TOTAL | 37 | | 51*** | |

*Million barrels per day of oil equivalent

**Less than 0.5 mbd

***Projected from US Department of Energy "conventional program" estimates, including increased conservation equivalent to 3 mbd.

*Source:* Compiled from Department of Energy estimates by Robert Stobaugh and Daniel Yergin, "After the Second Shock: Pragmatic Energy Strategies," *Foreign Affairs* Vol. 57 (Spring, 1979), p. 842.

vides about 24 percent of the nation's energy needs; it is almost all domestic, but in the future the United States will need to import more natural gas. Coal produces only about 19 percent of the nation's energy needs, even though it is the most abundant fuel in America. While proven reserves of American oil and gas are estimated to amount to only a ten- or twenty-year supply, we have at least a 300-year supply of coal in the ground. Nuclear plants provide only about 3 percent of the nation's energy needs. All of this nuclear energy is produced in sixty-seven licensed electrical generating plants; nuclear plants provide about 12 percent of the nation's electrical generating capacity. The remaining 3 percent of the nation's energy needs are produced by hydroelectric generating plants. Solar energy does not account for any significant share of energy production at the present time.

Projections for the future by the U.S. Department of Energy (DOE) (see Table 8–1) envision continued U.S. production of oil and gas at present levels, a feat which can only be achieved by advanced technological methods and incentives to oil companies to invest heavily in these technologies. DOE also projects a tripling of nuclear power generation, but political setbacks stemming from the Three Mile Island "incident," complicated licensing procedures, and heavy investment costs, make that projection unlikely. DOE is hopeful that the U.S. can almost double coal production in the next ten years, but this feat can only be achieved if utilities and industries are permitted to burn coal, if coal producers are permitted to strip mine, and if railroads (or new coal slurries) are rebuilt to carry large amounts of coal. Solar power, despite its romantic appeal, is not yet on the horizon. DOE now "projects" that the U.S. will have to import three-fifths of its oil supply and 29 percent of its total energy supply by the end of the decade. But we suspect that DOE is *under*estimating future U.S. dependence on imported oil and gas.

The failure to develop a national energy policy—to cope with a challenge as grave as any America has faced since World War II—is a serious threat to the American political system and its tradition of compromise and consensus. In 1973, in response to the Arab oil embargo against the United States, Republican President Richard Nixon announced "Project Independence" designed to achieve U.S. self-sufficiency in energy by 1980. Nixon called for deregulation of the prices of oil and natural gas, relaxation of clean air standards to allow coal burning, emergency gas rationing and conservation measures, federal authority to reduce red tape in new energy plants, including nuclear plants, and federal funding for research and development of alternative energy sources. At that time, the United States imported only 25 percent of its oil, at a cost of about three dollars per barrel, and the price of gasoline at the pump averaged about thirty-two cents per gallon. In 1979, Democratic President Jimmy Carter called for an almost identical program and termed the effort as "the moral equivalent of war." But by that time the United States imported almost 50 percent of its oil at a cost of nearly twenty dollars per barrel, and the price of gasoline at the pump averaged about one dollar per gallon. Despite the announced *goals* of reducing imports, becoming more self-sufficient, developing other sources of energy, and maintaining reasonable energy prices, government *activities* resulted in just the opposite outcomes. The failure to meet the energy challenge has in turn produced other effects which also contradict announced goals: energy prices have led to unacceptable inflation rates of 10, 14, and 18 percent per year, and to an increasingly unfavorable balance of trade with billions of U.S. dollars flowing out of the country each year.

For many years, *government price regulation* of oil and natural gas encouraged waste and discouraged exploration and production. In 1979, the President began a phased deregulation program. Of course, deregulation means higher (world market) prices for oil and natural gas, and higher prices contribute to inflation. Moreover, higher prices mean larger profits for oil and gas companies; if these profits are not used to expand energy research, exploration, and production, they would not contribute much to solving the nation's energy problem.

The cost of electrical power is regulated by *state* utility commissions, rather than by the federal government. Generally these commissions allow the utility companies to charge a rate which reflects their cost plus a small profit to investors. Historically, owning utility company stocks was considered a safe but slow-growth investment. There is not much incentive for power companies to take risks with new technologies because their profits are limited by law. Utilities can raise rates to offset the increasing cost of oil, but frequently state regulatory commissions delay granting these rate increases and otherwise hamper utilities in attracting new investors.

*Environmental regulations*—federal and state—are an even greater obstacle to energy production. New plant construction of any kind can be held up for years by active environmental opposition. Legal efforts by environmental groups, relying on a maze of federal and state laws, regulations, and agencies, have brought new plant construction to a standstill in many parts of the country. Legal delays themselves add to the cost and slow the development of new energy sources. Sometimes they even result in utilities cancelling new plant construction altogether. According to a leader of the Sierra Club, "Our strategy is to sue and sue and sue."

Federal environmental legislation also forced many utilities and industries to convert from coal burning to cleaner oil and gas burning power generators. Coal is the nation's most abundant fuel. But the mining of coal scars the land and the burning of coal pollutes the air. Natural gas is clean burning. And low-sulphur oil is also relatively clean burning. But conversions to these fuels make the United States more dependent on imports. Reconversion back to coal would reduce dependence on imports.

*Federal nuclear safety regulations* have brought nuclear power plant building to a halt. Despite its announced goal of doubling nuclear generating capacity over the next decade, federal policies raise serious doubts about the future of nuclear power. Nuclear power plants offer a means of generating electricity without discharging any pollutants into the air or water. Nuclear power does not diminish the world's supply of oil, gas, or coal. A "fast breeder" reactor can reprocess uranium fuel and "breed" more fuel for nuclear plants, thus solving the problem of uranium supply. However, used reactor fuel remains radioactive for hundreds of years and there are potential problems in burying this radioactive waste. Despite a thirty-year record of safety (no one has ever died or been seriously harmed by radioactivity from a nuclear power plant)[1], it is easy to generate fear about nuclear plants because of the devastation which nuclear weapons can cause. No responsible scientist or engineer would claim that there are *no* possibilities of a nuclear accident. But most would also contend that there are few other activities in modern society—automobile and air transport, coal mining, fuel transportation, etc.,—that could pass a test of one hundred percent proven safety that nuclear critics demand for atomic power plants. A nuclear plant could never create a nuclear detonation, but there is always a possibility of some radioactivity escaping. A "melt down" is a remote possibility, wherein the heat of the radioactive fuel destroys the container and building and escapes into the surrounding countryside. In 1979, at the Three Mile Island plant near Harrisburg, Pennsylvania, a small amount of radioactive steam escaped; for several hours there was concern, and some panic, over the possibility of a melt down. No one was hurt, but the accident gave nuclear critics new popular leverage to oppose nuclear power. More importantly, the incident fostered the mushroom cloud mentality, in which no technical or economic facts can erase the images and associations of nuclear war.

Nuclear power plant licensing, which came to a stop after the media coverage of the Three Mile Island "incident," has made the future expansion of nuclear power difficult, if not impossible. The Nuclear Regulatory Commission must issue site approvals, construction per-

---

[1]This record includes the seventy-one nuclear power plants operating in the United States, over eighty nuclear power plants operating outside the United States, and hundreds of nuclear-powered surface and submarine ships operated by the U.S. Navy. For an excellent, unbiased discussion of nuclear safety, see Harold W. Lewis, "The Safety of Fission Reactors," *Scientific American* vol. 242 (March 1980), 53–65.

mits, and operating licenses for nuclear power plants. But this process takes about twelve years! Licensing reform is badly needed; but in the wake of popular fears, licensing problems may get worse rather than better.

Perhaps the overriding problem is that the United States has no coordinated national energy policy. Industry, utilities, labor, environmentalists, the Congress, the President, DOE and other governmental agencies have failed to agree on such questions as

> whether to rely primarily on energy conservation or to stimulate the search for new energy sources;
>
> whether or not to "trade off" clean air standards in order to ensure adequate energy supplies;
>
> whether to proceed slowly in developing new oil, gas, and coal reserves and means of transporting these fuels in the interests of environmental protection, or to move rapidly in the interests of achieving independence from foreign powers;
>
> whether to reduce energy consumption by relying on voluntary conservation, or allowing fuel prices to rise to world market levels, or imposing governmental allocations and rationing;
>
> whether to finance a large-scale government investment in the development of synthetic fuels, or to give small tax breaks to individuals who buy insulation, solar equipment, and so forth;
>
> whether and how fast to "deregulate" oil and natural gas prices in the face of inflationary pressure, and whether to impose a "windfall profits" tax on the oil companies which benefit from deregulation;
>
> whether to encourage the development of nuclear power and speed up nuclear plant construction, or to turn away from nuclear power altogether.

These domestic issues are further complicated by delicate and dangerous Middle East politics. Arab countries are the largest oil producers in the OPEC cartel. It is clear that these countries will use their oil weapon for political gains, at the expense of the United States. Another international problem: as the United States buys more and more imported oil, it competes in the same market with Western Europe and Japan. As U.S. purchases force up prices, inflationary pressures are felt worldwide, with possible disastrous effects on our relationships with key friends and allies.

## Energy Policy Alternatives

Meeting the energy challenge is primarily a *political* problem. There are a variety of technical ways to provide the United States with all the energy it needs. The real problem is finding agreement over which ways, or combination of ways, the nation should adopt.

### Conservation

Conservation is a term that covers a wide variety of activities at many levels of society—federal, state, and local governments; large and small businesses; industries and banks; schools and hospitals; automobile and home owners; and virtually every citizen in the nation. It covers such diverse activities as mass transit, car pooling, insulation, building designs, space heating, utility rate pricing, home appliance usage, driving habits, air conditioning and water heating, recycling waste heat, rationing, and turning off the lights.

Politically, conservation is a fragmented topic that lacks glamor. There is no one technological "fix"—no Manhattan Project, or man-on-the-moon program—that can achieve energy conservation once and for all. Because conservation is such a broad and fragmented term, it is difficult for public policy to cope with it directly, and it is particularly difficult to pass a single law which would mandate so many forms of conservation at so many different levels of society. Nonetheless, a coordinated energy conservation effort might enable the United States to maintain or improve its standard of living at the same time as it uses considerably less energy. The Harvard School of Business Energy Project reports that European nations consume less than three-quarters as much energy for each dollar of goods produced as the United States.[2] In other words, the United States could reduce energy consumption by 25 percent or more without cutting production.

> The United States can use 30 to 40 percent less energy than it does, with virtually no penalty for the way Americans live—save that billions of dollars will be spared, save that the environment will be less strained, the air less polluted, the dollar under less pressure, save that the growing and alarming dependence on OPEC oil will be reduced, and Western society will be less likely to suffer internal and international tension.[3]

But, to date at least, there is little evidence to support such an optimistic prediction about conservation. It is true that *growth* in energy consumption has been reduced. Instead of the previous 4 or 5 percent annual growth in energy consumption, the United States is now increasing consumption at only 2 or 3 percent per year.

Gasoline consumption has actually declined slightly since 1978.

[2]Robert Stobaugh and Daniel Yerkin, eds., *Energy Future* (New York: Random House, 1979), p. 143.
[3]Ibid., p. 182.

Most of the decline can be attributed to increased gasoline prices. But government policies have also helped. The federal government imposes a national fifty-five-mile-per-hour speed limit and urges Americans to turn their thermostats down to sixty-five degrees in winter and their air conditioners up to seventy-eight degrees in summer. The federal Energy Policy and Conservation Act of 1975 ordered automobile companies to achieve greater gas mileage in new cars: company fleet averages (the average mileage of a company's entire production of cars) must increase from fourteen miles per gallon in 1975 to twenty-seven and a half miles per gallon in 1985. The National Energy Act of 1978 provides a 10 percent tax credit incentive for businesses to install energy conserving devices. The act also provides a 15 percent tax credit on investments in conservation by homeowners. Finally, the earlier Energy Policy and Conservation Act of 1975 provides direct grants to the states to assist the poor, elderly, and handicapped to "weatherize" their homes.

The energy crisis has provided radicals with a new weapon to attack the established socioeconomic system and lifestyle of the American people. There is a romantic view of America in a "postindustrial era" in which the absence of energy forces everyone back to a more natural "pastoral" lifestyle—windmills, solar collectors, bicycles, and clean air and water. This view usually includes the collapse of large industrial corporations, utilities, and particularly, the oil companies—who are singled out as the villains in the energy drama. Viewed in this fashion, conservation becomes a mechanism of changing the entire social order.

The energy crisis has provided conservatives with new arguments on behalf of the private market system. Because energy conservation is so fragmented and difficult to deal with by law, why not rely on the market system to do its work? Conservation activity will eventually respond to energy prices. If energy prices are allowed to rise to market levels, and government regulations are ended, conservation will be the natural result.

### Decontrol

The decontrol of prices on domestic oil and natural gas can accomplish several things.

1. Higher prices to consumers will provide an economic incentive to conserve.
2. Higher profits to producers will provide an economic incentive to increase production and stimulate efforts to extract "hard to get" oil.
3. Alternative energy sources, once considered too costly, will become economically competitive.

4. The nation's homes, factories, and cars will be more quickly adapted to use less oil.

Europeans and Japanese have paid the world market price for oil for many years—gasoline is regularly two to three dollars per gallon at the pump. They have long produced smaller, more gas-efficient cars, and they have long maintained good railroad systems. Pricing American energy at the world market level may assist this nation in its own efforts to improve gas mileage and mass transportation—using the market mechanism rather than government regulations. Voluntary conservation has not proven effective. Only when gasoline is two to three dollars per gallon can we expect large cutbacks in unnecessary driving and preferences for small cars or mass transit.

But as one commentator put it: "This country did not conserve its way to greatness. It produced its way to greatness." Removing price controls should also encourage oil companies to explore for more oil and to develop unconventional means for extracting more oil from known reserves. Actually, it is unlikely that anyone will discover any large new domestic reserves of oil or gas. Over two million wells have already been drilled in the United States—four times as many as in all of the rest of the world combined. But large quantities of oil—more than half—are left behind by conventional recovery methods. Higher prices may encourage more costly and sophisticated methods of forcing oil from the ground through heat or steam. Another costly but feasible source is oil-bearing shale rock, although extracting this oil involves large quantities of water and perhaps ugly scarring of the land. All sources of new production combined can only be expected to *maintain* current levels of domestic production.

Of course, decontrol means higher prices for gasoline and home heating oil. This is another economic setback for a nation already staggering under the burden of double-digit inflation. Moreover, it can also be argued that these price increases would be especially burdensome for the poor, although special programs like the food stamp program could be devised to offset this burden.

### Breaking Up the Big Oil Companies

Frustration with energy problems frequently results in the search for a scapegoat—someone to blame—and the oil companies are visible targets. But contrary to popular opinion, the oil and gas industry is not especially monopolistic. (For example, three auto makers control 90 percent of all domestic auto sales, but twenty oil companies control less than 70 percent of the domestic oil production.) There are eight large companies that operate "vertically," that is, they extract oil, transport it, refine it, and market it themselves.[4] Proposals have been made to force the separation of these functions—"divestiture." But no one ever claims that "breaking up the big oil companies" would increase oil supplies. Economists seem equally divided over whether or not it would increase or decrease prices, but they agree that any price effect would be very small.

### The Windfall Profits Tax

As controls are removed from prices, the value of oil reserves in the ground and in inventory increase. Companies which own domestic oil reserves benefit directly from the rise in price which results from decontrol. These benefits are frequently called "windfall profits." It is hoped that these revenues to the companies would go directly into new exploration or new recovery methods. Indeed, laws have been proposed to force companies to use their "windfall profits" in this fashion. But a more common proposal is to tax these "windfall profits"; the federal government might earmark these tax monies to fund its own energy research or simply to add to its revenue base. The tax on "windfall profits" might be 50 to 80 percent.

Yet, if the purpose of decontrol is to provide greater incentives to produce, then profits should not be taxed away. It is precisely these profits which are designed to increase production. It will be challenge enough to find enough new reserves of domestic oil and gas to maintain production at current levels.

### Conversion to Coal

Coal, as we know, is the nation's most abundant energy source. There are ample supplies of known coal reserves to last the nation for three hundred years. While domestic oil and natural gas are limited by supplies in the ground, coal is limited by *political* issues. The national Clean Air Acts, particularly the Clean Air Act of 1970, forced many industries and electrical utilities to convert from coal-burning to oil-burning plants. Environmentalists object to every step in coal production: mining the coal, transporting it, and particularly burning it. There has been a *decline* in the production of coal since 1969, variously attributed to mine safety regulations, labor union strife in the coal fields, the decline of rail transportation, and clean air and strip-mining

[4]Exxon, Gulf, Standard Oil of Indiana, Texaco, Shell, ARCO, Mobil, and Standard Oil of California.

regulations. Electric utilities are reluctant to shift back to coal, fearing new, uncertain, federal government regulations on smoke emissions. (For example, will the federal government require costly "smoke scrubbers" to remove the sulphur content from the emissions of coal-burning plants?) The nation's railroads are largely bankrupt anyhow; they cannot afford to invest in new tracks and cars to move large quantities of coal from the Western states where it is plentiful to the industrial Northeast. And stripmining cannot proceed in the face of legal uncertainties about federal and state environmental regulations. Companies do not now know what will be required of them to return stripmined land to its original contour and condition. Coal gasification and liquefaction are technically possible, but the cost is very high, still well above the world market price for oil.

In brief, coal is abundant, but the use of coal requires the development of a national energy policy governing its mining, transportation, and burning. So far, this challenge has exceeded the capacity of the American political system.

### Nuclear Power

Political obstacles also bar heavy reliance on nuclear energy. Nuclear power now provides about 12 percent of the nation's total electricity. Most early studies recommended that the U.S. strive for 50 percent nuclear power by 1990. But advocates of nuclear power have lost ground in recent years to a wide assortment of "no-nuke" groups. The mushroom cloud image of devastation of Japanese cities at the end of World War II is still with us, whether or not this image has anything to do with nuclear power. Fear plays an important role in nuclear politics. The mass media cannot resist accounts of the potential dangers of nuclear plants. Delay after delay has resulted from endless litigation, hearings, and vociferous demonstrations. These delays increase the costs of nuclear power, as do continuously changing safety regulations and construction designs.

The Carter Administration has confounded the problem of spent fuel storage by halting the development of the "breeder reactor" at Clinch River, Tennessee. Nuclear planners had assumed that the breeder reactor would reprocess spent fuel and provide a continuous supply of enriched uranium. But fears of "nuclear proliferation" (the same process which regenerates spent fuels can also produce high-grade plutonium for weapons use) have been cited by the federal government as a reason for halting construction of the breeder reactor. Spent fuel is now piling up in storage areas in specially designed pools of water at nuclear power sites. When these existing storage places are filled to capacity, spent fuel will have to be transported somewhere else, adding to new complaints about the dangers of radioactive waste. There are many technical alternatives in dealing with waste (all of the waste of this century could be stored in an area no larger than an average industrial warehouse), but there is no political consensus about which of these alternatives to choose.

### Solar Power

Solar power holds out the promise of cheap, clean renewable energy. But so far it is only a promise. There are no solar technologies available today which can provide significant energy resources in this century. The simple solar panel collector, designed to catch and concentrate the sun's rays, can heat water and air in sunny climates. But back-up devices are required, and the payback period (how fast a homeowner can recover the cost of investment) is very long, even with government tax incentives. "Small solar" for households may become increasingly attractive, if electric bills are allowed to rise significantly. But "big solar," expensive new technologies for large-scale solar power stations, is still very experimental. Nonetheless, there remains the hope that a new technological breakthrough in "photovoltaics" (small silicon cells which can change sunlight directly into electricity) will make solar energy a reality and not merely a promise. In the meantime, public policy, while supporting solar research, cannot rely on an unproven energy source.

### Synfuels

Synthetic fuels, especially synthetic oil derived from oil shale or made by liquefying or gasifying coal, are technically feasible, but very costly. It requires roughly 1.7 tons of shale rock to produce a single barrel of oil. Once the oil is removed by a heating process, the producer is left with more rock than he started with because of a "popcorn effect." The spent rock must be disposed of, and the process requires large amounts of water—and water is in short supply in the western states where shale oil is found. Coal liquefaction is also a massive task. It takes about one and a half tons of coal to produce one barrel of liquefied coal. South Africa operates a liquefying plant, and Germany produced synthetic oil in World War II. But a long time would be required to build a large-scale industry, and the costs would be very high. It might take ten years to build a plant and one billion to three billion dollars invested before a single barrel of oil was produced. Obviously, only heavy government involvement would make such a project possible. And we could expect the OPEC countries to try to price their oil so as to cause any synfuel producers to lose money and go out of business. So a government guaranteed price for synfuels would be essential.

### Licensing and Regulation

Perhaps the most important obstacle to a national energy policy is the maze of licensing and regulating procedures of federal, state, and local government agencies. Regulatory squabbling and court fights have created interminable delays, added greatly to the costs of projects, and created costly confusion over energy policy. Large-scale energy projects, such as coal development and transportation, nuclear power plants, pipelines, synfuel projects, etc., must be freed from unnecessary regulatory harrassment. Preferably, a single federal agency should have the authority to approve or disapprove all energy projects; all other agencies—federal, state, and local—would be subject to a single federal decision-making body. Environmentalists can be expected to oppose any "fast track" for licensing of energy projects. They are likely to feel that such an approach would threaten the nation's environmental legislation, and set back progress in cleaning up the air and water.

### Rationing

Rationing is the most extreme form of conservation. Yet in the event of a complete oil embargo against the United States or some other unforeseen energy disaster, a "stand-by" rationing program may be wise. All goods are "rationed" in the market place by prices. But government rationing substitutes a new form of money, ration stamps, for dollars. These stamps are allocated to the public according to the *government's* view regarding who should get how much gasoline. The total amount of ration stamps issued would equal the government's decision about the total amount of gasoline that should be used. The government could decide, for example, to issue twenty-five gallons of gas per month to every automobile owner. The government could allow the sale of the stamps, that is, a "white market." Or it could prohibit their sale, which would lead to the creation of an illegal "black market" in ration stamps. But rationing is only successful when the vast majority of Americans support it, as in World War II. A rationing program with little popular support would be a disaster. The federal government has proven to be an inefficient allocator of goods and services, compared to the market place. Indeed, Department of Energy "allocations" of bulk gasoline shipments in 1978–1979 turned out to be so misguided that unnecessary shortages and surpluses were artificially created in various parts of the country from time to time. Government rationing is bound to create tremendous administrative problems.

## A Presidential Program: "The Moral Equivalent of War"

In 1977 President Carter appeared on national television to make a dramatic appeal: "Our decision about energy will test the character of the American people and the ability of the President and Congress to govern this nation. This difficult effort will be the moral equivalent of war—except that we will be uniting in our efforts to build and not to destroy." Yet to date precious little of the President's program has become law, and the "moral equivalent of war" has become a squabble among interest groups.

### The Department of Energy

The President was successful in creating a new cabinet-level Department of Energy in 1977. The new department combined the functions of the old Federal Power Commission (regulating natural gas and wholesale electricity), Federal Energy Administration (pricing and allocating oil), and the Energy Research and Development Administration (including research on all energy sources and the development of nuclear power). However, the new Secretary of Energy was required to share power over oil, gas, and electricity prices with a five-member Federal Energy Regulatory Commission.

### Decontrol

In 1979, the President acquired discretionary power to allow "phased" decontrol of oil prices. All price controls lapse in 1981, unless Congress reimposes them. But conflict in Congress is so great over this issue that it is unlikely that Congress can do anything to extend controls. One problem with decontrol, of course, is that decontrol will mean that domestic U.S. prices will be set by the OPEC nations. The world market price of oil has skyrocketed from three dollars per barrel in 1972 to over twenty-five dollars per barrel in 1980. Increased prices may not lead to as much conservation as expected. Many people do not have any alternatives to auto transportation; they must drive their cars regardless of the price of gasoline. Both the President and most energy experts believe that decontrol is a necessary step.

### Oil Import Limits

The President also has the authority to limit the importation of oil from abroad. In 1979 Carter announced that he would keep oil imports under 9 mbd; this figure was very close to existing levels of imports. Oil import quotas are a good idea *if* U.S. domestic energy sources and conservation efforts can meet the nation's energy needs. However, if these needs outstrip our abilities to produce and conserve, oil import quotas will be difficult, if not impossible, to maintain.

### Windfall Profits Tax

President Carter linked his decontrol of oil prices to his own proposal to Congress to tax the profits of oil companies from oil that was already discovered. At first Carter proposed to give the tax revenues to low income families to pay fuel bills, but later Carter's emphasis was on using the revenues to pay for the government's own energy research efforts. The oil companies have opposed the tax; they argue that industry and not government is best equipped to determine how profits should be "plowed back" into research and development.

### Synfuel Development

The President has asked Congress to create a new "Energy Security Corporation" to provide financial support for the development of alternative energy supplies. The corporation would have broad authority to set up joint ventures with private industry, to build and operate its own facilities, to sell bonds to raise money, and to guarantee government purchases and prices for new fuels. The costs of this effort may be paid for from earmarked funds from the "windfall profits" tax. Hopefully, this effort will result in an entirely new synthetic fuels industry—liquefied and gasified coal, oil shale extraction, and methane from organic materials.

### Solar Bank

The President is calling for a new, separate federal effort in solar research and development, a Solar Bank. The Bank would make loans to private companies to develop solar technology and to businesses and individuals for solar-powered installations.

*Energy Mobilization*

To make sure that synfuels and other large energy projects do not bog down in endless delays, licensing procedures, regulatory hearings, court suits, and so on, the President has proposed an "Energy Mobilization Board" to handle energy projects with speed and efficiency. The board would be empowered to cut through red tape at the federal, state, and local level. The board would require all regulatory agencies to act promptly, and if they did not do so, the board would make all the necessary decisions itself. Needless to say, environmentalists are sharply opposed to the "energy mobilization" notion.

*Coal*

Coal was the initial focal point of the President's energy program. Indeed, the President had considered requiring industries and utilities to convert to coal. The President envisioned a doubling of coal production in ten years. However, a variety of problems have intervened to cause the President to back away from his early commitment to coal.

First of all, the President has been unwilling to squarely face the environmental lobby and push Congress to amend the Clean Air Acts to allow coal burning. Industries and utilities cannot be confronted with one law requiring them to convert to coal and another law prohibiting them from burning coal. Until the President and Congress amend the Clean Air Acts, coal cannot be much help in resolving the energy crunch.

Second, it is not clear that the coal industry can double its production. The industry has long been troubled by labor strife. Federal mine safety regulations and new surface mining and reclamation requirements reduce productivity. A great deal of new capital investment will be needed, and many new skilled miners will have to be trained.

Third, the nation's railroads are unprepared to carry large amounts of coal. About two-thirds of the nation's coal is carried on railroads; the rest on barges and trucks. Much of the railroad industry has been bankrupt for years. Coal is bulky and must be transported great distances over land. Costly new investments in trucks, cars, and locomotives will be required. Proposals for new coal slurry pipelines (that pump a mixture of coal and water) confront the usual objections of environmentalists.

*Nuclear Power*

The President is aware of the continuing need for nuclear power development. He also knows that to revive the nuclear industry the federal government must reform and speed up its nuclear plant licensing process. However, the President is painfully aware that the "incident" at the Three Mile Island nuclear power plant near Harrisburg, Pennsylvania, created panic and confusion in the minds of many Americans. Because of the current twelve-year delay in plant licensing and construction and the ever changing safety regulations, the costs of nuclear plants have skyrocketed. Electric utilities have been cancelling their orders for new nuclear plant construction. Unless the federal government acts decisively to reassure the public about nuclear safety and encourage the speedy licensing and construction of nuclear plants, the "nuclear option" will disappear.

## The Environmental Challenge

The United States has moved rapidly over the last decade to develop a comprehensive set of laws and regulatory agencies for environmental protection. In the late 1960s there was little or no effective opposition to "clean" legislation, and little or no concern for the ultimate costs of cleaning up the environment. The mass media generated one dramatic "crisis" after another, including lead, mercury, DDT, PCB, ozone, asbestos, and sulfur dioxide. Anyone who spoke reassuringly about the low levels of risk involved was regarded as an opponent of the environmental crusade. But increasingly we are coming to realize that environmental protection involves costs to all of us—in higher consumer prices, in slower economic growth, in larger regulatory bureaucracies, and, most of all, in meeting the energy challenge. Increasingly, we are trying to weigh the benefits of a particular environmental regulation against its cost. Nonetheless, the air we breathe and the water we drink is significantly cleaner than a decade ago, and no one wishes to reverse the nation's commitment to environmental protection.

### Air Pollution

The air we breathe is about one-fifth oxygen and a little less than four-fifths nitrogen with traces of other gases, water vapor, and the waste products we spew into it. Most air pollution is caused by gasoline-powered internal combustion engines—cars, trucks, and buses. Motor vehicles send over 700 million tons of contaminants into the atmosphere every year—about 51 percent of the total polluting material. Industries and governments contribute another 42 million tons. The largest industrial polluters are petroleum refineries, smelters (aluminum, copper, lead, and zinc), and iron foundries. Electrical power plants are another major source of air pollution. Forty-four million tons are produced by burning coal or oil for electrical power. Heating is also a major source of pollution; homes, apartments, and offices use coal, gas, and oil for heat. Another source of pollution is the incineration of garbage, trash, metal, glass, and other refuse by both governments and industries (see Table 8–2).

Air pollutants fall into two major types: particles and gases. The particles include ashes, soot, and lead, the unburnable additive in gasoline. Often the brilliant red sunsets we admire are caused by large particles in the air. Less obvious but more damaging are the gases: (1) sulfur dioxide, which in combination with moisture can form sulfuric acid; (2) hydrocarbons—any combination of hydrogen and carbon; (3) nitrogen oxide, which can combine with hydrocarbons and the sun's ultra-violet rays to form smog; and (4) carbon monoxide, which is produced when gasoline is burned.

It is difficult at the present time to assess the full impact of air pollution on health. We know that when the smog or pollution count rises in a particular city there are more deaths due to emphysema than would normally have been expected.

In the streets of certain cities at certain hours of heavy traffic, carbon monoxide can deprive the body of oxygen; persons exposed to it may exhibit drowsiness, headache, poor vision, impaired coordination, and reduced capacity to reason. Nitrogen oxide irritates the eyes, nose, throat, and respiratory system; it damages plants, buildings, and stat-

**TABLE 8–2**   Air pollution

| | | In Millions of Tons Per Year | | | | | |
| | $CO$ | $SO_2$ | $HC$ | $NO_x$ | Port. | Percent of Total | Adjustment of Total |
|---|---|---|---|---|---|---|---|
| Transportation | 77.5 | 1.0 | 14.7 | 11.2 | 1.0 | 51 | 19 |
| Fuel Combustion in Stationary Sources | 1.0 | 26.3 | .3 | 10.2 | 6.5 | 21 | 41 |
| Industrial | 11.4 | 5.1 | 5.6 | 5.2 | 13.6 | 17 | 29 |
| Solid Waste Disposal | 3.8 | .1 | 1.0 | .2 | .7 | 3 | 2 |
| Miscellaneous | 6.5 | .1 | 5.0 | .2 | 5.2 | 8 | 9 |
| Total | 100.2 | 32.6 | 26.6 | 27.0 | 27.0 | 100 | 100 |

*Note:* $CO$ = Carbon monoxide; $SO_2$ = sulfur dioxide; $HC$ = hydrocarbons; $NO_x$ = nitrogen oxides; Port. = particulate matter. The first column of percentages shows the pollution accounted for by each source by weight. The second column of percentages corrects for the amount of damage to health and safety done by the pollutants emitted from each source.

*Source:* U.S. Council on Environmental Quality, *Environmental Quality* (Washington, D.C.: Government Printing Office, 1973).

ues. Finally, urban residents have been found to be twice as likely to contract lung cancer as rural residents.

On the other hand, it is known that smoking is much more hazardous than the worst air pollution. As one expert testified: "If you want to pass all of these regulations because smog stinks, or because it burns your eyes, or because it blocks your view of the mountains, OK—fine, but if you are trying to pass all of these regulations because smog is a health hazard—forget it—because it is not."[5] Early reports published by the government that pollution is a health hazard were later discredited.[6]

Total amounts of pollution may be deceptive, however, because we are really more concerned about the damage done to health and safety rather than about the millions of tons of various pollutants in the air; for example, the damage done by a ton of sulfur dioxide is much greater than the damage done by a ton of carbon monoxide. So the Council on Environmental Quality has "adjusted" the percentages of emissions from various sources to correspond to the damage done to the environment. (These percentages are shown in the last column of Table 8–2.) Adjusted figures show that automobile emissions dropped from first to third place behind stationary power plants and industrial emissions, which are generally more dangerous to health than automobiles. Finally, meteorological conditions also affect the dangers of pollution. The phenomenon known as "inversion" is especially important: inversion occurs when cool air near the ground is trapped beneath a layer of warmer air. This air does not move and becomes heavy with pollutants. Inversions occur more frequently on the West Coast, notably in Los Angeles, than elsewhere in the nation.

What is being done? In a series of Clean Air Acts, culminating in the stringent Clean Air Act of 1970, Congress gradually raised the standards for clean air, tightened enforcement processes, and increased penalties for violators. Congress authorized the Environmental Protection Agency (EPA) to establish national air quality standards and national emission standards for air pollution sources. The requirement for *national* standards means that cities without air pollution problems are subject to the same regulations as cities with major problems.

The emission standards for automobiles were particularly stringent. The automobile industry was required to reduce auto emissions on new cars by 90 percent over a five-year period. The industry made significant early strides in reducing emissions, but further reductions hinged on the development of "catalytic converters," costly and unreliable additions to new cars. It turned out that these converters fre-

---

[5]Quote from Richard J. Lescoe, MD, former director of the California Lung Association, in *World Research Ink*, November/December, 1979, p. 10.
[6]Richard J. Tobin, *The Social Gamble* (Boston: Lexington, 1979).

quently do not work properly, especially when leaded fuel is used even for a short time. The response of some environmentalists has been to urge federal regulations of state auto inspections and to require drivers to periodically replace their converters.

Power plants were encouraged by the Act to switch from coal to oil in order to reduce sulfur emissions. Industries were also encouraged to build tall smoke stacks with costly "scrubbers" to reduce or eliminate pollutants. These "scrubbers" are supposed to eliminate sulfur emissions, but it is doubtful that their costs are commensurate with any gains in public health which might result from their use. Their use may be responsible for an addition of up to 25 percent in the cost of electricity, and they use 3 to 5 percent of the total electricity generated to run themselves. Finally, they produce a sulfuric sludge which may itself be an environmental hazard.

Needless to say, the Clean Air Acts have created many problems for industry and the consumer. These laws contribute to our dependence on costly foreign oil by forcing power plants to switch from coal to oil. Recent amendments to these laws allow the EPA to temporarily suspend emission standards in specific plants when it is in the national interest to do so. A controversy also arose regarding whether the Clean Air Acts prohibit the lowering of air quality in areas which were already cleaner than the national EPA standards. Despite these problems, industry has been pushed to make major investments in clear air and the Council of Environmental Quality reports that the air is cleaner now in most cities than it was in 1970.

### Water Pollution

Debris and sludge, organic wastes, and chemical effluents are the three major types of water pollutants. These pollutants come from (1) domestic sewage, (2) industrial waste, (3) agricultural run-off of fertilizers and pesticides, and (4) "natural" processes including silt and sedimentation which may be increased by nearby construction. A common standard for measuring water pollution is "biochemical oxygen demand" (BOD), which identifies the amount of oxygen consumed by wastes. This measure, however, does not consider chemical substances which may be toxic to humans or fish. It is estimated that domestic sewage accounts for 30 percent of BOD, and industrial and agricultural wastes for 70 percent.

Primary sewage treatment—screens and settling chambers where filth falls out of the water as sludge—is fairly common. Secondary sewage treatment is designed to remove organic wastes, usually by trickling water through a bed of rocks three to ten feet deep, where bacteria consume the organic matter. Remaining germs are killed by chlorination. Tertiary sewage treatment uses mechanical and chemical filtration processes to remove almost all contaminants from water. The present federal water pollution abatement goals call for the establishment of secondary treatment in 90 percent of American communities. In most industrial plants, tertiary treatment ultimately will be required to deal with the flow of chemical pollutants. But tertiary treatment is expensive; it costs two or three times as much to build and operate a tertiary sewage treatment plant as it does a secondary plant. Even today, however, one-third of all Americans live in communities where their sewage gets nothing but primary treatment.

Phosphates are major water pollutants which overstimulate plant life in water, which in turn kills fish. Paper manufacturing is another major industrial polluter. Municipalities are frequently unwilling to pay the high costs of secondary and tertiary sewage treatment. Once, the Cuyahoga River in Cleveland actually caught fire, suggesting the extent of chemical pollution in this waterway.

Waterfronts and seashores are natural resources that Americans can no longer take for granted. The growing numbers of waterfront homes, amusement centers, marinas, and pleasure boats together with the occurrence of offshore oil spills are threatening to alter the environment of the nation's coastal areas. Marshes and estuaries at the water's edge are essential to the production of seafood and shellfish, yet they are steadily shrinking with the growth of residential-commercial-industrial development. Oil spills are unsightly. Coastal pollution is much greater in Europe than in America, but America's coastal areas still require protection. The Water Quality acts make petroleum companies liable for the cleanup costs of oil spills, outlaw flushing of raw sewage from boat toilets, restrict thermal pollution, and set general water quality standards for all of the states. In addition, the federal government has purchased certain coastal areas to preserve the coastal wilderness.

The federal government has provided financial assistance to states and cities to build sewage treatment plants ever since the 1930s. Efforts to establish national standards for water quality began in the 1960s and culminated in the Water Pollution Control Act of 1972. This Act reinforced earlier laws against oil spills and thermal (heat) pollution. More importantly it set "national goals" of elimination of the discharge of *all* pollutants into navigable waters by 1985; it required industries and municipalities to install "the best available technology" by 1983; it gave EPA authority to initiate legal actions against polluters; and increased federal funds available to municipalities for the construction of sewage treatment plants.

The problem, of course, is that removing *all* pollutants may not be cost effective. There is a law of diminishing returns at work in environmental efforts which tells us that removing the last 1 percent of pollution is more costly than removing the first 99 percent. Setting unrealistic standards for clean air and clean water is self-defeating.

### Solid Waste Disposal

Every American discards between 6 and 8 pounds of solid waste per day. This per capita waste production is expected to double in weight in the next 20 years. The annual load of waste dumped on the environment includes 48 billion cans, 26 billion bottles and jars, 4 million automobiles and trucks, and 30 million tons of paper. Already the nation spends billions of dollars annually on hauling all this away from homes and businesses. Open dumps are eyesores and create health hazards. The Environmental Protection Agency urges cities to rely on sanitary landfills—where the waste is spread in thin layers over specific land areas and covered at least once a day with a layer of earth. But many cities are running out of landfill sites.

Solving the problem of solid waste disposal requires that we either find better methods of disposal, find ways to reduce the amount discarded, or recycle wastes. Recycling could decrease the volume of solid wastes which must be disposed, and at the same time reduce the amount of virgin materials taken from the earth. Yet recycling is hampered by the difficulties of separating reusable materials from other refuse. Given the present state of technology, it is frequently cheaper to use virgin materials than it is to separate refuse and recycle it.

## Strip Mining

About half of the United States' coal supply comes from surface mines. Millions of acres of land have been disturbed by surface mining, and many more millions of acres will be mined if we are to increase coal production. Much of the new mining will occur in the western United States with its large untapped coal reserves. In the East a great deal of surface mining has already been done, and much of this land has never been reclaimed.

The Surface Mining Control and Reclamation Act of 1977 was one of the few successful efforts to resolve energy and environmental concerns and achieve a clear national policy. The Act recognized both the nation's increased need for coal and its interest in preserving and reclaiming land and maintaining natural beauty and wildlife habitat. The Act removes surface mining from the requirements for "environmental impact" statements. It gives the Secretary of the Interior authority to issue regulations governing surface mining and reclamation;

EPA is only allowed to review air and water quality standards. These regulations will require mine operators to return surface lands to their approximate original contours, preserve topsoil, minimize disturbance to water flows, and "revegetate" the mined lands with cover native to the area. Some money was provided for federal reclamation of already abandoned strip mines.

Reclamation itself may not be the chief problem created by the Act for coal companies, but rather the regulatory bureaucracy with its required reports, applications, approvals, permits, etc. As one coal operator put it: "Every day they want more and more coal production, then they put more and more roadblocks."[7]

## The Environmentalists:
## Man Against Technology

Everyone is against pollution. It is difficult to publicly oppose antipollution laws—who wants to stand up for dirt? Thus, the environmentalists begin with a psychological and political advantage: they are "clean" and their opponents are "dirty." The news media, Congress, executive agencies, and the courts can be moved to support "environmental protection" measures with little consideration of their costs—in jobs lost, in price increases, in unmet consumer demands, in increased dependence on foreign sources of energy. Industry—notably the electric power companies, oil and gas companies, auto makers, and coal companies—must fight a rear guard action, continually seeking delays, amendments, and adjustments in federal standards. They must endeavor to point out the increased costs to society of unreasonably high standards in environmental protection legislation. But industry is suspect; the environmentalists can charge that industry opposition to environmental protection is motivated by greed for higher profits. And the charge is partially true, although most of the cost of antipollution efforts is passed on to the consumer in the form of higher prices.

The environmentalists are generally upper-middle-class or upper-class individuals whose income and wealth are secure. Their aesthetic preferences for a no-growth, clean, unpolluted environment may take precedence over jobs and income which new industries can produce. Workers and small businessmen whose jobs or income depend upon energy production, oil refining, mining, smelting, or manufacturing are unlikely to be ardent environmentalists. But there is a psychological impulse in all of us to preserve scenic beauty, protect

[7]See Congressional Quarterly, *Energy Policy* (Washington: Congressional Quarterly Inc., 1979), p. 87.

wildlife, and conserve natural resources. It is easy to perceive industry and technology as the villain, and "man against technology" has a humanistic appeal.

Who are the environmentalists? The Sierra Club is the oldest of the environmentalist groups. (It was founded in 1892 by the naturalist John Muir, who was instrumental in establishing the U.S. national park system.) Despite its age, it is a militant and aggressive group, fighting strip mining, dams, power plants, roads, and industrial and residential development with court actions, legislative lobbying, and appeals to executive agencies.

Another aggressive environmentalist group is the Audubon Society. (It was founded in 1905 and named for the noted nineteenth-century bird artist John James Audubon.) Originally concerned with saving birds from extinction, the Society now has joined in a wide variety of antipollution efforts, particularly the opposition to the use of herbicides, insecticides, pesticides, and fertilizers.

The largest conservation group is the National Wildlife Federation. It contains three million members and finances itself in part by issuing beautiful poster stamps depicting wildlife. The Federation includes many hunters and fishermen and generally opposes pollution and destruction of wildlife habitat, but it is not considered as militant as the Sierra Club or Audubon Society.

Several new organizations were formed in recent years as the environmental issue grew more popular. Friends of the Environment, League of Conservation Voters, Environmental Defense Fund, and similar organizations have been created at the national level. Numerous local and state groups have also sprung up, sometimes in response to specific projects or issues. And liberal groups such as Common Cause (Washington's heaviest spending lobby) have frequently given support to the environmental cause.

What tactics are employed by the environmentalists? Typically when we think of interest groups we think of Congressional lobbying, and certainly this is an important aspect of the work of the environmental groups. But increasingly *court actions* have replaced legislative lobbying in emphasis among environmental groups. Many class action suits (where a group represents a number of individuals who claim to be injured by the current or proposed activities of the defendant) have been filed by environmental groups against industries and governmental agencies. Even where there is little clear evidence proving that the activity of the defendant damages the environment, a lawsuit can delay action, halt construction, and tie up the defendant in litigation for months or years. Another common court action—against federal agencies—is to bring suit claiming the agency has failed to file an acceptable "environmental impact statement" as required by the National Environmental Policy Act of 1969. Frequently agencies must halt work until court controversy over their "environmental impact statement" is resolved. Finally, of course, environmental groups can bring suit for enforcement of the various Clean Air and Water Quality Acts when it feels that EPA is not adequately enforcing them. Again, often the point is to tie up industries and government agencies in court litigation so as to delay and discourage projects considered undesirable by the environmental groups.

## The Regulatory Quagmire

Within the federal bureaucracy, various agencies appear to represent competing interest groups. The Environmental Protection Agency and the Council on Environmental Quality both owe their existence to increased concern with the environment, and both therefore reflect the views of environmentalist groups. On the other hand, the Department of Energy is concerned with maintaining the nation's supply of gas and electric power, and it is charged with the responsibility of developing new sources of energy as well as a coordinated energy policy. The EPA and CEQ frequently come in conflict with these other executive agencies. Who wins frequently depends upon the strength of various interests, the stand of the news media and their impact on public opinion, and the access of various agencies and interest groups to the White House.

The Environmental Protection Agency was created by executive order in 1970 to bring together a number of separate agencies in different departments charged with enforcing environmental regulations. The EPA director reports to the president. The EPA administers and enforces federal programs and laws in water quality control, clean air, solid waste disposal, pesticide control, toxic substances, noise abatement, and even radiation control. Many of the laws it enforces grant much discretion to EPA itself. EPA has been obliged to make some difficult decisions—granting the auto industry more time to meet emission standards, banning DDT, banning Mirex to fight fire ants, publishing mileage reports on automobiles, etc. EPA also distributes grants to state and local governments and conducts research on the possible harmful effects of various products.

Another organization with a key role in environmental policy making is the Council on Environmental Quality. CEQ was established by Congress in the National Environmental Policy Act of 1969. The CEQ has no direct enforcement powers; instead it "advises" the president on environmental questions. For example, CEQ advised the president against the Cross-Florida Barge Channel (a project which was already under construction to minimize East-coast to Gulf-coast shipping time), and the president ordered the Corps of Engineers to cease its construction. But CEQ's real power derives from a provision in the National Environmental Policy Act of 1969 that all federal agencies must submit statements to CEQ on the impact of any action which affects the environment. These "environmental impact statements" require federal agencies as well as state, local, and private organizations receiving federal monies, to file lengthy reports on "environmental impacts." It is reliably reported that very few of the statements are actually read by anyone at CEQ;[8] however, if CEQ wants to delay or obstruct a project, it can ask for endless revisions, changes, additions, etc., in the environmental impact statement. CEQ cannot by itself halt a project, but it can conduct public hearings for the press, pressure other governmental agencies, and make recommendations to the president. The courts have ruled that the requirement for an environmental impact statement is judicially enforceable.

## Summary

Group theory suggests that public policy reflects the balance of group interests. But the group struggle over energy and the environment has resulted in a virtual stalemate over policy direction and a paralysis of government action. The result is a failure of government to develop reasoned, consistent, and coherent energy policy.

1. The nation's energy needs conflict directly with the interests of the environmentalists. Environmentalist groups have opposed offshore oil drilling, pipeline construction, hydroelectric dams, strip mining of coal, the burning of coal, and the construction of new power plants, particularly nuclear plants. Government regulation of the price of domestic oil and gas, and the price of electricity, has also helped to keep down energy production within the United States. The result is increased dependency on foreign sources of energy (oil).

2. Industry groups urge that environmental restrictions be relaxed, that controls on domestic oil and gas prices be removed, and that tax incentives be provided to encourage additional investment in energy. Environmentalist groups usually stress conservation as the answer to the energy crisis. The clash over nuclear energy is especially bitter, with many environmentalists seeking to ban "nukes" and power companies contending they are the safest, least polluting source of energy available.

3. Support for environmental legislation (e.g., the Sierra Club,

---

[8]J. Clarence Davies and Barbara S. Davies, *The Politics of Pollution*, 2nd ed. (Indianapolis: Bobbs-Merrill, 1975), p. 118.

Audubon Society, Environmental Defense Fund) is strongest among upper-middle class and upper-class groups whose preferences for a clean, unpolluted environment take precedence over jobs, incomes, and places to live for workers and industries. The environmentalists not only engage in traditional lobbying activities in Congress, states, and communities, but more importantly they support class action law suits designed to enforce environmental laws, collect for damages to the environment, and tie up private industry and public agencies in lengthy, costly court litigation.

4. Immediate environmental problems center around air pollution, water pollution, and solid waste disposal. Federal policy has produced a series of Clean Air Acts, Water Pollution Control Acts, and a National Environmental Protection Act which created an Environmental Protection Agency (EPA) with broad regulatory powers. In addition, a Council on Environmental Quality (CEQ) requires "environmental impact statements" from all public and private agencies receiving federal funds, and advises federal agencies on environmental matters.

5. The Carter Administration initially tried to speed up the development of nuclear energy. But the opposition of environmentalists, and technical difficulties and costs of getting nuclear plants "on line," forced the Administration to shift its emphasis from nuclear energy to coal. However, environmental opposition to strip mining and the burning of high sulfur content coal have obstructed efforts to utilize America's abundant coal reserves.

6. The United States has failed to develop a clear, consistent, and coherent energy policy. The group struggle over energy and the environment has produced a deadlock and a general paralysis of governmental action.

## Bibliography

COMMONER, BARRY, *The Closing Circle*. New York: Knopf, 1971.

Congressional Quarterly, *Energy Policy*. Washington: Congressional Quarterly, 1979.

DAVIES, J. CLARENCE, and BARBARA S. DAVIES, *The Politics of Pollution*. 2nd ed. Indianapolis: Bobbs-Merrill, 1975.

FISHER, JOHN C., *Energy Crisis in Perspective*. New York: Wiley, 1974.

JONES, CHARLES O., *Clean Air*. Pittsburgh: University of Pittsburgh Press, 1976.

STOBAUGH, ROBERT, and DANIEL YERGIN, *Energy Future*. New York: Random House, 1979.

Federal assistance for cities: New York faces bankruptcy. *The Port Authority of New York & New Jersey.*

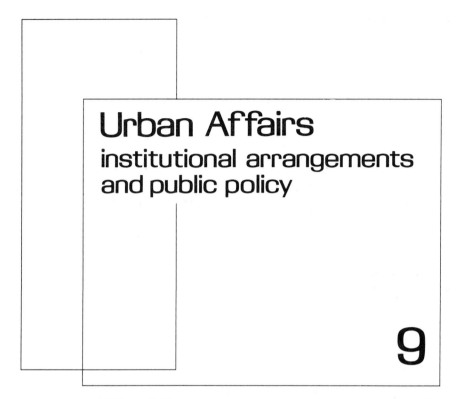

# Urban Affairs
## institutional arrangements and public policy

# 9

## Dilemmas of Urban Policy

Urban life has come under severe criticism in recent years. A newspaperman describes the dangers of the modern city:

> whose air grows fouler and more dangerous by the day, whose water is threatened increasingly by pollution, whose mobility is undermined by accumulations of vehicles and withering transit, whose educational systems reel under a growing variety of economic, social, and national emergencies, and whose entire pattern is assuming an ominous shape and sociological form, with well-to-do whites in their suburban cities ringing poverty-ridden minority groups widening at the core.[1]

The urban "crisis" is really a series of interrelated problems which affect the nation as a whole. Poverty, poor housing, racial conflict, crime and delinquency, social dependency, poor health, overcrowding, joblessness, ignorance, white flight to the suburbs, and fiscal imbalance are national problems. Yet their impact is increasingly concentrated in the nation's large cities.

The critical deficiency in federal urban policy is that there are no concrete goals or clear priorities in the hundreds of separate programs affecting cities. James Q. Wilson writes about urban policy:

[1]Mitchell Gordon, *Sick Cities: The Psychology and Pathology of American Urban Life* (Baltimore: Penguin, 1963), p. 3.

*We do not know what we are trying to accomplish. . . . Do we seek to raise stand-
ards of living, maximize housing choices, revitalize the commercial centers of our
cities, end suburban sprawl, eliminate discrimination, reduce traffic congestion, improve the quality of urban design, check crime and delinquency, strengthen the effectiveness of local planning, increase citizen participation in local government? All
these objectives sound attractive—in part, because they are rather vague—but unfortunately they are in many cases incompatible.*[2]

The institutional arrangements of American government have
proven remarkably well-suited for pursuing different policies toward
contradictory goals simultaneously. Government can maintain the support of competing groups in society by allowing different federal agencies to pursue incompatible goals and by permitting local communities
to follow competing policies with federal money.

For example, the two federal program areas that account for the
greatest expenditure of dollars for the physical improvement of cities
are (1) the federal highway and transportation programs, (2) the federal housing and urban renewal programs. The first is operated by the
Department of Transportation (DOT) and the second by the Department of Housing and Urban Development (HUD). The urban portion
of the interstate highway system cost billions of federal dollars; the effect of these dollars was to enable people to drive in and out of the
central city speedily, safely, and conveniently, and to open up suburban areas to business and residential expansion. Of course, these expressways also encouraged middle-class (mostly white) families to move
out of the central city and enabled commercial establishments to follow
them. This led to further racial segregation within the metropolitan region in housing and schools, and reduced the number of service jobs
available to the poor living in the city. The encouragement of longer
automobile trips from suburban residencies to downtown offices also
added to pollution, congestion, and energy consumption.

At the same time, the Federal Housing Administration (FHA),
and the Veterans Administration (VA), were encouraging home ownership by insuring mortgages that were written on easy terms for millions of middle-class (mostly white) Americans. Most of these mortgages were for new homes because it is cheaper to build on vacant land
and because so many prospective homeowners wanted to move to the
suburbs. So it turned out that these programs actually facilitated the
movement of middle-class people out of the central city.

In the meantime, the urban renewal was helping cities tear down
slum dwellings, often displacing the poor who lived there at considerable hardship, in order to make way for office buildings, hotels, civic
centers, industrial parks, and middle-class luxury apartments. In part,
this effort was intended to lure suburbanites back to the central city.

[2]James Q. Wilson, "The War on Cities," *The Public Interest* (Summer 1966), 10.

Although urban renewal reduced the overall supply of housing to the poor in cities, the federal government was assisting cities in building low-rent public housing units to add to the supply of housing for the poor.

Finally, the emphasis in federal urban programs has been on the *physical* characteristics of cities. Yet most observers now acknowledge that "the urban crisis" is not primarily, nor even significantly, a physical problem. It is not really housing, or highways, or urban rebuilding that lie at the heart of urban discontent. Instead when we think of the challenges confronting cities, we think of racial tension, crime, poverty, poor schools, residential segregation, rising welfare rolls, fiscal crisis— in short, all the major domestic problems facing the nation. In an urban society, *all* domestic problems become urban problems.

## HUD—Federal Housing and Urban Development Programs

The Department of Housing and Urban Development (HUD) is the federal agency concerned primarily with public housing, mortgage insurance, community development, and related programs. HUD administers federal programs in housing and urban affairs which were begun in the 1930s.

### Mortgage Insurance

The federal government began as early as 1934 to guarantee private mortgages against default by the individual home buyer, thereby enabling banks, savings and loan associations, and other lending agencies to provide long-term, low-interest, low-down payment mortgages for Americans wishing to buy their own homes. After checking the credit rating of the prospective buyer, HUD insures the private mortgage lender—bank, savings and loan company, or insurance company—of repayment of the loan in case the home buyer defaults. This reduces the risk and encourages mortgage lenders to make more loans at lower interest rates, lower down payments, and longer repayment periods. While these advantages in borrowing assist middle-class home buyers, the direct beneficiaries of mortgage insurance are the banks and mortgage-lending companies who are insured against losses. HUD also establishes minimum building standards for the homes it insures; these standards have raised the general quality of middle-class housing.

Mortgage insurance has been extremely successful in promoting home ownership among millions of middle-class Americans. Millions of families have financed their homes through federally-insured mortgages. (For many years, before the creation of the Department of

Housing and Urban Development, these federally insured mortgages were called FHA mortgages, referring to the Federal Housing Administration.) A great many of these mortgages financed suburban homes. In fact, the success of mortgage insurance programs may have contributed to the deterioration of the nation's central cities by enabling so many middle-class white families to acquire homes in the suburbs and to leave the city behind. HUD's mortgage insurance program is an entirely federal program, but its impact on city and suburban governments should not be underestimated.

In addition to a large mortgage insurance program, HUD also subsidizes the costs of flood insurance in flood-prone areas, riot reinsurance in urban areas which have experienced civil disturbances, and crime insurance in high-crime areas where private insurance is difficult to obtain.

### Public Housing

The Housing Act of 1937 initiated federal public housing programs to provide low-rent public housing for the poor who could not afford decent housing on the private market. The public housing program was designed for persons without jobs or incomes sufficient to enable them to afford home ownership, even with the help of mortgage insurance. HUD does *not* build, own, or operate its own housing projects; rather, it provides the necessary financial support to enable local communities to provide public housing for their poor if the communities choose to do so. HUD makes loans and grants to local public housing authorities established by local governments to build, own, and operate low-cost public housing. Local public housing authorities must keep rents low in relation to their tenants' ability to pay. This means that local public housing authorities operate at a loss and the federal government reimburses them for this loss. No community is required to have a Public Housing Authority; it must apply to HUD and meet federal standards in order to receive federal financial support.

Public housing has always been involved in more political controversy than mortgage insurance. Real estate and building interests, which *support* mortgage insurance because it expands their number of customers, have often opposed public housing on the grounds that it is socialist and wasteful. While in theory public housing serves individuals who cannot afford private housing, private real estate interests contend that public housing hurts the market for older homes and apartments. In addition, owners of slum dwellings seldom welcome competition from federally supported housing authorities. Political difficulties have also been encountered in the location of public housing units. Many Americans will support public housing for low-income persons, so long as it is not located in their own neighborhood. A majority of public housing occupants are black, and this automatically involves public housing in the politics of race.

In recent years many of the early supporters of public housing, including minority groups, labor, social workers, charitable organizations, and big-city political organizations have expressed doubts about the effects of public housing. Public housing, while providing improved living conditions, failed to eliminate poverty, ignorance, family disruption, juvenile delinquency, crime, and other characteristic troubles of the slums. Very often, the concentration of large numbers of poor persons with a great variety of social problems into a single, mass-housing project compounded their problems. The cost of central-city land required many big cities to build high-rise housing buildings of ten to twenty stories. These huge buildings frequently became unlivable due to such circumstances as crime in the hallways, elevators that seldom worked, drugs and human filth in halls and stairways, or families locking themselves in and alienating themselves from community life. Huge housing projects were impersonal and bureaucratic, and they often failed to provide many of the stabilizing neighborhood influences of the old slums. Children could be raised in public housing projects and never see a regularly employed male head of a household going to and from work. The behavior and value patterns of problem families were frequently reinforced.[3]

Moreover, removing thousands of people from neighborhood environments and placing them in the institution-like setting of large public housing developments very often increased their alienation from society and removed what few social controls existed in the slum neighborhood. A family living in public housing that became successful in finding employment and raising its income level faced eviction to make room for more "deserving" families. Finally, black groups often complained that public housing was a new form of racial segregation, and, indeed, the concentration of blacks among public housing dwellers does lead to a great deal of *de facto* segregation in housing projects.

Requests by cities for federal aid for public housing have far exceeded the amount of money appropriated by Congress. The result in most cities is a long list of those persons who are eligible for public housing for whom no space is available. An estimated two million people live in public housing in America, but ten million people are probably eligible for it under current standards.

To alleviate the shortage of public housing and to correct some of the problems involved in large-site housing projects, Congress authorized several additional approaches to supplement public housing—

[3]For the story of the virtual collapse of public housing in St. Louis, see Eugene J. Meehan, "Looking the Gift Horse in the Mouth," *Urban Affairs Quarterly* (June 1975), 423–63.

a rent subsidy program, a dispersed public housing site program, and a "turnkey" program of acquiring new public housing. The rent subsidy program authorizes federal grants to local housing authorities to give cash grants to assist families in meeting the rent in "approved" privately owned housing projects. The grants are paid to the housing owners; the tenants are required to contribute only a small portion of the rent. The dispersed site program provides federal grants to local housing authorities to encourage them to buy or lease single homes or small apartment complexes throughout the city as public housing units. The "turnkey" program encourages local authorities to purchase completed housing projects from private builders. The purpose of these programs is to speed up the availability of public housing units and, perhaps more importantly, to eliminate dependence upon large, institution-like public housing facilities and to achieve more dispersal of public housing residents throughout the community.

### The Private Market and Low Income Housing

The private homebuilding industry and mortgage market continues to play the dominant role in filling the nation's housing needs. Over two million new housing units are built each year in the United States. Only about 600,000 of these are financed through federally guaranteed mortgages. Only about 30,000 new public housing units are produced each year. Thus, the private sector continues to provide the bulk of housing and housing finance in America. The median sales price of a new single-family home in the private market is now over $60,000; this price excludes over half of the nation's families from the purchase of a *new* single family home. But private apartments play a major role in housing—slightly less than half of all new housing units are apartments.

The private sector also plays the major role in providing *low-cost* housing. The mobile home industry is generally ignored by public housing advocates, but in fact this industry has provided the great bulk of low-cost housing for America. Approximately 500,000 mobile home units are produced each year, compared to only 30,000 public housing units. If low-income Americans depended exclusively on public housing, most would be camping out in the cold. Fortunately, the mobile home industry has filled the gap in low-income housing without government assistance.

### Community Development

In the original Housing Act of 1937, the idea of "urban renewal" was closely tied to public housing. Slum residences were to be torn down as public housing sites were constructed. Later, in the Housing

Act of 1949, the urban renewal program was separated from public housing, and the federal government undertook to support a broad program of urban redevelopment to help cities fight a loss in population and to reclaim the economic importance of the core cities. After World War II, the suburban exodus had progressed to the point where central cities faced slow decay and death if large public efforts were not undertaken. Urban renewal could not be undertaken by private enterprise because it was not profitable; suburban property was usually cheaper than downtown property, and it did not require large-scale clearance of obsolete buildings. Moreover, private enterprise did not possess the power of eminent domain;[4] this power enables the city to purchase the many separately owned small tracts of land needed to insure an economically feasible new investment. For many years, the federal government provided financial support for specific removal projects in cities.

In the Housing and Community Development Act of 1974, federal grants to save the nation's central cities were consolidated into a *community development bloc grant* program. Cities and counties are authorized to receive these bloc grants to assist them in eliminating slums, increasing the supply of low-income housing, conserving existing housing, improving health, safety, welfare, and public service, improving planning, and preserving property with special value. Community development bloc grants are based on a formula which includes population, housing overcrowding, and extent of poverty. No local "matching" funds are required. Communities are required to submit an annual application which describes their housing and redevelopment needs and a comprehensive strategy for meeting those needs.

Community development bloc grants can be used by local authorities to acquire blighted land, clear off or modernize obsolete or dilapidated structures, and make downtown sites available for new uses. When the sites are physically cleared of the old structures, they can be resold to private developers for residential, commercial, or industrial use, and the difference between the costs of acquisition and clearance and the income from the private sale to the developers is paid for by the federal government. In other words, local authorities sustain a loss in their redevelopment activities and this loss is made up by federal grants.

No city is required to engage in redevelopment, but if one wishes federal financial backing, it must show in its application that it has developed a comprehensive program for redevelopment and the prevention of future blight. A city must demonstrate that it has adequate building and health codes, good zoning and subdivision control regu-

---

[4]The power to take private property for public purposes, with fair compensation to the owner, whether or not the owner wishes to sell.

lations, sufficient local financing and public support, and a comprehensive plan of development with provisions for relocating displaced persons.

Urban redevelopment is best understood from an economic standpoint. The key to success is to encourage private developers to purchase the land and make a heavy investment in middle- or high-income housing or in commercial or industrial use. In fact, before undertaking a project, local authorities frequently "find a developer first, and then see what interests him." The city cannot afford to purchase land, thereby taking it off the tax rolls, invest in its clearance, and be stuck without a buyer. A private developer must be encouraged to invest in the property and thus enhance the value of the central city. Over time, a city can more than pay off its investment by increased tax returns from redeveloped property and hence make a "profit." Thus, many people can come out of a project feeling successful—the city increases its tax base and annual revenues, the private developer makes a profit, and mayors can point to the physical improvements in the city that occurred during their administration.

Moreover, there are many favorable "spillover effects" of a successful urban renewal project:

> 1. Each project stimulates jobs, not only during demolition and construction but also later in servicing the new housing, business, or industry.
>
> 2. The city increases its ability to attract and maintain middle-class residents as well as business and industry.
>
> 3. Universities, hospitals, cultural centers, etc., can be built or expanded when all or part of a redevelopment project is turned over to public purposes.
>
> 4. Downtown areas can be revitalized and attract private development in areas adjacent to redevelopment projects.

However, there are also drawbacks to urban renewal. The concern for "profit" frequently leads to fiscal conservatism on the part of local authorities. They do not undertake to renew the very worst slum areas because of the excessive costs involved and because private developers may not wish to go into these areas even after renewal. More importantly, the financial considerations often dictate the choice of profitable middle- or upper-income housing or commercial or industrial use of renewed land, rather than low-cost private or public housing development. Developers make more profit on the former types of investments, and the city gets better tax returns. The effect of redevelopment is frequently to redistribute land from lower-income to higher-income purposes.

Relocation is the most sensitive problem in redevelopment. The vast majority of people relocated by redevelopment are poor and black. They have no interest in moving simply to make room for middle- or higher-income housing, or business or industry, or universities, hospitals, and other public facilities. Even though relocated families are frequently given priority for public housing, there is not nearly enough space in public housing to contain them all. They are simply moved from one slum to another. The slum landowner is paid a just price for his land, but the renter receives only a small moving allowance. Redevelopment officials assist relocated families in finding new housing and generally claim success in moving families to better housing. But frequently the result is higher rents, and redevelopment may actually help to create new slums in other sections of the city. Small businessmen are especially vulnerable to relocation. They often depend on a small, well-known neighborhood clientele, and they cannot compete successfully when forced to move to other sections of the city.

Political support for redevelopment has come from mayors who wish to make their reputation by engaging in large-scale renewal activities that produce impressive "before" and "after" pictures of the city. Businessmen wishing to preserve downtown investments and developers wishing to acquire land in urban centers have provided a solid base of support for downtown renewal. Mayors, planners, the press, and the good-government forces have made urban redevelopment politically much more popular than public housing. When the dislocated persons are poor and black, and the project is used for middle- or high-income predominantly white residents, the charge is leveled that urban renewal is simply "Negro removal."[5]

Originally liberal reform groups and representatives of urban minorities supported urban renewal as an attack on the slum problem. Over the years, however, many of these groups have become disenchanted with urban renewal, complaining that urban renewal has not considered the plight of the slum dweller. Too often, slum areas have been cleared and replaced with high-income residential developments or commercial or industrial developments that do not directly help the plight of the slum dwellers. Urban renewal authorities are required to pay landowners a just price for their land, but slum dwellers who rent their apartments are shoved about the city with only a minimal amount of support from the "relocation" division of urban renewal authority. Downtown areas have been improved in appearance, but usually at the price of considerable human dislocation.

[5]The original and now classic attack on federal urban renewal policies is Jane Jacobs, *The Death and Life of Great American Cities* (New York: Random House, 1961).

## DOT—Public Highway Policy

Few inventions have had such a far-reaching effect on the life of the American people as the automobile. Henry Ford built one of the first gasoline-driven carriages in America in 1893, and by 1900 there were eight thousand automobiles registered in the U.S. The Model T was introduced in the autumn of 1908. By concentrating on a single un-lovely but enduring model, and by introducing assembly line processes, the Ford Motor Company began producing automobiles for the masses. By 1921 there were over one million cars in existence, and the auto industry was established in the United States. Today there are nearly 150 million registered motor vehicles in the nation, one for every two persons living in the country.

It was in the Federal Aid Road Act of 1916 that the federal government first provided regular funds for highway construction under terms that gave the federal government considerable influence over state policy. For example, if states wanted to get federal money, they were required to have a highway department and to have their plans for highway construction approved by federal authorities. In 1921, federal aid was limited to a connected system of principal state highways, now called the "federal aid primary highway system." Uniform standards were prescribed and even a uniform numbering system was added, such as "US 1," or "US 30." The emphasis of the program was clearly rural.

Later the federal government also designated a federal aid "secondary" system of farm-to-market roads and provided for "urban extensions" of primary roads, in addition to the federal aid for the primary highway system. Federal funds for primary and secondary and urban extension roads, commonly called "ABC funds," are determined by three separate formulas, but all take into account area, population, postal routes, and mileage. These ABC funds are generally matched on a 70 percent federal and a 30 percent state basis. In the use of their federal funds, states make the surveys and plans, let the contracts, and supervise the construction. All ABC funds remain under the administrative control of the states, who are responsible for their operation and maintenance. All payments to contractors for work done on any federal project are made by the states; the federal government makes very few direct payments.

In 1956, Congress authorized a national system of interstate and defense highways ("I" highways)—now the most important feature of the federal highway policy. At that time, Congress provided for its completion by 1972, and allocated the costs on the basis of 90 percent federal and 10 percent state. The Federal Highway Act of 1956, as amended, authorizes 42,500 miles of highway, designed to connect principal metropolitan and industrial centers, and thereby shifts the emphasis of federal highway activity from rural to urban needs. Figure 9–1 shows the complete "I" highway system. Although the system constitutes less than 2 percent of the total surfaced roads in the nation, it carries over 20 percent of all highway traffic. The Department of Transportation has been given strong supervisory powers, including the selection of routes (it can even transfer interstate mileage and funds out of noncooperative states), but administration and execution are still left to state highway departments. Federal monies are paid to the states, not to the contractors, as the work progresses. The Federal Highway Trust Fund is responsible for the orderly scheduling of federal aid and the phasing out of reimbursement requests for the states.

Controversy has already developed about what to do with federal highway funds after the completion of the "I" highway system. The federal gasoline tax is currently the source of all federal highway funds. These tax receipts are currently deposited in the Federal Highway Trust Fund for disbursement as federal aid to the states for highway construction. Automotive and highway interests want to keep it that way. They want to use federal gasoline taxes exclusively for maintenance and repair and for the construction of additional links and connectors in the "I" highway system. But others have argued that the federal government should direct its attention and resources to mass

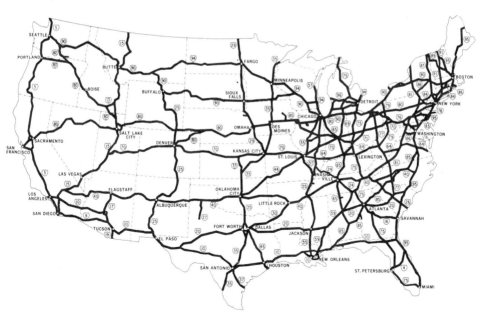

**Fig. 9–1**  The national system of interstate and defense highways
*Source:* U.S. Department of Transportation, Federal Highway Administration.

transportation projects. Urban interests, including mayors and planners, combined with railroad interests, have urged greater federal investment in urban mass transit—trains, subways, buses—and high-speed rail connections between major metropolitan areas, particularly on the eastern seaboard.

## The Metropolitan Transportation Mess

To date, expressways have failed in alleviating the transportation problems in large cities. City planners, transportation specialists, and nearly all who have studied the modern city's traffic picture readily agree that the only way to relieve traffic congestion and preserve central cities is to get people out of private automobiles and into public transit, that is, "to move people, not vehicles."[6] Technological and economic evidence points to rail transit as the only reasonable way to move persons in and out of the central city at rush hours. Automobiles on expressways can move about two thousand people per lane per hour, buses can move between six thousand and nine thousand, but rail systems can carry up to sixty thousand persons per hour. In other words, one rail line is estimated to be equal to that of twenty or thirty expressway lanes of automobiles in terms of its ability to move people.

Of course, as most commuters know all too well, privately-owned commuter railroads are generally in deplorable operating condition and even worse financial condition. The average citizen has a large investment in his or her automobile; the automobile has become a way of life for the nation's suburbanites. Few Americans want to see their financial investment sit in a garage all day. Americans clearly prefer private automobile transportation and costly expressways to mass transit, regardless of the arguments of transportation experts. The result is that existing private mass transit facilities have been steadily losing customers over the last two decades. As their operating costs increase and their patronage declines, many private bus and rail carriers resort to raising fares, reducing service, and putting off maintenance— all of which simply turns away more customers and accelerates the downward spiral. Very often service is poor and equipment is dirty and uncomfortable. Spokesmen for commuter railroads insist that the fault is not theirs—they must compete with automobiles operating on publicly subsidized, multimillion-dollar expressways. Most Americans cannot be lured away from their beloved automobiles and the privacy and convenience they think it gives them.

It is virtually impossible for the nation's major cities to continue

[6]See Francis Bello, "The City and the Car," *The Exploding Metropolis* (New York: *Fortune* Magazine, 1957).

to rely upon automobile transportation over expressways to handle projected increases in transportation needs. Most of our cities are already experiencing expressway traffic jams at rush hours and a resulting increase in time and cost to the average automobile commuter. Needless to say, the cost of mass transit facilities on a per capita basis is small compared with the cost of expressway building. It is necessary to provide public subsidies to commuter rail companies or to have city governments acquire these facilities at a loss if commuter service is to be restored. The cost of such public subsidies is very small in comparison with the cost of building and maintaining expressways. Thus, mass transit is a considerable savings to most cities, even if fares do not meet operating expenses. Moreover, new, speedier, more comfortable, air-conditioned, high-capacity trains with fewer stops and more frequent time schedules may lure many riders back to public transportation.

Mass transit facilities, while cheaper than expressways, are still quite costly, particularly for cities that do not already have commuter rail service. Proponents of greater federal aid for mass transit argue that cities and states do not have sufficient resources to build mass transit facilities. They argue that mass transit is cheaper than expressway construction and that expressways can never handle predicted traffic increases, anyhow. They emphasize the costs of traffic jams in time and wages lost and their economic impact on central cities. They point out that privately owned mass transportation facilities fail to show profits and that, therefore, these companies are not in a position to make improvements in equipment, facilities, and services at fare levels that would attract riders. Rural opposition stresses the increased centralization at the federal level that would be involved in federally aided mass transit. They object to the idea that the entire nation, including rural areas, should be asked to contribute to solving transportation problems of the nation's cities. Moreover, they are doubtful about the feasibility of convincing Americans that they should give up the convenience of their automobiles for mass transit.

For many years the federal government has subsidized the building of highways, particularly the interstate highways for which the federal government assumed 90 percent of the costs. But only recently has the federal government shown any comparable interest in mass transportation. The "interstate" highway system, despite its name, has carried a major share of intrametropolitan city-suburban traffic. However, the energy crisis has accelerated federal efforts in mass transit.

The Department of Transportation is authorized to make grants to cities for both construction and operation of mass transit systems. In many cities this has simply meant the creation of a local mass transit authority and the purchase of buses. But in some cities, massive new mass transit programs have been developed.

Perhaps the most striking new efforts in mass transit are San Francisco's BART (Bay Area Rapid Transit), Washington, D.C.'s METRO, and Atlanta's MARTA (Metropolitan Atlanta Rapid Transit Authority). These are large new projects in which the cities and the federal governments have pumped hundreds of millions of dollars. They incorporate all of the latest features of modern, pleasant, rapid, convenient, and efficient mass transit. If they turn out to be successful in terms of ridership and their ultimate costs do not balloon out of proportion to their benefits, they could become models for future federal urban policy. Despite the costs of these projects, the severe gasoline shortage may make new mass transit facilities a necessity in large cities.

## Evaluation:
## Structural Problems In Federal Urban Policy

For over thirty years the federal government has been directly involved in housing and urban development programs. Yet today we continue to speak of the "urban crisis"—racial conflict, inadequate housing, air and water pollution, poor schools, crime and delinquency, crowded hospitals, traffic congestion, crippling city tax burdens, poorly paid policemen and other municipal workers, and so on.

The failure of federal urban policy to resolve these problems is *not* merely a product of structural or organizational defects in federal programs. Indeed, it is a serious difficulty of the institutional approach that it focuses on structural or organization problems when in fact the real issues are much more deeply rooted in social or economic dimensions of urban life. Poverty, racism, crime, pollution, and other serious maladies afflicting humankind are not likely to be cured by tinkering with the organizational structure of government.

Yet it is possible to identify briefly a number of organizational and administrative problems that are serious obstacles to the development of an effective federal policy in housing and urban affairs:[7]

1. First of all, the major thrust of federal policy is now and always has been a commitment to the physical aspects of urban life—the provision of housing and transportation, the rebuilding of central cities, and development of community facilities, etc. It may be that the "urban crisis" is not primarily or even significantly a problem of housing or transit or facilities. It may be a problem of human conflict in crowded, high-density, socially heterogeneous areas.

[7]For a more detailed critique of federal urban policy, see James Q. Wilson, "The War on Cities," *The Public Interest* (Summer 1966), 1–12; and Edward C. Banfield, *The Unheavenly City* (Boston: Little, Brown, 1970).

2. Federal policy has frequently worked at cross-purposes, reflecting organizational fragmentation of programs. For example, community development tries to save central cities, while federal highway policy builds expressways making possible the suburban exodus and federal mortgage insurance has helped suburbanites to buy their own homes.

3. The public housing program has tried to increase the supply of low-rent housing for the poor, while the urban renewal program, together with highway building, has torn down low-rent housing.

4. Federal civil rights policy is committed to desegregation but many large public housing projects concentrate blacks in *de facto* segregated neighborhoods and schools.

5. Federal policy has stressed *local* administration with local autonomy, flexibility, and participation in decision making. Yet this has meant that housing and urban renewal have been employed in different places for different purposes—in some places to help get blacks out of white neighborhoods, in others to subsidize white middle-class residents to come back to the central city, in others to restore business to downtown department stores, in others to build dramatic civic monuments or assist university expansion, in others to build sports palaces, museums, or other middle-class centers, and in still others to improve the quality of life for urban blacks.

6. Direct federal-to-city grants for community development assist hard-pressed central cities, but generally overlook the possibilities for regional or metropolitan-wide housing and urban renewal programs. If it is true that segregation, slum housing, poverty, crime, and so on, are responsibilities of the entire metropolitan population, then grants to regional organizations for the implementation of housing and urban development policy would appear more appropriate than grants to cities.

7. Federal grant-in-aid programs provide money for specific purposes—frequently "new" or "innovative" or "demonstration" programs. Yet the real urban crisis may be occurring in the provision of traditional municipal services—policy protection, sewage disposal, sanitation—and what is required is the upgrading of existing services, not necessarily the initiation of "new" or "innovative" or "demonstration" programs.

8. The maze of federal grant-in-aid programs for cities (nearly 500 separate programs with separate purposes and guidelines) is uncoordinated and bureaucratic in character. Mayors and other municipal officials spend a great deal of time in "grantmanship"—learning where to find federal funds, how to apply, and how to write applications in such a way as to appear to meet the purpose and guidelines of the program.

9. The federal government has never set any meaningful priority among its hundreds of grant programs. The result is that too few dollars chase too many goals. Cities are sometimes pressured to apply for funds for projects they do not really need simply because federal funds are available, while they may receive little or no federal assistance for more vital programs.

The reason for many of these administrative and organization problems is not merely incompetency on the part of government planners. Institutional analysis is misleading when it implies that these problems are strictly institutional. Frequently conflicting policies, incompatible goals, and competing government programs reflect underlying conflicts over public policy. Government institutions often accommodate conflict over public policy by enacting conflicting policies and establishing separate agencies to implement these policies. We can only admire a political system that so neatly accommodates conflicting demands!

An alternative approach to the organizational and administrative problems in federal grant-in-aid programs is that of providing unrestricted *federal bloc grants* to states or cities with few or no strings attached. A related approach is that of *federal revenue sharing* where a certain percentage of federal tax collections would be turned back to states or cities for their own use. Bloc grants are given by the federal government for stated purposes, such as law enforcement or community development, and states or cities spend the money for these purposes largely as they see fit. Revenue sharing gives states and cities access to the fiscal resources of the federal government and ensures state and local control over the use of these funds.

In the State and Local Fiscal Assistance Act of 1972, the federal government adopted the principle of revenue sharing. Cities now enjoy a small but significant income from shared federal revenues which cities may use for purposes of their own choosing with few strings attached. (Revenue sharing is described in more detail in Chapter 10.)

In the Housing and Community Development Act of 1974 the notion of bloc grants was applied to the areas of urban renewal and community facilities. A single bloc grant is made available to cities for community development; this bloc grant program replaces separate categorical grant programs in urban renewal, model cities, water and sewer, open space land, and public facilities. The amount of each city's grant is calculated by a formula based on population, overcrowding, and poverty. The community bloc grant approach grew out of the nation's experience with overlapping and uncoordinated, specialized grant-in-aid programs for cities, and the unsuccessful attempt of the "Model Cities" program in the late-1960s to rationalize federal urban policy. The ill-fated Model Cities Program was announced in 1966 by President Lyndon Johnson as an effort to bring order to the maze of fragmented, uncoordinated, and often contradictory urban grant programs. The program designated 150 cities as demonstration cities in which federal City Demonstration Agencies would undertake to coordinate all federal grant programs. All federal grant applications from a demonstration city—public housing, urban renewal, community facilities, manpower training, transportation, antipoverty, education, etc.—were supposed to be "cleared" by the City Demonstration Agency. As might be expected, this created more mountains of red tape, and functional agencies resented interference with their activities by Model City staffers.[8] The Model Cities Program greatly underestimated institutional barriers to program coordination among federal agencies. The confusion and failure of the Model Cities Program, which was abandoned in 1974, paved the way for the new bloc grant approach. Both bloc grants and revenue sharing place responsibility for coordination in program development in the hands of local officials.

The issue of bloc grants and revenue sharing extends well beyond the area of housing and urban development. Indeed, the structure of American federalism is vitally affected by the direction of federal grant-in-aid policy. Bloc grants and revenue-sharing proposals are generally supported by those groups that fear centralization of power in federal bureaucracies. In addition, state and local officials welcome the notion of assigning the federal government the unhappy task of collecting money, while retaining for themselves the more agreeable task of deciding how the money should be spent. Many mayors support bloc grants and revenue sharing only on the guarantee that federal money will be given directly to cities and not allocated to state governments. Some urban groups—notably, blacks and poor people—are distrustful of state and local decision making, and would probably prefer the present arrangements, however chaotic, to any organizational shifts that would threaten their interests. The federal bureaucracies themselves are less than enthusiastic about relinquishing too much control over policy making to state and local authorities.

## Federal Assistance for Cities:
## New York Faces Bankruptcy

New York City's near bankruptcy has focused new attention on the fiscal problems facing large cities, and has raised the question of what, if anything, the federal government should do about it.

[8]See Bernard J. Frieden and Marshall Kaplan, *The Politics of Neglect: Urban Aid from Model Cities to Revenue Sharing* (Cambridge, Mass.: MIT Press, 1975); and Christopher C. Demuth, "Deregulating the Cities," *The Public Interest* (Summer 1976), 115–28.

Like other large cities, New York has been losing much of its middle-class residential tax base. As the new immigrants arrived, the need for social services increased, and this required higher taxes. But higher taxes, together with social problems in the schools, rising crime rates, drug abuse, and so on, hastened the exodus of the white middle class from the city. Even more worrisome in financial terms was that many of the large industrial corporations which had maintained their headquarters in New York began to leave the city, often at the request of their office employees.

Yet New York had always taken pride in its treatment of the poor, welcoming wave after wave of new immigrants. From the early days of the Tammany Hall machine, through the flamboyant days of Mayors Jimmy Walker and Fiorello La Guardia, to the liberal visions of recent Mayors Robert Wagner and John Lindsay, the city political organization catered to the needs, and won the votes, of the city's large needy population. The city provided liberal welfare benefits; a costly school system; libraries, parks, and playgrounds; day-care centers and drug abuse programs; scores of publicly financed city hospitals; and a large tuition-free City University of New York, which accepted any city high-school graduate, whatever his or her grades. The city paid high salaries to a large number of city employees (338,000 for a city of 7 million). Most city employees could retire at half-pay after 20 or 25 years of service. As a result of these many benefits and services, the per capita cost of running New York City was higher than any other city in the nation. (However, New York carries some burdens, like welfare and education, that other cities share with county, special district, or state governments.)

New York City spends more than any other state or local government in the nation—over $15 billion in a year. The problem was that the city was collecting less than $12 billion a year in revenue. The resulting deficits have been piling up over the years; in 1975 the city was $15 billion in debt and falling deeper into red ink each year. How are New York debts financed? Like other cities, New York sells municipal bonds to banks, investment companies, and private individuals. To help cities keep down the cost of borrowing, the federal government does not tax the interest income on municipal bonds, thus encouraging wealthy investors to buy "munies" even at lower interest rates rather than corporate bonds with taxable interest. So most cities have little trouble borrowing money. Indeed, as old debts come due, cities can usually borrow anew to pay them off, thereby continuing to "float" their municipal indebtedness.

But what happens when banks and investors realize that a city is getting deeper and deeper into the red with little prospect of ever balancing its budget or reducing its debt? If banks and investors decline to purchase new city bonds and turn in bonds which have become due for payment, and the city has no money to meet these obligations, the result is *municipal bankruptcy*. This probably means that a federal bankruptcy court would take over the city—cutting budgets, reorganizing agencies, and removing most of the power over spending from elected city officials.

For many years, under popular Mayors Robert Wagner and John Lindsay, the city's comptroller, Abraham Beame, postponed New York City's financial crisis by budgetary gimmicks. Many current expenses, salaries, and supplies were shifted to the capital construction budget which should cover only long-term projects for which the city can borrow money. Other strategies included deliberately overestimating revenues, allowing semi-independent city "authorities" to borrow money, asking for "advances" on federal and state grant-in-aid programs, and draining various trust funds. In 1973 Abraham Beame was elected mayor, but he was no longer able to hide the city's financial plight.

The New York City banks insisted that the city balance its budget and undertake a long-range program to reduce its debts. The banks would no longer lend the city money unless the city displayed greater fiscal responsibility. The real financial "crunch" came in the fall of 1975. The city was unable to borrow money, outstanding debts were falling due, and there was not enough cash to pay city employees, welfare recipients, or bondholders. The State of New York itself was also threatened with bankruptcy because banks and investors began to distrust any bonds with a "New York" label. Indeed, the entire market for municipal bonds of cities everywhere began to dry up; investors began to flee the municipal bond markets; and cities throughout the nation were forced to pay higher interest rates to borrow money. For several hours New York City teetered on the verge of default and bankruptcy. New York State also appeared headed for bankruptcy. The State of New York, under the leadership of Governor Hugh Carey, created a new Municipal Assistance Corporation ("Big Mac") to help sell city bonds and oversee the city's budget. But without spending restraint by the city and new responsible accounting procedures, even Big Mac could not sell New York city bonds on the open market. So, Governor Hugh Carey and Mayor Abraham Beame went to Washington in a last-ditch attempt to stave off bankruptcy.

Initially New York's request for federal aid was met with strong presidential opposition. Republican President Gerald Ford quickly perceived a campaign issue for 1976: liberal Democratic fiscal irresponsibility leads to bankruptcy. The president threatened to veto any congressional "bail-out" of the city, and his tough stand was widely applauded in the Midwest and West. The New York Daily News headlined the president's stand: "FORD TO CITY: DROP DEAD."

While Ford's opposition to federal aid was politically popular, the specter of a New York City and New York State bankruptcy was an economic nightmare. It is estimated that 30 percent of all municipal bonds are from New York City or State, and the "ripple effect" of such a massive bankruptcy might lead to the fiscal collapse of many other cities throughout the nation. Over 500 banks have more than 20 percent of their reserve in New York City or State bonds, and widespread bank closings might occur with default. In a recession-weakened economy, a massive city-state bankruptcy could plunge the nation into another 1930s depression.

Eventually, all of the participants in New York's fiscal crisis were forced to come to an agreement. The federal government agreed to provide the city with over $2 billion in annual revolving credit; sales taxes in the city were increased to 9 percent (the highest in the nation); the banks which were holding city bonds were forced to accept delays in principal and interest payments; the city was forced to make additional budget cuts; the unions were obliged to accept additional manpower cuts and to invest some of their pension funds in New York City bonds.

In the 1977 mayoral election, a moderate and fiscally responsible Democrat, Edward Koch, defeated the incumbent Abraham Beame and the flamboyant Bella Abzug. The new mayor gradually reduced the number of city employees and whittled away at some of the city's debt. The Carter Administration was friendlier to the city than the Ford Administration. The New York City Loan Guarantee Act of 1978 gave federal guarantees to some New York City and Big Mac bonds and enabled the city to begin a long program designed to restore financial solvency.

But New York's future is still uncertain. Increased taxes and reduced services may speed the exodus of taxpaying citizens and corporations from the city, creating more financial problems in the future.

## Summary

The urban crisis is not only, or even primarily, a problem of governmental organization or administration. The institutional approach is misleading to the extent that it implies that reforming governmental institutions in the metropolis can solve problems of urban blight, inadequate housing, crime and delinquency, poverty and poor health, pollution, racial tension, and other urban ills. Yet institutional arrangements are linked to the nature of the urban environment and even to the content of urban policy. Let us summarize our ideas about these linkages:

1. Federal housing and urban development policy centers around direct federal-to-city grants-in-aid for public housing, urban renewal, community facilities and related programs, together with mortgage insurance programs administered by the federal government itself. These programs are organized and administered separately from federal grants programs in education, welfare, economic opportunity, and transportation. These programs have emphasized the physical aspects of urban life.

2. Frequently federal programs in urban areas have worked at cross-purposes, reflecting organizational fragmentation. However, competing goals and conflicting policies reflect underlying conflicts over urban affairs rather than merely organizational problems.

3. The question of federal control versus state or local autonomy in urban policy raises broad questions of centralization and decentralization in the American federal system. For example, *local* housing authorities may pursue policies desired by community majorities but run afoul of *national* housing policy.

4. The maze of different federal agencies and programs distributing grants-in-aid for different purposes results in serious problems for local officials who are trying to maximize the amount of federal money available for their communities.

5. Institutional barriers between federal agencies make it difficult to coordinate federal programs at the local level. Bloc grants, as well as federal revenue sharing, turn over responsibility for program development and coordination to local officials.

6. The nation's largest cities, especially New York, are confronted with problems which transcend their own boundaries. The flight of white middle-class residents to the suburbs, the influx of the poor and unskilled, the concentration of social problems in the inner cities, and erosion of the cities' tax bases have all contributed to financial problems of these cities—problems which only federal assistance may be able to resolve.

## Bibliography

BANFIELD, EDWARD C., *The Unheavenly City*. Boston: Little, Brown, 1970.

BANFIELD, EDWARD C., and JAMES Q. WILSON, *City Politics*. Cambridge, Mass.: Harvard University Press, 1963.

BOLLENS, JOHN C., and HENRY J. SCHMANDT, *The Metropolis*, 2nd ed. New York: Harper & Row, 1970.

HAWKINS, BRET W., *Politics and Urban Policies*. New York: Bobbs-Merrill, 1971.

WOLMAN, HAROLD, *Politics of Federal Housing*. New York: Dodd, Mead, 1971.

TVA's Wheeler Dam: dimensions of government spending.

# Priorities
# and Price Tags
## incrementalism at work

# 10

Too often we think of budgeting as the dull province of clerks and statisticians. Nothing could be more mistaken. The budget is the single most important policy statement of any government. The expenditure side of the budget tells us "who gets what" in public funds, and the revenue side of the budget tells us "who pays the cost." There are few government activities or programs that do not require an expenditure of funds, and no public funds may be spent without budgetary authorization. Deciding what goes into a budget (the budgetary process) provides a mechanism for reviewing government programs, assessing their cost, relating them to financial resources, making choices among alternative expenditures, and determining the financial effort that a government will expend on these programs. Budgets determine what programs and policies are to be increased, decreased, lapsed, initiated, or renewed. The budget lies at the heart of public policy.[1]

## Dimensions of Government Spending

Governments do many things that cannot be measured in dollars. Nevertheless, government expenditures are the best available measure

[1]See Aaron Wildavsky, *The Politics of the Budgetary Process* (Boston: Little, Brown, 1964).

of the overall dimensions of government activity. There are few public policies that do not require an expenditure of funds. Budgets represent government policies with price tags attached.

The expenditures of *all* governments in the United States—federal, state, and local—grew from $1.7 billion in 1902 to over $900 billion in 1980 (see Table 10–1). A great deal of the increase in government activity can be attributed to growth in the nation's population. And a great deal of the increase in dollar amounts spent by government is exaggerated by the diminishing value of the dollar—that is, by inflation. If we are to measure the growth of government activity accurately, we must examine government expenditures *per person*, and do so in *constant dollars*. This enables us to view past and present government activity in relation to the size of the population and the value of the dollar. It turns out that *per capita* expenditures of all governments *in constant dollars* increased from $84 to over $1,650 from 1902 to 1980. Thus, we note that the increase in government spending cannot be attributed merely to increases in population or the devaluation of the dollar; government activity has grown much faster than both the population and inflation.

**TABLE 10–1**   Growth in Population, Wealth, and Government Activities Over Eight Decades

|  | GNP | | All Government Spending | | |
|---|---|---|---|---|---|
|  | Population Millions | Billions | Billions | Per Capita Constant Dollars | Percent of GNP |
| 1902 | 79.2 | 21.6 | 1.7 | 84 | 7.7 |
| 1913 | 97.2 | 39.1 | 3.2 | 107 | 8.2 |
| 1922 | 110.1 | 74.0 | 9.3 | 174 | 12.5 |
| 1927 | 119.0 | 96.0 | 11.2 | 190 | 11.6 |
| 1932 | 124.9 | 58.5 | 12.4 | 254 | 21.3 |
| 1936 | 128.2 | 82.7 | 16.8 | 316 | 20.8 |
| 1940 | 132.6 | 100.6 | 20.4 | 353 | 20.3 |
| 1944 | 138.9 | 211.4 | 109.9 | 1,429 | 52.0 |
| 1946 | 141.9 | 210.7 | 79.7 | 866 | 37.8 |
| 1950 | 152.3 | 284.6 | 70.3 | 593 | 24.7 |
| 1952 | 157.6 | 347.0 | 99.8 | 751 | 28.8 |
| 1955 | 165.9 | 397.5 | 110.7 | 762 | 27.9 |
| 1960 | 180.7 | 502.6 | 151.3 | 848 | 30.1 |
| 1962 | 186.6 | 554.9 | 175.8 | 933 | 31.7 |
| 1967 | 199.1 | 789.7 | 257.8 | 1,102 | 32.6 |
| 1970 | 203.2 | 959.6 | 312.1 | 1,156 | 32.5 |
| 1972 | 208.2 | 1,155.0 | 371.6 | 1,222 | 32.2 |
| 1976 | 215.0 | 1,887.0 | 664.5 | 1,439 | 35.1 |
| 1980 (est.) | 220.0 | 2,565.0 | 900.0 | 1,650 | 35.1 |

*Source:* U.S. Bureau of the Census, *Historical Statistics on Governmental Finances and Employment* (Washington, D.C.: Government Printing Office, 1967); updating from U.S. Bureau of the Census, *Statistical Abstract of the United States,* and *The Budget of the United States Government, 1980.*

An even more important yardstick of the growth of government activity is found in the relationship of government expenditures to the Gross National Product (GNP). The GNP is the dollar sum of all goods and services produced in the nation's economy. The growth of the GNP in the twentieth century reflects the expansion of the nation's economy: the GNP in dollar amounts grew from $21.6 billion to over $2.5 *trillion* today.

Government expenditures in relation to the Gross National Product have risen, somewhat bumpily, from 7.7 percent in 1902 to 35 percent in the late 1970s. If public programs financed by the government had grown at the same rate as private economic activities, this percentage figure would have remained at the same level over the years. But government activity over the long run has grown even *faster* than private enterprise. By any yardstick, then, we find the growth of government activity in America has been substantial. Government activity now accounts for over one-third of all economic activity in the nation.

## Wars, Depressions, and Government Activity

What accounts for the growth of government activity? Years ago, a European economist, Adolph Wagner, set forth a "law of increasing state activity" roughly to the effect that government activity increased faster than economic output in all developing societies.[2] He attributed his law to a variety of factors: increasing regulatory services required to control a more specialized, complex economy; increasing involvement of government in economic enterprise; increasing demands in a developed society for social services such as education, welfare, public health, etc. Thus the "law of increasing state activity" portrayed growth in government activity as an inevitable accompaniment of a developing society.

But the American experience raises serious doubts about the "law of increasing state activity." Although it is true that governmental activity has grown in relation to the economy over the last seven decades, this growth has occurred in spurts rather than as a steady acceleration. Government expenditures in relation to the GNP have *not* increased predictably as if governed by a "law"; instead they have remained stable over periods of time and then spurted upward in response to wars and depressions.

Wars and depressions bring about significant increases in government activity. National emergencies provide the opportunity for gov-

[2]Adolph Wagner's major work is *Grundlegung der politischen oekonomie* (Leipzig, 1893). This work is discussed at length in Alan T. Peacock and Jack Wiseman, *The Growth of Public Expenditures in the United Kingdom* (Princeton, N.J.: Princeton University Press, 1961).

ernments to increase the scope and magnitude of their activities, both in national defense and domestic affairs. When an emergency ends, government activities do not decline to their old levels. Postcrisis expenditures level out on a higher plateau than precrisis expenditures. Thus national emergencies provide the occasion for government activities to rise to successively higher plateaus (see Figure 10–1).

Scholars have summarized the American experience as follows:

> Whether the rule of "normal peacetime" stability would continue over large periods without crisis is unknown; unfortunately, such periods have in the past been of relatively short duration. The experience does, however, suggest a hypothesis that, over the short run at least, the political pressures in this democratic society are such as to prevent any substantial change in the total levels of expenditures upward or downward in relation to the economy as a whole. And it appears probable that the fixing of expenditure levels is a consequence of the stickiness of revenues, principally taxes, rather than of the shifting of expenditure needs. Crises, on the other hand, "unfreeze" revenue levels, permit them to rise and then, once the crises are past, they again congeal.

> In sum, it is clear that expenditures of American governments have increased substantially by every measure, but that these increases have occurred spasmodically with the occurrences of international and domestic crises.[3]

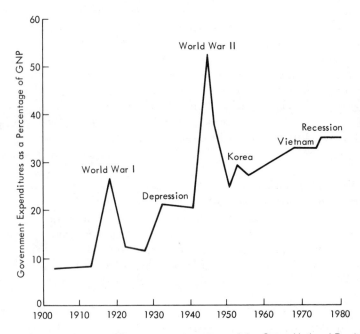

FIG. 10–1   Government expenditures as a percentage of the Gross National Product

[3]Frederick C. Mosher and Orville F. Poland, *The Costs of American Governments* (New York: Dodd, Mead, 1964), pp. 28–29.

*Defense* spending rises sharply during war, then declines after hostilities. During periods of peace, defense spending gradually declines as a proportion of the GNP. In contrast, *domestic* spending declines during wartime. During peacetime periods it tends to rise.

These trends indicate that defense and domestic spending move in different patterns, and sometimes compensate for each other. During World War II *defense* spending grew to over 40 percent of the entire economic product of the nation. In contrast, during World War II *domestic* spending dropped to 10 percent of the GNP, from highs of nearly 18 percent during the Depression. (See Table 10–2.) After World War II, domestic spending gradually regained momentum, with a brief drop-off during the Korean War. War tends to displace domestic spending with defense spending during the period of hostilities. But war also conditions citizens to tolerate major increases in government activity, and thus, after the war, government activity remains on a higher plateau than before the war. Domestic spending gradually displaces defense spending during peacetime periods.

During the Vietnam War, a deliberate effort was made by the Johnson and Nixon administrations to prevent the war from becoming a drain on domestic programs. National policy stressed "guns *and* butter." The effort was successful. Domestic expenditures did *not* decline

**TABLE 10–2**   Defense and Domestic Spending of Federal, State, and Local Governments as a Percentage of GNP

|  | All Government Spending | Defense[1] | Domestic[2] | Federal[3] | State-Local |
|---|---|---|---|---|---|
| 1902 | 7.7 | 1.6 | 6.1 | 2.6 | 5.1 |
| 1913 | 8.2 | 1.2 | 7.0 | 2.5 | 5.7 |
| 1922 | 12.5 | 3.2 | 9.3 | 5.0 | 7.5 |
| 1927 | 11.6 | 2.1 | 9.5 | 3.6 | 8.0 |
| 1932 | 21.3 | 3.8 | 17.4 | 7.1 | 14.2 |
| 1936 | 20.8 | 2.4 | 17.4 | 10.2 | 10.6 |
| 1940 | 20.3 | 2.5 | 17.8 | 9.8 | 10.5 |
| 1944 | 52.0 | 41.6 | 10.4 | 47.2 | 4.8 |
| 1946 | 37.8 | 27.0 | 10.8 | 31.7 | 6.1 |
| 1950 | 24.7 | 6.8 | 17.9 | 16.4 | 8.3 |
| 1955 | 27.9 | 11.2 | 16.7 | 18.1 | 9.8 |
| 1960 | 30.1 | 9.9 | 20.2 | 18.6 | 11.5 |
| 1965 | 31.7 | 8.2 | 23.5 | 18.1 | 13.6 |
| 1970 | 32.5 | 8.8 | 23.7 | 20.6 | 13.4 |
| 1975 | 35.1 | 5.1 | 30.0 | 22.0 | 13.1 |
| 1980 | 35.6 | 5.0 | 30.6 | 21.2 | 14.4 |

[1]Defense and international relations.
[2]All other, including social insurance.
[3]Including social insurance.

*Source: The Budget of the United States Government 1980* and past volumes of the *Statistical Abstract of the United States.*

as a percentage of the GNP, as had been the case in previous wars. (See Figure 10–2.) Domestic expenditures continued to rise even in relation to the economy. The serious economic recession in 1973–1975 caused government expenditures to move upward again in relation to the GNP. Both the Ford and Carter administrations made a deliberate effort to prevent further erosion of defense spending as a percentage of the GNP.

In recent years total state and local government spending has grown more rapidly than federal spending. There are 18,000 state and local governments in America—states, counties, cities, townships, school districts, special districts, etc.—and collectively they spend nearly 15 percent of the GNP. Education—elementary, secondary, and higher education—take the largest share of state and local funds.

## Changing National Priorities

A great deal of political rhetoric centers around national "priorities." The problem is to separate rhetoric from reality. We must distinguish between what is *said* to be a national priority from what is actually given priority in the allocation of national resources. To identify *actual*

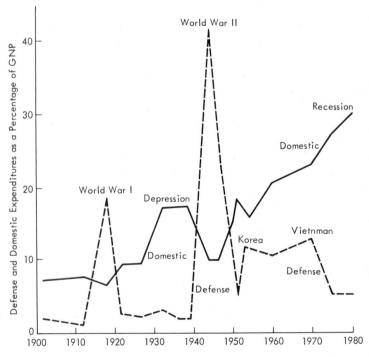

FIG. 10–2  Defense and domestic expenditures as a percentage of the Gross National Product

priorities, we have determined the percentage of the federal budget devoted to various government activities. The results are summarized in Table 10–3. Obviously all private needs are given priority over all public needs, because total public expenditures of federal, state, and national governments are only about one-third of the Gross National Product. This is what one might reasonably expect in a private enterprise, capitalist society.

Until recently, national defense was the nation's highest priority

**TABLE 10–3**   Federal Expenditures Over Two Decades

| | Billions of Dollars | | | | | | | |
|---|---|---|---|---|---|---|---|---|
| | *1960* | *1965* | *1968* | *1970* | *1972* | *1975* | *1978* | *1981 est.* |
| National Defense | 45.9 | 49.6 | 80.5 | 79.4 | 78.3 | 87.7 | 111.9 | 146.2 |
| International Affairs | 3.0 | 4.3 | 4.6 | 4.1 | 3.7 | 9.1 | 7.8 | 9.6 |
| Space and Science | .4 | 5.1 | 4.7 | 3.9 | 3.4 | 3.3 | 4.7 | 6.4 |
| Agriculture | 3.3 | 4.8 | 5.9 | 6.3 | 7.1 | 2.7 | 2.3 | 2.8 |
| Natural Resources | 1.0 | 2.0 | 1.7 | 2.5 | 3.8 | 3.1 | 20.5 | 20.9 |
| Commerce and Transportation | 4.8 | 7.4 | 8.0 | 9.4 | 11.2 | 13.4 | 20.1 | 20.8 |
| Community Development and Housing | 1.0 | .3 | 4.0 | 3.0 | 4.3 | 5.7 | 10.0 | 8.8 |
| Health and Welfare | 18.7 | 27.2 | 43.5 | 57.1 | 82.1 | 126.4 | 191.0 | 282.4 |
| Education and Manpower | 1.3 | 2.5 | 7.0 | 7.5 | 9.8 | 11.5 | 26.5 | 32.0 |
| Veterans' Benefits | 5.4 | 5.7 | 6.9 | 8.7 | 10.7 | 13.6 | 19.1 | 21.7 |
| Interest | 8.3 | 10.3 | 13.7 | 17.8 | 20.6 | 29.1 | 41.8 | 67.2 |
| General Government | 1.3 | 2.3 | 2.6 | 3.6 | 4.9 | 6.8 | 7.8 | 9.6 |
| Revenue Sharing | — | — | — | — | — | 6.2 | 9.7 | 9.6 |
| Total* | 92.2 | 118.4 | 178.8 | 197.9 | 231.9 | 304.4 | 459.4 | 615.8 |
| | Percentage Distribution | | | | | | | |
| National Defense | 48.8% | 41.9% | 45.0% | 40.1% | 32.6% | 28.8% | 24.4% | 23.7% |
| International Affairs | 3.3 | 3.7 | 2.6 | 2.1 | 1.6 | 1.3 | 1.7 | 1.1 |
| Space and Science | 0.4 | 4.3 | 2.6 | 2.0 | 1.4 | 1.1 | 1.0 | 1.0 |
| Agriculture | 3.6 | 4.1 | 3.3 | 3.2 | 2.9 | .9 | 0.5 | 0.4 |
| Natural Resources | 1.1 | 1.7 | 1.0 | 1.3 | 1.6 | 1.0 | 4.5 | 3.4 |
| Commerce and Transportation | 5.2 | 6.2 | 4.5 | 4.7 | 4.7 | 4.4 | 4.4 | 3.3 |
| Community Development and Housing | 1.1 | 0.2 | 2.3 | 1.5 | 1.9 | 1.9 | 2.2 | 1.4 |
| Health and Welfare | 20.3 | 23.0 | 24.3 | 28.8 | 34.2 | 41.5 | 41.6 | 45.8 |
| Education and Manpower | 1.4 | 2.1 | 3.9 | 3.8 | 4.1 | 3.8 | 5.8 | 5.2 |
| Veterans' Benefits | 5.9 | 4.8 | 3.8 | 4.4 | 4.5 | 4.5 | 4.2 | 3.5 |
| Interest | 9.0 | 8.7 | 7.7 | 9.0 | 8.6 | 9.6 | 9.1 | 10.9 |
| General Government | 1.4 | 1.9 | 1.5 | 1.8 | 2.0 | 2.2 | 1.7 | 1.4 |
| Revenue Sharing | — | — | — | — | — | 2.0 | 2.1 | 1.5 |

*Figures may not total correctly because of "offsetting receipts" from various programs.

*Source:* Data derived from *The Budget of the United States Government, 1980,* (Washington, D.C.: Government Printing Office, 1979).

in public spending. Indeed, for many years the common argument on behalf of liberalized social welfare programs followed clear lines: (1) the United States was spending the largest proportion of its budget for defense; (2) programs for the poor, the sick, the aged, and minorities were underfinanced; (3) the nation should "change its priorities" and spend more for social programs and less on war. The argument ended with a call for a "revolution" in national priorities.

But revolutions in public spending patterns were considered unlikely. The prevailing model in public budgeting was (and continues to be) that of *incrementalism*. Incrementalism views public policy as a continuation of past government activities with only incremental modifications from year to year. Thus, neither the history nor the theory of public spending prepared the nation for the revolution in national priorities which occurred between 1965 and 1975.

In a single decade America's "national priorities" in defense and social welfare were reversed. In 1965 national defense expenditures accounted for 41.9 percent of the federal budget, while health and welfare expenditures accounted for only 23 percent of the budget.

The Changing Priorities in the Federal Budget Constant 1980 Dollars

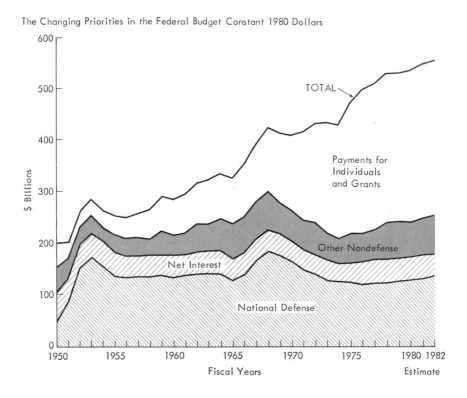

FIG. 10–3   The changing priorities in the federal budget

(See Figure 10–3.) While the mass media focused attention on the war in Vietnam and on Watergate, national budget priorities were reversed. By 1975, only a decade later, defense accounted for only 28.8 percent of the federal budget, while health and welfare expenditures had grown to 41.5 percent of the budget. This reversal of national "priorities" occurred during both Democratic (Johnson) and Republican (Nixon and Ford) administrations in Washington, *and* during the nation's longest war. In short, what we thought we "knew" about the effects of politics and war on social welfare spending turned out to be wrong.

Interestingly, not many people really noticed this reversal of national priorities. Many people still believe the federal government spends more on defense than anything else. Old beliefs die hard.

Federal budget outlays over two decades for major programs are shown in Table 10–3, in both dollars and percentages of the total federal budget. Note how spending for *national defense* has grown very slowly in dollars and declined very rapidly as a percentage of total federal spending. In contrast, spending for health and welfare (including social security, public assistance, Medicare, and Medicaid) has grown very rapidly, both in dollars and in percentages of the federal budget.

## Incrementalism in Budget Making

The incremental model of public policy making is particularly well suited to assist in understanding the budgeting process. Budgeting is *incremental* because decision makers generally consider last year's expenditures as a base. Active consideration of budget proposals is generally narrowed to new items or requested increases over last year's base. The attention of presidents, congressmen, governors, legislators, mayors, and councils is focused on a narrow range of increases or decreases in a budget. A budget is almost never reviewed as a whole every year, in the sense of reconsidering the value of all existing programs. Departments are seldom required to defend or explain budget requests which do *not* exceed current appropriations; but requested increases in appropriations require extensive explanation. To eliminate the accumulated waste of obsolete programs which remain in government budgets, reformers have proposed the "zero base" budget. This is designed to force agencies to justify every penny requested—not just requested increases. In theory, zero base budgeting would eliminate unnecessary spending protected by incrementalism. But in practice, zero base budgeting may require so much wasted effort in justifying already accepted programs each year that executive agencies and legislative committees will grow tired of the effort and return to incrementalism.

Budgeting is very *political*. As Aaron Wildavsky was told by a federal executive, "It's not what's in your estimates, but how good a politician you are that matters."[4] Being a good politician involves (1) the cultivation of a good base of support for requests among the public at large and among people served by the agency, (2) the development of interest, enthusiasm, and support for a program among top political figures and legislative leaders, and (3) skill in following strategies that exploit opportunities to the maximum. Informing the public and the clientele of the full benefit of the services they receive from the agency may increase the intensity with which they will support the agency's request. If possible, the agency should inspire its clientele to contact congressmen, governors, mayors, legislators, and councilmen, and to help work for the agency's request. This is much more effective than the agency trying to promote its own requests.

Budgeting is also quite *fragmented*. In theory, the Office of Management and Budget (OMB), in the executive branch, and the Congressional Budget Office (CBO), in the legislative branch, are supposed to bring together budget requests and fit them into a coherent whole, while at the same time relating them to revenue estimates. But often these budget offices do little more than staple together the budget requests of individual departments, and it is very difficult for the President, and almost impossible for the Congress, to view the total policy impact of a budget. Wildavsky explains that the fragmented character of the budgetary process helps to secure agreement to the budget as well as reduce the burden of calculation. If each Congressional subcommittee challenged the result of the others, conflict might be so great that no budget would ever be passed. It is much easier to agree on a small addition or decrease to a single program than it is to compare the worth of one program to that of all others. However, to counter the fragmentation in the federal budget, Congress not only established a Congressional Budget Office, but also new House and Senate Budget Committees to examine the budget as a whole. We will describe their operation in the next section. But it is interesting to note that their purpose is to overcome the fragmentation in federal budget making.

Finally, budgeting is *nonprogrammatic*. For reasons that accountants have so far kept to themselves, an agency budget typically lists expenditures under the ambiguous phrases: "personnel services," "contractual services," "travel," "supplies," "equipment." It is impossible to tell from such a listing exactly what programs the agency is spending its money on. Such a budget obscures policy decisions by hiding programs behind meaningless phrases. Even if these categories are broken down into line items (for example, under "personnel services," the

[4]Aaron Wildavsky, *The Politics of the Budgetary Process* (Boston: Little, Brown, 1964), p. 19.

line-item budget might say, "John Doaks, Assistant Administrator, $25,000"), it is still next to impossible to identify the costs of various programs. Reform-oriented administrators have called for budgeting by programs for many years; this would present budgetary requests in terms of end products or program packages, like aid to dependent children, vocational rehabilitation, administration of fair employment practices laws, highway patroling, and so on. Chief executives generally favor *program budgeting* because it will give them greater control over policy. But very often administrative agencies are hostile toward program budgeting—it certainly adds to the cost of bookkeeping, and many agencies feel insecure in describing precisely what it is they do. Wildavsky points out that there are some political functions served by *non*program budgeting. He notes that

> Agreement comes much more readily when the items in dispute can be treated in dollars instead of basic differences in policy. Calculating budgets in monetary increments facilitates bargaining and logrolling. It becomes possible to swap an increase here for a decrease there or for an increase elsewhere without always having to consider the ultimate desirability of the programs blatantly in competition. . . . Problems of calculation are vastly increased by the necessity, if program budgeting is to have meaning, of evaluating the desirability of every program as compared to all others, instead of the traditional practice of considering budgeting in relatively independent segments.[5]

The most important influence over the size and content of this year's budget is last year's budget. One of the reasons for this is the continuing nature of most governmental programs and outlays. Over two-thirds of the federal budget is officially labeled "uncontrollable." The "uncontrollable" items are expenditures that are mandated by previous programs—for example, commitments to recipients of social security, Medicare, Medicaid, and public assistance; commitments to veterans; interest that must be paid on the national debt; and so on. (See Figure 10–4.)

Another reason for using last year's budget as a base is the cost that would be involved in generally reconsidering every government program and expenditure. There is not enough time and energy for the decision-making process required to do this, so past programs are assumed to be worthy of continuation at previous levels of expenditures. It is considered a waste of time to view every budget as a blank slate and to ignore past experience. Moreover, the political instability that would ensue if every program were reevaluated every year would be too much for the system; every political battle that has ever been fought over a program would have to be fought all over again every year. Obviously, it is much more practical and political to accept past

[5]Ibid., pp. 136–38.

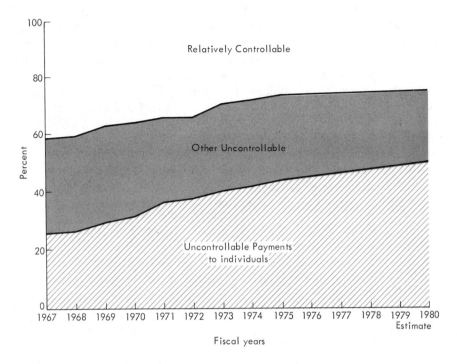

FIG. 10–4  Controllability of federal expenditures (percentage)
*Source:* The Budget of the United States Government *1980.*

decisions on programs and expenditures as a base, and concentrate attention on new programs and increases and decreases in expenditures. For all these reasons, the range of decision making actually confronting legislative and executive officials is really quite small, generally within 10 percent of the previous budget.[6]

## The Formal Budgetary Process

It is difficult to imagine that prior to 1921 the president played no direct role in the budget process. The secretary of the treasury compiled the estimates of the individual agencies, and these were sent, without revision, to Congress for its consideration. The Budget and Accounting Act of 1921 provided for an executive budget giving the president responsibility for budget formulation, and thereby giving him impor-

[6]Richard F. Fenno, *The Power of the Purse: Appropriations Politics in Congress* (Boston: Little, Brown, 1966). See also Otto A. Davis, M. A. H. Dempster, and Aaron Wildavsky, "A Theory of the Budgetary Process," *American Political Science Review,* 60 (September 1966), 529–47.

tant means of controlling federal policy. The Office of Management and Budget (OMB), located in the Executive Office, has the key responsibility for budget preparation. In addition to this major task, the OMB has related responsibilities for improving the organization and management of the executive agencies, for coordinating the extensive statistical services of the federal government, and for analyzing and reviewing proposed legislation to determine its effect on administration and finance.

Preparation of the federal budget starts more than a year before the beginning of the fiscal year for which it is intended. OMB, after preliminary consultation with the executive agencies and in accord with presidential policy, develops targets or ceilings within which the agencies are encouraged to build their requests. This work begins a full sixteen to eighteen months before the beginning of the fiscal year for which the budget is being prepared. In other words, work would begin in January 1980, on the budget for the fiscal year beginning October 1, 1981, and ending September 30, 1982.

Budget materials and instructions go to the agencies with the request that the forms be completed and returned to OMB. This request is followed by about three months' arduous work by agency-employed budget officers, department heads, and the "grass roots" bureaucracy in Washington and out in the field. Budget officials at the bureau level check requests from the smaller units, compare them with the previous year's estimates, hold conferences, and make adjustments. The process of checking, reviewing, modifying, and discussing is repeated on a larger scale at the department level.

The heads of agencies are expected to submit their completed requests to OMB by mid-September or early October. Occasionally a schedule of "over ceiling" items (requests above the suggested ceilings) will be included.

With the requests of the spending agencies at hand, OMB begins its own budget review. Hearings are given each agency. Top agency officials support their requests as convincingly as possible. On rare occasions dissatisfied agencies may ask the budget director to take their cases to the president.

In December, the president and the OMB director will devote time to the document which by now is approaching its final stages of assembly. They and their staffs will "blue-pencil," revise, and make last-minute changes, as well as prepare the president's message which accompanies the budget to Congress. After the budget is in legislative hands, the president may recommend further alterations as needs dictate.

Although the completed document includes a revenue plan with general estimates for taxes and other income, it is primarily an expenditure budget. Revenue and tax policy staff work centers in the Treasury Department and not in the Office of Management and Budget.

Congress has two responsibilities in making money available for spending—authorization and appropriation. Authorization in a technical sense refers to the substantive legislation that establishes a program and enables an agency to spend money when appropriations are made. An appropriations measure, on the other hand, allows an agency to obligate the government to pay out funds and spend specified amounts. Before authorization legislation goes to the House or Senate floor, it is considered by appropriate program committees (for example, Aeronautical and Space Sciences, Education, Labor, or Interior and Insular Affairs).

Until recently, Congressional consideration of the budget was divided between House and Senate Appropriations Committees and subcommittees, the House Ways and Means Committee, and the Senate Finance Committee. Moreover, consideration of proposed government spending was divided over twelve to fifteen different appropriations bills, each covering separate broad categories, which arrived on the Congressional calendar at different times of the year. Finally, taxing measures were considered separately from appropriations measures and by different committees. In short, Congress never took an overall view of the budget—setting priorities among major categories, considering the overall impact of the budget on the economy, or balancing revenues with expenditures. As a result Congress was open to the charge that it dealt irresponsibly with government spending.

Congress attempted to remedy problems of budgetary oversight in 1974 by establishing new Congressional budgetary procedures. Congress created two new House and Senate Budget Committees and a Congressional Budget Office to review the president's budget soon after its submission to Congress. These Committees draft a concurrent resolution setting forth target totals to guide Congressional actions on appropriations and revenue measures considered throughout the year. This initial budgetary guide is enacted by the Congress prior to consideration of specific taxing or spending measures. Thus, Congressional committees considering taxing and spending bills not only have presidential recommendations to guide them, but also the guidelines established earlier by the Budget Committees. If an appropriation measure exceeds the target set by the earlier resolution, it is sent back to the Budget Committees for reconciliation. A final Congressional budget including all appropriations measures, tax measures, and the debt ceiling is passed by Congress before October 1, the date set for the start of the fiscal year. Of course, it is still too early to judge whether the new procedures will make Congress any more responsible in government spending. But the new procedures clearly reduce Congressional dependence on executive budget making.

Consideration of specific appropriations measures are functions of the Appropriations Committees in both houses. Committee work in the House of Representatives is usually more thorough than it is in the Senate; the committee in the Senate tends to be a "court of appeal" for agencies against House action. Each committee, moreover, has about ten largely independent subcommittees to review the requests of a particular agency or a group of related functions. Specific appropriations bills are taken up by the subcommittees in hearings. Departmental officers answer questions on the conduct of their programs and defend their requests for the next fiscal year; lobbyists and other witnesses testify.

The appropriation subcommittees are of primary importance in Congressional consideration of the budget. Because neither Congress nor the full committees have the time or understanding necessary to conduct adequate reviews, the subcommittee has become the locus of Congressional budget analysis. Several factors contribute to its preeminent position. Each subcommittee specializes in a relatively small fraction of the total budget. It considers the same agencies and functions year after year. The long tenure characteristic of the membership of the prestigious Appropriations Committees guarantees decades of experience in dealing with particular programs. Although the work of the subcommittee is reviewed by the full committee, in practice it is routinely accepted with the expenditure of little time and debate.

The House Committee on Ways and Means and the Senate Finance Committee are the major instruments of Congress for consideration of *taxing* measures. Through long history and jealous pride they have maintained formal independence of the Appropriations Committees, further fragmenting legislative consideration of the budget.

In terms of aggregates, Congress does not regularly make great changes in the executive budget, rarely changing it more than five percent. The budget is approved by Congress in the form of appropriations bills, from twelve to fifteen of them, each ordinarily providing for several departments and agencies. The number of revenue measures is smaller. As with other bills that pass Congress, the president has ten days to approve or veto appropriations legislation. He lacks the power to veto items in bills, and only rarely exercises his right to veto appropriations bills in their entirety.

Once the budgeted funds are authorized, controls over their expenditure shift to the executive establishment, although not immediately to the departments and agencies. OMB may establish reserves against appropriations in order to provide for emergencies and to effect economies. OMB, after consultation with the agencies, apportions the appropriations, usually on a quarterly basis. A major purpose of apportionment is to prevent an agency from depleting its appropriation before the end of the fiscal year.

## Public Policy and the Federal System

At the beginning of the twentieth century, most government activity was carried on at the *local* level. Table 10–4 reveals that local governments once made about 59 percent of all government expenditures, compared to 35 percent for the federal government and 6 percent for state governments. Yet by 1960 centralization in the American federal system had proceeded to the point where local governments were spending only 24 percent of all government expenditures, compared to 65 percent for the federal government and 13 percent for state governments. Then, in the 1970s, despite the war in Vietnam and a host of new and expanding federal social security and welfare programs, state and local spending outpaced federal spending. The federal percentage of total government spending declined to about 58 percent.

**TABLE 10–4**  A Comparison of the Expenditures of Federal, State, and Local Governments over Seven Decades

|             | Percentages of Total General Expenditures | | |
|-------------|-----------|-----------|-----------|
|             | *Federal*[2] | *State*[3] | *Local*[3] |
| 1902        | 35%       | 6%        | 59%       |
| 1913        | 31        | 9         | 60        |
| 1922        | 40        | 11        | 49        |
| 1927        | 31        | 13        | 56        |
| 1932        | 34        | 16        | 50        |
| 1936        | 50        | 14        | 36        |
| 1940        | 48        | 15        | 37        |
| 1944        | 91        | 3         | 7         |
| 1946        | 82        | 6         | 12        |
| 1948        | 64        | 13        | 23        |
| 1950        | 64        | 12        | 24        |
| 1952        | 71        | 9         | 20        |
| 1955        | 66        | 11        | 23        |
| 1960        | 65        | 12        | 23        |
| 1965        | 62        | 14        | 24        |
| 1970        | 62        | 15        | 23        |
| 1975        | 59        | 15        | 24        |
| 1980 (est.) | 58        | 17        | 24        |

[1]Figures may not total correctly because of rounding.
[2]Figures include social security and trust fund expenditures.
[3]State payments to local governments are shown as local government expenditures; federal grants-in-aid are shown as federal expenditures.

Wars and depressions had a great deal to do with the shift away from local reliance on American government. During national emergencies, both foreign and domestic, Americans have turned to the federal government for help. After the emergency, federal activity decreases somewhat in relation to state and local activity, but federal activity never returns to the precrisis level. Thus, during World War I, World War II, and the Korean War, the federal government increased its percentages of total government activity, while local and state government percentages declined. Because the federal government has the primary responsibility for national defense, we would expect this to occur during wartime. But the federal government also expands its activities in response to domestic crisis—it was during the 1930s that federal expenditures first surpassed those of all local governments.

Although foreign and domestic crises have brought about increasing centralization in American government, we noted that expanded federal activity has not come at the expense of state and local activity. Federal power and state-local power are not at the opposite ends of a seesaw; the growth of federal power has not necessarily curtailed the power of states and localities. National activity has expanded in the twentieth century but so has the activity of state and local governments.

Over the years, the federal government has steadily increased its share of responsibility in every important policy area of American government. Many feel that the date 1913, when the *Sixteenth Amendment* gave the federal government the power to tax incomes directly, was the beginning of a new era in American federalism. Congress had been given the power to tax and spend for the general welfare in Article I of the Constitution. But the Sixteenth Amendment helped to shift the balance of financial power from the states to Washington when it gave Congress the power to tax the incomes of corporations and individuals on a progressive basis. The income tax gave the federal government the power to raise large sums of money, which it proceeded to spend for the general welfare as well as for defense. It is not coincidence that the first major grant-in-aid programs (agricultural extension in 1914, highways in 1916, vocational education in 1917, and public health in 1918) all came shortly after the inauguration of the federal income tax.

The federal grant-in-aid has become the principal instrument for the increased involvement of the federal government in domestic policy areas. The *Depression of the 1930s* put pressure on the national government to use its tax and spending powers in a wide variety of areas formerly reserved to states and communities. The federal government initiated grant-in-aid programs to states and communities for public assistance, unemployment compensation, employment services, public housing, urban renewal, and so on; it also expanded federal grants-in-aid programs in highways, vocational education, and rehabilitation. The inadequacy of state and local revenue systems to meet the financial crises created by the Depression contributed significantly to the development of cooperative federalism. States and communities called upon the superior taxing powers of the national government to assist them in many fields in which the federal government had not previously involved itself.

Today *grant-in-aid programs* are the single most important source of federal influence over state and local affairs. The growth of federal grants is depicted in Figure 10–5. Approximately one-fifth of all state and local government revenues are from federal grants. This money is paid out through a staggering number and variety of programs. There are probably 500 different federal grant programs in existence today. So numerous and diverse are federal aid programs that a substantial information gap surrounds the availability, purpose, and requirements of these programs. Learning about their availability and mastering the art of grant application places a serious burden on state and local officials. Moreover, the problem of program coordination, not only be-

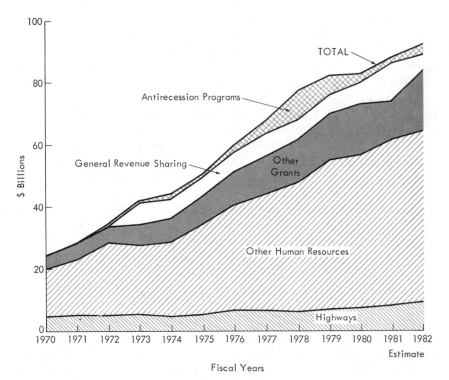

FIG. 10–5   Federal aid to state and local governments

tween levels of government but also among federal agencies, is a truly difficult one.

Federal grants are available in nearly every major category of state and local government activity. Federal grants may be obtained to assist in everything from the preservation of historic buildings, the development of minority-owned businesses, and aid for foreign refugees, to the drainage of abandoned mines, riot control, and school milk. However, federal aid for welfare, Medicaid, food stamps, and highways accounts for over two-thirds of total federal aid money.

Not only have federal grants-in-aid to the states expanded rapidly in terms of the numbers of programs and the dollar amounts involved, but states and communities have also come to *rely* on the national government for an ever increasing share of their total revenues (see Table 10–5). Prior to the New Deal, federal grants amounted to only 2 or 3 percent of total state-local revenue. The New Deal itself, in spite of all of its innovations in federal aid programs, raised this proportion only to 7 or 8 percent. State-local reliance on federal aid has continued to increase over the last two decades, from 8 percent over total state-local revenues in 1946 to over 23 percent today. More than one-third of *state* revenues are derived from federal sources. Thus, no matter how it is measured—increased numbers of programs, increased dollar amounts, increased reliance by states and communities—federal aid has grown into a major influence over state and local governmental activity.

**TABLE 10–5**  Federal Grants-in-Aid and State-Local Finances

|  | Total Federal Grants-In-Aid in Millions of Dollars | Federal Grants as a Percentage Of State-Local Revenue |
|---|---|---|
| 1902 | 7 | * |
| 1913 | 12 | * |
| 1922 | 118 | 2.1% |
| 1927 | 123 | 1.6 |
| 1932 | 232 | 2.9 |
| 1938 | 800 | 7.2 |
| 1940 | 945 | 8.1 |
| 1944 | 954 | 6.8 |
| 1948 | 1,861 | 8.6 |
| 1950 | 2,486 | 9.7 |
| 1955 | 3,131 | 8.3 |
| 1960 | 6,974 | 11.6 |
| 1962 | 7,871 | 11.3 |
| 1967 | 15,366 | 14.0 |
| 1970 | 25,029 | 18.0 |
| 1972 | 35,940 | 21.3 |
| 1975 | 51,732 | 22.4 |
| 1980 (est.) | 82,937 | 23.6 |

*Less than 1 percent.

## The Debate Over Governmental Centralization

There are several reasons for this growth of federal aid.[7] First, these grants permit the federal government to single out and support those state and local government services in which it has a particular interest. Grants permit the national government to set national goals and priorities in all levels of government without formally altering the federal structure. Thus, as problems of public assistance, community development, highway construction, education, poverty, and so on, acquire national significance, they can be dealt with by the application of national resources.

Second, the grant-in-aid system helps to overcome the inadequacies of state-local revenue resources. Contrary to the political rhetoric charging the states with fiscal conservatism, the states have actually demonstrated a great deal of fiscal courage, effort, and ingenuity in trying to cope with money problems. In the last decade state-local expenditures have risen at a faster *rate* than have federal expenditures. These fiscal efforts have meant increased income or sales tax rates in nearly every state in the past ten years as well as increased liquor and gasoline tax rates. Yet in spite of these efforts by states, their fiscal problems continue to multiply.

States and communities must raise revenues and at the same time carry on interstate and interlocal competition for industry and wealth. Although the influence of tax considerations on industrial locations decisions may be overstated by most lawmakers, this overstatement itself is part of the political lore at statehouses and courthouses that operates to impede revenue raising. Not only do competitive considerations inhibit state-local taxing efforts but they also tend to push them in regressive directions.

Debates over finances in state capitals invariably include references to the "preemption" of income taxes by the national government. There are no compelling economic reasons for the argument that the federal income tax preempts this source of revenue for the states (particularly because the federal government permits the deduction of state income taxes from total taxable income). Nonetheless, in the minds of most state lawmakers and probably in the minds of their constituents as well, there is the belief that the federal government already takes all the income taxes they wish to pay. This means states are stuck with sales taxes and localities with property taxes, and, in contrast to income taxes, these taxes respond sluggishly to rises in the GNP.

[7]See George F. Break, *Intergovernmental Fiscal Relations in the United States* (Washington, D.C.: Brookings Institution, 1967); Deil S. Wright, *Federal Grants-in-Aid: Perspectives and Alternatives* (Washington, D.C.: American Enterprise Institute, 1968).

Another argument in behalf of federal grants-in-aid centers about the greater progressivity of the federal tax structure. If a particular government program is funded through state and local taxes, it is funded on a tax structure that is regressive or only mildly progressive; but if it is funded out of federal taxes, it is funded on a more progressive basis. This may help to explain the "liberal" predisposition for federal financial involvement.

Finally, grants-in-aid provide an opportunity for the national government to insure a uniform level of public service throughout the nation as a minimum or foundation program—for example, federal grants-in-aid to help achieve equality in educational opportunity in all parts of the nation, or to help to insure a minimum level of existence for the poverty-stricken regardless of where they live. This aspect of federal policy assumes that in some parts of the nation, state and local governments are unable, or perhaps unwilling, to devote their resources to raising public service levels to minimum national standards.

Whenever the national government contributes financially to state or local programs, state and local officials have less freedom of choice than they would have without federal aid. They must adhere to federal standards or "guidelines," which invariably accompany federal grants-in-aid, if they are to receive their federal money. The national government gives money to states and communities only if they are willing to meet conditions specified by Congress. Often Congress delegates to federal agencies the power to establish the "conditions" that are attached to grants.

No state is required to accept a federal grant-in-aid. In other words, states are not required to meet federal standards or guidelines that are set forth as conditions for federal aid because they have the alternative of rejecting the federal money—and they have sometimes done so. But it is very difficult for states and communities to resist the pressure to accept federal money.

In short, through the power to tax and spend for the general welfare, and through "conditions" attached to federal grants-in-aid, the national government has come to exercise great powers in many areas originally "reserved" to the states—highways, welfare, education, housing, natural resources, employment, health, and so on. Of course, federal grants-in-aid have enabled many states and communities to provide necessary and desirable services that they could not have afforded otherwise. Federal guidelines have often improved the standard of administration, personnel policies, and fiscal practices in states and communities. More important, federal guidelines have helped to insure that states and communities will not engage in racial discrimination in federally aided programs.

The centralization of power in Washington has also created some serious problems in the implementation of public policy. First of all, federal grant programs frequently work at cross-purposes, reflecting fragmentation of federal programs. For example, community development grants attempt to save central cities from deterioration and population loss, while federal highway grants have built expressways to make possible the suburban exodus. The federal public housing programs have tried to increase the supply of low-rent housing for the poor, but federally funded urban renewal and highway programs have torn down low-rent housing.

Second, the federal government has never set any significant priorities among its hundreds of grant programs. The result is that too few dollars chase too many goals. Cities are pressured to apply for funds for projects they do not really need, simply because federal funds are available, although they may receive little or no federal assistance for more vital programs. Federal grant money is frequently provided for "new" or "innovative" or "demonstration" programs, when the real crisis facing states and communities may be in traditional public services, such as policy, sewage, sanitation, and so forth.

Third, the administrative quagmire created by the maze of separate federal grant programs threatens to drown state and local officials in red tape. The 500 separate federal grant programs with separate purposes and guidelines are uncoordinated and bureaucratic. State and local officials spend a great deal of their time in "grantmanship," that is, learning where to find federal funds, how to apply, and how to write applications in such a way as to appear to meet purposes and guidelines.

Finally, the current grant-in-aid system assumes that federal officials are better judges of goals and priorities at all levels of government than state or local officials. State and local officials do not determine what activities in their states and communities will receive federal money; federal officials determine these priorities. Whether federal officials or state and local officials are better judges of public goals and priorities is, of course, a political question.

## Attempts at Decentralization: Revenue Sharing and Bloc Grants

Over the years, power in the American federal system has flowed toward Washington, largely because the national government has the superior taxing powers and therefore the money to deal more effectively with the nation's domestic problems. But the many dissatisfactions with the conditional grant-in-aid system led to appeals for a new approach to federal financial assistance to state and local governments—unrestricted federal grants with no strings attached. For many years Congress debated the idea of "revenue sharing"—the turnover of federal tax dollars to state and local governments for use as they see fit. The idea of revenue sharing assumes that the federal government is better at *collecting* revenue than state or local governments, but state and local governments are better at *spending* it. Consequently, revenue sharing was said to combine the best features of each level of government. More importantly, revenue sharing promised to reverse the flow of money and power to Washington, to end excessive red tape, and to revitalize state and local governments.

The State and Local Fiscal Assistance Act of 1972 is a true landmark in American federalism. This Act establishes *general revenue sharing* and provides for the distribution of federal monies to states and communities with very few restrictions on its use. This Act was strongly supported by state and local government officials. Two-thirds of these shared revenues go to local governments and one-third to state governments. The formula for allocation to states and cities is based on three factors: population, tax effort, and the income level of the population. These revenues may be used for police and fire protection, sewage and garbage disposal, pollution abatement, transportation, physical facilities, parks and recreation, and most other recognized state-local functions.

Revenue sharing does not replace any existing grant-in-aid programs, but does provide states and communities with new unrestricted revenues. No applications are required; the United States Treasury Department sends revenue sharing money to states and communities on a formula basis which considers population, income, and local tax effort. Discrimination by governments receiving such funds is prohibited, public hearings must be held on its use to insure public participation, federal labor laws and wage rates must be observed, and reports must be filed on how the money was spent. But these restrictions are minor compared to the maze of restrictions surrounding categorical federal grants.

Revenue sharing promises to check the trend toward centralization of power in Washington. Of course, Congress will always be under pressure to attach restrictions to the use of any money coming out of the federal treasury. But revenue sharing marks a reassertion of states and cities in the American federal system.

Another approach to cutting federal strings in grant-in-aid programs is the "bloc grant." Bloc grants may be used by states and communities for specific projects decided at the local level within a broad category—"community development" or "law enforcement," for example. Bloc grants carry many of the requirements and restrictions of ordinary categorical federal grants. However, in the Housing and

Community Development Act of 1974, for example, specific public housing projects, urban renewal projects, and community facilities projects, were incorporated into a general bloc grant program. The federal Department of Housing and Urban Development still supervises "community development bloc grants," but specific projects are supposed to be decided at the local level. Obviously, bloc grants do *not* give states and communities the same freedom as revenue sharing money. But bloc grants provide greater flexibility than traditional categorical grants.

While revenue sharing and bloc grants promise to breathe new financial life into the notion of "federalism," we should remember that most federal grant money is still allocated directly from Washington under categorical grant programs. Indeed, today over 75 percent of all federal money going to state and local governments flows through specific, categorical grants. Only about 10 percent of federal aid flows through revenue-sharing and 15 percent through bloc grants.

## Summary

Government budgeting lies at the heart of public policy making. Incrementalism is a helpful model in understanding the budgetary process. But there have been many "nonincremental" changes in American priorities, as reflected in budgetary changes over time.

1. Government activity has grown in relation both to the size of the population and to the economy. Government activity now accounts for about one-third of all economic activity in the United States.

2. Government expenditures as a proportion of all economic activity in the nation spurt upward in response to wars and depressions. When these crises subside, government expenditures associated with them decline somewhat, but stabilize at levels higher than before the crisis. War conditions citizens to tolerate major increases in government activity. During war, government domestic spending declines; but after a war, domestic spending displaces defense spending and achieves a higher plateau than before the war.

3. Among public expenditures, national income security (social security, welfare, and social services) now takes highest priority. In recent years national defense spending has declined as a percentage of the GNP. This shift in national priorities occurred between 1965 and 1975, during both a Democratic and a Republican administration and during the nation's longest war. This reversal of federal budget priorities raises questions about whether budgeting is truly "incremental."

4. Nonetheless, the budgetary process itself is incremental, political, fragmented, and nonprogrammatic. Policy makers generally con-

sider last year's expenditure as a base and focus their attention on a narrow range of increases and decreases in expenditures. Despite efforts at Congressional reform (including the establishment of House and Senate budget committees) most agencies and legislative committees deal with specific segments of the budget. Evaluating the desirability of *every* public program *every* year might create politically insoluble conflict, as well as exhaust the energies of budget makers.

5. The range of decisions available to policy makers in the development of a budget is really quite small, generally within 10 percent of the previous budget. "Uncontrollable" items account for more than three-quarters of the federal budget.

6. Wars and depressions have helped to shift responsibilities from local and state governments to the national government. However, national power and state-local power are not at opposite ends of a seesaw; national activity has expanded rapidly in the twentieth century, but so has the activity of state and local governments.

7. Federal grants-in-aid to state and local governments have been the principal instrument of the national government's involvement in domestic policy areas. These federal area payments now make up 24 percent of all state and local government revenue.

## Bibliography

BREAK, GEORGE F., *Intergovernmental Fiscal Relations in the United States*. Washington, D.C.: Brookings Institution, 1967.

FENNO, RICHARD, *The Power of the Purse: Appropriations Politics in Congress*. Boston: Little, Brown, 1966.

SHARKANSKY, IRA, *The Politics of Taxing and Spending*. New York: Bobbs-Merrill, 1969.

WILDAVSKY, AARON, *The Politics of the Budgeting Process*. Boston: Little, Brown, 1964.

Howard Jarvis: tax reform and Proposition 13. *Wide World Photos*.

# Tax Policy
## revolting against incrementalism

# 11

Everyone talks about a tax revolt. Jimmy Carter's 1976 campaign rhetoric captured the common mood: "America's tax system is a disgrace to the human race." *Forty* percent of personal income in the nation goes to taxation—to the bewildering array of complex, chaotic, and inequitable taxes of federal, state, and local governments. Yet a serious nationwide revolt against taxes has yet to appear. It is true that some states, following the lead of California's "Proposition 13" movement, have slashed property taxes. And tax reduction notions are frequently praised by Washington politicians. But the incremental character of national policy making has prevented any significant overhaul of the nation's tax structure. Indeed, quite the opposite is true: tax burdens have grown *heavier* each year under current tax laws, as inflation has pushed taxpayers into higher tax brackets.

### The Inflation Ratchet

Under the federal government's progressive personal income tax (the nation's largest source of tax revenue), the percentage of income captured by government rises with increases in income. Currently, the federal personal income tax begins at 14 percent of the *first* $1,000 of taxable income (after exemptions and deductions), and moves up to higher percentages for each $1,000 of additional income: a tax of 51 percent is levied on taxable income over $38,000, and the highest tax bracket of 70 percent is levied on taxable income over $200,000.

For example, for a family of four, the first $7,000 of income is currently free of most federal income taxes. A combination of personal exemptions, tax credits, and low income allowances frees most poverty-level families from any income taxes. (Welfare assistance and social security payments are not taxed.) Thus, federal personal income taxes for a family of four currently start on income over $7,000. The initial rate is 14 percent of each *marginal* dollar, that is, each dollar *over* $7,000. So, a family with an $8,000 income would pay approximately $140 in federal personal taxes. (Note: this is not 14 percent of their *total* income, but rather 14 percent of their first $1,000 of "taxable income.") Rates on taxable income then increase in steps from 14 percent to a high of 70 percent on taxable income over $200,000.

Under this *progressive* system of taxation, it is unnecessary for Congress to vote tax increases during inflationary periods. Tax increases occur automatically when salaries and wages increase with inflation.

What does the combination of inflation and progressive taxation mean to the average American? Let us consider a worker who earned $10,000 in 1960. This worker would have paid $1,362 in taxes and kept $8,638 in *buying* power. This worker would have paid an "effective tax rate" (taxes paid as a percent of total income) of 13.6 percent. (See Table 11–1.) But in 1978 this same worker would have had to earn $22,671 just to keep the same $8,638 in buying power. This is because $10,098 of the salary increase (from $10,000 to $22,671) would go to inflation and $3,935 to taxes. The "effective tax rate" would now be 17.5 percent. Thus, salaries go up and taxes go up—even as a percentage of income—but buying power remains the same, even for workers who more than doubled their salary.

The same is true for higher paid executives. Executives who were paid $50,000 in 1960 would have to earn $118,482 in 1978 in order to have the same *buying* power that they enjoyed in 1960. And even with

**TABLE 11–1**   Inflation, Taxes, and Buying Power

|  | Worker | | Executive | |
|---|---|---|---|---|
|  | *1960* | *1978* | *1960* | *1978* |
| Salary | $10,000 | $22,671 | $50,000 | $118,482 |
| Taxes | 1,362 | 3,935 | 14,187 | 40,804 |
| Inflation | — | 10,098 | — | 41,865 |
| Buying Power | $ 8,638 | $ 8,638 | $35,813 | $ 35,813 |
| Effective Tax Rate | 13.6% | 17.5% | 28.4% | 34.5% |

no increase in buying power, their "effective tax rate" would increase from 28.4 percent in 1960 to 34.5 percent in 1978.

A family's "real" income, that is, its purchasing power, is not increased by an increase in salary which barely matches the increase in inflation. So while progressive taxation assumes that the family is able to pay more in taxes because its income increased, it turns out that during inflationary periods a movement into a higher tax bracket may mean a *reduction* in purchasing power.

Politically, this means that Congress can finance steadily increasing federal budgets *without voting for tax increases*. Increasing public spending can be funded largely by automatic increases in personal income taxes which are stimulated by inflation. Thus, incremental spending is aided and abetted by incremental taxing. And Congressmen are not obliged to go on record as having voted for tax increases.

While there is not yet an effective "tax revolt" movement in Washington, it is clear that resentment and cynicism are growing. The federal tax system, particularly the personal income tax, rests primarily on voluntary compliance. Millions of taxpayers must voluntarily declare their income on their 1040 forms, compute their own taxes, and turn in their calculations before April 15th each year. Across the country, opinion surveys find the overwhelming majority of Americans think that their taxes are too high, too complicated, and unfair. The voluntary compliance upon which the tax system is based may be in danger of collapse. The incidence of tax evasion is increasing. The "underground" economy (financial transactions hidden from the tax collectors) is estimated to be over $100 billion or 5 percent of the GNP. If cynicism becomes widespread, and tax cheating and evasion become the norm, the entire tax system could come tumbling down, because there are not enough Internal Revenue Service (IRS) agents to investigate these tax evasions.

## The Federal Tax Bite

Federal taxes are derived from five major sources:

### Individual Income Taxes

This source of tax money accounts for 43 percent of the federal government's total income. Not only is the personal income tax the largest source of revenue, it is also one of the fastest growing, due to the effect inflation has in pushing individuals into higher tax brackets. The tax is very progressive in its rate structure, but various exemptions, deductions, and special treatments tend to moderate its progres-

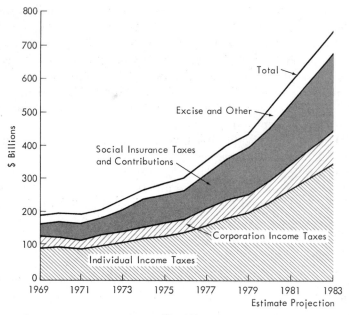

(In billions of dollars)

| Source | 1977 actual | 1978 estimate | 1979 estimate | 1980 estimate |
|---|---|---|---|---|
| Individual income taxes | $156.7 | $178.8 | $190.1 | $223.9 |
| Corporation income taxes | 54.9 | 58.9 | 62.5 | 69.1 |
| Social insurance taxes and contributions | 108.7 | 124.1 | 141.9 | 160.1 |
| Excise taxes | 17.5 | 20.2 | 25.5 | 31.1 |
| Estate and gift taxes | 7.3 | 5.6 | 6.1 | 6.5 |
| Customs duties | 5.2 | 5.8 | 6.4 | 7.0 |
| Miscellaneous receipts | 6.5 | 6.9 | 7.2 | 7.5 |
| Total | $356.9 | $400.4 | $439.6 | $505.4 |

**FIG. 11–1**   Sources of federal revenue
*Source:* Budget of the United States Government 1980

sivity. (See the section titled "Tax Reform and Tax Loopholes," which appears later in this chapter.)

The federal income tax is generally based on the notion of "ability to pay." This is determined not only by income, but also by family size, sickness, age, debt, and other situations, which are recognized in deductions, exemptions, and special treatments. All of these factors are subtracted from an individual's total income to arrive at "taxable income."

The federal individual income tax was adopted in 1913, but for many years it was very modest and it applied only to a small number of high-income people. But during the Second World War, rates were increased and revenue collected by this tax rose dramatically. Since then, inflation has increased the yield of the tax manyfold.

The income tax is automatically deducted from the paychecks of all employees except farm and domestic workers. This "withholding" system is the backbone of the individual income tax. There is no withholding of non-wage income but taxpayers with such income must file a "declaration of estimated taxes" and pay this estimate in quarterly installments. Before April 15th of each year, all income-earning Americans must report their taxable income to the Internal Revenue Service on its Form 1040.

Taxable income is computed by taking total income and (1) subtracting welfare payments, social security benefits, unemployment compensation, interest from state and local bonds, and other forms of untaxed income; (2) subtracting personal exemptions for each member of the family (currently $750), additional exemptions for persons over 65 or blind, charitable contributions, interest paid, state and local taxes paid, medical and dental expenses above 3 percent, losses from casualty or theft over $100, and a "low income" allowance (currently $2,100 for married couples). Instead of itemizing deductions, the taxpayer may use a standard deduction and consult a tax table showing taxes due for various size families. Most taxpayers receive a refund on their withholding taxes.

Capital gains—profits made from the buying and selling of stock, real estate, or other assets, held for at least a year—are taxed at about half the rate of salaries and wages. Since "earned" income is taxed at rates from 14 to 70 percent, the rates on "unearned" capital gains run from 7 to 35 percent. The reason given for taxing capital gains at a lower rate than earned income is to encourage business investment, risk-taking, job creation, and economic growth.

In the Tax Reform Act of 1969 the maximum tax rate on "earned" income was limited to 50 percent. A combination of earned income, dividends, interest, rents, etc., could still be taxed at the maximum rate of 70 percent. But Congress believed that it was necessary to increase the work and incentives of professional people and managers and executives by limiting the tax bite on salaries to 50 percent.

### Corporate Income Tax

The corporate income tax is 48 percent of corporate profits. Corporations, even very large ones, that do not make a profit in a given year, are not taxed in that year. (It is always an interesting news item to report that some large corporations paid no taxes in some years; rarely does the news report indicate whether the corporation lost money.) Corporations that lose money in a particular year may use this loss to offset profits in three preceding years (carry back), and thereby lessen their taxes on these earlier years. Religious, educational, and charitable organizations and their unions are exempt, except for their "unrelated business income."

Who pays the corporate income tax? Economists differ over whether this tax is "shifted" to consumers or whether corporations and their stockholders bear its burden. The evidence on the incidence of the corporate income tax is inconclusive.[1]

The strongest criticism against the corporate income tax centers around its effect on investment and saving and corporate debt. The tax is said to discourage private investment in stocks because the income (dividends) from stocks are taxed twice, first at 48 percent as corporate income and then as personal income to stockholders at rates from 14 to 70 percent. For example, $100 of corporate income taxed at 48 percent leaves only $52 for stockholders; stockholders in the 70 percent bracket would have to pay $36.40 of this remaining $52 in personal income tax. The combination of both taxes means that $84.40 out of $100 of corporate income goes to federal taxation. This leads wealthy investors *out* of the stockmarket. To raise money for new growth, corporations must increasingly turn to bank loans rather than investment capital. To pay the interest on bank loans and at the same time make a profit, corporations must expect a high rate of return—usually 20 percent or more—in order to justify a new expansion. The result has been slowing of industrial growth in America over the years. Partly to offset the ill-effects of current tax policy on investment, the federal government has instituted an "investment tax credit" which allows businesses to deduct as credit against their income tax, 10 percent of the cost of new investment.

The corporate income tax is *not* growing as a proportion of federal revenue; corporate taxes have remained about 13 percent of total federal revenues for several years.

### Social Security Taxes

The second largest, and fastest growing, source of federal revenue is the social security tax. To keep up with the rising number of beneficiaries and the higher levels of benefits voted by Congress, the social security tax is scheduled to rise incrementally each year through 1984 in two ways: (1) a gradual increase in the combined employer-employee tax rate (percent); and (2) a gradual increase in the taxable earnings base.

[1] Joseph A. Pechman, *Federal Tax Policy*, 3rd ed. (Washington: Brookings Institution, 1977).

| | 1978 | 1979 | 1980 | 1981 | 1982 | 1983 | 1984 |
|---|---|---|---|---|---|---|---|
| Tax Rate | 12.1 | 12.26 | 12.26 | 13.3 | 13.4 | 13.4 | 13.4 |
| Earnings Base | 17,000 | 22,900 | 25,900 | 29,700 | 32,100 | 34,500 | 36,900 |

Note that the middle class (those whose incomes range from $17,000 to $36,900) receive double blows during these years—the increase in the rate of social security tax, *and* an increase in the base, the proportion of their earnings subject to the tax.

The taxes collected under social security are earmarked (by social security number) for the account of each taxpayer. Workers, therefore, feel they are receiving benefits as a right rather than as a gift of the government. Benefits are slightly related to the earnings record of the individual worker; there are both minimum and maximum benefit levels which prevent benefits from corresponding closely to payments.

The social security tax now provides about 32 percent of the federal government's revenue.

### Excise Taxes

Federal taxes on liquor, tobacco, gasoline, telephones, air travel, and other so-called luxury items account for only about 1 to 2 percent of total federal revenue.

### Custom Duties

Taxes on imports provide another 1 to 2 percent of total federal revenues.

## Tax Burdens: Progressivity and Regressivity

The politics of taxation centers around the question of who actually bears the burden or "incidence" of a tax—that is, which income groups must devote the largest proportion of their income to taxes. Taxes that require high-income groups to pay a larger percentage of their incomes in taxes than low-income groups are said to be *progressive*, while taxes that take a larger share of the income of low-income groups are called *regressive*. Note that the *percentage of income* paid in taxes is the determining factor. Most taxes take more money from the rich than the poor, but a progressive or regressive tax is distinguished by the *percentages of income* taken from various income groups. The percentage of income paid in taxes is called the "effective tax rate."

Progressive taxation is generally defended on the principle of ability to pay; the assumption is that high-income groups can afford to pay a larger percentage of their incomes into taxes at no more of a sacrifice than that required of lower-income groups to devote a smaller proportion of their income to taxation. This assumption is based on what economists call "marginal utility theory" as it applies to money: each additional dollar of income is slightly less valuable to an individual than preceding dollars (for example, a $5,000 increase in the income of an individual already earning $100,000 is much less valuable than a $5,000 increase to an individual earning only $3,000 or to an individual with no income). Hence, added dollars of income can be taxed at higher *rates* without violating equitable principles.

Opponents of progressive taxation generally assert that equity can only be achieved by taxing everyone at the *same* percentage of their income, regardless of the size of their income. Progressivity penalizes initiative, enterprise, and risk, and reduces incentives to expand and develop the nation's economy. Moreover, by taking incomes of high-income groups, governments are taking money that would otherwise go into business—investments, stocks, bonds, loans, etc.—and hence government is curtailing economic growth.

Regressive taxation is seldom defended as equitable in itself. However, some regressive taxes—notably the general sales tax imposed by most state governments—are such good revenue producers that they have many adherents. Sales taxes are less visible than income taxes; consumers generally consider them part of the price of an item. They can reach mobile populations whose income or property cannot be taxed by a state or local jurisdiction. When a major segment of the *national* tax structure is progressive, it is sometimes argued that some regressivity in state and local taxation is not inequitable in the light of the overall tax picture. Finally, it can be argued that the benefits to low-income groups of increased government expenditures outweigh whatever burdens are imposed by the regressivity of sales taxation.

In considering the burden of incidence of a tax it is important not only to consider the *rate*, but also *economic behaviors* that affect burdens, and the problem of tax shifting. The *rate* simply states the percentage of the *base* (the object of the tax) which will go to taxes—for example, a 5 percent tax on all sales, or 10 percent tax on airline tickets, or a progressive sliding rate from 14 to 70 percent on income. A *rate* may appear to be neither progressive nor regressive, but economic behaviors may operate to make certain income groups more likely to bear the greater burden of the tax, that is, to pay a higher "effective tax rate." For example, a 10 percent tax on jewelry or yachts does not have a progressive rate, but because high-income groups are presumed to spend a greater percentage of their income on these items than low-income groups, the tax is presumed to be progressive. A 5 percent tax on all sales of consumer items is considered regressive because low-income groups devote a larger percentage, sometimes all, of their income to consumer items and hence bear the full brunt of the tax. High-income groups, which save or invest a sizable proportion of their income and spend only part of it for consumer items, do not allocate the same proportion of their incomes to the payment of a sales tax as low-income groups.

When the person taxed, such as a property owner, can pass on the impact of the tax to other persons, such as renters, the burden of the tax is said to "shift." Because poor people usually rent, and they must spend a large percentage of their income for housing, property taxes shifted onto them in the form of higher rents are generally considered regressive. Thus, state and local sales taxes are generally considered regressive, as are local property taxes.

The federal income tax is indeed progressive and the largest share of it is paid by middle-class Americans. The Congressional Quarterly reports that the poorest one-fifth of all taxpayers in 1975 (those with adjusted gross incomes of $7,300 a year or less) earned 4.3 percent of all taxable income, but paid less than 1 percent of all income taxes (see Table 11–2). In contrast, the richest one-fifth of all taxpayers, those with incomes above $22,000, earned 42.3 percent of all taxable income and paid 60.3 percent of all income taxes. If income and the income tax burden were divided evenly, each group would have earned 20 percent of the taxable income and paid 20 percent of income taxes.

Finally, it should be noted that the social security system is financed on a regressive revenue structure. Social security payments are made only on wage and salary income, not on profits, capital gains, interest, and dividends, which provide a large share of the income of upper-income groups. More importantly, the social security payments are only collected on the first $29,700 (in 1981) of wage income; thus, per-

**TABLE 11–2**  Tax Burdens: Federal Individual Income Tax

| Income Earners | 1975 Incomes | Proportion of Taxable Income | Percentage of Federal Tax Paid (in percent) |
|---|---|---|---|
| Lowest Fifth | under $7,300 | 4.7 | 0.6 |
| Second Fifth | $7,300–$12,000 | 12.0 | 5.8 |
| Third Fifth | $12,000–$16,300 | 17.9 | 13.1 |
| Fourth Fifth | $16,300–$22,000 | 23.0 | 20.1 |
| Highest Fifth | over $22,000 | 42.3 | 60.3 |

*Source:* Congressional Quarterly, Inc., *Taxes, Jobs, and Inflation* (Washington: Congressional Quarterly, Inc., 1978), p. 40.

sons earning more than this amount pay a lower percentage of their total income into social security than persons earning less than this amount. Of course, this financing system was established on the principle that social security is an "insurance" program in which participants only received what they paid for; it was not established as an income redistribution system.

## Federal, State, and Local Tax Sources

Although there is no constitutional requirement that assigns different types of taxes to federal, state, and local governments in America, over the years, these three levels of government have come to rely on separate tax bases (see Figure 11–2). The federal government's principal reliance is on personal and corporate *income* taxes. State governments also rely on income taxes to some extent, but the principal source of state tax revenues is *sales taxation.* Consumers are a notoriously weak pressure group. And it seems easy for taxpayers to dribble pennies away two or three at a time. Sales tax does not require obvious payroll deductions as income taxation or year-end tax bills as property taxation. It is a steady producer of large amounts of revenue. Local governments rely primarily on *property* taxes. Real estate is relatively easy to find for tax purposes, and it cannot be easily moved out of the local jurisdiction. A local sales tax can result in merchants moving beyond city boundaries, and a city income tax can speed the population exodus to suburbia.

## Proposition 13 in the States

Office seekers regularly attack the burdens of taxation. Opinion polls generally show that large majorities of Americans believe their taxes are "too high." But are Americans ready yet to *do anything* about tax burdens?

If there really is a national "tax revolt," it might be traced to a 1978 California referendum known as "Proposition 13." California citizens were sufficiently aroused to ignore the pleas and warnings of business, labor, and government leaders and vote themselves a healthy property tax cut by a two-to-one margin. Specifically, Proposition 13 amended the California constitution to

> limit property tax collections by local governments to 1 percent (10 mills) of the "full cash value" of 1977 assessments.
>
> limit increases in assessments to 2 percent each year.

allow reassessments only when property is sold.

require a two-thirds vote of both houses of the state legislature to levy any new taxes.

prohibit local government from imposing any new property taxes, and require two-thirds vote approval for *any* other new form of local taxation.

The impact of Proposition 13 falls most heavily upon local governments and school districts, which rely primarily on property taxation. The state of California has a general sales tax of 4.75 percent and an income tax ranging up to 11 percent, in addition to alcoholic bev-

FEDERAL TAX SOURCES

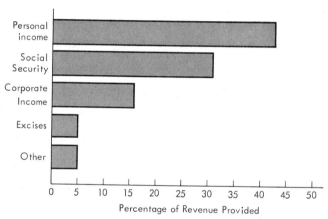

STATE AND LOCAL TAX SOURCES

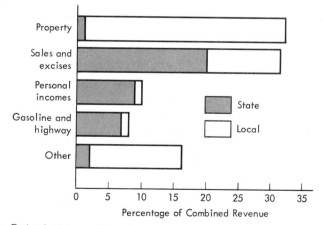

FIG. 11–2   Federal, state, and local tax sources

erages, cigarette, gasoline and other taxes. Indeed, the state had accumulated a $5 billion budget surplus in 1978, a surplus which may have contributed to the voters' urge to reduce taxation. Another contributing factor to the California outcome was the rapid rise in property values and the accompanying rapid rise in property value tax assessments. Finally, California was one of the heaviest tax burden states in the nation. No doubt all of these factors contributed to the success of Proposition 13.

However, despite predictions of a *national* tax revolt, voters have not yet been stampeded into slashing taxes at every opportunity, regardless of the consequences. Since California's Proposition 13, many more states have voted on tax limitation referenda. The results have been mixed. Some states have voted to limit state and local taxing and spending, while other states have voted against identical taxing and spending limitations. Opinion polls which face respondents with a *direct tradeoff* between reducing taxes or cutting public services, show pluralities favoring keeping taxes "about the same," rather than "increasing" or "reducing" them. In other words, the largest group of voters seem willing to accept current tax levels if they are convinced that these burdens are directly tied to services such as education, police, fire, sanitation, highways, and even welfare for the "truly deserving."

Much of the popular grievance about tax burdens is (accurately) directed against *federal* taxation. However, the United States Constitution does not provide for national initiatives or referenda. This means that taxpayers can only strike out against "government" taxes in state and local referenda voting, even though their real grievance may be with high levels of federal taxation.

Tax limitation proposals fall into several general categories. Of course, any specific plan may vary in details from the outlines described here.

### 1. Property Tax Limits

First of all, there is the "Proposition 13" (or "Jarvis-Gann," named after the cosponsors of the California referendum) type of proposal which is directed at property taxes. These proposals usually limit allowable tax rates to 10 to 15 mills of full value of property, limit annual assessment increases, and/or allow reassessments only when the property is sold. This form of limitation applies mainly to local governments and school districts and may actually increase state taxes if state governments simply take over local services. There is also controversy over the real beneficiaries of a Proposition 13 proposal. If two-thirds of a state's assessed property value is owned by financial, commercial, or industrial firms, rather than private homeowners, then the bulk of tax relief goes directly to these firms. Of course, tax relief to business firms may stimulate economic growth, but homeowners may feel "cheated" when they learn that the bulk of relief goes to business and not to them.

### 2. Personal Income Limits

A somewhat more complex scheme, yet one which promises to limit *all* forms of state and local taxes, involves limiting state and local taxes to a certain percentage of the state's personal income. For example, if state and local taxes amount to 10 percent of a state's total personal income, a constitutional amendment could be offered to voters which limits all future state and local taxes to a total of no more than 10 percent of personal income. This prevents state and local government from growing at a faster rate than personal income, but it does allow tax revenues to rise.

### 3. Expenditure Limits

Similar restrictions can be placed on total state and local *expenditures*—limiting spending to a certain percentage of a state's total personal income. Presumably, expenditure limits would hold down taxes over the long run, and therefore expenditure limits can be considered as an indirect form of tax limitation.

### 4. Public Employment Limits

Another indirect method of limiting taxation is to limit state and local government employment. For example, in the United States as a whole, 4.75 percent of the population is employed by state and local governments. A state could fix this public employment percentage by law or by constitutional amendment to 4.75 percent or lower, and thereby prohibit state and local government employment from growing at a faster rate than the state population. Presumably, such a limit would hold down taxes over the long run.

## Evaluation: The Sputtering Tax Revolt

Proposals to lighten the national tax burden, or to reform and simplify federal taxation, run afoul amongst a tangle of political calculations, social goals, practical limits, and basic confusion over the purposes of the tax system. Who should receive tax relief? How much tax relief can be granted without cutting essential federal programs or increasing the federal debt and the rate of inflation? What should the tax system do— simply raise revenue, redistribute income from the rich to the poor, or reward investment and economic growth, or punish people for smoking or drinking or using gasoline, or all these things at once? Any proposal to radically alter the nation's tax structure raises all these difficult political questions. To avoid these conflicts, both the president and Congress generally fall back upon *incrementalism*—minor tinkering with the tax laws each year, but with no serious changes in tax policy.

Nonetheless, significant changes in federal tax policy have been offered and deserve some consideration. Economist Arthur Laffer has stimulated a great deal of thought about tax reduction with his simple suggestion that heavy taxes discourage work, productivity, investment, and economic growth. Reduce taxes, he urges, and the paradoxical result will be an *increase* in governmental revenue because more people will work longer and harder knowing they can keep a larger share of their earnings. Hence, productivity will increase, investors will be persuaded to put their money back into business enterprises in the hope of winning financial rewards, more new jobs will be created, and all of this increased economic activity will actually produce more governmental revenues even though tax rates are lower.

Laffer's notion is expressed in the "Laffer curve" shown in Figure 11–3. Initially, governmental revenues will rise with increases in tax rates; but when these rates become too high, they discourage workers and businessmen from producing and investing. When this discouragement occurs, production and investment decline, and government revenues also fall. For example, *no one* would work or invest if a 100 percent tax rate were imposed, that is, if everything they worked for was confiscated by the government. Since no one would work under

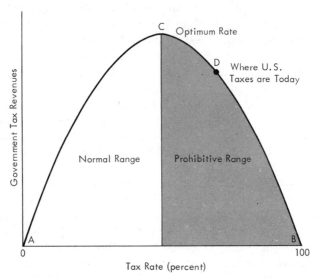

FIG. 11–3  The Laffer curve

such a tax, government tax revenues would decline to zero (point B on Figure 11–3). Of course, if the government imposed no taxes (a zero tax rate) the government would not receive any revenues (point A). According to the Laffer curve, modest increases in tax rates will result in increased tax revenues, up to an optimum point (point C), at which further increases discourage work, investment, and economic growth, and thereby reduce government revenues. Laffer does not claim to know exactly what the optimum rate of taxation should be. But Laffer believes the United States is currently operating in the "prohibitive range" (point D) at which taxes discourage work, productivity, investment, and growth. He believes a tax reduction would actually increase total tax revenues.

Notions such as those put forward by economist Arthur Laffer have stimulated some interest in Washington in general tax reduction. Representative Jack Kemp (Rep., N.Y.) and Senator William Roth (Rep., Del.) have proposed a 30 percent cut in federal taxes over a three-year period. Presumably—if Laffer is correct—such a drastic cut would eventually stimulate sufficient economic activity and resulting tax revenues so as to overcome any temporary budget deficits.

A less drastic reform is the elimination of personal income taxes on interest from investments and dividends from stock. It is frequently argued that taxing these sources of personal income is a form of "double taxation": (1) corporations are taxed first on their corporate profits, and then (2) when corporations distribute the remainder to their stockholders, the stockholders must pay a personal income tax on the dividends. More important, it is argued that eliminating or reducing the tax on interest and dividends would encourage more people to invest in banks and corporations. More money would be available for economic growth; productivity would increase with new plant investments; new jobs would be created; and we would all be better off in an expanding economy. However, eliminating or reducing taxes on "unearned income" would be viewed as a tax break for the wealthy since they receive more income from interest and dividends than the poor. It is difficult to justify politically any tax reduction which would mainly benefit the rich.

With runaway inflation, increasing attention has been given in recent years to automatically adjusting personal income tax rates to rises in prices. (This is often referred to as "indexing" taxes to the cost of living.) This would end the ratchet effect whereby inflation pushes individuals into ever higher income tax brackets. Each year tax brackets would be automatically raised with the inflation rate, so that individuals would pay taxes in proportion to their buying power after inflation. This "indexing" of taxes would offset the effects of inflation. However, it would also force Congress either to vote tax increases each year to meet rising governmental budgets or to cut the budgets. Congressmen usually do not like to do either of these things. Moreover, "indexing" would remove some Congressional flexibility in dealing with changing fiscal conditions through tax policy.

## Tax Reform and Tax "Loopholes"

Incrementalism is a characteristic of tax policy just as it is a characteristic of expenditure policy. A review of major tax decisions of the federal government over the last decade clearly indicates the obstacles to significant change in the tax structure.

Since the adoption of the Sixteenth Amendment in 1913, the income tax has been the chief producer of revenue for the federal government and the chief object of political conflict. Yet despite many efforts at tax "reform"—efforts which, if successful, would result in a reallocation of burdens among income groups—Congress has never undertaken any comprehensive rewriting of federal tax laws. Instead, tax policy has been characterized by a gradual accretion of decisions.

The actual incidence of the federal income tax is a matter of great controversy. Although nominal rates are very progressive, the actual effective tax rate on income—the rate that income is taxed after exemptions, deductions, capital gains, and other provisions are considered—is much less progressive than generally believed. The Internal Revenue Code is hundreds of pages long, and it contains a long list of exemptions, deductions, and special treatments; these have been expanded by administrative and court decisions. Almost ritualistically, Congressmen and presidents have pledged to eliminate "loopholes" and "reform" the tax structure. Yet only modest changes have been made in tax laws over the years.

The problem in closing tax loopholes is that what one person regards as a loophole may be regarded as a socially useful tax provision by someone else. (For example, deductions from taxable income for charitable contributions are generally applauded as a useful incentive to charitable giving; but this is also a major source of lost tax revenue.) Almost *half* of total personal income in America is not taxed because of all the exemptions and deductions written into the tax laws.

A great deal of personal income escapes federal income taxation because of the following deductions and exemptions:

1. Personal exemption of $1,000 per dependent, with double exemptions for the blind and the aged
2. Medical expenses over 3 percent of income and drug expenses over 1 percent
3. Charitable contributions

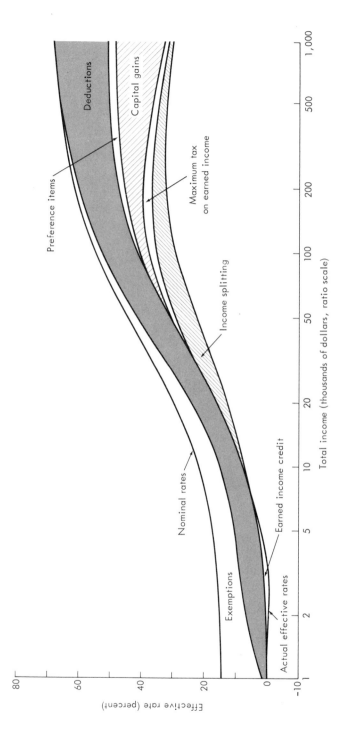

**FIG. 11—4** Influence of various provisions on effective rates of federal individual income tax, 1976

[a]Preference items as defined by the Tax Reform Act of 1969, except excluded net long-term capital gains.

*Source:* Joseph A. Pechman *Federal Tax Policy* 3rd ed. (Washington: Brookings Institution, 1977), p. 72.

4. Taxes paid to state and local governments
5. Child-care expenses and alimony payments
6. Casualty losses
7. Interest payments, including home mortgages
8. Income from social security, public assistance, unemployment insurance, and veterans' disability

Although these provisions account for the great bulk of lost revenue, they are seldom the object of political controversy. So many Americans make use of these provisions that they are rarely called "loopholes." In contrast, certain other exemptions and deductions are frequently cited as "loopholes":

1. *Capital gains*—profits from the sale of investments held over six months—are taxed at only one-half of the rate of "earned" income (up to a maximum of 35 percent, rather than 70 percent). This special treatment for "unearned income" is regarded by some as a necessary incentive for business investment; but regarded by others as special treatment for income derived from investment that is not afforded to income from wages and salaries.

2. *State and local bond interest* is completely exempt from federal income taxation. This is regarded by some as an incentive to buy state and local government bonds for roads, hospitals, schools, environmental improvement, etc.; but regarded by others as a way in which wealthy people can escape taxation on income from their investments.

3. *Oil and gas depletion allowance* permits individuals and companies to deduct 22 percent of income from oil and gas production in recognition of the depreciation of these reserves. This is regarded by some as a necessary incentive in the search for new sources of energy; but regarded by others as a special privilege to oil and gas interests.

4. *Accelerated depreciation of property* permits individuals and companies to calculate the depreciation of their income-producing property in ways that overestimate the actual decline in value. This is regarded by some as a spur to capital investment and economic growth; but regarded by others as an unfair "fast tax write-off."

The history of tax reform legislation reveals a reluctance to radically restructure the tax system and a tendency instead to make only incremental changes in the tax laws. In 1964 Congress reduced the progressivity of tax rates—from the previous 20 to 91 percent to a range of 14 to 70 percent—but retained nearly all the traditional exemptions, deductions, and special treatments. In 1968, the costs of the Vietnam War moved Congress to consider an increase in the personal income tax. Again there was considerable controversy over loopholes, but the device finally settled upon was a "surtax" of 10 percent—a uniform 10 percent increase over whatever the individual was already paying. This device again left the basis of the tax structure untouched.

The Tax Reform Act of 1969 caused the most comprehensive review of tax exemptions and deductions, but only minor changes were incorporated into law. For example, after much debate, the oil and gas depletion allowance was reduced from 27.5 to 22 percent. The tax on capital gains was increased up to 35 percent. The tax rates on single persons were reduced to rates at or below the rates paid by married taxpayers. The personal exemption was raised from $600 to $750, and taxes were eliminated on the lowest incomes. Finally, a 10 percent minimum tax was imposed on high incomes, regardless of exemptions, deductions, or exclusions. But these were clearly *incremental* changes, rather than a major restructuring of the tax laws.

Contrary to widespread belief, "soaking the rich" would not lead to any major increase in federal government revenue. For example, if all incomes over $50,000 a year were confiscated by the government, the additional tax revenues would amount to less than $20 billion, or 6.5 percent of the federal government's budget. Closing four tax loopholes (capital gains, state and local bond interest, oil and gas depletion allowance, accelerated depreciation) would increase federal revenues less than $10 billion, or 2 percent of the budget (perhaps less if the changes caused shifting of investments). Taxing the rich may provide some symbolic satisfaction, but it will not produce great revenue. The bulk of taxable income in America is concentrated in the middle classes. Unquestionably, continued increases in governmental activities will result in greater tax burdens on the middle classes.

## Spending Policy:
## Who Enjoys the Benefits of Government?

Expenditures as well as taxes can be progressive or regressive in their impact. Obviously public assistance payments are *progressive* expenditures because they are of greater benefits to low-income families than high-income families. In contrast, interest payments—interest on government bonds paid out to investors—are *regressive* expenditures because they are likely to go to high-income rather than low-income groups. In determining the distributional impact of expenditures, assumptions must be made about the use of government services by various income classes, and the relationship of this use to their total income. We must consider education, health, public assistance, recreation, police and fire, etc., and the use that is made of these governmental services by various income groups.

As we might expect, the most progressive of all government services in its distributional impact is welfare. Three-quarters of all welfare expenditures go to the two lowest-income classes. Social security benefits are also very progressive. Expenditures for public schools and highways tend to benefit middle-income groups more than the poor or the rich. Apparently the poor do not get as much out of public education as the middle class; neither do the wealthy, who limit the size of their family and make greater use of private schools. Public expenditures for higher education are generally regressive, because it is the middle and upper-middle classes who are most likely to send their children to college. Only in the very highest income categories are the benefits of public higher education expenditures diminished, probably because this group relies more on private colleges and universities. In general, the distributional impact of total government expenditures is moderately progressive.

## Summary

Incrementalism is characteristic of tax policy in that comprehensive restructuring of federal taxes is unlikely. Despite rumors of a national tax revolt, relatively little has been done by Congress or the president to revise federal tax policy. The political costs appear to be too great; it is easier to consider minor tinkering with exemptions and credits than to overhaul the entire tax system.

1. Under the federal progressive personal income tax, tax increases occur automatically each year with inflation. This continuous growth in revenues from the nation's largest revenue source, the personal income tax, fuels ever increasing federal expenditures. Thus, incremental growth in expenditures is accompanied by incremental growth in tax revenues.

2. Tax increases brought about by inflation do not require officeholders to vote on the record in favor of tax increases. Thus, the current "inflation ratchet," which increases the *proportion* of income paid into taxes with increases in inflation, whether or not real income is higher, allows Congress and the president to escape political "blame" for raising taxes.

3. The impact of heavy taxation on economic growth is unclear. But many economists believe that high personal income tax brackets, taxes on interest and dividends, and the corporate income tax, all combine to discourage investment and real economic growth. Congress has allowed modest investment tax credits—a 10 percent deduction of new business investment against income taxes—to partially offset the adverse impact of taxation on economic growth. But no overhaul of federal taxes with a view toward stimulating growth is currently being considered.

4. Although there is no constitutional requirement to separate revenue sources, federal, state, and local governments rely on different taxes. The federal government relies primarily on personal and corporate income taxes and social security contributions, while state governments rely primarily on sales taxes and local governments rely primarily on property taxes.

5. The national "tax revolt" has occurred in a limited number of states where popular referenda (such as California's Proposition 13) allow voters to express their concern about tax rates. The U.S. Constitution does not provide for *national* referenda on taxation or anything else. Congress has devoted only fragmented and incidental consideration to proposals to lighten the national tax burden. No serious changes in national tax policy have emerged from the "tax revolt."

6. Policies that distribute government burdens and benefits among income groups can be identified by calculating the progressivity and regressivity of both taxes and expenditures. Progressivity means that the tax burden is a higher percentage of income of high-income groups than of low-income groups, or that the expenditure benefit is a higher percentage of the income of low-income groups than of high-income groups. Regressivity in tax burdens and expenditure benefits means just the opposite.

7. The burden of all federal taxes is progressive, although not steeply so. The most progressive of all taxes is the federal personal income tax. In contrast, state and local taxes are regressive, owing to the reliance of state and local governments on sales and property taxation.

8. The distributional impact of most government expenditures is moderately progressive. Welfare and social security expenditures are very progressive. Expenditures for schools and highways tend to benefit middle-income groups more than the rich or poor. Expenditures for public higher education are generally regressive because more middle- and upper-class families send their children to college.

## Bibliography

BREAK, GEORGE F., and JOSEPH A. PECHMAN, *Federal Tax Reform: The Impossible Dream*. Washington: Brookings Institution, 1975.

BUCHANAN, JAMES M., and MARILYN R. FLOWERS, *The Public Finances: An Introductory Textbook*, 4th ed. New York: Richard D. Irwin, 1975.

GOODS, RICHARD, *The Individual Income Tax*. Washington: Brookings Institution, 1976.

PECHMAN, JOSEPH A., *Federal Tax Policy*, 3rd ed. Washington: Brookings Institution, 1977.

Strategic weapons: peace versus nuclear confrontation. *Wide World Photos*.

# Defense Policy
## strategies
## for serious games

# 12

Many years ago the Nobel prize-winning mathematician and peace advocate Bertrand Russell observed that the game of "Chicken" was played by youthful degenerates and world leaders. The statement is true. But whether we like it or not, our life, liberty, and security depend upon our national leaders being willing to play the game. For as Russell himself observes:

> Practical politicians may admit all this [the dangers and destructiveness of war], but they argue that there is no alternative. If one side is unwilling to risk global war, while the other side is willing to risk it, *the side which is willing to run the risk will be victorious in all negotiations and will ultimately reduce the other side to complete impotence.* . . . We are, therefore, faced quite inevitably with the choice between brinkmanship and surrender.[1]

Game theory provides an interesting way of thinking about defense policy. Defense policies of major world powers are interdependent. Each major power must adjust its own defense policies to reflect not only its own national objectives but also its expectations of what other major powers may do. Outcomes depend on the combination of choices made in world capitals. Moreover, it is not unreasonable to as-

[1]Bertrand Russell, *Common Sense and Nuclear Warfare* (New York: Simon & Schuster, 1959), p. 30.

sume that major powers strive for rationality in defense policy making. Nations choose defense strategies (policies) that are designed to achieve an optimum payoff even after considering all their opponents' possible strategies. Thus, national defense policy making conforms to basic game-theoretic notions. Our use of game-theoretic ideas is limited, however, to suggesting interesting questions, posing dilemmas, and providing a vocabulary for dealing with policy making in a competitive, interdependent world.

## Deterrence Strategy and Nuclear War

In order to maintain peace and protect the national interest of the United States, primary reliance is placed upon the strategy of *deterrence*. In a general sense, deterrence means that war and aggression are prevented by making the consequences of such acts clearly unacceptable to rational leaders of other nations. This is the irony of deterrence: massive destruction of civilization is prevented by maintaining weapons capable of inflicting the massive destruction they seek to prevent. The United States does not wish to use its nuclear deterrent *physically*, but rather *psychologically*, to inhibit potential enemies from engaging in war or aggression.

### Minimum Deterrence

This is the notion that potential enemies can be dissuaded from war or aggression by the mere possession of enough nuclear weapons to destroy their homeland. The minimum deterrence strategy rests on the belief that nuclear war is now "unthinkable" because of the destruction involved and that no rational leader would choose war as an instrument of national goals. A related notion is that of "overkill"— that if the United States has enough explosive force at its disposal to kill every Russian six times, this is enough (or too much) defense. The only capability required in minimum deterrence, then, is the possession of some nuclear weapons and some aircraft or missiles to deliver them.

Perhaps it is the widespread ignorance of the American public about defense policy that accounts for the popularity of the notions of minimum deterrence, "overkill," and the "unthinkable" nuclear war. Or perhaps these notions are comfortable substitutes for serious thinking about defense requirements. But no serious military analyst today believes that minimum deterrence is sufficient insurance against war, and this view has never prevailed in American defense policy.

## Assured Destruction Deterrence

This is the notion that a potential enemy can be dissuaded from aggression or war only by maintaining the capability to destroy his society even after absorbing a well-executed surprise attack. Assured destruction deterrence considers the enemy's most menacing attack—a surprise, full-salvo, first-strike against our own offensive forces. It emphasizes our "second-strike capability"—the ability of our forces to survive such an attack by the enemy and then to inflict an unacceptable level of destruction on his homeland in retaliation. Generally, U.S. defense analysts believe that an enemy will consider one-third to one-half of his population killed and two-thirds to three-quarters of his industrial capacity destroyed to be "unacceptable," and hence this level of damage is believed to be sufficient to deter a nuclear attack.[2]

Note that the "second-strike capability" required for assured destruction deterrence is far more complex than minimum deterrence. It is not sufficient to merely count missiles or megatonnage or "overkill" capacity. The key question is the *survivability* of an effective deterrent strike force. Assured destruction deterrence considers what can be done *after* a successful surprise attack by the enemy. The surviving forces will be damaged and not fully coordinated because of the enemy's attacks on communications and command installations. These forces must operate in the confusion of a post-attack environment. The enemy's defenses will be alerted. Yet the surviving forces must still retain a credible capability of penetrating the best-alerted defenses and inflicting unacceptably high casualties.

It is extremely important to realize that second-strike capability must be *communicated* to the enemy if it is to serve as a deterrent. It would be irrational to keep your second-strike capacity a secret. (Even if you did not have such a capability, you might bluff that you did.) Hence, U.S. policy makers regularly publicize the strength and size of U.S. strategic offensive forces. Deterrence is achieved only if the enemy knows that you have the capacity to deliver unacceptable damage even after absorbing a first strike.

Moreover, a second-strike deterrent must be *credible*. A potential enemy must never begin to suspect that in the event of attack you would lack the will to use your weapons. Even if you doubt the morality of a retaliatory strike which would kill millions of people, you must hide this doubt in order to preserve deterrence. Consistently backing

[2]Testimony of Robert S. McNamara, Committee on Armed Services, U.S. House of Representatives, 89th Congress, 1st session, February 1965. Reprinted in Mark E. Smith and Claude J. Johns, eds., *American Defense Policy*, 2nd ed. (Baltimore: Johns Hopkins Press, 1968), p. 98.

down in international confrontations may also erode credibility. In contrast, occasional "saber rattling" or "shows of force" can serve a useful psychological purpose.

Finally, deterrence strategy assumes that potential enemies are *rational*. In this context, rationality means that an enemy would not deliberately choose a course of action that would produce mass death and destruction in his own country. Needless to say, an irrational world leader (or a terrorist group) with nuclear weapons is an immense danger to the world.

In summary, assured destruction deterrence is a psychological concept. It requires (1) second-strike capability, (2) communication, (3) credibility, and (4) a rational opponent. The capability of this nation's forces to survive a surprise, full-salvo, nuclear attack must not be allowed to erode; potential aggressors must be informed of these capabilities; and the threat to use these capabilities in case of attack must be credible. If these requirements are met, then there should never be any need to use our nuclear weapons physically, that is, peace should be the outcome.

### Damage Limitation

Damage limitation is the capacity to reduce the damage inflicted by an enemy. A damage limitation strategy assumes that assured destruction deterrence has been provided, but it adds that in the event of the failure of deterrence, whether by accident or miscalculation, it is still essential that forces be provided to limit the damage of an enemy attack. Although most defense analysts accept the assured destruction deterrence notion, there is disagreement over the utility, costs, and effectiveness of damage limitation efforts.

The major dispute over damage limitation centers on the development of defensive antiballistic missile systems (ABMs). ABMs are surface-to-air missiles designed to intercept and destroy incoming missiles. Because an ICBM requires less than forty minutes to travel from the USSR to the U.S., the reaction time of an ABM must be less than twenty minutes. An ABM system could be placed around our ICBM silos in order to protect them and reinforce our assured destruction deterrence, and it could be placed around Washington to insure the survival of command and communications facilities. Or ABM could be used to defend major population centers, but this would require nationwide coverage and very large numbers of missiles.

There are several deficiencies in ABM, however, aside from its costs. First of all, virtually all defense analysts believe that it is technically impossible to build an ABM system capable of keeping U.S. casualties to "acceptable" levels (under 40 million?) in the event of a Soviet first strike against cities. Just as bomber forces have been able to penetrate SAM (surface-to-air missile) defenses, ABMs are unlikely to stop any significant proportion of an attacking missile force. Moreover, offensive countermeasures are cheaper and easier to develop than effective antiballistic missiles. In other words, even if a heavy ABM system were constructed at great cost, the enemy could easily offset its effect by a modest increase in his offensive forces.

The U.S. built one ABM complex with 100 missiles to defend its ICBM sites. The USSR built two complexes each with 100 missiles, protecting Moscow and some of its ICBM sites. The SALT I agreement prohibited both nations from having more than two ABM sites each with 100 missiles. The U.S. never built its second allowed site and deactivated its first site.

An effective nationwide civil defense program could reduce U.S. fatalities from an all-out enemy first strike against cities to 80 million out of a 215-million population. (Without *any* civil defense, U.S. casualties in such an attack might run to 150 million.) The additional civil defense required to reduce casualties below 80 million would be very costly and easily offset by less costly increases in the enemy's offensive striking force. For example, to limit fatalities to 40 million in a large first strike against cities, we would have to spend four times as much as a potential aggressor would have to spend on his offensive forces to offset our efforts. Thus, it is difficult to justify a *heavy* civil defense effort. Nonetheless, the U.S. has failed to provide even a modest civil defense program, while the U.S.S.R. has long maintained an impressive system of civil defense shelters with provisions for thirty days or more.

More important than the technical and cost problems in damage limitation policy is the strategic dilemma that the policy creates. *An increase in one nation's damage limitation capabilities is a reduction in the other nation's assured destruction capabilities.* A heavy emphasis on damage limitation by one player might be viewed by another player as an attempt to take away his second-strike capability and hence leave him open to a surprise attack. If both players possess credible assured second-strike destruction capabilities, then a reasonably stable "balance of terror" situation is said to exist. Each nation is deterred from a first strike by the knowledge that the other nation will have enough forces left to inflict unacceptable damage levels. *But* if either nation builds an effective damage limitation capability (a heavy ABM system, a strong civil defense program with deep shelters or city evacuation plans, etc.), this action may be viewed as an attempt to take away the other nation's second-strike capability and free oneself from the consequences of surprise first strike. Thus, damage limitation may be viewed by an opponent as a very aggressive move—perhaps even preparation for a deliberate first strike. At the very least, damage limitation would oblige one's opponent to add new strength to his offensive forces to insure that his assured destruction deterrent remains credible and effective.

### Credible First-Strike Capability

First-strike capability is the capacity to threaten the enemy with a first strike and to make the threat a credible one. Although the notion that " we will never strike first" is a common one, for many years the United States provided a protective nuclear shield over Western Europe by pledging to come to the aid of NATO nations in the event of an attack. This commitment included an implied pledge to use our strategic nuclear forces against the Soviet heartland in the event that Soviet troops invaded Western Europe. It is generally assumed that this threat played a major role in halting Soviet expansion in Europe in the years following World War II. The history of Soviet expansion into Eastern Europe—postwar Communist takeovers in Poland, Hungary, Czechoslovakia, Bulgaria, Rumania; the use of Soviet troops in East Germany, Poland, and particularly Hungary to maintain Communist governments in these nations; military pressures and blockades of Berlin—all combine to suggest that the Soviets can and will use force in Europe to further their political goals. They clearly have superiority in conventional military strength—troops, tanks, artillery, support aircraft, etc. Hence, most defense analysts believe that the threat of nuclear retaliation was an essential component of the defense of Western Europe.

In recent years, the credibility of our threat has been seriously eroded. In the decade following the end of World War II, the United States indeed possessed a credible first-strike threat. It possessed the atomic bomb and long-range bombers to deliver it. More importantly, the Soviet Union did *not* possess atomic weapons and had no significant second-strike capability. The U.S. could threaten to use nuclear weapons knowing that the other side had to believe the threat because the U.S. *could* use them without risking damage to itself. But after the Soviet Union acquired its own second-strike assured destruction capability, the U.S. threat lost much of its credibility. The Soviets began to doubt that the U.S. would risk nuclear destruction on itself in order to save Western Europe. They felt freer to increase pressure on Berlin, building the Berlin Wall and creating a Berlin crisis in 1961 that necessitated President Kennedy's historic trip to Berlin and pledge of U.S. support. France also began to doubt the credibility of the U.S. commitment and embarked on its own nuclear weapons development program. Indeed, the whole fabric of European relations in recent years reflects the decline in the credibility of the U.S. shield.

Note that credible first-strike capability does not simply mean the capability of hurting the other side on a first strike. *Credible* first-strike capability really depends on how much harm the enemy can do in retaliation. A first-strike threat is not really credible if the enemy knows that you know he can inflict unacceptable damages on you in response.

Developing a credible first-strike capability would entail (1) a massive buildup of offensive weapons—enough to take out all or nearly all of the enemy's offensive weapons on a first strike; (2) a massive buildup of damage limitation systems to reduce his second-strike damage to acceptable levels; or (3) both of these moves in combination.

Current U.S. defense policy does *not* include the force levels required for a credible first-strike capability. Indeed, in the last few years defense policy makers have avoided references to "superiority" of force levels and talked instead about "sufficiency" and "rough equivalency." This means that U.S. defense policy has emphasized assured destruction deterrence; but we now recognize the loss of our credible first-strike capability.

But the real question remains whether the *Soviets* have given up the quest for a credible first-strike capacity. Until the mid-1970s, U.S. defense policy makers generally assumed that the Soviets were striving only to maintain assured second-strike capability, in the same fashion as the U.S. In other words, it was as generally believed that U.S. and Soviet objectives were the same—each was content with a "stable" balance of terror where neither nation could attack the other without bringing excessive damage upon itself. However, today defense analysts are divided, with many seeing a build-up of new, heavy, Soviet ICBMs with MIRVs, together with a strong civil defense system in the USSR, as an attempt to gain first-strike capacity. These analysts do not believe the USSR would actually initiate a first strike, but they would use their capacity to intimidate the U.S. psychologically—forcing the U.S. to back down in a series of confrontations.

### Mutual Assured Destruction—MAD

If *both* sides possess second-strike capability, each side can deter the other from launching a first strike. The mutual development of second-strike capability by both the U.S. and the USSR provides *stability* in strategic nuclear relations between the superpowers. *If* (1) both the U.S. and the USSR possess sufficient, protected retaliatory forces, so that either side could absorb any conceivable first strike by the other and still retain sufficient power to strike back and destroy the other; and *if* (2) each side communicates this retaliatory power to the other side; and *if* (3) both sides believe that the other side can survive a first strike; *then* the situation is one of mutual assured destruction or "MAD." MAD's balance of terror—each side restrained by knowledge of the second-strike capability of the other side—has maintained stability and protected the world from nuclear war for the past twenty years. MAD produces stability because each side knows that any offensive action it might take could lead to *its own destruction* and thus be suicidal. MAD removes the need for trust and replaces it with the calculated self-interest in not being devastated. World peace under MAD does not rest on trust or love or brotherhood, but on rational calculation of what is in each side's self-interest.

MAD reduces the prospects of miscalculation. Because of each side's ability to retaliate even after absorbing the other side's full-salvo attack, there is no need for either side to try to launch first in a crisis situation. MAD removes the "itchy trigger finger" effect that would exist if one or both nations believed that their own offensive forces would be destroyed in a first strike.

MAD has the effect of holding the populations of each nation hostage against the possibility of a first-strike attack. The population of the USSR can be destroyed by a retaliatory strike by the U.S., and the population of the U.S. can be destroyed by a retaliatory strike by the USSR. Hence, both nations are threatened with the annihilation of their own populations if they launch a first-strike attack.

The United States has officially embraced the notion of mutual assured destruction. The U.S. has no objection to the maintenance of a Soviet second-strike capability, as long as the U.S.'s own second-strike capability is maintained. U.S. defense policy does not envision the development of strategic superiority, or credible first-strike capability. Instead, the U.S. has concentrated on maintaining second-strike capability. The Soviet Union, however, has never publicly acknowledged the existence of MAD. More important, it has not renounced the intention of developing a credible first-strike capability against the U.S.

## Strategic Weapons: The Embattled TRIAD

In striving to maintain assured destruction deterrence, the United States, over the past twenty years, has relied on a "TRIAD" of weapons systems—launched missiles (ICBMs), submarine-landed missiles (SLBMs), and manned bombers (B52s). The strategic concept of the TRIAD includes the notion that any *one* of three sets of forces would give the United States assured destruction deterrence, that is, for example, if the ICBMs were destroyed in their silos by an enemy first strike, and all of the manned bomber force were destroyed, the United States could still retaliate with an SLBM attack which would itself inflict unacceptable damages on the enemy. Each "leg" of the TRIAD is supposed to be an independent, survivable, second-strike force. Each "leg" of TRIAD poses separate and unique problems for an enemy in devising a way to destroy the U.S. second-strike deterrent.

### ICBMs

Both the United States and the Soviet Union have developed long-range intercontinental ballistic missiles (ICBMs) that can travel between the U.S. and USSR in less than forty minutes. To insure their survivability, both sides have placed their ICBMs in "hardened" (concrete and steel) underground silos—designed and constructed so that they can be destroyed only by a direct hit. The U.S. built 1,000 "Minuteman" ICBMs in the early 1960s in addition to fifty-four larger Titan missiles. These twenty-year-old missiles continue to be this nation's complete ICBM force. The Minuteman is a solid-fuel missile which can be launched on short notice and can strike within one-quarter mile of any target in the Soviet Union. Each Minuteman ICBM can carry a one megaton warhead (equivalent to one million tons of TNT). About half of the Minuteman force carries multiple independently targeted reentry vehicles (MIRVs) which are smaller nuclear warheads that separate from the missile itself and can be accurately directed to separate targets. MIRV allows the U.S. to triple the number of deliverable nuclear warheads from its Minuteman force. The newest Minuteman III missiles carry three MIRVed warheads with 335 kiloton weapons. (While these weapons are small by today's standards, they are sixteen times more powerful than the 20 kiloton "Little Boy" A-bomb dropped on Hiroshima.) The destructiveness of various U.S. and Soviet missiles at various distances from the center of detonation is shown in Table 12–1.

**TABLE 12–1**  The Destructiveness of Nuclear Weapons

| | Weapon Size | | | |
|---|---|---|---|---|
| | 40 KT U.S. Polaris, Poseidon | 170 KT U.S. MIRVed Minuteman III, One Warhead | 1 MT U.S. Minuteman II UnMIRVed Warhead; USSR MIRVed SS18, One Warhead | 5 MT USSR SS9, SS18 |
| Crater Diameter[1] | .08 | .13 | .25 | .70 |
| Fireball radius | .20 | .35 | .70 | 1.40 |
| 150 PSI blast[2] (100% dead) | .20 | .30 | .60 | 1.00 |
| 5 PSI blast[3] (50% dead) | 1.00 | 1.60 | 3.00 | 5.00 |
| 2 PSI blast[4] (5% dead) | 1.60 | 2.70 | 5.00 | 8.00 |

[1] All figures expressed as miles or percentage thereof. Destruction of all facilities including hardened silos and underground command and control facilities.

[2] Fatal blast level for all unprotected populations, survival in reinforced concrete construction.

[3] Severe damage to unprotected populations, commercial buildings, and homes. However, standard fallout shelters can protect most of the population from blast pressures up to 7 PSI.

[4] Fatal injuries begin at 2 PSI. Population and buildings will survive outside this radius.

*Source:* Michael B. Donley, ed., *The SALT Handbook* (Washington: The Heritage Foundation, 1979).

Beyond replacing earlier Minuteman missiles with the MIRV-carrying Minuteman III, and improving the accuracy of the Minuteman guidance system, the United States has not deployed any follow-on ICBM program for the last twenty years. Moreover, no ICBM has ever been fired from an operational silo to test its reliability. ICBMs have only been fired from test facilities at Vandenberg Air Force Base in California and from Cape Kennedy in Florida under highly controlled conditions.

In contrast, the Soviet Union, during the past twenty years, has continued the development of newer, larger, and more accurate MIRVed missiles. The result is a diversified Soviet Strategic Rocket Force which includes over 1,600 ICBMs of various types, as shown in the following table:

| Type | Year | Size in Throw-Weight | Warhead | Number |
|------|------|---------------------|---------|--------|
| SS-9 | 1965 | 15 | 18-25 MT | 190 |
| SS-11 | 1966 | 2 | 1-2 MT | 780 |
| SS-13 | 1968 | 1 | 1 MT | 60 |
| SS-17 | 1975 | 6 | 5 MT | 60 |
| SS-18 | 1975 | 18 | 10 × 1 MT (MIRV) | 314 |
| SS-19 | 1975 | 7 | 6 × 1 MT (MIRV) | 200 |

The SS-18 is currently the Soviet's major land-based ICBM. It dwarfs the Minuteman III. It carries *ten* MIRV warheads, each with a *one-megaton* weapon, and there is no reason to doubt its accuracy. The Soviets have 314 of these large ICBMs, which means that their SS-18 force can deliver 3,140 one-megaton weapons.

The Soviet SS-18 missile is a "cold launch" missile; older Soviet ICBMs and all U.S. ICBMs are "hot launch." A hot-launch missile is fired *in* the silo and burns the silo in the launch process. A cold-launch missile is propelled out of the silo by gas or steam and fired *after* it clears the silo. The silo can then be reloaded immediately with a new missile. (All U.S. and USSR submarine missiles are cold launch to protect the boat and crew.) Thus, the Soviets, but not the U.S., have more ICBMs than launchers.

The debate in Congress over the second Strategic Arms Limitation Treaty (SALT-II) exposed Soviet superiority in numbers and size of their ICBM force. With their improved accuracy, the Soviets can now destroy the entire U.S. missile force using only a small portion of their own ICBM force. This danger to the survivability of our ICBM force compelled President Carter to announce plans for the development of a new mobile ICBM system called the MX. The chief purpose of the MX system is to provide *mobile* launch sites for ICBMs in order to make it very difficult for the Soviets to destroy our ICBMs in a surprise first strike. The MXs will be mounted on large mobile carriers. Each of 200 MXs can be moved secretly and at random to one of 25 or 30 hardened sites spaced along track. The Soviets will not know which sites are empty and which sites contain operational MX missiles. Therefore, to insure destruction of such a force in a surprise attack, the Soviets would have to accurately target over 6,000 separate sites. It is hoped that the Soviets will believe that the possibility of destroying such a mobile force would be very unlikely, and that they would therefore be deterred from trying to do so. Moreover, the MX missile itself, although not large, will carry *ten* MIRVed warheads. This will warn the Soviets that even if they should destroy 80 or 90 percent of the MX force, the remaining 20 or 40 MXs could deliver 200 or 400 nuclear warheads on the Soviet Union. Assuming the rationality of Kremlin leaders, the MX force should be an effective deterrent.

### Manned Bombers

The second "leg" of the TRIAD is the intercontinental bomber. Manned bombers can survive a first strike if they are in the air. A certain portion of a manned bomber force can be kept in the air during crisis periods. Given adequate warning (knowledge that the enemy has fired his ICBMs or SLBMs), a significant percentage of bombers can get off the ground before incoming missiles arrive. The range of intercontinental bombers (a 6,000-mile two-way mission range, with added range from inflight refueling), allows the United States to keep its bombers at home bases. Unlike missiles, manned bombers can be called back if the alert is an error; they can be redirected to other targets in flight; and they can be used in conventional, nonnuclear war if needed. Manned aircraft can be equipped with short-range (25-75 mile) air-to-surface missiles (ASMs) or long-range air-launched Cruise missiles (ALCMs) to give the aircraft "stand off" capability, that is, the capability to launch nuclear attacks on targets without ever flying over the target area. The U.S. intercontinental manned bomber force is composed exclusively of aged, slow, and large B-52s. This bomber was developed in 1952 as a high-penetration aircraft (a plane that would fly high over enemy air defenses), with a 6,000-mile range and a capability of carrying large numbers of nuclear weapons as bombs and short-range air-to-surface missiles. But the B-52 is subsonic, that is, it flies at a maximum speed of 550 miles per hour. It is large, and therefore it presents a better target to enemy air defense missiles and interceptor aircraft. It was produced between 1952 and 1962, and it is predicted to "wear out" in the 1980s. Indeed, many of the original force of 600 B-52s have been cannibalized to keep 348 aircraft "operational." (However, the

U.S. must count stored B-52 aircraft as part of its overall SALT II limits, so we officially have 573 of them.) The B-52 has undergone eight
major improvements (to the B-52 G and B-52 H models) to try to offset Soviet strategic air defenses. The latest improvement is the equip-
ping of a small number of B-52s to carry long-range Cruise missiles.
Soviet surface-to-air missiles (SAMs) now make high-altitude penetration very risky. Low-altitude penetration (as low as 100 to 200 feet) is
preferred to make radar detection difficult and radar-guided SAMs
ineffective. An advanced manned-bomber, the B-1, was developed as
a smaller supersonic (over 2,000 miles per hour) bomber, of low-
altitude penetration, which can actually deliver more warheads than
the larger, slower B-52. After successful development and test flying of
the B-1, the Carter Administration cancelled the program as too costly.
The U.S. Air Force had requested a force of 224 B-1s at nearly $100
million each.

The Soviet Union has developed a new, supersonic, low-altitude
penetration bomber, the TU22M, known in the U.S. as the "Backfire."
The Soviets claim that this plane is not an intercontinental bomber and
not a "strategic" weapon, because its range is less than 5,000 miles. But,
of course, with in-flight refueling the Backfire can penetrate any target
in the United States. The Soviets have over 100 operational Backfires,
and they are building thirty each year. The development of the speedy
Backfire is clear evidence that the Soviets do *not* regard manned bombers as outmoded.

### SLBMs

The third "leg" of the TRIAD is the submarine-launched ballistic
missile (SLBM) force. At present, this is the most "survivable" force
and therefore the best second-strike component of the TRIAD. Most
defense policy analysts agree that Soviet antisubmarine warfare (ASW)
capability is not now, nor will it be in the foreseeable future, capable of
destroying a significant portion of our SLBM force.

The U.S. SLBM force consists of 41 Polaris nuclear-powered submarines, each carrying 16 SLBMs which can be fired while submerged.
This is a total force of 656 SLBMs, but at any given time only about
two-thirds of the submarine force can be at sea in a position to fire
their missiles. The first Polaris submarines were completed in 1960 and
now have twenty years of high-tempo use. Most of the Polaris submarines are armed with new Poseidon missiles, which have a 4,000-mile
range and can carry 7 to 10 MIRVed warheads. The U.S. is now building a small force of new nuclear-powered Trident submarines. Each
Trident will carry 24 missiles with a 6,000-mile range and 10 MIRVed
warheads. The first Trident was completed in 1979. The longer range
of the Trident's missiles will enable it to fire from Boston harbor and

**TABLE 12–2** The Language of Defense Policy

MINUTEMAN. U.S. solid-fuel missile with intercontinental range. 1,000 Minuteman are dispersed in hardened underground silos. Minuteman I carries one MT warhead; advanced Minuteman III carries three 175-KT MIRVed warheads.

MIRV. Multiple independently targetable reentry vehicle. A U.S. system capable of directing three to ten nuclear warheads at separate targets after being launched from one missile. MIRVs on Minuteman III missiles carry three 175-KT warheads; MIRVs on Poseidon carry ten 40-KT warheads.

ASM or SRAM. Air-to-surface missiles or short-range attack missiles. Airborne short-range (60-75 miles) missile with nuclear warhead for attack against surface target designed to give bombers "standoff" capability, that is, the ability to hit a target without flying over it.

STRATEGIC WEAPON. Any weapon, plan, or policy designed to strike the enemy's homeland and destroy his ability to wage war.

TACTICAL WEAPON. Any weapon, plan, or policy designed to defeat the enemy's armies in the field.

SLBM. Submarine-launched ballistic missile. Missile in Polaris and Poseidon nuclear-powered submarines capable of firing under the surface and delivering a 1-MT warhead, or in the case of MIRVed Poseidon, ten 40-KT warheads.

HARDENING. Protecting a land-based missile against nuclear attack by enclosing it in underground silos of concrete and steel.

B-1. An advanced manned strategic aircraft. Long-range U.S. supersonic bomber developed to replace the antiquated B-52s. Production cancelled.

BACKFIRE. Soviet advanced manned supersonic bomber. Shorter range than U.S. B-1, but capable of strategic attack with in-flight refueling.

POLARIS and POSEIDON. U.S. submarines and submarine-launched missile systems. Polaris submarines carry sixteen missile launching tubes. New Poseidon missiles are MIRVed to carry up to ten separately targetable warheads.

TRIDENT. A new submarine with twenty-four missile launching tubes that will double the range (3,000 to 6,000 miles) of underwater-launched missiles over current Polaris type. This will give submarines greater hiding space in the oceans. The first Trident was completed in 1979.

CRUISE MISSILE. Small, inexpensive, subsonic, low-flying, guided missile that can be launched from aircraft, surface ships, or submarines, and can carry nuclear warheads.

ALCM. Air-launched cruise missile.

GLCM. Ground-launched cruise missile, or "Glicum."

SLCM. Sea-launched cruise missile, or "Slicum."

ABM. Antiballistic missile system. Missiles designed to intercept and destroy incoming offensive missiles.

SAM. Surface-to-air-missiles. Short-range missiles designed to intercept and destroy enemy aircraft. U.S. B-52 pilots successfully attacked targets in North Vietnam defended by Soviet SAMs with less than 1 percent attrition rate.

KT or MT. Kilotons or megatons. Measures of destructive power of weapons. One KT is equivalent to one thousand tons of TNT and one MT is equivalent to one million tons of TNT.

ASM or SRAM. Air-to-surface missile or short-range air missile. Missiles designed to give bombers "standoffs" capability, to allow them to fire at targets 25 to 100 miles away without flying directly over the target.

ASW. Antisubmarine warfare. Any efforts to detect, locate, intercept, and destroy enemy submarines.

hit targets in the Soviet Union. The Trident will have a faster speed and run more quietly than the Polaris.

The Soviets also have an SLBM force of nuclear-powered submarines. Their "Hotel," "Yankee," and "Delta" class submarines cannot match the Trident in speed, range, sophistication, and numbers of missiles. The Soviet Delta is roughly equivalent to the Polaris. However, the Soviets are believed to have 83 operational nuclear-powered strategic submarines with 950 SLBMs.

### The Cruise Missile

The Cruise missile is usually viewed as an extension of the TRIAD, rather than as a replacement for it. Cruise missiles are small, subsonic, low-flying guided missiles that can be fired from the ground (Ground Launched Cruise Missiles, GLCM), or from the air (Air Launched Cruise Missiles, ALCM), or from surface ships or submerged submarines (Sea Launched Cruise Missiles, SLCM). Cruise missiles can deliver small but powerful nuclear warheads. Cruise is very inexpensive to build compared to other weapons; tens of thousands could be built to overwhelm any possible air defense system and frustrate any possible attempt to destroy all of them on a first strike. Cruise missiles are very small (under 30 feet long); their size makes them mobile and difficult to locate; a single B-52 can carry twenty; and attack submarines can fire them under water from torpedo tubes. Although they are very slow-flying, their radar guidance system allows them to fly close to the ground; very few could be intercepted in a full-salvo attack; and they are very accurate.

Currently, the Soviet Union does not have the sophisticated guidance technology required to build an effective Cruise missile. The present SALT II Protocol, effective through 1981, prevents the United States from building a Cruise missile with a range of more than 600 kilometers. However, experts believe that the U.S. has the technological capability of building *intercontinental* cruise missiles (6,000-mile range) should it decide to do so.

Potentially, the Cruise missile is a major threat to the USSR. When President Carter cancelled the B-1 program, he announced the United States' intention of arming part of the existing B-52 force with ALCMs. The prospects of a large intercontinental, mobile, land-based missile force, together with large numbers of surface ship and submarine-launched (GLCM and SLCM) Cruise missiles, doubtlessly contributes to the Soviet desire to continue the Strategic Arms Limitation talks (SALT).

## The SALT Game

In the Strategic Arms Limitation Talks (SALT), the United States has tried to advance three goals: (1) to maintain "essential equivalence" between the strategic forces of the U.S. and USSR; (2) to maintain and enhance the stability of the strategic balance by insuring "survivability" of second-strike forces so that neither side has an incentive to strike first in a crisis; (3) to improve the political relationship between the U.S. and USSR ("detente") so that military tensions might be reduced and expenditures for strategic forces controlled. It is unrealistic, however, to expect that SALT will end competition between the superpowers, eliminate all threats against U.S. forces, or sharply reduce U.S. defense spending.

SALT I in 1972 concluded over two years of negotiation between the U.S. and USSR about limiting the strategic arms race. SALT I was a milestone in that it marked the first effort by the superpowers to limit strategic weapons. SALT I consisted of a formal treaty halting further development of ABMs, and an executive agreement placing numerical limits on offensive missiles. The ABM treaty limited each side to one ABM site for defense of its national capital and one ABM site for defense of an offensive ICBM field. The total number of ABMs permitted was 200 for each side, 100 at each location. (The USSR already has both of its ABM sites constructed; the U.S. had one site at the Grand Falls, North Dakota, Minuteman field, which was deactivated in 1975.) Under the offensive arms agreement, each side was frozen at the total number of offensive missiles completed or under construction. The Soviet Union was permitted 1,618 land-based missiles. The U.S. was permitted to maintain 1,054 land-based missiles. Both sides were limited to the missile-carrying submarines operational or under construction at the time of the agreement; this meant 43 for the Soviets and 41 for the U.S. The U.S. was permitted 656 SLBMs and the USSR 740 SLBMs. Both sides could construct new missiles if they dismantled an equal number of older missiles. Each nation agreed not to interfere in the electronic and satellite intelligence-gathering activities of the other nation. The SALT I agreements were to last until October 1977. Both nations pledged to continue efforts at further arms control—the SALT II talks.

Why would the U.S. and USSR enter into such an agreement? First of all, the USSR achieved what it had been struggling toward for decades: the U.S. officially recognized in a treaty Soviet superiority in the number and size of offensive weapons. The U.S. hoped to achieve a slowing of the Soviet momentum in the building of ICBMs and missile-carrying submarines—a momentum which would have given the Soviet Union even greater superiority in the years to come. Bombers were not covered by the agreement, and at that time (prior to the deployment of the Soviet "Backfire") the U.S. had superiority in numbers of long-range bombers. U.S. nuclear weapons in Europe, which were designed to defend NATO but *could* be used against the Soviets, were not included in the agreement, nor were the British and French

SLBMs or bombers. Both sides agreed not to build large-scale ABM systems to defend their own cities. This meant that each agreed to curtail its damage limitation efforts. Each nation holds the population of the other as hostage (a "stabilizing" condition) as long as neither develops a credible first-strike capability. Satellite reconnaissance made the SALT agreement self-enforcing; without satellite photography the question of inspection would have doomed negotiations.

Soviet weapons development after SALT I continued at a rapid pace and soon began to threaten U.S. second-strike capability. SALT I did *not* limit MIRVs, nor the size and throw weight of missiles, nor the accuracy of missiles or manned bombers. In all these areas, the Soviets made impressive gains. By 1976, the Soviet MIRV program was roughly on a par with our own. More importantly, because their existing missiles were larger than ours, their eventual ability to deliver larger numbers of warheads than the U.S. was virtually assured. Perhaps of even greater importance was the fact that by 1976 Soviet missile accuracy had improved to one-quarter mile radius at a 6,000-mile range—the same accuracy previously enjoyed only by the United States. This degree of accuracy is equivalent to a direct hit. The newest large Soviet missile, the SS-18, carries ten one-megaton weapons. The Soviets built 314 of these giant missiles—enough to carry 3,140 one megaton warheads. The Soviets could destroy our ICBM forces using only a fraction of the SS-18s and keep the bulk of their ICBM and SLBM forces in reserve for threatened use against American cities if the U.S. attempted to retaliate. Finally, the Soviets deployed a new supersonic manned bomber, the Backfire, which is capable, with in-flight refueling, of penetrating U.S. air defenses and hitting any remaining targets.

The SALT II Agreement is a complex one. Its major provisions include:

1. An overall limit on the number of strategic nuclear delivery vehicles (ICBMs, SLBMs, manned bombers) to 2,250 in 1981.

Since the U.S. does not have 2,250 delivery systems, no U.S. forces will be dismantled to reach this limit. However, the Soviets will be obliged to dismantle 250 older missiles or bombers.

2. An overall limit of 1,320 on the total number of MIRVed ballistic missiles, ICBMs, and SLBMs and strategic bombers with long-range Cruise missiles.

Over half of the ballistic missiles forces on both sides will be MIRVed; a U.S. bomber carrying Cruise missiles will be counted under this limit.

3. An overall limit of 1,200 on the total number of launchers of MIRVed ballistic missiles.

This provision, together with provision 2, means that the U.S. will be allowed only 120 bombers carrying Cruise missiles.

4. A ban on the construction of additional *heavy* ICBMs.

This is a controversial item because the USSR currently has 314 heavy ICBMs (the SS-18) while the U.S. has none. The treaty prevents the U.S. from building a heavy missile and recognizes the USSR monopoly in this weapon.

5. A ban on the testing or deployment of new types of ICBMs, with the exception of one new type of light ICBM for each side. A new type of missile is one which exceeds current types by more than 5 percent in size, weight, or throw-weight.

This provision allows the U.S. to build its new MX mobile missiles. The USSR has at least four new missiles under development; the Soviets will have to choose one of these.

6. A limit of 10 MIRVed warheads on a single ICBM; a limit of 14 MIRVed warheads on a single SLBM; and a limit of 20 Cruise missiles on a single bomber.

These limits represent current technology; they do not require changes in programs of either side.

7. A ban on the rapid reload of ICBM launchers.

This affects the USSR program because only Soviet ICBMs can refire. Soviet reload missiles must be kept away from launch sites.

8. An agreement by both sides not to interfere with national technical means (NTM) of verification of the provisions of the treaty. Neither side will interfere with photo reconnaissance satellites or use deliberate concealment measures which impede verification. Electronic signals from test missiles, known as telemetry, cannot be encoded.

This is an extension of the SALT I provision prohibiting interference in satellite and electronic intelligence. Periodically, the U.S. will be obliged to reveal all of its MX missiles simultaneously for verification and then hide them again.

9. A protocol to the treaty states that the U.S. will not test or deploy a mobile missile, or deploy a ground-launched Cruise missile (GLCM) or sea-launched Cruise missile (SLCM) with a range in excess of 600 kilometers before 1982. The USSR will not build more than 30 Backfire bombers per year.

The U.S. State Department contends that this provision will not slow the development of the MX, or of GLCM and SLCM. However, the Soviets are likely to demand an extension of the protocol as a first step in any SALT III negotiations.

The Carter Administration recommended the SALT II treaty for several reasons. According to former Secretary of State Cyrus Vance, SALT II was signed

. . . First, because it enhances the security of the U.S. and our allies. Second, it will help maintain strategic stability; it will reduce uncertainties with respect to the force structures of the two sides and thus enable each to plan forces in a more intelligent, less destabilizing way. Third, the treaty is based on adequate verification—not on trust. Fourth—and this is what I'd like to emphasize—we should never lose sight of the awesome horror of nuclear weapons and the incredible effects of a nuclear exchange. Anything that makes those horrors less likely is of fundamental importance to us, to the Soviets and to the whole world.[3]

The United States believes that SALT II reduces some of the uncertainties about levels and types of strategic forces the USSR will develop. SALT II does not end the arms race, but without SALT II there are *no boundaries* to the race. Any reduction in uncertainty (that is, any increase in intelligence) is preferable to uncertainty and ignorance. Second, SALT II recognizes "essential equivalence" as a strategic relationship, even though its realization depends upon continued U.S. development of the MX, the Trident, and Cruise missiles. "Essential equivalence" does not mean that the U.S. has forces equal to the USSR in every category, but rather that in combined overall strategic force the U.S. and USSR can be roughly equivalent. (See Table 12–3.) While the USSR still does not officially recognize mutual assured destruction (MAD) as a strategic concept, they *are* willing to recognize "the princi-

**TABLE 12–3**   The Strategic Balance: U.S. and USSR, 1982*

|  | Strategic Nuclear Launch Vehicles | | Numbers of Deliverable Warheads | | Deliverable Megatonnage | |
|---|---|---|---|---|---|---|
|  | *U.S.* | *USSR* | *U.S.* | *USSR* | *U.S.* | *USSR* |
| *ICBMs* |  |  |  |  |  |  |
| MIRV | 550 | 820 | 1,650 | 5,752 | 430 | 4,314 |
| nonMIRV | 504 | 390 | 504 | 970 | 1,026 | 1,935 |
| Total | 1,054 | 1,210 | 2,154 | 6,722 | 1,456 | 6,249 |
| *SLBMs* |  |  |  |  |  |  |
| MIRV | 640 | 296 | 5,456 | 2,912 | 364 | 582 |
| nonMIRV | 160 | 680 | 480 | 1,080 | 105 | 777 |
| Total | 800 | 976 | 5,936 | 3,992 | 469 | 1,359 |
| *Bombers* |  |  |  |  |  |  |
| ALCM | 15 | 64 |  |  |  |  |
| nonALCM | 331 |  |  |  |  |  |
| Total | 346 | 64 | 2,824 | 260 | 1,624 | 260 |
| *TOTAL* | 2,200 | 2,250 | 10,914 | 10,974 | 3,549 | 7,868 |

*This table does *not* include the Soviet Backfire aircraft, expected to number 190 by 1982. It assumes continued modernization programs planned for both countries, consistent with SALT II.

*Source:* Figures derived from *The SALT Handbook* (Washington: The Heritage Foundation, 1979).

[3]*Time,* May 21, 1979, p. 33.

ple of equality and equal security" (words used in the treaty itself). And last, given the rapid Soviet buildup of strategic forces over the last ten to fifteen years, the imbalance in real military investment with the USSR outspending the U.S. two to one, and the tremendous momentum of the Soviet strategic forces development, SALT II's limitations may slow the Soviet forward momentum. In contrast, the U.S. will have to increase its strategic forces in order to reach the levels envisioned by the Treaty. In other words, the U.S. was falling increasingly behind in strategic arms. The treaty may slow Soviet development and simultaneously spur the U.S. into moving ahead with the MX, the Trident, Cruise, and perhaps a manned bomber.

The case against SALT II is equally convincing. The treaty recognizes the Soviet monopoly in "heavy" missiles (SS-18s). The treaty does not require the dismantling of this large Soviet ICBM force, and it does not permit the U.S. to build a comparable force. With its SS-18s, the Soviets continue to have a first-strike capability against our aging Minuteman ICBM force. This Soviet first-strike advantage against our land-based missiles will exist until the US MX missile is fully deployed—and MX deployment may not be completed until 1990. The treaty also recognizes Soviet advantage in size, numbers, weight, deliverable warheads, and deliverable megatonnage in ICBMs. SLBM forces are roughly equal, provided, of course, that the U.S. continues the Trident program. The only "advantage" enjoyed by the U.S. is in "intercontinental" bombers—B-52s—which few people believe can be effective today. The treaty does *not* cover the Soviet Backfire bomber (except to limit its production to 30 per year), and this bomber *is* an effective modern weapon.

The U.S. is prevented by the treaty from testing or deploying long-range Cruise missiles or MXs until 1982. These are the only areas in which the U.S. has a significant qualitative advantage. While work can continue on these weapons systems, the Soviets can be expected to demand a continued ban on their testing and deployment as a first step in SALT III. The U.S. has set a precedent for slowing the only significant threats to Soviet superiority.

Finally, the long-term political effect of a SALT II Treaty in the U.S. may be to slow down weapons development and deployment. Of course, initially the president and Congress may promise increased spending for MX, Trident, Cruise, and perhaps even a new manned bomber, in order to quiet opposition to SALT II. But once the treaty is passed, U.S. defense programs may be set aside in the hopes that disarmament agreements will make them unnecessary. However, we can be reasonably certain that the *Soviets* will not deemphasize defense because of SALT II. We can expect that they will build right up to the limits of SALT II and continue work on weapons systems not covered by the agreement. In other words, SALT II may be a ploy by the Soviets to bring about a relaxation of U.S. defense efforts while their own programs continue to move ahead rapidly.

## Nuclear War Games

Thus far, we have examined the major strategies available to the superpowers in confronting nuclear war. Now let us confront some of the dilemmas of choice by examining a few possible "scenarios"—potential events, choices, and outcomes.[4]

### The Preemptive Strike

One possible cause of nuclear war is accident—mechanical failure or human error. For years, Americans have been entertained in movies and novels by the thought of inadvertent war—the failure of "fail-safe" mechanisms or the crazed actions of "Dr. Strangeloves." The actual probability of inadvertent war has been rendered very low by a variety of elaborate safety precautions and devices. But it is important to realize that an increase in safety lengthens reaction time and may allow incoming missiles to reach their targets, thereby reducing second-strike capability. Moreover, if command and control is centralized in the hands of the president, it is more vulnerable to attack. In contrast, assured "survivability" of weapons reduces the possibility of inadvertent war, because it gives a decision maker time to evaluate and decide about the size and intentions of incoming attack forces. The defender is not under overwhelming pressure to get his own attack forces safely into the air. Nonetheless, in a period of tension, with exchanges of threats and perhaps limited aggression, an accident or sequence of multiple accidents could be very dangerous.

A more likely cause of a first-strike surprise nuclear attack would be the loss of assured destruction second-strike capability by one or both nations. If a nation has no second-strike capability, it may come to believe that its survival depends upon a preemptive strike. Such a first strike would not be undertaken to achieve political goals, but rather to prevent a feared enemy attack. If a nation has no second-strike deterrent, the advantages of striking first are so great that should there appear to be a high probability of the enemy's actually attacking, it may be more rational to accept a relatively small retaliatory

[4]For further inquiry into nuclear war strategies, see Herman Kahn, *On Thermonuclear War* (Princeton, N.J.: Princeton University Press, 1961); Herman Kahn, *Thinking About the Unthinkable* (New York: Horizon Press, 1962); Henry A. Kissinger, ed., *Problems of National Strategy* (New York: Praeger, 1965).

strike rather than to risk a high probability of receiving a much more destructive first blow. Reciprocal fear of surprise attack may pressure one side to launch a preemptive strike if only because he knows the other side is under similar pressure! Note that such a war would not be a product of accident, but rather the product of rational calculation.

If both sides possess credible first-strike capability (which means that neither side possesses second-strike assured destruction capability), the pressure to preempt would be overwhelming. Defense analysts refer to such a situation as "unstable." In contrast, if both sides possess second-strike assured destruction capability (which means that neither can launch a first strike without expecting to receive unacceptable damage in a retaliating blow), then it is said that a "balance of terror" exists. War is still a possibility, but defense analysts label such a situation as "stable."

An enemy first-strike should be detected as soon as his missiles are fired. Electronic and satellite reconnaissance should detect a full-salvo enemy attack on launch and provide the defender with nearly forty minutes to respond before incoming ICBMs strike their targets. *If* the defender is prepared to launch on such "unambiguous information of attack," then the defender's retaliatory missiles would be in the air before the attacker's first-strike missiles arrived. Thus, good intelligence and alert response should remove any advantage from a first-strike attack. However, we can reasonably expect that an enemy first-strike would be preceded by a jamming effort against, or a direct attack on, electronic and satellite intelligence equipment. Would the president be willing to launch nonrecallable ICBMs and SLBMs merely on information that our electronic and satellite intelligence equipment had been destroyed? Simply posing this question points to the necessity of maintaining *survivable* second-strike forces—forces which can still retaliate after a worse case, surprise, full-salvo first strike.

### The Intelligence Game

Satellite reconnaissance is a major stabilizing force in the nuclear war game. Good intelligence reduces uncertainty about offensive and defensive capabilities, and hence reduces the likelihood of war through miscalculation. One result of the U.S. space program was the development of "spy in the sky" satellites capable of constant photo reconnaissance of enemy territory. These satellites can take amazingly detailed pictures from outer space. (High-altitude airplane over-flights of enemy territory—"U-2" flights—are no longer essential.) It is now virtually impossible for the enemy to deploy offensive or defensive weapons without the president knowing about it as soon as construction begins. The development of these satellites also makes arms limitations agreements possible because each nation can identify cheating in their space photography.

A destabilizing element is the Soviet development and testing of "killer" satellites, that is, antisatellite systems (ASAT) designed to destroy satellite reconnaissance. In the SALT I treaty, the USSR pledged not to interfere in satellite reconnaissance. They have not technically violated SALT I by developing and testing ASAT, but ASAT certainly violates the spirit of SALT I. Why build an ASAT system that you pledged never to use?

### Controlled Reprisal—"Tit for Tat"

Even if assured destruction deterrence prevents a surprise all-out nuclear attack, a limited strategic nuclear exchange is still a possibility. Although many lay people have visualized *any* nuclear war beginning with a full-salvo city-busting attack, most defense policy analysts consider a "controlled," limited nuclear exchange as a more likely prospect. For example, consider the following "scenario": The USSR decides that the U.S. would not really go to nuclear war to defend Berlin and Western Europe. Soviet troops quickly capture Berlin, and heavy Soviet divisions pour into West Germany. The Soviets make no direct attack on the U.S. but they warn the U.S. that nuclear retaliation on our part will result in the complete destruction of American society. American "deterrence" has failed to protect Berlin, West Germany, and Western Europe from a conventional military attack, and neither the U.S. nor other NATO countries have sufficient conventional forces—troops, tanks, artillery, tactical air support—to halt the Russian advance. Is the president faced with the choice between all-out nuclear war or the surrender of Western Europe? Perhaps not—even if he has previously told the USSR that he would order an all-out nuclear attack in response to such aggression. (It may be rational to *threaten* to go to all-out war to deter an aggression, and also rational *not* to do so even if the threat fails to deter the aggression.) Instead, the president may choose to launch a controlled demonstration attack on a single Soviet city to convince the Soviets of our firm resolve to resist aggression; at the same time he would demand a halt to the Soviet advance and threaten additional damage if they did not acquiesce in our demand. This move might convince the Soviets of our seriousness of purpose and strength of will. On the other hand, the Soviets might retaliate with a limited controlled attack of their own on three or four American cities, demonstrating their *greater* firmness of will. They would couple such an attack with a peace offering and a threat that we had better acquiesce in the surrender of Europe or face even greater destruction.

At this point, both sides would be engaged in a superdestructive game of Chicken.

As bizarre as the scenario may appear, most defense policy analysts believe that the threat of controlled reprisal is a more credible deterrent to aggression than the threat of mutual annihilation.

### The Disarmament Game

Disarmament schemes place the superpowers in a classic "game" known as *The Prisoner's Dilemma.* The Prisoner's Dilemma is a situation in which each of the two participants, if they act rationally, will engage in behavior which will result in outcomes detrimental to both. Both could gain if they cooperated, but the consequences for one cooperator would be disastrous if the other did not cooperate.[5]

The disarmament dilemma is portrayed in Table 12–4. The numbers are arbitrary, but they represent outcomes of simultaneous decision making by two nations. Each nation may choose to "Disarm" or "Continue Arming." Both nations would benefit if they both "Disarm" (+5 for both), because each saves the money that continued arming costs. If both nations "Continue Arming," they continue to spend money on arms and both lose (−5 for both). However, if one disarms and the other continues arming, the nation that disarms risks losing

**TABLE 12–4**   Disarmament as Prisoner's Dilemma Game

| | Nation's 2 Choices: | |
| --- | --- | --- |
| | *Disarm* | *Continue Arming* |
| **Nation's I Choices:** | Nation 1 = +5 <br> Nation 2 = +5 | Nation 1 = −100 <br> Nation 2 = +100 |
| Disarm <br> Continue Arming | Nation 2 = +100 <br> Nation 2 = −100 | Nation 1 = −5 <br> Nation 2 = −5 |

[5]The classic Prisoner's Dilemma is this: two prisoners are confronted with a crime that either could blame on the other. The police call in each prisoner separately, allowing no communication between them. The police offer each the same bargain: If he will "rat" on the other, he will go free while his companion will be given a life sentence. If both refuse to talk, they can both go free because the police will have no witnesses and no case. If both "rat" on each other, each will be convicted of a minor offense and serve only a year or two in jail. Both prisoners must make their choice to "rat" or not, without knowing what the other has done. Obviously, the best *outcome* for both would occur if neither "ratted." But fear that the other prisoner will rat and that a life sentence will result if he does not also rat, encourages each prisoner to rat. Indeed, the minimax strategy—acting so as to minimize the maximum loss—dictates that each prisoner rat, because the worst loss is a life sentence and each cannot trust the other with his life. Thus, "rational" prisoners will both rat on each other; it is the rational thing to do even though both lose.

everything—the arming nation gains first-strike capability and therefore the ability to "blackmail" the other with the threat of a preemptive strike. Thus, the outcomes are represented as $-100$ for the disarming and $+100$ for the arming nation.

There is an advantage in both sides' disarming ($+5$ for both). The problem, however, is that without trust (or without continuous unmistakable verification) each nation cannot risk the threat of strategic disadvantage which would occur if one nation disarmed and the other did not. The "rational" thing for both to do is to minimize their maximum possible loss, and choose the course that does not threaten their national existence. Thus, both nations must choose to "Continue Arming."

This is the underlying logic of the arms race. Of course, in the real world, the game is much more complicated. And in the real world, some knowledge of the decision made by the opponent is available through national technical means of intelligence. However, all the theoretical problems of choice, minimax, trust, and verification are analogous to the Prisoner's Dilemma.

## Conventional War Games

Because of the high risks and costs of all-out nuclear war, and the *recognition* of these risks and costs by the U.S. and the USSR, limited conventional war is a more likely occurrence than a nuclear exchange. The notion of deterrence in nuclear war strategy involves the *psychological* use of very destructive weapons. But conventional war strategy is much more likely to involve the *actual* use of less destructive weapons—artillery, tanks, troops, and tactical aircraft.

America's active involvement in limited conventional wars in Korea and Vietnam has made most Americans realize that "war" is not a single, simple, or uniform action. Wars come in different varieties and sizes. Sometimes it is difficult for Americans to understand why this is so—why the United States does not seek "total victory" in every war and use any and every weapon in its arsenal to achieve that victory.

War is an instrument of national policy. Victory in war is not an end in itself; the purpose of war is to achieve some national objective—security, survival, credibility, protection of an ally, vital territory, resources, etc. Nations are continually asserting their wills in conflict situations with other nations and using a variety of means of influence and coercion. At some point these conflicts become "war." War, then, is a matter of the degree and intensity of international conflict. It is not undisciplined mass violence. The size and nature of a war must be related to its political purposes. Karl Von Clauswitz, the famous German military theorist of the nineteenth century, explains the importance of keeping the political purposes of a war constantly in the forefront of military operations:

> War is nothing but a continuation of politics by other means . . . war can never be separated from political intercourse, and if this occurs, all the threads of relations are broken, and we have before us a senseless thing without an object.

War, then, if it is to be employed at all, must be employed in a rational fashion to serve national purposes. War is not simply a way of giving vent to hatred, malevolence, or sadism. Crushing the enemy is not the measure of success, but whether we have achieved our national purposes at a reasonable cost. For war to be a rational policy—that is, for its benefits to outweigh its costs—several conditions must be met. First of all, policy makers must clearly understand the objectives of the war and commit military forces in rough proportion to the value of these objectives. War is a very crude instrument of policy. Its violence and destruction can set off a chain of consequences that overshadow and defeat the original purposes of the war. Costs in lives and resources can easily spiral all out of proportion to the original objectives of the war. An increase in costs may itself cause a nation to expand its original objectives in order to rationalize higher costs. The enemy must then commit larger forces to prevent greater losses. Hence the necessity for close control and supervision of the level of violence. Diplomats must make continuing efforts to maintain political talks toward a negotiated settlement on the basis of national objectives.

If the object of war becomes total victory over the enemy, there will be no limit on the enemy's use of force. Total victory for one nation implies total defeat for its opponent—a threat to national survival, justifying unlimited levels of violence. Political objectives are set aside for possible resolution after the war, and every effort is directed toward the complete destruction of the enemy's war-making power. As the dimensions of violence and destruction increase, the war arouses passionate fears and hatreds, which themselves come to replace rational objectives in the conflict. As the level of suffering and sacrifice increases, the goal becomes the blind unreasoning destruction of the enemy.

In a "stable" nuclear balance of terror—in which each side possesses assured destruction second-strike capability—conventional war becomes a more likely possibility. America's strategic nuclear forces have been designed to deter a direct attack on continental United States and a major attack on Western Europe. In *all* other conflicts the United States will probably rely on conventional weapons, or perhaps in extremely rare circumstances, "tactical" nuclear weapons. *Exclusive* reliance on nuclear weapons would place the United States in a terrible dilemma in confronting limited aggression—involving a choice between either surrender or nuclear war. In contrast, if the United States maintains a balance of forces—strategic nuclear, tactical nuclear, and conventional—it will be able to confront aggression anywhere in the world with weapons and forces appropriate to the situation.

Apart from their strictly military purposes, conventional forces also have an important psychological role to play. The deployment of U.S. troops in Berlin, West Germany, and Western Europe serves notice to the USSR that it cannot send Soviet divisions across the borders without engaging U.S. troops. Even though these U.S. troops are no match for the massive Soviet armies, nonetheless, the very fact that American troops would have to be killed in a Soviet attack in Western Europe *insures* U.S. involvement in such a conflict. U.S. troops in Europe form a "plate-glass window": the Soviets know that to take Western Europe they would have to kill American troops, and this knowledge is a further deterrent to such an attack.[6] Deploying U.S. troops in Europe notifies friend and foe alike of the seriousness of our commitment to defend the area.

U.S. troops in Europe are equipped with tactical nuclear weapons. Obviously this fact has additional deterrent value. Not only do the Soviets know that U.S. troops would be immediately involved in any defense against aggression, but they also know that such a defense would involve the use of nuclear weapons, at least at the tactical level.

Perhaps the most important objectives at stake in conventional war situations are the perceived political effects of various outcomes. The actual territories, resources, or people being fought over may be relatively unimportant. In general, the superpowers have justified military intervention in local conflicts by citing the long-range threats that might occur if a particular area is allowed to fall. In any limited conventional war, the U.S. and the USSR must consider what conclusions its allies and enemies might draw from humiliation or defeat. For example, the U.S. withdrawal from Vietnam led not only to a collapse of the South Vietnamese government, but also to the loss of Laos and Cambodia, the loss of Thailand as an ally, and the encouragement of Soviet and Cuban military activity in Angola. It is now more difficult for the U.S. to convince both allies and enemies of the seriousness of its military commitments. It would have been better for the mainte-

---

[6]Likewise, the deployment of U.S. forces in South Korea is a crucial psychological deterrent to another invasion by North Korea. North Korea has pledged itself to "reunification" of Korea and has built large, paved, and lighted tunnels under the border in preparation for invasion. But the presence of U.S. troops—so far, at least—has deterred or postponed invasion plans.

nance of American credibility had we never gone into Vietnam in the first place.

In the Kennedy and Johnson Administrations, the policy of flexible response and balanced forces meant that the U.S. should prepare itself to respond to various levels of aggression with weapons and forces appropriate to the threat. Moreover, the U.S. should be prepared to fight several of these conflicts simultaneously. Specifically, this country should be prepared to fight simultaneously two conventional wars, with or without tactical nuclear weapons, on two continents (presumably Europe and Asia), with a small military contingent left over to handle one minor conflict. This became known as the "2½ war" force level.

Today, however, the U.S. asserts that nations being threatened by aggression must assume primary responsibility for their own security. The U.S. will no longer provide military advisors or counterinsurgency forces to governments threatened by Communist-inspired "wars of national liberation"; U.S. aid would be limited to economic assistance and military supplies. In the case of a conventional war, the U.S. now expects any nation under attack by the conventional forces of another nation to be responsible for the burden of providing its own ground forces. Even in a major conventional war (e.g., the North Korean attack on South Korea, the Chinese attack on Taiwan, etc.) the U.S. would attempt to limit its military role to sea and air support.

U.S. force levels have been reduced to a "1½ war" capability—the capability of fighting one conventional war, with or without tactical nuclear weapons, and a minor conflict simultaneously. This reduction in force levels from the Kennedy-Johnson years permitted the U.S. to end the draft and rely on an all-volunteer army.

Limited wars are wars fought in relatively small geographic areas with restrictions on both sides on weapons and targets. The Korean War was limited to the Korean peninsula and the Vietnam War to Indochina. In the Korean War the Chinese never attacked U.S. bases in Japan and the U.S. never attacked Chinese territory. In the Vietnam War the U.S. did not target population centers or industry, although these were occasionally hit in attacks aimed at nearby military or transportation facilities. Not using nuclear weapons has been the most significant limitation on U.S. actions in limited wars. But it is difficult to predict the specific military actions that would be taken in any *future* limited war. The conduct of limited wars is determined by specific international and local political conditions at the time of the conflict. Limits are not a product of any agreement between the countries involved, but instead a product of internal decisions about the benefits and costs of various military actions.

## Soviet Superiority in Conventional Forces

The USSR has enjoyed a vast superiority in ground combat troops, tanks, and artillery since the end of World War II. The Soviets maintain 4.5 million persons under arms, compared to slightly more than 2 million for the United States. The Soviets maintain 173 combat divisions, while the U.S. maintains sixteen Army divisions and three Marine divisions. The Soviets have an arsenal of 50,000 tanks of all types compared to 12,000 for the U.S.; the Soviets have 8,000 tactical aircraft, compared to 5,364 for the U.S.; and the Soviets have over 20,000 artillery pieces, compared to 5,500 for the U.S.

Part of the Soviet tactical superiority is dictated by the multiple missions assigned to the Soviet military: (1) to confront the NATO alliance in Europe; (2) to keep the nations of Eastern Europe inside the Soviet bloc through armed intimidation; and (3) to defend against a growing Chinese threat in the Eastern Soviet Union. Indeed, defending its eastern boundaries against potential Chinese incursions now divert nearly one-third of the Soviet ground combat forces. The USSR must also divert about 20 percent of its ground combat forces to hold in check the populations of Poland, Hungary, East Germany, Rumania, Bulgaria, and Czechoslovakia. (In contrast, the U.S. can count on support, rather than opposition, from its NATO allies, including British, French, German, Belgian, Dutch, Italian, Greek, and Turkish forces.) Thus, it can be argued that the USSR needs a larger ground combat capability than the U.S.

However, the overwhelming superiority of the USSR in conventional forces (see Table 12–5) clearly exceeds their dual missions of protecting the USSR from the Chinese and maintaining control of their Eastern European satellite nations. It is this *excess* capability that worries U.S. and NATO military commanders. The only off-setting element in the European equation is superiority in U.S. tactical nuclear weapons. (The U.S. is estimated to have 7,000 tactical nuclear weapons in Europe, compared to a maximum of 3,000 for the Soviets.) But clearly the Soviets have a preponderance of conventional ground combat forces.

American conventional arms—tactical aircraft, conventional bombs, tanks, antitank missiles, artillery, and battlefield missiles—are technologically equal or superior to Soviet conventional arms. But the USSR produces so many more conventional arms than the U.S. that the Soviets can send advanced arms to their client nations in the Middle East, Asia, and Africa without depleting their own armies. In contrast, to assist the Israelis in the Yom Kippur War in 1973, the U.S. had to seriously deplete its NATO forces as well as its home arsenal.

The USSR has five separate military services. They are (1) stra-

**TABLE 12–5** Balance of Conventional Forces, U.S. and USSR

|  | U.S. | USSR |
|---|---|---|
| Total Armed Forces Personnel | 2.1 million | 4.5 million |
| *Army Divisions* | 16 | 173[1] |
| deployment | 5 Europe | 31 Eastern Europe |
|  | 1 S. Korea | 66 European USSR |
|  | 10 U.S. | 6 Central USSR |
|  |  | 24 Southern USSR |
|  |  | 46 Chinese border |
| Tanks (all types) | 12,100 | 50,000 |
| Artillery | 5,500 | 20,000 |
| Marines[2] | 3 divisions |  |
|  | 550 aircraft |  |
| *Air Force* |  |  |
| Combat aircraft | 3,400 | 4,350 |
| *Navy* |  |  |
| Major combat-surface ships | 161 | 275 |
| Attack submarines | 80 (73 nuclear) | 255 (86 nuclear) |
| Aircraft carriers | 13[3] | 2[4] |
| Aircraft | 1,100 | 870[4] |

[1]At full strength, Soviet combat divisions include 8,000 to 10,000 men compared to 14,000 to 16,000 men in full-strength U.S. combat divisions.

[2]USSR "Naval Infantry" is organized in brigades and assigned to fleets; they have no separate air support units.

[3]U.S. carriers include the new nuclear-powered *Enterprise* and *Nimitz* at 90,000 tons capable of carrying 140 combat aircraft.

[4]The Soviet Navy relies primarily on missile-carrying cruisers rather than aircraft carriers; only two 40,000-ton carriers have been put in operation; most Soviet naval aircraft are shore-based.

*Source:* Institute for Strategic Studies, *The Military Balance 1979–1980* (London: Institute for Strategic Studies, 1979).

tegic rocket forces, (2) air defense forces, (3) ground forces, (4) air forces, and (5) navy. The strategic rocket forces have responsibilities for all intercontinental and intermediate range ballistic missiles. The Soviet navy is responsible for SLBMs, and the air force is responsible for bombers. The Soviets have a very heavy air defense system of SAMs, and their civil defense system is well-developed.

The U.S. and USSR have different kinds of navies. The U.S. has large, aircraft carrier forces and a large Marine Corps, which together can mount amphibious landing operations anywhere in the world with close air support. The Soviets have no such forces. They rely instead on missile cruisers and attack submarines, which give them the capacity to interrupt naval operations anywhere in the world. It would be difficult to estimate the outcome of a sea battle between U.S. forces relying on naval air attacks from carriers and Soviet forces relying on surface-to-surface missiles and submarine attacks. Perhaps the most worrisome aspect of Soviet naval power is its spectacular growth over the last decade. The Soviets built the largest combat surface fleet in the world in a very short period of time, and its ships are generally newer than those of the U.S. Navy.

The United States currently maintains total armed forces of 2.1 million, compared to 4.5 million for the Soviet Union. But the U.S. may not be able to maintain current manpower levels under the "All Volunteer" concept, that is, without the draft. In the first place, the "All Volunteer" army is expensive, because pay and benefits must be made attractive. The result is that personnel costs have soared to more than half of the entire defense budget, leaving less money for weapon research and development. Secondly, the Army consistently encounters difficulty in attracting new recruits and holding experienced soldiers. An economic recession helps enlistments when other jobs are hard to find; but it is difficult to keep up enlistments in a full employment economy. Finally, a disproportionate number of the poor and black find life in the military better than life at home. The U.S. Army, which was about 12 percent black during the Vietnam War (approximately the same percentage black as the U.S. population), is now over 30 percent black. If we are committed to an integrated society, it is difficult to justify a predominantly black army, assuming this trend continues. Thus, the president and Congress may be forced to consider a new draft law. (A new draft would probably drop the college student deferment and apply a lottery system to all young men. It may also allow substitute "national service" for persons who object to military service.) The Soviets, of course, have no problem in maintaining a permanent four- to six-million man army. Moreover, they are able to place a larger proportion of these men in combat divisions, because "civilian" employees perform many military tasks.

The Soviet Union spends about 15 percent of its Gross National Product on defense, compared to 5 percent for the United States. (However, since the GNP of the United States is larger than that of the Soviet Union, the ratio of Soviet to U.S. defense spending is closer to two-to-one, rather than three-to-one.) If current trends in defense spending continue in both nations, eventually the Soviets will gain superiority in *all* aspects of war-making power. To maintain a reasonable balance of forces, the U.S. must either increase its defense spending or achieve some agreement with the Soviet Union that would limit both strategic and conventional arms.

## Evaluation: The Price of Peace

The continuing decline in U.S. defense spending, coupled with the continuing buildup of Soviet forces at all levels, requires that the U.S. respond with a large-scale program to revitalize the nation's defense.

SALT II does not affect this requirement; indeed, large-scale expenditures will be required for the U.S. to build up to the strategic limits of the treaty. Moreover, the conventional balance of forces against the U.S. invites increased Soviet military adventurism throughout the world.

In 1955 defense spending claimed 58.1 percent of all federal expenditures and equaled 10.5 percent of the Gross National Product. Ten years later, in 1965, defense spending had shrunk to 40.1 percent of federal spending and 7.2 percent of the GNP. In 1980 defense spending was down to only 23 percent of federal spending and 4.9 percent of the GNP. This is the lowest defense "effort" the U.S. has made since before World War II.

Defense outlays have no discernible effect on either social welfare spending or inflation. Total spending for welfare, social security, health, housing, and education is more than double the defense budget. There is no evidence that increases in the defense budget come at the expense of social spending; indeed, during the years of the Vietnam War, social welfare spending more than doubled. The inflationary effects of increased defense spending are very mild. From 1955 to 1965, when defense spending was heavy, there was very little inflation in the country.

Because of the Soviet strategic buildup (SS-18s, SLBMs, Backfires) and modernization (particularly improved accuracy), the U.S. will confront a "window of vulnerability" in the 1980s. This is a period of time, before the MX or long-range Cruise missiles are deployed, when the U.S. land-based ICBM force will be subject to destruction by a surprise USSR attack. Already there is very little that can be done about this period of vulnerability; it results from the failure to develop a replacement for the Minuteman system speedily enough, the demise of the B-1 bomber, the slow progress on the Trident submarine force, and general restraint in defense spending over the past decade. The only possibility of narrowing the "window of vulnerability" is speedy development and deployment of long-range Cruise missiles (probably launched from B-52s). But SALT II prevents deployment of long-range Cruise missiles until 1982.

Soviet conventional superiority may be an even greater concern. The Soviets are out-producing the U.S. in nearly every category of military equipment and their equipment is no longer inferior in quality. The threat of a conventional attack in Western Europe is especially worrisome.

To partially offset Soviet superiority in Europe, the U.S. has pledged to its NATO allies a continuing *3 percent increase in total defense spending over inflation rates*. This spending would assist in modernizing and increasing U.S. conventional capabilities as well as strategic forces. For example, the U.S. needs to deploy more tanks, antitank missiles, mobile artillery pieces, ammunition, and trained personnel in Europe. The Air Force, and the air forces of our allies, need increased numbers of the new and highly sophisticated F-15 and F-16 tactical aircraft, and the A-10 ground support (antitank) aircraft. The Navy has been steadily reducing the size of its fleet, from 955 ships in 1960 to 458 today. The Navy is particularly short of Marine landing ships. Indeed, the total military requirements add up to a continuing 5 percent real increase in defense spending, in contrast to the proposed 3 percent.

Another strategy to offset Soviet superiority in Europe involves the deployment of medium-range Pershing II nuclear missiles in Europe, as well as the deployment of the enhanced radiation warhead (the "neutron bombs") in Europe. The range of the Pershing II missile is 1,000 to 1,500 miles; stationing such missiles in Europe would allow the U.S. or NATO to launch an attack on the Soviet Union itself. Because of its limited range the Pershing II is not considered a "strategic weapon" in SALT II. The Soviets have complained bitterly about the deployment of these medium-range missiles in Europe (despite the fact that the Soviets have already deployed their own multiwarhead SS-20 medium-range missile against European targets), and the Soviets have threatened European nations which allowed them on their soil. But the NATO nations have requested the weapons and their presence in Europe will be an obvious deterrent against Soviet aggression. The enhanced radiation warhead (or "neutron bomb") is a nuclear warhead for use by artillery and short-range missiles; its purpose is to destroy tank formations but limit damage to surrounding cities and towns. Increased radiation generated by deterioration would penetrate armor, but blast and fire effects would be minimal. Clearly, such a weapon would be preferred by allied nations in Europe, who can expect much of the fighting to occur on their own territory.

But perhaps the most serious American military shortcoming is manpower. The absence of highly skilled personnel makes sophisticated weapons systems useless. The quality of recruits in the All-Volunteer Army is low and dropping, yet already personnel costs exceed 50 percent of the defense budget. Not only would increasing pay and benefits be very costly, but there is no clear evidence that these inducements actually bring in higher quality personnel. And manpower problems will become worse in the 1980s because of lower birth rates in the 1960s. Thus, the price of defense in the 1980s may also include some form of compulsory military service.

## Summary

Decisions about defense policy in Washington, Moscow, Peking, and other world capitals are interdependent—the future of mankind depends on what is done at each of these major power centers and how each responds to the decisions of others. Game theory provides a vocabulary and a way of thinking rationally about decision making in competitive interdependent situations. Let us set forth several summary ideas about defense policy.

1. Minimum deterrence strategy is the belief that potential enemies can be dissuaded from war simply because the U.S. possesses nuclear weapons and delivery systems. It is considered insufficient by most military analysts because it fails to consider the enemy's best possible move—a surprise first strike against our offensive forces.

2. Assured destruction deterrence strategy is the basis of current national defense policy. It seeks to prevent nuclear war by making the consequences of a first strike unacceptable to a potential enemy by providing assured second-strike capability. The key to assured destruction deterrence is the *survivability* of one's forces—what can be done on a "second strike" after absorbing a successful surprise first strike by the enemy. To maintain peace through assured destruction deterrence requires (1) second-strike capability, (2) communication of that capability to the enemy, (3) the enemy's belief in the credibility of the threat, and (4) a rational enemy.

3. Damage limitation strategy attempts to limit the damage inflicted by an enemy attack. But damage limitation measures including antiballistic missiles are expensive, unreliable, and easily offset by increases in the enemy's offensive capabilities. More important, damage limitation reduces the enemy's assured second-strike capability and encourages him to strike first; it replaces a "balance of terror" in which each side has assured second-strike capability, with an unstable relationship.

4. If both sides maintain second-strike capability—that is, *mutual* assured destruction, or MAD—then a stable "balance of terror" is said to exist. Each side is restrained from launching an attack because it knows of the second-strike capability of the other side. World peace does not rest on trust or love or brotherhood, but on a rational calculation of what is in each side's self-interest.

5. To implement its assured destruction deterrence, the U.S. has attempted to maintain a "TRIAD" of strategic forces—land-based missiles, submarine-launched missiles, and manned bombers. However, declines in defense spending, opposition to the military generated during the Vietnam War, and underestimation of Soviet technological developments, has threatened the survivability of land-based missiles and manned bombers. Defense planners are hopeful that the MX, the Cruise missile, and the Trident submarine will modernize the TRIAD. The advanced manned bomber (B-1) has been cancelled.

6. In the SALT agreements the U.S. has sought to maintain "essential equivalence" with the USSR, to protect its own second-strike ca-

pability, and to improve political relations with the world's other superpower ("detente"). Negotiations are carried on simultaneously with improvements in weapons systems by both sides. In SALT I (1972), both sides renounced large-scale damage limitation (ABM) programs and placed overall numerical limits on strategic weapons. But the arms race continued, and so did Soviet momentum in heavy missiles, MIRV, and Backfires. The SALT II agreement recognized Soviet monopoly in heavy ICBMs and placed no restrictions on Backfire bombers. Nonetheless, a series of limits on strategic nuclear launch vehicles, combined with guarantees of national technical means of verification, help to reduce uncertainty in strategic nuclear relationships.

7. Rational policy making in a nuclear world requires defense analysts to "think about the unthinkable." For example, a preemptive surprise nuclear attack might be rational if one or both nations lose their second-strike capability. A nation which knows it has no second-strike capability may be pressured into launching a first-strike nuclear attack. Such a situation is considered unstable. Technological advances may be "destabilizing" if they threaten the second-strike capability of one or both nations. In contrast, good intelligence, particularly satellite reconnaissance, is "stabilizing" because it reduces uncertainty. The choice of targets depends upon whether a nation is planning for a first strike or a second strike. First-strike targets are offensive missile sites, bomber bases, and strategic submarines. Second-strike targets are population and industrial centers. However, most defense analysts believe that nuclear war, if it comes at all, will come in the form of controlled reprisal attacks—"tit for tat."

8. It is widely assumed that Soviet expansion into Western Europe after World War II was halted by America's credible first-strike threat. The Soviets have always enjoyed supremacy in conventional military strength in Europe, but in the early Cold War years the U.S. maintained supremacy in nuclear weapons and strategic bombers. However, when the Soviets developed their own second-strike capability, the credibility of our threat declined, the NATO alliance eroded, and Western European nations began to make their own security arrangements.

9. Rational thinking in conventional war requires that the political purposes of the war should guide military operations. Unlimited, uncontrolled violence is not a rational strategy in a conventional war. For conventional war to be a rational policy, the benefits must outweigh the costs. Soviet conventional forces far outnumber U.S. conventional forces. This poses a conventional military threat to Western Europe and allows the Soviets to supply arms to satellite nations in the Middle East, Asia, Africa, and Latin America. The U.S. and NATO plan to counter the Soviet threat in Europe with medium-range ballistic mis-

siles on European territory—missiles which are capable of reaching the USSR.

## Bibliography

DONLEY, MICHAEL B., *The SALT Handbook.* Washington: Heritage Foundation, 1979.

KISSINGER, HENRY A., *Nuclear Weapons and Foreign Policy.* New York: Harper & Row, 1957.

SCHELLING, THOMAS C., *Arms and Influence.* New Haven: Yale University Press, 1966.

STAFFORD, ROY W., and JOHN E. ENDICOTT, eds., *American Defense Policy*, 4th ed. Baltimore: Johns Hopkins Press, 1977.

Alabama State Capitol. Alabama Bureau of Publicity and Information.

# Inputs, Outputs, and Black Boxes

## a systems analysis of state policies

**13**

### Extending the Boundaries of Policy Analysis

Political science has been so preoccupied with describing political institutions, behaviors, and processes that it has frequently overlooked the overriding importance of social and economic forces in shaping public policy. Of course, political scientists generally recognize that socioeconomic variables affect politics and public policy, but these variables are often slighted, and occasionally ignored, in specific policy explanations. The problem seems to be that the concepts and methods of political science predispose scholars to account for public policy largely in terms of the *internal* activities of political systems. Political science never lacked descriptions of what goes on within political systems; what it has lacked is a clear picture of the *linkages* between the socioeconomic environment, political activity, and public policy.

What is the socioeconomic environment? By the socioeconomic environment we mean anything that lies outside the boundaries of the political system yet within the same society. Needless to say, this takes in a great deal of territory. Socioeconomic variables include such things as the level of technological development, the extent of urbanization, the literacy rate, the level of adult education, the character of the economic system and its level of development, the degree of modernization of the society, the occupational structure, the class system, racial composition and ethnic diversity, mobility patterns, prevailing myths and beliefs, and so on. Any variable that is distinguishable from the political system itself yet lies within the same society is part of the socioeconomic environment.

From the almost unlimited number of socioeconomic conditions that might influence public policy outcomes, we must choose only a limited number for inclusion in our research. We are obliged to reduce our studies to manageable proportions by making some selection. Let us begin by reviewing the research literature on the impact of *economic development* on public policy.

## Economic Resources and Public Policy: Previous Research

Economists have contributed a great deal to the systematic analysis of public policy. Economic research very early suggested that government activity was closely related to the level of economic development in a society.[1] Economic development was broadly defined to include levels of wealth, industrialization, urbanization, and adult education.

Systematic analysis of the economic determinants of *state and local* government expenditures began with the publication of Fabricant's *The Trend of Government Activity in the United States Since 1900*.[2] Fabricant employed comparative analysis of state and local spending in all of the states to observe relationships between three socioeconomic measures (per capita income, population density, and urbanization) and per capita expenditures of state and local governments. Using data for 1942, Fabricant found that variations in these environmental variables in the states accounted for more than 72 percent of the variation among the states in total state and local spending. Of these three variables, he found that per capita *income* showed the strongest relationship to expenditures.

Another economist, Glenn F. Fisher, continued Fabricant's analysis into the 1960s.[3] He found that Fabricant's original three socioeconomic variables were somewhat *less* influential in determining levels of state and local government spending than they had been two decades before. The three variables that had explained 72 percent of the variation in state and local spending in 1942 explained only 53 percent

[1]See, for example, Bruce R. Morris, *Problems of American Economic Growth* (New York: Oxford, 1961); Walter Krause, *Economic Development* (Belmont, Calif.: Wadsworth, 1961); W.W. Rostow, *The Process of Economic Growth*, 2nd ed. (New York: Norton, 1962).

[2]Solomon Fabricant, *Trend of Government Activity in the United States Since 1900* (New York: National Bureau of Economic Research, 1952).

[3]Glenn F. Fisher, "Interstate Variation in State and Local Government Expenditures," *National Tax Journal*, 17 (March 1964), 57–74.

variation in spending in 1962. However, by adding other economic variables (e.g., percentage of families with less than $2,000 annual income, percentage increase in population, percentage of adult education with less than five years schooling), Fisher was able to explain even *more* of the interstate differences in state and local per capita spending than Fabricant's original analysis. And, like Fabricant, Fisher found that per capita *income* was the strongest single environmental variable associated with state and local expenditures.

Economists Seymour Sachs and Robert Harris added to this research literature by considering the effect of federal grants-in-aid on state and local government expenditures.[4] By 1960 it appeared that economic resources were losing some of their explanatory power in relation to state-local spending, particularly in the areas of welfare and health. Sachs and Harris also noted that the ability of income, population density, and urbanization to explain interstate variation in total state-local spending had declined from 72 percent in 1942 to 53 percent in 1960 (see Table 13–1). They particularly noted the decline in the explanatory power of these three variables in the areas of welfare (from 45 percent in 1942 to 11 percent in 1960) and health (from 72 percent in 1942 to 44 percent in 1960).

**TABLE 13–1** The Linkages Between Environmental Resources, Federal Aid, and State-Local Spending

| | Percent of State-Local Spending Determined By: | | | | | | |
| | Economic Development[1] | | | | | Economic Development Plus Federal Aid[2] | |
| State-Local Expenditures | 1942 | 1957 | 1960 | 1970 | 1976 | 1970 | 1976 |
|---|---|---|---|---|---|---|---|
| Total Expenditures | 72 | 53 | 53 | 62 | 45 | 72 | 91 |
| Education | 59 | 62 | 60 | 52 | 47 | 67 | 79 |
| Highways | 29 | 34 | 37 | 50 | 41 | 86 | 75 |
| Public Welfare | 45 | 14 | 11 | 17 | 32 | 48 | 57 |
| Health and Hospitals | 72 | 46 | 44 | 37 | 35 | 38 | 36 |
| Police | 81 | 74 | 79 | 69 | 59 | 70 | 66 |

*Note:* Figures are coefficients of multiple determination ($R^2$) for 48 states.

[1]Economic development is defined as per capita income, population density, and percent urbanization.

[2]Three economic development variables plus per capita federal aid.

*Source:* Adapted from Seymour Sachs and Robert Harris, "The Determinants of State and Local Government Expenditures and Intergovernmental Flow of Funds, *National Tax Journal,* 17 (March 1964), 78–85; 1970 and 1976 findings by the author.

[4]Seymour Sachs and Robert Harris, "The Determinants of State and Local Government Expenditures and Intergovernmental Flow of Funds," *National Tax Journal,* 17 (March 1964), 78–85.

They suggested that the decline in the explanatory power of economic resources could be attributed to the intervening effect of federal grants-in-aid, particularly in the welfare and health fields. They reasoned that federal grants were freeing the states from the constraints of their own economic resources. Federal grants were "outside money" to state and local government officials, which permitted them to fund programs at levels beyond their own resources. Hence the decline in the closeness of the relationship between economic resources and state-local spending, particularly in the fields with the heaviest federal involvement: welfare and health.

Table 13–1 is a replication of the Sachs and Harris study. We have updated their research to 1970 and 1976. The table shows some decline over time in the importance of economic resources in explaining state-local spending. But it also shows what happens when federal grants-in-aid are included among the explanatory variables: federal grants add considerably to the explanation of state-local spending. For example, in 1976 the proportion of total state-local spending explained by economic resources alone is 45 percent; but by considering federal grants-in-aid in addition to economic resources, 91 percent of total state-local spending can be explained. Note that in the welfare field the proportion of explained variance rises from 32 percent to 57 percent by the inclusion of federal aid. This means that a state's economic resources have relatively little to do with its welfare spending; federal policy is the primary determinant of state-local spending in this field. Indeed, in recent years federal aid has become one of the most important determinants of state-local spending for many functions. A state's own income, together with federal aid, largely determines what services it can provide.

## Economic Resources and Levels of Public Spending and Service

There is little doubt that levels of government revenue, expenditures, and services are closely linked to economic resources. Although there are some notable exceptions, virtually all the systematic evidence points to this fact: economic resources (particularly income) are the most important determinants of *levels* of government taxing, spending, and service. Socioeconomic measures, such as per capita income, adult education, and urbanization, consistently turn out to be the most influential variables in systematic analysis of public policies when public policies are defined as levels or amounts or averages of taxes, expenditures, or services.

Table 13-2 presents a typical selection of public policies in the American states defined in terms of levels of taxing, spending, bene-

**TABLE 13–2**  The Relationship Between Environmental Resources, Federal Aid, and Levels of Spending and Service in the Fifty States, 1970

| Levels of Spending and Service | Simple Correlation Coefficients | | | Total Explained Variance | |
|---|---|---|---|---|---|
| | Environmental Resources | | | | Percent Explained by Environmental Resources and Federal Aid |
| | | | | Percent Explained by Environmental Resources | |
| | Income | Education | Urban | | |
| *Education* | | | | | |
| Per Pupil Expend. | .76 | .53 | .30 | 63 | 64 |
| Average Teacher Salary | .90 | .54 | .54 | 83 | 85 |
| Teacher-Pupil Ratio | −.12 | −.32 | −.18 | 23 | 24 |
| Per Capita Educ. Expend. | .56 | .63 | .14 | 52 | 67 |
| *Welfare* | | | | | |
| Per Capita Welfare Expend. | .32 | .18 | .41 | 17 | 48 |
| Per Capita Health Expend. | .54 | .14 | .31 | 37 | 38 |
| Unemploy. Benefits | .80 | .49 | .61 | 66 | 66 |
| AFDC Benefits | .70 | .59 | .33 | 55 | 56 |
| Gen. Assist. Benefits | .79 | .53 | .56 | 64 | 64 |
| AFDC Recipients | −.02 | −.21 | .32 | 26 | 32 |
| Unemploy. Recipients | .58 | .20 | .31 | 39 | 39 |
| Gen. Assist. Recipients | .58 | .35 | .55 | 40 | 43 |
| *Highway* | | | | | |
| Per Capita Highway Expend. | .07 | .29 | −.43 | 50 | 86 |
| *Public Regulation* | | | | | |
| Numbers of Laws | .47 | .30 | .41 | 22 | 22 |
| Public Employees Per Popul. | .13 | .41 | .00 | 21 | 62 |
| Public Employee Salary | .90 | .55 | .51 | 81 | 85 |
| Per Capita Corrections Expend. | .69 | .58 | .32 | 52 | 52 |
| Police Protection | .57 | .37 | .73 | 56 | 58 |
| *Finance* | | | | | |
| Per Capita Total Expend. | .78 | .54 | .34 | 62 | 66 |
| Per Capita Total Revenue | .64 | .26 | .08 | 45 | 75 |
| Per Capita Tax Revenue | .77 | .65 | .54 | 64 | 64 |
| Per Capita Debt | .59 | .30 | .61 | 45 | 45 |

fits, and service. These are important policies in education, health and welfare, highways, public regulation, and taxing and spending.

Let us summarize the linkages between state policies and environmental resources (income, urbanization, and education) and federal aid, revealed in this table. First of all, differences in educational expenditures among the fifty states are closely related to differences in income. (Figure 13–1 is a graphic portrayal of this relationship.) Income also explains most of the differences among the states in measures reflecting the level of educational service, such as average teacher salaries and pupil-teacher ratios. In contrast, economic resources are not as influential in explaining health and welfare expenditures as they are in explaining education expenditures. Per capita welfare expenditures do not correlate with measures of economic resources, and this can be attributed to the effect of federal participation in welfare financing. (The federal government provides over half the funds spent on public assistance, and federal percentages of total public assistance expenditures decline with increases in state income levels. This means that federal policy offsets the effect of wealth so that per capita welfare expenditures do not reflect income levels in the states.) However, the impact of economic resources on benefit levels in health and welfare programs is quite obvious. Benefits per recipient for unemployment, aid to families with dependent children (AFDC), and general assistance are closely related to income levels in the states.

Highway expenditures in the states are also related to socioeconomic conditions, although in a somewhat different fashion than health, welfare, and education expenditures. Rural states spend *more* per capita on highways than do urban states.

The legislatures of wealthy urban states introduce and enact more laws than do the legislatures of poor rural states. Moreover, there are more public employees per capita in wealthy urban states than in poor rural states. Finally, the average monthly salaries of public employees in wealthy urban states is greater than in poor rural states. All this suggests that the level of government activity and public service is a function of the availability of resources. Police protection (as well as the crime rate) is related to urbanization, and per capita correctional expenditures are related to wealth.

There is little doubt that the overall ability of states to raise revenue and spend money is a function of their level of economic resources. Both per capita expenditures and per capita revenues are closely related to wealth. Per capita tax levels are also related to wealth, as is the ability to carry larger per capita debt levels.

In short, there are many significant linkages between environmental resources and public policies in the states. Levels of government taxing, spending, benefits, and service are related to income, urbanization, education. It is possible, of course, to focus attention on *un*explained variations in policy outcomes. (Unexplained variation is 1 minus the explained variation: for example, environmental resources explain 63 percent of variations among the states in per pupil expend-

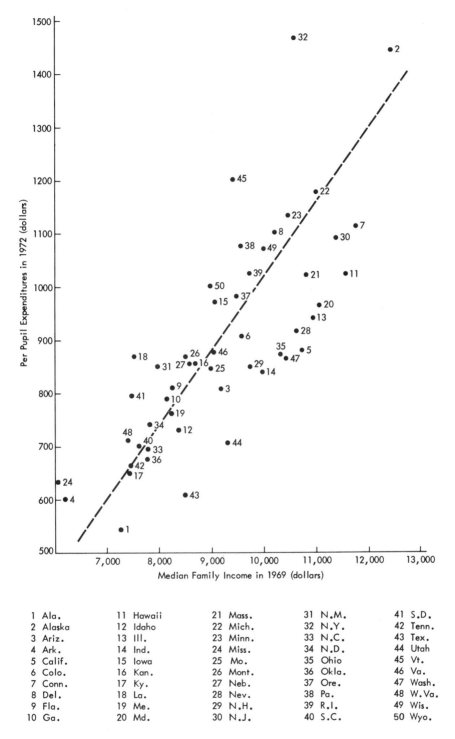

FIG. 13–1  The fifty states arranged according to median family income and per pupil expenditures for education

| | | | | |
|---|---|---|---|---|
| 1 Ala. | 11 Hawaii | 21 Mass. | 31 N.M. | 41 S.D. |
| 2 Alaska | 12 Idaho | 22 Mich. | 32 N.Y. | 42 Tenn. |
| 3 Ariz. | 13 Ill. | 23 Minn. | 33 N.C. | 43 Tex. |
| 4 Ark. | 14 Ind. | 24 Miss. | 34 N.D. | 44 Utah |
| 5 Calif. | 15 Iowa | 25 Mo. | 35 Ohio | 45 Vt. |
| 6 Colo. | 16 Kan. | 26 Mont. | 36 Okla. | 46 Va. |
| 7 Conn. | 17 Ky. | 27 Neb. | 37 Ore. | 47 Wash. |
| 8 Del. | 18 La. | 28 Nev. | 38 Pa. | 48 W.Va. |
| 9 Fla. | 19 Me. | 29 N.H. | 39 R.I. | 49 Wis. |
| 10 Ga. | 20 Md. | 30 N.J. | 40 S.C. | 50 Wyo. |

itures, and the remaining 37 percent is unexplained by environmental resources.) Environmental variables fail to explain half of the total variation in half of our policy variables. Certainly there is room for continued research on additional determinants of public policy. But social science rarely produces complete explanations of anything. Unexplained variation may be a product of poor measurement or a product of the combined efforts of thousands of other factors influencing political systems. The fact that only three environmental variables—income, education, and urbanization—can explain half of the variation in levels of public spending and service is evidence of the importance of the socioeconomic environment in explaining public policy.

### Federal Grants as "Outside Money"

Federal grant-in-aid money is now a very important resource of state and local governments in America. Federal grants now account for one-third of all state government revenues and one-sixth of all local government revenues. State and local government officials tend to view federal grants as "outside money" to help support programs in education, welfare, health, highways, housing, urban renewal, and a myriad of other programs. This "outside money" tends to free states and communities from some of the constraints of their own limited economic resources and, therefore, reduce somewhat the impact of state and local economic resources on levels of public spending and service. Thus, in explaining levels of public spending and service, we must consider federal grant money as well as environmental resources.

Our own analysis of the effect of federal grant money on public policy in the states confirms the ideas of many economists. Federal money is indeed an important resource that helps explain interstate variation in levels of spending and service. This is particularly true in the two areas of greatest federal involvement—welfare and highways. The last column of figures in Table 13–2 shows the explanatory value of adding federal aid to income, education, and urbanization, in determining levels of taxing, spending, benefits, and services in the states. Note how adding federal aid significantly improves our ability to explain welfare and highway expenditures.

### Stability and Change
### in Input-Output Relationships

Do relationships between environment and public policy persist over time? Most of the linkages described so far are based on data from the last two decades. Can these same linkages be observed in other time periods? Are there any changes over time in the nature of the relationships between environment and public policy?

To explore these questions, we traced the relationships between several environmental variables and levels of public spending in the states over a period of eight decades—1890 to 1970. The results are shown in Figure 13–2. Each of the three diagrams traces the strength of the relationships (measured in terms of the size of the simple correlation coefficients) between environmental variables and total state-local spending, spending for education, and spending for welfare, in the fifty states.

Wealth has *always* been an important determinant of levels of total spending for public services in the American states. A half-century ago, states and communities relied primarily on property taxes and hence the value of property for revenue. Property value was the principal determinant of total state-local spending. In more recent decades personal income has been an even more influential determinant of public spending and services. There is no indication of any weakening over time in the relationships between wealth and government spending.

In contrast, urbanization, and particularly industrialization, are losing their influence over time as determinants of public spending. At one time, differences in the degree of industrialization among the fifty states helped to account for differences in spending policies. But in recent years, as all states became industrialized, differences in the degree of industrialization ceased to be a determinant of public policy. The same decline in influence of public policy can be observed in urbanization, although this variable has not yet lost all of its influence. But certainly urbanization is not as important today as it was a few decades ago.[5]

Education has a strong and persistent impact on public policy. The educational level of the adult population has a significant impact on total spending, and an even greater impact on spending for education.

In general, then, we can say that income and education are persistent determinants of levels of government spending in the states.

## Politics, Economics, and Policy: Previous Research

The political system functions to transform demands generated in the environment into public policy. The traditional literature in American

[5]See also Richard I. Hofferbert's "Ecological Development and Policy Change in the American States," *Midwest Journal of Political Science*, 10 (November 1966), 481–92; and his "Socioeconomic Dimensions of the American States: 1890–1960," *Midwest Journal of Political Science*, 12 (August 1968), 401–18.

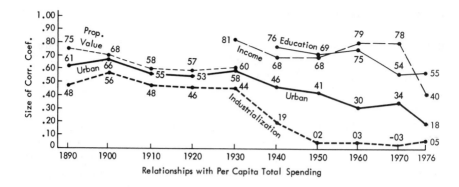

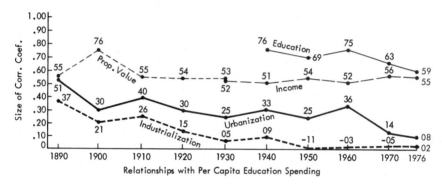

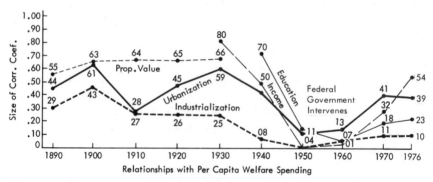

FIG. 13–2 Stability and change in relationships between environmental resources and levels of public spending over time

politics instructed students that characteristics of the political system, particularly two-party competition, voter participation, and apportionment had direct bearing on public policy.[6] Because political scientists

[6]V.O. Key, Jr., *American State Politics: An Introduction* (New York: Knopf, 1956); also his *Southern Politics in State and Nation* (New York: Knopf, 1951); Duane Lockard, *New England State Politics* (Princeton, N.J.: Princeton University Press, 1959); Malcolm Jewell, *The State Legislature* (New York: Random House, 1962); Duane Lockard, *The Politics of State and Local Government* (New York: Macmillan, 1963); John H. Fenton, *People and Parties in Politics* (Glenview, Ill.: Scott, Foresman, 1966).

devoted most of their time to studying what happened *within* the political system, it was easy for them to believe that the political processes and institutions which they studied were important determinants of public policies. Moreover, the belief that competition, participation, and equality in representation had important consequences for public policy squared with the value placed upon these variables in the prevailing pluralist ideology.

The assertion that political variables, such as party competition and voter participation, affected public policy rested more upon a priori reasoning than upon systematic research. It seemed reasonable to *believe* that an increase in party competition would increase educational spending, welfare benefits, numbers of welfare recipients, highway spending, health and hospital care, and so on, because competitive parties would try to outbid each other for public favor by offering such inducements, and the overall effect of such competition would be to raise levels of spending and service. It also seemed reasonable to believe that increased voter participation would influence public policy, presumably in a more liberal direction.

The earliest system model in the state policy field was a "competition-participation" model:

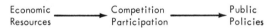

where economic resources determined political competition and participation and these political factors in turn determined public policies in welfare, education, health, highway, taxation, and spending. The early work of V.O. Key, Jr., Duane Lockard, John Fenton, and others, asserted the central place of political factors in shaping state policy.[7] For many years there was no empirical evidence to contradict this model: poor, rural, agrarian states tended to have less competitive parties ("one-party" or "modified one-party" systems, in contrast to "two-party" systems), and these same states spent less per capita for education, welfare, health, and other social services.

However, in order to assess the *independent* effect of politics on public policy, it is important to control for the intervening effects of socioeconomic variables. For example, if it is shown that, in general, wealthy states have more party competition than poor states, it might be that differences in the level of welfare benefits of competitive and noncompetitive states are really a product of the fact that the former are wealthy and the latter are poor. If this is the case, policy differences between the states might be attributable to wealth rather than to

[7]V. O. Key, Jr., *American State Politics* (New York: Knopf, 1956); Duane Lockard, *The Politics of State and Local Government* (New York: Macmillan, 1963); John H. Fenton, *People and Parties in Politics* (New York: Scott, Foresman, 1966).

party competition. In order to isolate the effect of party competition on education and welfare policies from the effect of economic resources, it is necessary to control for these variables.

The first hint that political variables might not be as influential in determining levels of public taxing, spending, and service as commonly supposed came in an important research effort by Richard E. Dawson and James A. Robinson in 1963.[8] These political scientists examined the linkages between socioeconomic variables (income, urbanization, industrialization), the level of interparty competition, and nine public *welfare* policies. They concluded that "high levels of interparty competition are highly interrelated both to socioeconomic factors and to social welfare legislation, but the degree of interparty competition does not seem to possess the important intervening influence between socioeconomic factors and liberal welfare programs that our original hypothesis and theoretical schemes suggested."

A comprehensive analysis of public policy in the American states was published in 1965 by Thomas R. Dye.[9] Employing a systems model, the linkages between the four economic development variables, four political system characteristics, and over ninety separated policy output measures in education, health, welfare, highways, corrections, taxation, and public regulation were described. This research produced some findings that were very unsettling for many political scientists. Four of the most commonly described characteristics of political systems—(1) Democratic or Republican control of state government, (2) the degree of interparty competition, (3) the level of voter turnout, and (4) the extent of malapportionment—were found to have less effect on public policy than environmental variables reflecting the level of economic development—urbanization, industrialization, wealth, and education. The conclusion: "The evidence seems conclusive: economic development variables are more influential than political system characteristics in shaping public policy in the states." The reasoning in this was similar to that of Dawson and Robinson; most of the associations that occur between political variables and policy outcomes are really a product of the fact that economic development influences both political system characteristics and policy outcomes. When political factors are controlled, economic development continues to have a significant impact on public policy. But when the effects of economic development are controlled, political factors turn out to have little influence on policy outcomes. Several policy areas were pointed out where political factors remained important, and certain policy areas were also identi-

[8]Richard E. Dawson and James A. Robinson, "Inter-Party Competition, Economic Variables, and Welfare Policies in the American States," *Journal of Politics*, 25 (May 1963), 265–89.

[9]Thomas R. Dye, *Politics, Economics, and the Public* (Chicago: Rand McNally, 1966).

fied in which federal programs tended to offset the impact of economic development levels on state policies. Yet in an attempt to generalize about the determinants of public policy, it was concluded that, on the whole, economic development was more influential in shaping state policies than any of the political variables previously thought to be important in policy determination.

The resulting "economic resources" model may be viewed as follows:

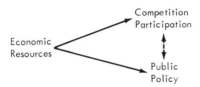

In this view, economic resources shape both the political system characteristics (competition and participation) and public policy, but characteristics of the political system have no direct causal effect on public policy.

These findings—regarded as commonplace by economists—were very disturbing to political scientists who were committed to a *pluralist ideology* which asserted the importance of competition and participation in politics. Now, of course, most of us would prefer to live in a political system in which there are high levels of competition and participation, since these conditions are highly valued in any democracy. *But* it remains a scientific question whether these political conditions produce different kinds of policies than noncompetitive, nonparticipating political systems. We cannot *assume* that competition and participation will produce "better" public policies simply because we prefer a competitive, participating political system.

Nonetheless, the challenge to political scientists to prove that "politics count" in shaping public policy inspired a new systematic reexamination of the determinants of public policy. A number of scholars were stimulated to reexamine systematically the traditional wisdom in the state politics field. New and more sophisticated methods were introduced;[10] additional political variables were tested for their policy impact; [11] some policy variables other than levels of public expenditures

[10]Ira Sharkansky and Richard Hofferbert, "Dimensions of State Politics, Economics, and Public Policy," *American Political Science Review*, 63 (September 1969), 867–79; James C. Strouse and Oliver J. Williams, "A Non-Additive Model for State Policy Research," *Journal of Politics*, 35 (May 1972), 648–57.

[11]Ira Sharkansky, "Agency Requests, Gubernatorial Support, and Budget Success in State Legislatures," *American Political Science Review*, 62 (December 1968), 926–39; Thomas R. Dye, "Executive Power and Public Policy in the States," *Western Political Quarterly*, 22 (December 1969), 926–39.

and sources were examined;[12] changes over time were described and analyzed;[13] some more sophisticated conceptual notions were explored;[14] and policy innovation became an important topic itself.[15] In short, a whole subfield grew to maturity in a short period of time.

Implicit in much of this literature, however, was a reluctance to accept the view that political system characteristics, particularly those reflecting the pluralist values of competition and participation, possessed less policy relevance than social needs or economic resources. Indeed, there seemed to be a great deal of scrambling about by political scientists ideologically committed to proving that party competition, voter participation, partisanship, and apportionment did indeed influence public policy.[16] Of course, there is nothing wrong with trying to find the policy relevance of differing governmental structures or political processes, but we should not insist that political variables *must* influence public policy simply because our traditional training and wisdom in political science has told us that political variables are important.

One interesting model of policy determination to emerge from this research was a "hybrid model" suggested by political scientists Charles F. Cnudde and Donald J. McCrone, illustrated in the following diagram:[17]

[12]Bryan R. Fry and Richard Winters, "The Politics of Redistribution," *American Political Science Review*, 64 (June 1970), 508–22; Ronald E. Weber and William R. Schaffer, "Public Opinion and American State Policy-Making," *Midwest Journal of Political Science*, 16 (November 1972), 683–99; Anne H. Hopkins, "Public Opinion and Support for Public Policy in the American States," *American Journal of Political Science*, 18 (February 1974), 167–78.

[13]Virginia Gray, "Models of Comparative State Politics: A Comparison of Cross-Sectional and Time Series Analyses," *American Journal of Political Science*, XX, 2 (May 1976), 235–56; Richard Hofferbert, "Socioeconomic Dimensions of the American States, 1890–1960," *Midwest Journal of Political Science*, 2 (August 1968), 401–18; Richard Hofferbert, "Ecological Development and Policy Change," *Midwest Journal of Political Science*, 10 (November 1966), 464–83.

[14]Ira Sharkansky, "Environment, Policy, Output and Input: Problems of Theory and Method in the Analysis of Public Policy," in *Policy Analysis in Political Science*, ed. Ira Sharkansky (Chicago: Markham, 1970); James C. Strouse and Oliver J. Williams, "A Non-Additive Model for State Policy Research," *Journal of Politics*, 34 (May 1972), 648–57.

[15]Jack L. Walker, "The Diffusion of Innovation Among the American States," *American Political Science Review*, 63 (September 1969), 880–89; Virginia Gray, "Innovation in the States," *American Political Science Review*, 67 (December 1973), 1174–85.

[16]John Crittenden, "Dimensions of Modernization in the American States," *American Political Science Review*, 61 (December 1967), 982–1002; Alan G. Pulsipher and James L. Weatherby, "Malapportionment, Party Competition, and the Functional Distribution of Government Expenditures," *American Political Science Review*, 62 (December 1968), 1207–20; Guenther F. Schaefer and Stuart Rakoff, "Politics, Policy, and Political Science," *Politics and Society*, 1 (November 1970), 52.

[17]Charles F. Cnudde and Ronald J. McCrone, "Party Competition and Welfare Policies in the American States," *American Political Science Review*, 62 (December 1968), 1220–31.

In this model, economic resources shape public policy both *directly* and *indirectly* through affecting competition and participation, which in turn affect public policy. This study focused on only one policy field—welfare—rather than on the broader array of policies in education, health, highways, spending, taxation, and so on. Welfare policy was thought to magnify the conflict between "haves" and "have nots" and therefore to magnify the effect of competition and participation. Presumably, the overwhelming influence of economic resources in determining other state policies was acknowledged.

Recently, more complex "path analytic" models have been introduced into the research on the determinants of public policy in the states. Path analysis was designed to portray ideas about causes and consequences of public policy in diagrammatic fashion. Path analytic models can help us think about *how* economic resources or social conditions might influence political system characteristics and public policy. To construct a path analytic model one must think about causal sequences, mechanisms of influence, and developmental processes in policy making. One must think about *how* economic resources, social conditions, political system characteristics, and public policies influence each other, and then construct a diagram which portrays these causal notions. The method of path analysis then allows one to test these notions.

The path analytic technique has been employed to shed more light on the effect of political competition and participation on welfare spending in the American states. As we observed in Chapter 2, pluralist ideology had posited an important role for competition and participation in determining levels of assistance for "have nots," including expenditures per recipient in AFDC programs. However, a number of empirical studies had suggested that economic development—income, urbanization, industrialization—had a more important impact on public policy, including welfare policy, than participation or competition. Political scientist Gary Tompkins designed a model to clarify these relationships—a model in which industrialization was perceived as antecedent to participation and competition; and all these variables were perceived as factors influencing levels of aid to dependent children in the states.[18]

This model succeeds in explaining 69 percent of the variation among the states in levels of aid to dependent children, but the inter-

[18]Gary Tompkins, "A Causal Model of State Welfare Expenditures," *Journal of Politics*, 37 (May 1975), 392–416.

esting aspect of the causal model (see Figure 13–3) and the path analysis employed to test it is the sorting out of significant causal sequences. Figure 13–3 presents only those linkages for which significant path coefficients were obtained. Note that ethnicity is related to income (immigrants came to wealthier states); higher incomes produce party competition which has some direct effect on welfare benefits; but it is ethnicity which is most closely related to welfare benefits. This model shows no direct path between income and welfare benefits when ethnicity is part of the model. This finding contrasts with earlier research which indicated a direct linkage between income and welfare benefits; the difference in outcomes appears to be a result of adding ethnicity to the model. In short, Tompkins uses this path analytic model to suggest that neither income nor competition-participation are as important in determining welfare benefits as ethnicity.

A similar, but less complex, path analytic model was devised by political scientist Michael Lewis-Beck to reexamine the earlier "competition-participation" and "economic resources" models.[19] Lewis-Beck

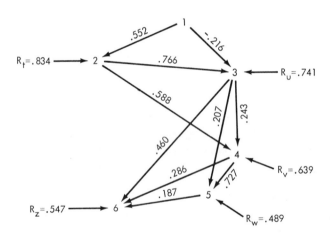

1 = industrialization
2 = income
3 = ethnicity
4 = interparty competition
5 = voter turnout
6 = per recipient aid to dependent children

**FIG. 13–3** A causal model of state welfare spending

*Source:* Gary Tompkins, "A Causal Model of State Welfare Expenditures," *Journal of Politics,* 37 (May 1975), 392–416.

[19]Michael Lewis-Beck, "The Relative Importance of Socioeconomic and Political Variables in Public Policy," *American Political Science Review,* 71 (June 1977), 559–66.

proposes a three-variable model to determine the *relative* impact of "economic affluence" and "competition turnout" on "welfare-education" policies:

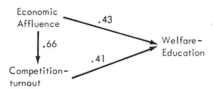

The strength of the causal paths is represented by the numbers adjacent to each arrow. "Economic affluence" is clearly the major direct determinant of "competition-turnout," and "economic affluence" also directly affects "welfare-education." Moreover, "economic affluence" affects "welfare-education" *through* its effect on "competition-turnout." Lewis-Beck concludes: "When the effects coefficients for a common model of welfare policy are estimated in a data-based example, socioeconomic variables are found to be considerably more important than political variables."[20]

## The Political System as a Conversion Process

The general failure of political variables to be influential determinants of public policy raises the question of whether we should view politics as a conversion system, rather than a direct cause of public policy. In other words, politics does not *cause* public policy, but rather, it *facilitates* the conversion of demands and resources into public policy.

If we accept this view, we would not really expect variations in political systems—variations in competition, participation, partisanship, reformism, and soon—to directly cause public policy. Instead, we would expect variations in political systems to affect *relationships* between demands and resources and public policies. For example, we would not expect highly competitive political systems to produce different policies than noncompetitive systems, but instead we might inquire whether the relationships between population characteristics and public policy are closer in competitive than in noncompetitive systems. Our focus would shift to the impact of political system variables on relationships between environmental conditions (measures of demands and resources) and public policies.

As a hypothetical example, we might portray relationships be-

[20]*Ibid.*, p. 566.

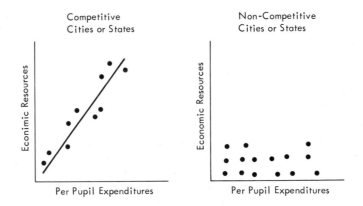

FIG. 13–4   Possible relationships between economic resources and educational expenditures in competitive and noncompetitive political systems

tween economic resources and educational policies in two different
kinds of cities/states—competitive and noncompetitive.

Among the competitive political systems (cities or states), it may turn
out that per pupil expenditures rise in direct proportion to increases
in economic resources. (See left drawing in Figure 13–4.) However,
among the noncompetitive political systems, it may turn out that there
is *no* relationship between economic resources and per pupil expenditures. (See right drawing in Figure 13–4.) In other words, competition
may *facilitate* relations between resources and public policy, but noncompetitive systems *obstruct* relationships between economic resources
and public policy. This would suggest that competitive political systems
are more *responsive* to socioeconomic conditions of the population than
noncompetitive political systems.

Not enough research has been completed to really tell us whether
our hypothetical example applies to the real world, that is, to cities,
states, or nations, and to policies in education, welfare, health, housing,
and so on.[21] However, an early study of "reformism" in American city
governments suggested that the type of government could indeed af-

[21]However, there is some evidence that "professional" state legislatures produce
welfare policies more closely linked to their states resources than "nonprofes-
sional" state legislatures. See Edward C. Carmines, "The Mediating Influence of
State Legislatures on the Link Between Interparty Competition and Welfare Policies," *American Political Science Review*, 68 (September 1974) 1118–24. There is also
some evidence that elected officials and the general public "concur" on policy issues more often in politically competitive cities than in noncompetitive cities. See
Susan B. Hansen, "Participation, Political Structure and Concurrence," *American
Political Science Review*, 69 (December 1975), 1181–99.

fect the responsiveness of public policy to characteristics of city populations.

In a study of 200 American cities, Robert L. Lineberry and Edmund D. Fowler found that reformed cities tended to tax and spend less than unreformed cities.[22] Cities with manager governments and at-large council constituencies were less willing to spend money for public purposes than cities with mayor-council governments and ward constituencies. In short, reformism does save tax money.

Lineberry and Fowler also found that environmental variables had an important impact on tax and spending policies. For example, they found that

1. the more middle class the city (measured by income, education, and occupation), the lower the general tax and spending levels
2. the greater the homeownership in a city, the lower the tax and spending levels
3. the larger the percentage of religious and ethnic minorities in the population, the higher the city's taxes and expenditures.

What turned out to be an even more important finding in the Lineberry and Fowler study was the difference in *responsiveness* of the two kinds of city governments—reformed and unreformed—to the socioeconomic composition of their populations. These researchers simply grouped their cities into subsamples—reformed cities (cities with manager governments, nonpartisan elections, and at-large constituencies) and unreformed cities (cities with mayor-council governments, partisan elections, and ward constituencies). Among reformed cities there were no significant correlations between tax and spending policies and income and educational, occupational, religious, and ethnic characteristics of their population. In contrast, among unreformed cities there were many significant correlations between taxing and spending policies and these socioeconomic characteristics of the population.

They concluded that reformism tends to reduce the importance of class, homeownership, ethnicity, and religion in city politics. It tends to minimize the role that social conflicts play in public decision making. In contrast, mayor-council governments, ward constituencies, and partisan elections permit social cleavages to be reflected in city politics and public policy to be responsive to socioeconomic factors. These findings suggest that reformed cities have gone a long way toward accomplishing the reformer's goal; that is "to immunize city governments from

[22]Robert L. Lineberry and Edmund D. Fowler, "Reformism and Public Policies in American Cities," *American Political Science Review*, 61 (September 1967), 701–17.

'artificial' social cleavages—race, religion, ethnicity, and so on." Thus, political institutions seem to play an important role in policy formation:

> . . . a role substantially independent of a city's demography. . . . Nonpartisan elections, at-large constituencies, and manager governments are associated with a lessened responsiveness of cities to the enduring conflicts of political life.[23]

## Summary

We have employed a systems model, and variations based on this model, to describe linkages between economic resources, political system characteristics, and public policies in *the American states*. Some general propositions about public policy which are suggested by our system model might include:

1. Economic development is an important determinant of overall levels of government taxing, spending, and service. Wealth, as measured by per capita personal income, is the single most important environmental variable associated with levels of government taxing, spending, and service.

2. Federal grants-in-aid, considered "outside" money to state and local governments, help to release these governments from their dependence upon economic conditions within their jurisdictions and permit them to spend at higher levels than they would otherwise be able to do. Federal grants reduce the impact of a state's own economic resources on its level of spending and service. Thus, in explaining levels of public spending and service in the states, one must consider federal grants as well as environmental resources.

3. Wealth and education have been consistent determinants of the level of government spending and service over time. In contrast, industrialization has been losing influence as a determinant of government spending. Where the federal government has intervened and offset disparities among the states, the influence of environmental variables has been significantly reduced.

4. The traditional literature in American politics asserted that characteristics of political systems—particularly party competition and voter participation—had an important impact on the content of public policy. But recent systematic research suggests that the characteristics of political systems are not as important as economic resources in shaping public policy. Most of the correlations between political system variables and public policy measure are a product of the fact that economic resources shape *both* the political system and public policy.

5. The ideology of "pluralism" implies that factors such as party

[23]*Ibid.*, p. 717.

competition and voter participation are important determinants of public policy. And it is true that states with competitive parties and high voter turnouts have generally higher levels of taxing, spending, benefits, and service in a variety of policy areas. But these same states also tend to be wealthy urban states with well-educated adult populations.

6. Multivariable analysis indicates that, in many policy areas, economic resources—income, urbanization, education, and federal aid—are more influential in determining levels of taxing, spending, benefits, and service, than either competition or participation in the political system.

7. The testing of alternative causal models in policy determination leads us to reject the proposition that economic resources shape public policy *only* through changes which are made in the political system. We must also reject the idea that the character of the political system must be changed in order to change public policy. Economic resources can affect public policy directly regardless of the character of the political system. However, in some policy areas, especially welfare, economic resources shape public policy both directly and indirectly through political variables.

8. Rather than think of the political system as *causing* public policy, perhaps we should think of it as *facilitating* public policy. Competition and participation may not affect public policy itself but these political variables may affect the relationship between environmental resources and public policies.

## Bibliography

DYE, THOMAS R., *Politics, Economics, and the Public: Policy Outcomes in the American States.* Chicago: Rand McNally, 1966.

DYE, THOMAS R., and VIRGINIA GRAY, *Determinants of Public Policy.* Boston: Lexington, 1980.

HOFFERBERT, RICHARD I., and IRA SHARKANSKY, eds., *State and Urban Politics.* Boston: Little, Brown, 1971.

SHARKANSKY, IRA, *Spending in the American States.* Chicago: Rand McNally, 1968.

Session of Interstate and Foreign Commerce Committee: getting inside the system. *Stan Wakefield.*

# The Policy-Making Process
## getting inside the system

# 14

## The Black Box Problem

It is important that we understand what goes on in the little black box labeled "political system." The systems approach employed in the previous chapter deals with aggregate characteristics of *whole* political systems; this model does not say much about what goes on *within* political systems. Our comparative analysis focused attention on the linkages between environmental resources, system characteristics, and public policy, and dealt with whole political systems. But we also want to know what happens *within* political systems. We want to know how public policy is generated within the political system, how institutions and processes function to handle demands generated in the environment, and how parties, interest groups, voters, governors, legislators, and other political actors behave in the policy-making process.

Let us try to illustrate the differences between a *comparative systems* approach and a *within-system* approach. Finding a high correlation between cigarette smoking and the incidence of cancer among human systems is important. But this correlation does not in itself reveal the functioning of cells within the human body: we still want to know *how* cancers are formed and how they behave. So also, finding a high correlation between urbanization and police protection does not in itself reveal the functioning of political systems; we will want to know *how* a political system goes about transforming demands arising from the socioeconomic environment into public policy.

The process model of public policy assists in identifying various processes occurring *within* the political system. They are:

> the identification of policy problems through public demands for government action
>
> the formulation of policy proposals through the initiation and development of policy proposals by policy-planning organizations, interest groups, government bureaucracies, and the president and Congress
>
> the legitimation of policies through political actions by parties, interest groups, the president, and Congress
>
> the implementation of policies through organized bureaucracies, public expenditures, and the activities of executive agencies
>
> the evaluation of policies by government agencies themselves, outside consultants, the press, and the public

We have already talked about most of these processes in the chapters covering specific policy fields: civil rights, criminal justice, poverty and welfare, health, education, energy and the environment, urban affairs, government spending, taxation, and national defense. In the final chapter of this book, "Policy Evaluation: Finding Out What Happens after a Law Is Passed," we will examine more closely the "policy evaluation" phase of the policy process model. In this chapter, we shall add a few general comments about the influence of mass opinion, elite attitudes, the mass media, interest groups, and political parties, in the policy-making process.

In describing these political processes, however, it is important to remember that the activities of the various political actors are greatly constrained by environmental conditions. We have already described the great influence environmental resources have on the character of the political system and the content of public policy. It is true that not *all* the variance in public policy can be explained by environmental resources. However, the activities of parties, groups, and individuals *within* the political system are heavily influenced by the nature of the environment. So our systems model has warned us not to expect the activities of individuals, groups, parties, or decision makers to produce policies at variance with environmental resources and constraints.

## Identifying Policy Issues: Public Opinion

The influence of public opinion over government policy has been the subject of great philosophical controversies in the classic literature on democracy. Edmund Burke believed democratic representatives should serve the *interest* of the people but not necessarily conform to their *will* in deciding questions of public policy. In contrast, some democratic theorists have evaluated the success of democratic institutions by whether or not they facilitate popular control over public policy.

The philosophical question of whether public opinion *should* be an important independent influence over public policy may never be resolved. But the empirical question of whether public opinion *does* constitute an important independent influence over public policy can be tackled by systematic research. However, even this empirical question has proved very difficult to answer.

The problem in assessing the independent effect of mass opinion on the actions of decision makers is that their actions help to mold mass opinion. Public policy may be in accord with mass opinion but we can never be sure whether mass opinion shaped public policy or public policy shaped mass opinion.

In V. O. Key's most important book, *Public Opinion and American Democracy*, he wrote:

> Government, as we have seen, attempts to mold public opinion toward support of the programs and policies it espouses. Given that endeavor, perfect congruence between public policy and public opinion could be government *of* public opinion rather than govern *by* public opinion.[1]

Although Key himself was convinced that public opinion did have some independent effect on public policy, he was never able to demonstrate this in any systematic fashion. He lamented:

> Discussion of public opinion often loses persuasiveness as it deals with the critical question of how public opinion and governmental action are linked. The democratic theorist founds his doctrines on the assumption that an interplay occurs between mass opinion and government. When he seeks to delineate that interaction and to demonstrate the precise bearing of the opinions of private citizens on official decision, he encounters almost insurmountable obstacles. In despair he may conclude that the supposition that public opinion enjoys weight in public decision is a myth and nothing more, albeit a myth that strengthens a regime so long as people believe it.[2]

Yet Key compiled a great deal of circumstantial evidence supporting the notion that elections, parties, and interest groups do institutionalize channels of communication from citizens to decision makers. But there is very little *direct* evidence in the existing research literature to

[1]V. O. Key, Jr., *Public Opinion and American Democracy* (New York: Knopf, 1967), pp. 422–23.
[2]Ibid., p. 411.

support the notion that public opinion has an important influence over public policy.

Public opinion rarely affects public policy; instead, public policy shapes public opinion. There are several reasons why policies are relatively unconstrained by public opinion. First, few people have opinions on the great bulk of policy questions confronting the nation's decision makers. Second, public opinion is very unstable. It can change in a matter of weeks in response to "news" events precipitated by leaders. Third, leaders do not have a clear perception of mass opinion. Most communications received by decision makers are from other elites—newsmakers, interest-group leaders, and other influential persons—and not from ordinary citizens.

We must not assume that the opinions expressed in the news media are public opinion. Frequently, this is a source of confusion. Newspersons believe *they* are the public, often confusing their own opinions with public opinion. They even tell the mass public what its opinion is, thus actually helping to mold it to conform to their own beliefs. Decision makers, then, may act in response to news stories or to the opinions of influential newsmakers in the mistaken belief that they are responding to "public opinion."

Most people do not have opinions on most policy issues. Public opinion polls frequently create opinions by asking questions that respondents never thought about until they were asked.[3] Few respondents are willing to say they have no opinion; they believe they should provide some sort of answer, even if their opinion is weakly held or was nonexistent before the question was asked. Thus pollsters produce "doorstep" opinions. But it is unlikely that many Americans have seriously thought about, or gathered much information on, such specific issues as government reorganization, zero-based budgeting, the B-1 bomber, investment tax credits, municipal bond interest exemption, and similar specific questions; nor do many Americans have information on these topics.

Public opinion is also very unstable. Mass opinion on a particular issue is often very weakly held. Asked the same question at a later date, many respondents fail to remember their earlier answers and give the pollster the opposite reply. These are not real changes in opinion, yet they register as such. One study estimates that less than 20 percent of the public holds meaningful, consistent opinions on most issues, even though two-thirds or more will respond to questions asked in a survey.[4]

Opinions also vary according to the wording of questions. It is

[3]Robert S. Erikson and Norman R. Luttbeg, *American Public Opinion* (New York: John Wiley, 1973).

[4]Phillip Converse, "Attitudes and Non-attitudes," in *Quantitative Analysis of Social Problems*, ed. Edward R. Tufte (Reading: Addison-Wesley, 1970).

relatively easy to word almost any public policy question in such a way as to elicit mass approval or disapproval. Thus, differently worded questions on the same issue can produce contradictory results. For example, in a California poll about academic freedom,[5] a majority of respondents (52 to 39) agreed with the statement: "Professors in state-supported institutions should have freedom to speak and teach the truth as they see it." However, a majority of respondents (by the same 52 to 39 ratio) also agreed with the statement: "Professors who advocate controversial ideas or speak out against official policy have no place in a state-supported college or university."

Opinion polls that ask the exact same question over time are more reliable indicators of public opinion than one-shot polls. Respondents in a one-shot poll may be responding to the wording of the question. But if the same wording is used over time, the bias in the wording remains constant and changes in opinion may be observed. This is why only verbatim wording used continuously over time produces reasonably accurate information about the public mood, and also why it is usually a mistake to rely on one-shot polls.

Finally, decision makers can easily misinterpret public opinion because the communications they receive have an upper-class bias. Members of the masses seldom call or write their senators or representatives, much less converse with them at dinners, cocktail parties, or other social occasions. Most of the communications received by decision makers are intraelite communications—communications from newspersons, organized group leaders, influential constituents, wealthy political contributors, and personal friends—people who, for the most part, share the same views. It is not surprising, therefore, that Congressmen say that most of their mail is in agreement with their own position; their world of public opinion is self-reinforcing. Moreover, persons who initiate communication with decision makers, by writing or calling or visiting their representatives, are decidedly more educated and affluent than the average citizen.

In a careful study of the relationship between mass opinion and Congressional voting on policy issues, Warren E. Miller and Donald Stokes found very low correlations between the voting records of Congressmen and the attitudes of their constituents on social welfare issues, and even lower correlations on foreign policy issues.[6] Only in the area of civil rights did Congressmen appear to vote according to the views of a majority of their constituents. In general, "the representative

---

[5]Erikson and Luttbeg, *American Public Opinion*, p. 38.
[6]Miller and Stokes, "Constituency Influence in Congress," *American Political Science Review*, 57 (March 1963), 55–65; see also Charles F. Cnudde and Donald J. McCrone, "The Linkage Between Constituency Attitudes and Congressional Voting Behavior," *American Political Science Review*, 60 (March 1966), 66–72.

has very imperfect information about the issue preferences of his constituency, and constituency's awareness of the policy stands of the representative is ordinarily slight." With the possible exception of civil rights questions, most Congressmen are free from the influence of popular preferences in their legislative voting.

This is not to say that policy makers are completely free from the influence of mass opinion. On the contrary, the voting behavior of Congressmen on roll call votes correlates very closely with characteristics of their constituencies. Districts of different social and economic makeup produce different political orientations and voting records for Congressmen. For example, Congressmen from urban-industrial districts are more likely to vote "liberal" than are Congressmen from rural, agricultural districts, regardless of party affiliation. Congressmen from suburban, high-income, white-collar districts have different voting records than do Congressmen from big-city, low-income, political machine-dominated districts. Because a Congressman is a product of the social system of his constituency, he shares its dominant goals and values. He has deep roots in the social system of his constituency— many organizational memberships, many overlapping leadership positions, lifetime residency, close ties with social and economic elites, shared religious affiliations, and so on. A Congressman is so much "of" his constituency that conflicts seldom occur between his own views and the dominant views in his constituency.

## Identifying Policy Issues: Elite Opinion

When V. O. Key wrestled with the same problem confronting us— namely, the determination of the impact of popular preferences on public policy—he concluded that "the missing piece of the puzzle" was "that thin stratum of persons referred to variously as the political elite, the political activists, the leadership echelons, or the influentials."

> The longer one frets with the puzzle of how democratic regimes manage to function, the more plausible it appears that a substantial part of the explanation is to be found in the motives that activate the *leadership echelon*, the values that it holds, the rules of the political game to which it adheres, in the expectations which it entertains about its own status in society, and perhaps in some of the objective circumstances, both material and institutional, in which it functions.[7]

In view of our inability to find any direct links between public policy and popular preferences, it seems reasonable to ask whether the pref-

---

[7]Key, *Public Opinion and American Democracy*, p. 537.

erences of elites are more directly reflected in public policy than the preferences of masses. Do elite attitudes independently affect public policy? Or are elite attitudes so closely tied to environmental conditions that elites have relatively little flexibility in policy making and therefore little independent influence over the content of public policy?

Elite preferences are more likely to be in accord with public policy than mass preferences. This finding is fairly well-supported in the existing research literature. Of course this does not *prove* that policies are determined by elite preferences. It may be that government officials are acting rationally in response to events and conditions, and well-educated, informed elites understand the actions of government better than masses. Hence, it might be argued that elites support government policies because they have greater understanding of and confidence in government, and they are more likely to read about and comprehend the explanations of government officials. On the other hand, the correspondence between elite opinion and public policy may also indicate that elite opinion determines public policy.

### Elite Opinion and the War in Vietnam

Let us consider, for example, the relationship between elite and mass opinion and the Vietnam War. Early in the war, well-educated Americans gave greater support to the war than less-educated Americans. The masses had greater doubts about the advisability of the war than the elites. However, the Johnson Administration went ahead with a policy of escalation, increasing U.S. combat forces in Vietnam. By 1968 elite opinion was divided, and in the 1968 elections both Democratic and Republican presidential candidates gave only guarded support for the policy of the administration. By 1969, elite opinion had shifted dramatically; nearly two out of every three well-educated Americans had come to believe that U.S. involvement in Vietnam was a "mistake." Mass opposition to the war had also grown to a point where a majority now felt U.S. policy was a mistake. But mass opinion never shifted as dramatically as elite opinion. It was at this point that the policy of escalation was reversed, and President Nixon began his policy of gradual U.S. combat troop withdrawal and "Vietnamization" of the war. Figure 14–1 shows that the greatest *shift* in opinion on the Vietnam War occurred among college educated groups—the groups from which elites are largely drawn. These groups gave the greatest support for the war in 1966 and the greatest opposition in 1969. In 1966 the U.S. government was escalating the war; in 1969 the government began withdrawing U.S. troops.

Nothing arouses patriotism more than decisive military victory;

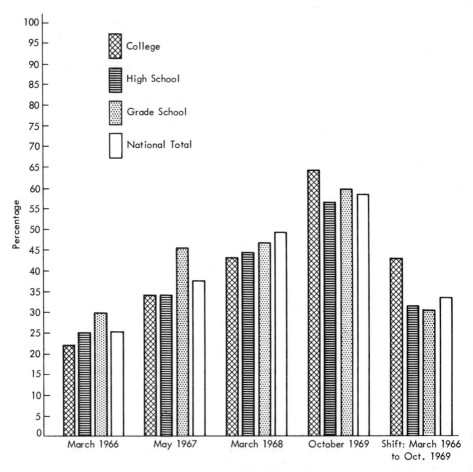

FIG. 14–1  Agreement that U.S. involvement in Vietnam was a mistake, by education
levels

*Source: Gallup Opinion Index* (October 1969), p. 15.

and nothing loses support for war efforts more than military defeat. When the United States was forced to retreat from North Korea after the Chinese invaded it in December, 1950, popular support for the war plunged. Likewise, after the successful communist "Tet" offensive in 1968, support of the Vietnam War by college-educated Americans declined and President Lyndon Johnson announced that he would not seek reelection and would open peace negotiations in Paris with the North Vietnamese. Support for both wars lasted a little over two years after the introduction of American combat ground troops. Analysis reveals that support for these two wars declined in direct relationship to the numbers of casualties and the length of the war. "To summarize, then, when one takes support or opposition for the wars in Korea or Vietnam and correlates them with (1) the casualties suffered at the time of the poll or (2) the direction of the war at the time of the poll, one gets a reasonably good fit."[8] The initial support of all population groups for the military action indicates that the masses will support the military adventures of the leadership. This support will evaporate only when military actions fail to bring a speedy victory.

Perhaps more importantly, policy making in both wars followed elite, not mass, opinion. Mass opinion never supported the Vietnam War. When elites supported these wars in their early stages, the United States "escalated" its participation—despite little enthusiastic support by less-educated groups. The United States withdrew from both wars and sought negotiated settlements after elites, not masses, made a dramatic shift in opinion. Elites agreed on escalation in the early phases of the Vietnam War, and they agreed on withdrawal in its later phases. The only disagreements occurred over how quickly we should withdraw. The student antiwar protesters had no significant effect on the course of the war. Indeed, if anything, the protesters strengthened the war effort. After a careful analysis of change in elite and mass opinion on the war, John E. Mueller concludes: ". . . the protest against the war in Vietnam may have been counterproductive in its impact on public opinion: that is, the war might have been somewhat more unpopular if protest had not existed."[9] Disagreement over the speed of withdrawal occurred *within* elite circles. Elites were not responding to mass opinion in their decision to withdraw.

Finally, elites can initiate events that profoundly shape public opinion. Any successful use of force will win widespread public approval in its initial phases. Indeed, even a crisis will strengthen the support of national leaders. Polls showed dramatic increases in support for Truman after the beginning of the Korean War, for Eisenhower after the invasion of Lebanon, for Johnson after committing U.S. combat troops to Vietnam, for Nixon after the Cambodian invasion, for Ford after the Mayaguez attack, and for Carter after the Iranian kidnapping of the U.S. embassy staff. Thus, the president's ability to "make something happen" is an important tool in shaping mass opinion.

Many other policy areas display the same elite-mass opinion linkages. It is usually the most highly educated, prestigiously employed,

[8]John Mueller, *War, Presidents and Public Opinion* (New York: Wiley, 1973), p. 61.
[9]Ibid., p. 164.

wealthy people who are highly supportive of government policies. Policy change more closely corresponds to changes in elite opinion than to changes in mass opinion.

## Agenda-Setting and "Nondecisions"

Who decides what will be decided? Defining the problems of society, and suggesting alternative solutions, is the most important stage of the policy-making process. We can refer to this stage as "agenda setting." Conditions in society which are not defined as a problem, and for which alternatives are never proposed, never become policy issues. They never get on the "agenda" of decision makers. Government does nothing and conditions remain the same. On the other hand, if certain conditions in society are defined as problems and alternative solutions put forward, the conditions become policy issues. Governments are forced to decide what to do.

Clearly then, the power to decide what will be a policy issue is crucial to the policy-making process. Deciding what will be the problems is even more important than deciding what will be the solutions. Political scientist E. E. Schattschneider once wrote:

> . . . As a matter of fact, the definition of the alternative is the supreme instrument of power; the antagonists can rarely agree on what the issues are because power is involved in the definition. He who determines what politics is about runs the country, because the definition of the alternatives is the choice of conflicts, and the choice of conflicts allocates power.[10]

Many civics textbooks imply that agenda setting just "happens." It is sometimes argued that in an open plural society such as ours, channels of access and communication to government are always open, so that any problem can be discussed and placed on the agenda of national decision making. Individuals and groups, it is said, can organize themselves to assume the tasks of defining problems and suggesting solutions. People can define their own interests, organize themselves, persuade others to support their cause, gain access to government officials, influence decision making, and watch over the implementation of government policies and programs. Indeed, it is sometimes argued that the absence of political activity such as this is an indicator of "satisfaction."

But, in reality, policy issues do not just "happen." Creating an is-

---

[10]E. E. Schattschneider, *The Semisovereign People* (New York: Holt, Rinehart & Winston, 1961), p. 68.

sue, dramatizing it, calling attention to it, and pressuring government to do something about it are important political tactics. These tactics are employed by influential individuals, organized interest groups, policy planning organizations, political candidates and officeholders, and perhaps most importantly, the mass media. These are the tactics of "agenda setting."

On the other hand, *preventing* certain conditions in society from becoming policy issues is also an important political tactic. "Nondecision making" occurs when influential individuals or groups, or the political system itself, operate to prevent the emergence of challenges to the dominant values or interests in society. According to political scientists Peter Bachrach and Morton Baratz:

> A nondecision, as we define it, is a decision that results in the suppression or thwarting of a latent or manifest challenge to the values and interests of the decision-maker. To be more clearly explicit, non-decision-making is a means by which demands for change in the existing allocation of benefits and privileges in the community can be suffocated before they are even voiced; or kept covert; or killed before they gain access to the relevant decision-making arena; or failing all these things, maimed or destroyed in the decision-implementing stage of the policy process.[11]

Nondecision making may occur when dominant elites act openly or covertly to suppress an issue because they fear that if public attention is focused on it something will be done and what is done will not be in their interest.

Nondecision making may also occur when political candidates or officeholders, or administrative officials, anticipate that elites will not favor a particular idea and therefore these officeholders and officials drop the idea. They do not want to "rock the boat." Elites do not have to *do* anything. Officials are acting in anticipation of what they *might* do.

Finally, and perhaps most importantly, nondecision making occurs because the political system itself is structured in such a way as to facilitate the resolution of some kinds of issues and to obstruct the resolution of others. There is a "mobilization of bias" within the political system itself, that is, "a set of predominant values, beliefs, rituals, and institutional procedures . . . that operate systematically and consistently to the benefit of certain persons and groups at the expense of others."[12] For example, many scholars believe that the interest group system is the key to understanding how issues are identified, solutions

---

[11]Peter Bachrach and Morton S. Baratz, *Power and Poverty* (New York: Oxford University Press, 1979), p. 7.

[12]Bachrach and Baratz, *Power and Poverty*, p. 43.

proposed, and policies adopted. However, we know that the political system responds well to large-scale, well-organized, wealthy, active interest groups with good access to government officials. It responds less well to smaller, unorganized, poorer, inactive interest groups with few available channels of communication to government officials. According to Schattschneider the interest group system "has an upper-class bias":

> The business or upper class bias of the pressure system shows up everywhere.
> . . . The data raise a serious question about the validity of the proposition that special interest groups are a universal form of political organization reflecting all interests.[13]

The same observations might be made for the party system—that parties respond to well-organized, wealthy, skilled, active, and knowledgeable individuals and groups rather than to the disorganized, poor, unskilled, inactive, or unknowledgeable. Indeed, all governmental bodies—elected and appointed; legislative, executive, and judicial; federal, state, and local—contain this same bias.

Thus, it is difficult to maintain the fiction that anyone in a democracy can raise any policy issue anytime one wishes. Who, then, is responsible for "agenda setting"? Who decides what will be decided?

## Agenda Setting and Mobilizing Opinion: The Mass Media

Television is the major source of information for the vast majority of Americans. Over two-thirds of Americans report that they receive all or most of their "news" from television. The importance of television in transmitting information is a relatively recent occurrence: in 1952 only 19.8 percent of all American homes had TV sets, compared to 99.8 percent in 1972. Newspapers had always reported wars, riots, scandals, and disasters, just as they do today, but the masses of Americans did not always read the news sections of their daily paper—and fewer still chose to read the editorials on these topics. But today television is really the first form of *mass* communication, that is, communication which reaches nearly everyone, including children. The television viewer *must* see the news or else turn off the set; the newspaper reader can turn quickly to the sports and comics without confronting the political news. More importantly, television presents a *visual* image, not merely a printed word. The visual quality of television—the emo-

---

[13]E. E. Schattschneider, *The Semisovereign People*, p. 31.

tional impact that is conveyed by pictures—enables the television networks to convey emotions as well as information.

The power to determine what the American people will see and hear about their world is vested in three private corporations—the American Broadcasting Company (ABC), the National Broadcasting Corporation (NBC), and the Columbia Broadcasting System, Inc. (CBS). These networks determine what will be seen by the mass viewing audience; there is no public regulation whatsoever of network broadcasting. Individual television stations are privately owned and licensed to use public broadcast channels by the Federal Communication Commission. But these stations are forced to receive news and programming from the networks because of the high costs involved in producing news or entertainment at the local station level. The top officials of these corporate networks, particularly the people in charge of the news, are indeed "a tiny, enclosed fraternity of privileged men."[14] Nicholas Johnson, a member of the Federal Communications Commission and a self-professed liberal, has said:

> The networks in particular . . . are probably now beyond the check of any institution in our society. The President, the Congress of the United States, the FCC, the foundations, and universities are reluctant even to get involved. I think they may now be so powerful that they're beyond the check of anyone.[15]

The news media generally credit themselves with the success of the civil rights movement: the dramatic televised images of nonviolent civil rights demonstrators of the early 1960s being attacked by police with night-sticks, cattle prods, and vicious dogs helped to awaken the nation and its political leadership to the injustices of segregation. These leaders also credit TV with "decisively changing America's opinion of the Vietnam War," and forcing Lyndon Johnson out of the presidency. Television news, together with the Washington press corps, also lays claim, of course, to the expulsion of Richard Nixon from the presidency. The *Washington Post* conducted the "investigative reporting" that produced a continuous flow of embarrassing and incriminating information about the President and his chief advisers. But it was the television networks that maintained the continuous nightly attack on the White House for nearly two years and kept Watergate in the public eye. Richard Nixon's approval rating in public opinion polls dropped

[14]The phraseology is courtesy of former Vice President Spiro Agnew, who also used the more colorful description of the network top brass—"supersensitive, self-anointed, supercilious electronic barons of opinion." See *Newsweek*, November 9, 1970, p. 22.

[15]Quoted by Edward Jay Espstein, *News from Nowhere* (New York: Random House, 1973), p. 6.

from an all-time high of 68 percent in January 1973 following the Vietnam Peace Agreement to a low of 24 percent less than one year later.

Yet the leadership of the mass media frequently claim that they do no more than "mirror" reality. Although the "mirror" argument contradicts many of their more candid claims to having righted many of America's wrongs (segregation, Vietnam, Watergate), the leadership of the three television networks claim that television "is a mirror of society." Of course, the mirror analogy is nonsense. Newsmen decide what the news will be, how it will be presented, and how it will be interpreted. As David Brinkley explained "News is what I say it is. It's something worth knowing by my standards."[16]

The power of television is not really in persuading viewers to take one side of an issue or another. Instead, *the power of television is in setting the agenda for decision making*—deciding what issues will be given attention and what issues will be ignored. Systematic research has shown that issues which receive greatest attention in the media are more likely to be viewed by voters as important.[17]

The television network executives and producers who decide which issues and events will be covered interact daily with their counterparts in the national press—the executives and editors of the *New York Times,* the *Washington Post, Time, Newsweek,* and so on. Even at the working level, the television and newspaper reporters interact in the "Washington Press Corps." This interaction reinforces decisions about what the "news" should be. As a result, there is not much diversity in news reporting. All three networks, as well as the major newspapers and news magazines, will carry stories on the same topics at the same time.

In exercising their judgment regarding which stories should be given television time and newspaper space, the media executives must rely on their own political values and economic interests as guidelines in determining what will be "news." In general, the media executives are more "liberal" in their views than other segments of the nation's leadership. Topics selected weeks in advance for coverage reflect, or often create, current liberal issues: concern for the poor and blacks, women's liberation, opposition to defense spending and the CIA, ecol-

---

[16]*TV Guide,* April 11, 1964.

[17]J. M. McCleod, L. B. Becker, and J. E. Byrne, "Another Look at the Agenda-Setting Function of the Press," *Communications Research* (April 1974), 131–66; and "The Political Consequences of Agenda-Setting," *Mass Communication Review* (Spring 1976), 8–15; M. E. McCombs, "Agenda-Setting Research: A Bibliographic Essay," *Political Communication Review* (March 1976), 1–7; D. L. Shaw and M. E. McCombs, eds., *The Emergence of American Political Issues* (New York: West, 1977).

ogy, migrant farm labor, tax loopholes, Indian rights, and for nearly two years, Watergate. But liberalism is *not* the major source of bias in the news.

The principal source of distortion in the news is caused by the need for drama, action, and confrontation to hold audience attention. NBC news executive producer Reuben Frank advised his producers in a memorandum: "The highest power of television journalism is not in the transmission of information but in the transmission of experience—joy, sorrow, shock, fear—these are the stuff of news.[18]

Television must entertain. To capture the attention of jaded audiences, news must be selected which includes emotional rhetoric, shocking incidents, dramatic conflict, overdrawn stereotypes. Race, sex, violence, and corruption in government are favorite topics because of popular interest. More complex problems such as inflation, government spending, and foreign policy, must either be simplified and dramatized or ignored. To dramatize an issue the newsmakers must find or create a dramatic incident; film it; transport, process, and edit the film; and write a script for the introduction, the "voice-over," and the "recapitulation." All this means that "news" must be created well in advance of scheduled broadcasting.

However, the networks' concentration on scandal, abuse, and corruption in government has not always produced the desired liberal, reformist notions in the minds of the masses of viewers. Contrary to the expectations of network executives, their focus on governmental scandals—Watergate, illicit CIA activities, FBI abuses, Congressional scandals, and power struggles between Congress and the executive branch—has produced feelings of general political distrust and cynicism toward government and "the system." These feelings have been labeled "television malaise"—a combination of social distrust, political cynicism, feelings of powerlessness and disaffection from parties and politics which seem to stem from television's emphasis on the negative aspects of American life.[19]

Network executives do not intend to create "television malaise" among the masses. But scandal, sex, abuse of power, and corruption attract large audiences and increase "ratings." "Bad" news is placed up front in the telecast, usually with some dramatic visual aids. Negative television journalism ". . . is concerned with what is wrong with our governmental system, our leaders, our prisons, schools, roads, auto-

---

[18]Epstein, *News From Nowhere*, p. 39.

[19]Michael J. Robinson, "Public Affairs Television and the Growth of Political Malaise," *American Political Science Review*, 70 (June 1976), 409–32; and "Television and American Politics," *The Public Interest* (Summer 1977), pp. 3–39.

mobiles, race relations, traffic systems, pollution laws, every aspect of
our society. In Europe, there is much less emphasis on exposing what
is wrong, much more satisfaction with the status quo."[20] The effect of
negative television coverage of the American political system is to "turn
off" the masses from participation in government.


## Formulating Policy:
## The Policy-Planning Organizations

It is the policy-planning organizations which are central coordinating
points in the policy-making process. Certain policy-planning groups—
for example, the Council on Foreign Relations, the Committee on Economic Development, and the Brookings Institution—are influential in
a wide range of key policy areas. Other policy planning groups—The
Urban Institute, Resources for the Future, The Population Council,
for example—specialize in a particular policy field.

These organizations bring together the leadership of corporate
and financial institutions, the foundations, the mass media, the leading
intellectuals, and influential figures in the government. They review
the relevant university and foundation-supported research on topics of
interest, and more important, they try to reach a consensus about what
action should be taken on national problems under study. Their goal
is to develop action recommendations—explicit policies or programs
designed to resolve national problems. These policy recommendations
of the key policy-planning groups are distributed to the mass media,
federal executive agencies, and the Congress. The purpose is to lay the
groundwork for making policy into law. Soon the results of elite decision making and consensus building will be reflected in the actions of
elected officials—the "proximate policy makers."

Let us illustrate these propositions by examining one of the nation's leading policy-planning organizations, the Council on Foreign
Relations. The CFR is the most influential private policy-planning organization in foreign affairs. It was founded in 1921 and supported by
grants from the Rockefeller and Carnegie Foundations and later by
the Ford Foundation. Its early directors were internationally minded
Wall Street corporation lawyers: Elihu Root, also Secretary of State;
John W. Davis, also 1924 Democratic presidential nominee; Paul Cravath, founder of the prestigious New York law firm of Cravath,
Swaine, and Moore.

The history of the CFR accomplishments is impressive: it developed the Kellogg Peace Pact in the 1920s, stiffened U.S. opposition to

[20]Merrit Panitt, "America Out of Focus," *TV Guide,* January 15, 1972, p. 6.

Japanese Pacific expansion in the 1930s, designed major portions of the United Nation's Charter, and devised the "containment" policy to halt Soviet expansion in Europe after World War II. It laid the groundwork for the NATO agreement and devised the Marshall Plan for European recovery.[21] When top elites began to suspect that the U.S. was overreliant upon nuclear weapons in the late 1950s, the CFR commissioned a young Harvard professor to look into the matter. The result was Henry Kissinger's influential book, *Nuclear Weapons and Foreign Policy*, which challenged the "massive retaliation" doctrine of John Foster Dulles and urged greater flexibility of response to aggression.[22]

The Council on Foreign Relations limits itself to approximately 700 individual resident members. There are few elites with an interest in foreign affairs who are not CFR members. Its list of former members includes every man of influence in foreign affairs from Elihu Root, Henry Stimson, John Foster Dulles, Dean Acheson, Robert Lovett, George F. Kennan, and Averill Harriman to Dean Rusk, Henry Kissinger, and Cyrus Vance.

Political scientist Lester Milbraith observes that the influence of CFR throughout the government is so pervasive that it is difficult to distinguish CFR from government programs. "The Council on Foreign Relations, while not financed by government, works so closely with it that it is difficult to distinguish Council actions stimulated by government from autonomous actions."[23]

A discussion of the CFR would be incomplete without some reference to its multinational arm, the Trilateral Commission. The Trilateral Commission was established by CFR Board Chairman David Rockefeller in 1972 with the backing of the Council and the Rockefeller Foundation. The Trilateral Commission is a small group of top officials of multinational corporations and governmental leaders of industrialized nations who meet periodically to coordinate economic policy among the United States, Western Europe, and Japan. At the request of J. Paul Austin, Chairman of the Board of Coca-Cola Co., with its headquarters in Atlanta, Rockefeller appointed the then little-known governor of Georgia, Jimmy Carter, to the Trilateral Commission. The Executive Director of the Commission was Columbia University Professor Zbigniew Brzezinski, now President Carter's National Security Advisor. The Commission's membership was a compendium of power and prestige: it included Cal Tech President Harold Brown

[21]See Joseph Kraft, "School for Statesmen," *Harper's*, July, 1958, pp. 64–68.
[22]Henry Kissinger, *Nuclear Weapons and Foreign Policy* (New York: Council on Foreign Relations, 1957).
[23]Lester Milbraith, "Interest Groups in Foreign Policy," in *Domestic Sources in Foreign Policy*, ed. James R. Rosenau, (New York: Free Press, 1967), 247.

(now Secretary of Defense); Coca-Cola's J. Paul Austin; *Time* magazine editor Hedley Donovan; Paul Warnke (later U.S. Arms Control and Disarmament Advisor); Alden Clausen, President, Bank of America, the nation's largest bank; United Auto Worker's President Leonard Woodcock (now U.S. representative to the People's Republic of China); Bendix Corporation President W. Michael Blumenthal (later Secretary of the Treasury); Cyrus Vance (later Secretary of State); and U.S. Senator Walter Mondale (now Vice President of the United States).

It is clear that the CFR not only provides policy direction in foreign affairs, but also recruits leaders for high government posts.

## Policy Legitimation:
## The "Proximate Policy Makers"

What is the role of the proximate policy makers?[24] The activities of the "proximate policy makers"—the president, Congress, federal agencies, congressional committees, White House staff, and interest groups—in the policy-making process have traditionally been the central focus of political science. Political scientists usually portray the activities of the proximate policy makers as the whole of the policy-making process. But our notion of public policy making views the activities of the proximate policy makers as only the *final phase* of a much more complex process. This final stage is the open, public stage of the policy-making process, and it attracts the attention of the mass media and most political scientists. The activities of the "proximate policy makers" are much easier to study than the private actions of corporations, foundations, the mass media, and the policy-planning organizations.

Many scholars concentrate their attention on this final phase of public policy making and conclude that policy making is a process of bargaining, competition, persuasion, and compromise among interest groups and governmental officials. Undoubtedly, bargaining, competition, persuasion, and compromises over policy issues continue throughout this final "law making" phase of the policy-making process, and admittedly many recommendations fail to win the approval of the president in the first year or two in which they are proposed. Conflict between the president and Congress, or between Democrats and Re-

---

[24]The phrase "proximate policy maker" is derived from political scientist Charles E. Lindbloom who uses the term to distinguish between citizens and elected officials: "Except in small political systems that can be run by something like a New England town meeting, not all citizens can be the immediate, or proximate, makers of policy. They yield the immediate (or proximate) task of decision to a small minority. "See Charles E. Lindbloom, *The Policy-Making Process* (Englewood Cliffs, N.J.: Prentice-Hall, 1968), p. 30.

publicans, or liberals and conservatives, and so forth, may delay or alter somewhat the final actions of the "proximate policy makers."

But the agenda for policy consideration has been set before the "proximate policy makers" become actively involved in the policy-making process—the major directions of policy change have been determined, and the mass media has prepared the public for new policies and programs. The formal law-making process concerns itself with details of implementation: who gets the "political" credit; what agencies get control of the program; and exactly how much money will be spent. These are not unimportant questions, but they are raised and decided within the context of policy goals and directions which have already been determined. The decisions of the "proximate policy makers" tend to center around the *means* rather than the *ends* of public policy.

## Party Influence on Public Policy

Parties are important institutions in the American political system, but it would be a mistake to overestimate their impact on public policy. It makes relatively little difference in the major direction of public policy whether Democrats or Republicans dominate the political scene. American parties are largely "brokerage" organizations, devoid of ideology and committed to winning public office rather than to advancing policy positions. Both the Democratic and Republican parties and their candidates tailor their policy positions to societal conditions. The result is that the parties do not have much independent impact on policy outcomes.

Both American parties subscribe to the same fundamental political ideology. Both share prevailing democratic consensus about the sanctity of private property, a free enterprise economy, individual liberty, limited government, majority rule, and due process of law. Moreover, since the 1930s both parties have supported the same mass-welfare domestic programs of social security, fair labor standards, unemployment compensation, and graduated income tax, a national highway program, a federally aided welfare system, countercyclical fiscal and monetary policies, and government regulation of public utilities. Finally, both parties have supported the basic outlines of American foreign and military policy since World War II—international involvement, anticommunism, the cold war, European recovery, NATO, military preparedness, and even the Korean and Vietnam wars. A change in party control of the presidency or Congress has not resulted in any significant shifts in the course of American foreign or domestic policy.

Yet there are nuances of differences between the parties that can be observed in the policy-making process. The social bases of the Democratic and Republican parties are slightly different. Both parties draw support from all social groups in America, but the Democrats draw disproportionately from labor, big-city residents, ethnic voters, blacks, Jews, and Catholics; while Republicans draw disproportionately from rural, small-town, and suburban Protestants, businessmen, and professionals. To the extent that the policy orientations of these two broad groups differ, the thrust of party ideology also differs. However, the magnitude of this difference is not very great.

Conflict between parties occurs most frequently over issues involving social welfare programs, housing and urban development, Medicare, antipoverty programs, and the regulation of business and labor. On some issues, such as civil rights and appropriations, voting will follow party lines during roll calls on preliminary motions, amendments, and other preliminary matters, but swing to a bipartisan vote on passage of the final legislation. This means that the parties have disagreed on certain aspects of the bill, but compromised on its final passage.

What are the issues that cause conflict between the Democratic and Republican parties? In general, Democrats have favored federal action to assist labor and low-income groups through social security, public assistance, housing, and wage-hour regulation; and generally a larger role for the federal government in launching new projects to remedy domestic problems. Republicans, on the other hand, have favored less government involvement in labor and welfare matters, and greater reliance on private action (see Table 14–1).

## Policy Innovation

Policy innovation has been a central concern of students of the policy processes.[25] Policy innovation is simply the readiness of a government to adopt new programs and policies. Several years ago, Jack L. Walker constructed an "innovation score" for the American states based upon elapsed time between the first state adoption of a program and its later adoption by other states. Walker monitored eighty-eight different programs adopted by twenty or more states, and he averaged each state's

[25]Victor Thompson, *Bureaucracy and Innovation* (Tuscaloosa: University of Alabama Press, 1969); Lawrence B. Mohr, "Determinants of Innovation in Organizations," *American Political Science Review*, 63 (March 1969), 111–26; Michael Aiken and Robert R. Alford, "Community Structure and Innovation: The Case for Public Housing," *American Political Science Review*, 64 (September 1970), 843–64; Jack L. Walker, "The Diffusion of Innovations Among the American States," *American Political Science Review*, 63 (September 1969), 880–99.

**TABLE 14–1**  Party Division on Selected Votes in Congress

| | House Votes | | | |
| --- | --- | --- | --- | --- |
| | Republicans | | Democrats | |
| | Yes | No | Yes | No |
| Medicare (1965) | 65 | 73 | 248 | 42 |
| Establish Department of Housing and Urban Development (1965) | 9 | 118 | 208 | 66 |
| Model Cities Programs (1966) | 16 | 81 | 162 | 60 |
| Turnover Poverty Program to states (1970) | 103 | 63 | 60 | 168 |
| Public service jobs expansion (1976) | 23 | 102 | 216 | 52 |
| Continue regulating natural gas prices (1976) | 13 | 117 | 192 | 84 |
| Make Martin Luther King Jr.'s birthday a holiday | 39 | 101 | 213 | 32 |
| Chrysler loan guarantee (1979) | 62 | 88 | 209 | 48 |
| No abortion funds under Medicaid (1979) | 119 | 23 | 116 | 132 |
| Implement Panama Canal Treaty (1979) | 19 | 125 | 173 | 78 |

| | Senate Votes | | | |
| --- | --- | --- | --- | --- |
| | Republicans | | Democrats | |
| | Yes | No | Yes | No |
| Medicare (1965) | 13 | 14 | 55 | 7 |
| Repeal Taft-Hartley "right to work" provisions (1965) | 5 | 26 | 40 | 21 |
| Antiballistic missile (ABM) system (1970) | 29 | 14 | 21 | 36 |
| Reverse presidential cutback on foodstamps (1976) | 13 | 18 | 39 | 4 |
| Delay production of B-1 bomber (1976) | 7 | 22 | 37 | 15 |
| Reduce amount of "windfall profits" tax on oil (1979) | 24 | 13 | 8 | 40 |
| Establish new cabinet level Department of Education (1979) | 18 | 17 | 51 | 5 |

*Source: Congressional Quarterly, various issues, 1965–1980.*

score on each program adoption to produce an index of innovation for each state. The larger the innovation score, the faster the state has been on the average in responding to new ideas or policies."[26] Walker proceeded to explore relationships between innovation scores in the 50 states and socioeconomic, political, and regional variables. It turned out that innovation was more readily accepted in urban, industrialized, wealthy states.

However, in a subsequent study of policy innovation in the American states, Virginia Gray argued persuasively that no general tendency toward "innovativeness" really exists—that states which are innovative in one policy area are not necessarily the same states which are innovative in other policy areas. She examined the adoption of twelve specific innovations in civil rights, welfare, and education, including the adoption of state public accommodations, fair housing and fair employment laws, and merit systems and compulsory school attendance.

[26]Diffusion of Innovations Among the American States," p. 883.

States that were innovative in education were not necessarily innovative in civil rights or welfare. Nonetheless, she discovered that "first adopters" of most innovations tended to be wealthier states.[27]

Let us try to explain why wealth, urbanization, and education are associated with policy innovation. First of all, *income* enables a state to afford the luxury of experimentation. Low incomes place constraints on the ability of policy makers to raise revenues to pay for new programs or policies: high incomes provide the *tax resources* necessary to begin new undertakings. We can also imagine that *urbanization* would be conducive to policy innovation. Urbanization involves social change and creates demands for new programs and policies, and urbanization implies the concentration of creative resources in large cosmopolitan centers. Rural societies change less rapidly and are considered less adaptive and sympathetic to innovation. Finally, it is not unreasonable to expect that *education* should facilitate innovation. An educated population should be more receptive toward innovation in public policy, and perhaps even more demanding of innovation in its appraisal of political candidates. In summary, wealth, urbanization, and education considered together, should provide a socioeconomic environment conducive to policy innovation.

We might also expect both party competition and voter participation to affect policy innovation. Closely contested elections should encourage parties and candidates to put forward innovative programs and ideas to capture the imagination and support of the voter. Competitive states are more likely to experience turnover in party control of state government. Innovations in policy are more likely when a new administration takes office. An increase in political participation should also encourage policy innovation.

The decision-making milieu itself—characteristics of the legislative and executive branches of state government—can also be expected to influence policy innovation. Specifically, we expect that the ethic of "professionalism" among legislators and bureaucrats is a powerful stimulus to policy innovation. Professionalism involves, among other things, acceptance of professional reference groups as sources of information, standards, and norms. The professional bureaucrat attends national conferences, reads national journals, and perhaps even aspires to build a professional reputation that extends beyond the boundaries of his own state. Thus, he constantly encounters new ideas, and he is motivated to pursue innovation for the purpose of distinguishing himself in his chosen field. Moreover, one might argue that professional bureaucrats are also moved to propose innovative pro-

[27]Virginia Gray, "Innovation in the States," *American Political Science Review,* 67 (December 1973), 1174–85.

grams in order to expand their authority within the bureaucracy— "empire building."

All these factors—income, urbanization, education, tax revenue, party competition, voter participation, civil service coverage, and legislative professionalism—are *related* to policy innovation. Table 14–2 shows the simple correlation coefficients between each of these explanatory variables and the policy innovation scores.

Further causal analysis reveals that "professionalism" in the legislative and executive branches of state government appears to be the most direct source of policy innovation. We might speculate that professionalism among both legislators and bureaucrats encourages the development of national standards for governmental administration. Professionals know about programmatic developments elsewhere through professional meetings, journals, newsletters, etc. More importantly, they view themselves as professional administrators and governmental leaders and they seek to adopt the newest reforms and innovations for their own states. As Jack Walker comments, "They are likely to adopt a more cosmopolitan perspective and to cultivate their reputations within a national professional community rather than merely within their own state or agency."[28] Even if individual legislators themselves do not think in professional terms, legislatures with professional staffs may be influenced by these values.

Education, participation, and innovation appear to be linked in a causal fashion. This lends some limited support to the *pluralist* contention that an educated and active political constituency can have an impact on public policy—at least to the extent that such a constituency seems to promote novelty and experimentation in programs and policies. In summary, the explanation of policy innovation turns out to be one that emphasizes professionalism in legislature and bureaucracies, and an educated and politically active population.

**TABLE 14–2** Correlates of Policy Innovation in the American States

| Figures are simple correlation coefficients for relationships with the innovation index | | | |
| --- | --- | --- | --- |
| Income | .56 | Party Competition | .34 |
| Urbanization | .54 | Voter Participation | .28 |
| Education | .32 | Civil Service Coverage | .53 |
| Tax Revenue | .28 | Legislative Professionalism | .62 |

[28]Jack Walker, "Diffusion of Innovations Among the American States," *American Political Science Review*, 63 (September 1969), 880–99.

## Summary

Systems theory helps us to conceptualize the linkages between the environment, the political system, and public policy, but it does not really describe what goes on inside the "black box" labeled "political system." The *process model* identifies a variety of activities which occur *within* the political system, including identification of problems and "agenda setting," formulating policies proposals, legitimating policies, implementing policies, and evaluating their effectiveness. Although political science has traditionally concerned itself with describing political institutions and processes, seldom has it systematically examined the impact of political processes on the *content* of public policy. Let us try to set forth some general propositions about the impact of political processes on policy content.

1. It is difficult to assess the independent effect of public opinion on public policy. Public policy may accord with mass opinion but we can never be certain whether mass opinion shaped public policy or public policy shaped mass opinion. The "public" does not have opinions on many major policy questions; public opinion is unstable; and decision makers can easily misinterpret as well as manipulate public opinion.

2. Public policy is more likely to conform to elite opinion than mass opinion. Elite opinion has been particularly influential in the determination of foreign policy. However, it is unlikely that elites can operate independently of environmental resources and demands for very long.

3. Deciding what will be decided—agenda setting—is a crucial stage in the policy process. Policy issues do not just "happen." Preventing certain conditions in society from becoming policy issues—"nondecision making—is an important political tactic of dominant interests.

4. The mass media, particularly the three television networks, play a major rule in agenda setting. By deciding what will be "news," the media sets the agenda for political discussion, whether or not the media can persuade voters to support one candidate or another. The continuing focus on the dramatic, violent, and negative aspects of American life may unintentionally create apathy and alienation—"television malaise."

5. A great deal of policy formulation occurs outside the formal governmental process. Prestigious, private, policy-planning organizations—such as the Council on Foreign Relations—explore policy alternatives, advise governments, develop policy consensus, and even supply top governmental leaders. The policy-planning organizations bring together the leadership of the corporate and financial worlds, the mass

media, the foundations, the leading intellectuals, and top government officials.

6. The activities of the "proximate policy makers"—the President, Congress, executive agencies, etc.—attract the attention of most commentators and political scientists. But nongovernmental leaders, in business and finance, foundations, policy-planning organizations, the mass media, and other interest groups may have already set the policy agenda and selected major policy goals. The activities of the "proximate policy makers" tend to center around the *means,* rather than the *ends,* of public policy.

7. The Democratic and Republican parties have agreed on the basic outlines of American foreign and domestic policy since World War II. Thus, partisanship has not been a central influence on public policy. However, there have been some policy differences between the parties. Differences have occurred most frequently over questions of welfare, housing and urban development, antipoverty efforts, health care, and the regulations of business and labor.

8. Most votes in Congress and state legislatures show the Democratic and Republican party majorities to be in agreement. However, when conflict occurs it is more likely to occur along party lines than any other kind of division.

9. Policy innovation—the readiness of a government to adopt new programs and policies—is linked to urbanization, education, and wealth, as well as competition, participation, and professionalism. Specifically, policy innovation appears to be a product of professionalism in legislatures and bureaucracies, and an educated and politically active population.

## Bibliography

EDELMAN, MURRAY, *The Symbolic Uses of Politics.* Urbana: University of Illinois Press, 1964.

KEY, V. O., JR., *Public Opinion and American Democracy.* New York: Knopf, 1967.

LIPSET, SEYMOUR MARTIN, *Political Man.* New York: Doubleday, 1963.

POMPER, GERALD, *Elections in America.* New York: Dodd, Mead, 1968.

SCHATTSCHNEIDER, E.E., *The Semisovereign People.* New York: Holt, Rinehart & Winston, 1960.

ZEIGLER, HARMON, *Interest Groups in American Society.* Englewood Cliffs, N.J.: Prentice-Hall, 1964.

Policy evaluation: the symbolic impact of policy. *Irene Springer.*

# Policy Evaluation
## finding out what happens after a law is passed

# 15

## Does the Government Know What It Is Doing?

Americans generally assume that once we pass a law, create a bureaucracy, and spend money, the purpose of the law, the bureaucracy, and the expenditure should be achieved either in whole or in part. We assume that when Congress adopts a policy and appropriates money for it, and when the executive branch organizes a program, hires people, spends money, and carries out activities designed to implement the policy, the effects of the policy will be felt by society and will be those intended by the policy. Unfortunately, these assumptions are not always warranted. The national experiences with the "war on poverty," public housing, public assistance, energy "independence," and many other public programs indicate the need for careful appraisal of the real impact of public policy. There is a growing uneasiness among policy makers and the general public about the effectiveness and the costs of many public service and social action programs. America's problems cannot always be resolved by passing a law, creating a new bureaucracy, and throwing a few billion dollars in the general direction of the problem in the hope that it will go away.

Does the government really know what it is doing? Generally speaking, no. Governments usually know how much money they spend, how many persons ("clients") are given various services, how much these services cost, how their programs are organized, managed, and operated, and perhaps how influential persons and groups regard their programs and services. But even if programs and policies are well-organized, efficiently operated, widely utilized, financially possible, and generally supported by major interest groups, we may still want to ask: "So what?"; "Do they work?"; "Do these programs have any beneficial effects on society?"; "Are the effects immediate or long-range? positive or negative?"; "What about persons *not* receiving these services?"; "What is the relationship between the costs of the program and the benefits to society?"; "Could we be doing something else with more benefit to society with the money and manpower devoted to these programs?" Unfortunately, governments have done very little to answer these more basic questions.

A candid report on federal evaluation effort is worth quoting at length:

> The most impressive finding about the evaluation of social programs in the federal government is that substantial work in this field has been almost nonexistent.
>
> Few significant studies have been undertaken. Most of those carried out have been poorly conceived. Many small studies around the country have been carried out with such lack of uniformity of design and objective that the results rarely are comparable or responsive to the questions facing policy makers.
>
> There is nothing akin to a comprehensive federal evaluation system. Even within agencies, orderly and integrated evaluation operations have not been established. Funding has been low. Staffing has been worse, forcing undue reliance on outside contractors by agencies that lack the in-house capacity to monitor contract work. The most clear-cut evidence of the primitive state of federal self-evaluation lies in the widespread failure of agencies even to spell out program objectives. Unless goals are precisely stated, there is no standard against which to measure whether the direction of a program or its rate of progress is satisfactory.
>
> The impact of activities that cost the public millions, sometimes billions, of dollars has not been measured. One cannot point with confidence to the difference, if any, that most social programs cause in the lives of Americans.[1]

This is a damning appraisal. It is just as true today as it was ten years ago when it was first issued. The government does not know how to tell whether or not most of the things it does are worth doing at all.

## Policy Evaluation:
## Assessing the Impact of Public Policy

Policy evaluation is learning about the consequences of public policy. Other, more complex, definitions have been offered: "Policy evalua-

[1] Joseph S. Wholey and others, *Federal Evaluation Policy* (Washington: Urban Institute, 1970), p. 15.

tion is the assessment of the overall effectiveness of a national program in meeting its objectives, or assessment of the relative effectiveness of two or more programs in meeting common objectives."[2] "We should reserve the name 'program evaluation' for when we are referring to a comprehensive evaluation of the entire system under consideration, and call it 'problem or procedure evaluation' when we refer to some segment within that system."[3] "Policy evaluation research is the objective, systematic, empirical examination of the effects ongoing policies and public programs have on their targets in terms of the goals they are meant to achieve."[4]

Note that some of these definitions tie evaluation to the stated "goals" of a program or policy. But since we do not always know what the "goals" of a program or policy really are, and because we know that some programs and policies pursue conflicting "goals," we will not limit our notion of policy evaluation to the achievement of goals. Instead, we will concern ourselves with the *all* of the consequences of public policy, that is, with "policy impact."

The impact of a policy is all its *effects on real-world conditions*. The impact of a policy includes:

1. Its impact on the target situation or group
2. Its impact on situations or groups other than the target ("spillover effects")
3. Its impact on future as well as immediate conditions
4. Its direct costs, in terms of resources devoted to the program
5. Its indirect costs, including loss of opportunities to do other things.

All the benefits and costs, both immediate and future, must be measured in terms of both *symbolic* and *tangible* effects.

Identifying the *target groups* means defining the part of the population for whom the program is intended—e.g., the poor, the sick, the ill-housed, etc. Then the desired effect of the program on the target group must be determined. Is it to change their physical or economic circumstances—for example, the percentage of blacks or women employed in professional or managerial jobs, the income of the poor, the housing conditions of ghetto residents? Or is it to change their knowledge, attitudes, awareness, interests, or behavior? If multiple effects are intended, what are the priorities among different effects—for example, is a high payoff in terms of positive attitudes toward the politi-

---

[2]Ibid., p. 25.
[3]Paul R. Binner, cited in Jack L. Franklin and Jean H. Thrasser, *An Introduction to Program Evaluation* (New York: John Wiley, 1976), p. 22.
[4]David Nachmias, *Public Policy Evaluation* (New York: St. Martin's Press, 1979), p. 4.

cal system more valuable than tangible progress toward the political system more valuable than tangible progress toward the elimination of black-white income differences? What are the possible unintended effects (side effects) on target groups—for example, does public housing achieve better physical environments for many urban blacks at the cost of increasing their segregation and alienation from the white community? What is the impact of a policy on the target group in proportion to that group's total need? Accurate data describing the unmet needs of the nation are not generally available, but it is important to estimate the denominator of total need so that we know how adequate our programs are. Moreover, such an estimate may also help in estimating symbolic benefits or costs; a program that promises to meet a national need but actually meets only a small proportion of it may generate great praise at first but bitterness and frustration later when it becomes known how small its impact is relative to the need.

"Policy impact" is not the same as "policy output." It is important *not* to measure benefits in terms of government activity. For example, the number of dollars spent per member of a target group (per pupil educational expenditures, per capita welfare expenditures, per capita health expenditures) is not really a measure of the *impact* of a policy on the group. It is merely a measure of government activity—that is to say, a measure of *policy output*. We cannot be content with measuring how many times a bird flaps its wings, we must assess how far the bird has flown. In *describing* public policy, or even in *explaining* its determinants, measures of policy output are important. But in assessing the *impact* of policy, we must find identity changes in the environment that are associated with measures of government activity.

All programs and policies have differential effects on various segments of the population. Identifying important *nontarget groups* for a policy is a difficult process. For example, what is the impact of the welfare reform on groups other than the poor—government bureaucrats, social workers, local political figures, working-class families who are not on welfare, taxpayers, others? Nontarget effects may be expressed as benefits as well as costs, such as the benefits to the construction industry of public housing projects. And these effects may be symbolic as well as tangible—for example, wealthy liberals enjoy a good feeling from participation in an antipoverty program, whether the program helps the poor or not.

When will the benefits or costs be felt? Is the program designed for short-term, emergency situations? Or is it a long-term, developmental effort? If it is short-term, what facts will prevent the processes of incrementalism and bureaucratization from turning it into a long-term program, even after immediate need is met? Many impact studies show that new or innovative programs have short-term positive effects—for example, operation Head Start and other educational programs. However, the positive effects frequently disappear as the novelty and enthusiasm of new programs wear off. Other programs experience difficulties at first, as in the early days of social security and Medicare, but turn out to have "sleeper" effects, as in the widespread acceptance of the social security idea. Not all programs aim at the same degree of permanent or transient change.

Programs are frequently measured in terms of their direct costs. We generally know how many dollars go into program areas, and we can even calculate (as in Chapter 10) the proportion of total governmental dollars devoted to various programs. Government agencies have developed various forms of cost-benefit analysis, such as Program, Planning, and Budgeting Systems (PPBS) and operations research, to identify the direct costs (usually, but not always, in dollars) of government programs.

But it is very difficult to identify the indirect and symbolic costs of public programs. Rarely can all these cost factors be included in a formal decision-making model. Often political intuition is the best guide available to the policy maker in these matters. What are the indirect symbolic costs for poor whites of the federal government's activities on behalf of blacks? What are the costs of public housing and urban renewal in the effects of relocation on the lives of slum dwellers? What are the symbolic costs for the working poor of large numbers of welfare recipients? What were the costs of the Vietnam War in terms of American morale and internal division and strife?

Moreover, it is very difficult to measure benefits in terms of general social well-being. Cost accounting techniques developed in business were designed around units of production—automobiles, airplanes, tons of steel, etc. But how do we identify and measure units of social well-being? In recent years, some social scientists have begun the effort to develop "social indicators"—measures of social well-being of American society.[5] This movement is just beginning; we are still a long way from assessing the impact of public policy on general social indicators or rationally evaluating alternative public policies by weighing their costs against gains in social indicators.

All these aspects of public policy are very difficult to identify, describe, and measure. Moreover, the task of calculating *net* impact of a public policy is truly awesome. The *net* impact would be all the symbolic and tangible benefits, both immediate and long-range, minus all the symbolic and tangible costs, both immediate and future (see Table

---

[5]See U.S. Department of Health, Education and Welfare, *Toward a Social Report* (Washington, D.C.: Government Printing Office, 1969); Bertram M. Gross, ed., *Social Intelligence for America's Future* (Boston: Allyn & Bacon, 1969).

**TABLE 15–1**  Assessing Policy Impact

| | Benefits | | Costs | |
|---|---|---|---|---|
| | *Present* | *Future* | *Present* | *Future* |
| Target Groups and Situations | Symbolic Tangible | Symbolic Tangible | Symbolic Tangible | Symbolic Tangible |
| Nontarget Groups and Situations (Spillover) | Symbolic Tangible | Symbolic Tangible | Symbolic Tangible | Symbolic Tangible |
| | Sum | Sum | Sum | Sum |
| Sum | | | | |
| | Present Benefits | Future Benefits | Present Costs | Future Costs |
| | Sum All Benefits | | Sum All Costs | |
| | | Net Policy Impact | | |

15–1). Even if all the immediate and future and symbolic and tangible costs and benefits are *known* (and everyone *agrees* on what is a "benefit" and what is a "cost"), it is still very difficult to come up with a net balance. Many of the items on both sides of the balance would defy comparison—for example, how do you subtract a tangible cost in terms of dollars from a symbolic reward in terms of the sense of well-being felt by individuals or groups?

## The Symbolic Impact of Policy

The impact of a policy includes both its *symbolic* and *tangible* effects. Its symbolic impact deals with the perceptions that individuals have of government action and their attitudes toward it. Even if government policies do not succeed in reducing dependency, or eliminating poverty, or preventing crime, and so on, this may be a rather minor objection to them if the failure of government to *try* to do these things would lead to the view that society is "not worth saving." Individuals, groups, and whole societies frequently judge public policy in terms of its good intentions rather than its tangible accomplishments. The general popularity and public appraisal of a program may be unrelated to the real impact of a program in terms of desired results. The implication is that very popular programs may have little positive impact, and vice versa.

The policies of government may tell us more about the aspirations of a society and its leadership than about actual conditions. Policies do more than effect change in societal conditions; they also help hold men together and maintain an orderly state. For example, a government "war on poverty" may not have any significant impact on the poor, but it reassures moral men, the affluent as well as the poor, that government "cares" about poverty. Whatever the failures of the antipoverty program in tangible respects, its symbolic value may be more than redeeming. For example, whether the fair housing provisions of the Civil Rights Act of 1968 can be enforced or not, the fact that it is national policy to forbid discrimination in the sale or rental of housing reassures men of all races that their government does not condone such acts. There are many more examples of public policy serving as a symbol of what society aspires to be.

The subjective condition of the nation is clearly as important as the objective condition. For example, white prejudices about blacks in schools, in public accommodations, or in housing may be declining over time. But this may not reduce racial tension if blacks *believe* that racism is as prevalent as it ever was. Blacks may be narrowing the gap between black and white income, jobs, and housing through individual initiative and opportunity within the existing system. But if the blacks *believe* that only massive government intervention in income, employment, and housing will assist them, this belief will become a critical factor in policy making.

Once upon a time "politics" was described as "who gets what, when, and how." Today it seems that politics centers about "who *feels* what, when, and how." The smoke-filled room where patronage and pork were dispensed has been replaced with the talk-filled room where rhetoric and image are dispensed. What governments *say* is as important as what governments *do*. Television has made the image of public policy as important as the policy itself. Systematic policy analysis concentrates on what governments *do*, why they do it, and what difference it makes. It devotes less attention to what governments *say*. Perhaps this is a weakness in policy analysis. Our focus has been primarily upon activities of governments rather than the rhetoric of governments.

## Program Evaluation: What Governments Usually Do
## To Learn the Impact of Their Own Policies

Most government agencies make some effort to review the effectiveness of their own programs. But these reviews usually take one or another of the following forms:

### Hearings and Discussions

This is the most common type of program review. Government administrators are asked by chief executives or legislators to give testimony (formally or informally) regarding the accomplishments of their own programs. Frequently, written "Annual Reports" are provided by program administrators. But testimonials and reports of administrators are not very objective means of program evaluation. They frequently magnify the benefits and minimize the costs of programs.

### Site Visits

Occasionally teams of high-ranking administrators, or expert consultants, or legislators, or some combination of these people, will decide to visit agencies or conduct inspections in the field. These teams can pick up impressionistic data about how programs are being run, whether programs are following specific guidelines, whether they have competent staffs, and sometimes whether or not the "clients" (target groups) are pleased with the services.

### Program Measures

The data developed by government agencies themselves generally cover policy *output* measures: the number of recipients in various welfare programs; the number of persons in manpower training programs; the number of public hospital beds available; the tons of garbage collected; or the number of pupils enrolled in Head Start programs. But these program measures rarely indicate what *impact* these numbers have on society: the conditions of life confronting the poor; the success of manpower trainees in finding and holding skilled jobs; the health of the nation's poor; the cleanliness of cities; and the subsequent academic success of children who participated in Head Start.

### Comparison with Professional Standards

In some areas of government activity, professional associations have developed standards of excellence. These standards are usually expressed as a desirable level of output: for example, the number of pupils per teacher, the number of hospital beds per 1,000 people, the number of cases for each welfare worker. Actual governmental outputs can be compared with "ideal" outputs. While such an exercise can be helpful, it still focuses on government outputs and not the *impact* of governmental activities on the conditions of target or nontarget groups. Moreover, the standards themselves are usually developed by professionals who are really guessing at what ideal levels of benefits and services should be. There is rarely any hard evidence that ideal levels of governmental output have any significant impact on society. (For example, the Coleman Report found that teacher-pupil ratios had little to do with student learning, see Chapter 1.)

### Evaluation of Citizen Complaints

Another common approach to program evaluation is the analysis of citizen complaints. But not all citizens voluntarily submit complaints or remarks regarding governmental programs. Critics of governmental programs are self-selected and they are rarely representative of the general public or even of the target groups of government programs. There is no way to judge whether the complaints of a vocal few are shared by the many more who have not spoken up. Occasionally, administrators develop questionnaires to give to participants in their program in order to learn what their complaints may be and whether they are satisfied or not. But these questionnaires really test *public opinion* toward the program and not its real impact on the lives of participants.

## Program Evaluation: What Governments Can Do To Learn the Impact of Their Own Policies

None of the common evaluative methods mentioned above really attempts to weigh *costs* against *benefits*. Indeed, administrators seldom calculate the ratio of costs to services—the dollars required to train one worker, to provide one hospital bed, to collect and dispose of one ton of garbage. It is even more difficult to calculate the costs of making specific changes in society—the dollars required to raise student reading levels by one grade, to lower the infant death rate by one point, to reduce the crime rate by one percent. To learn about the real *impact* of governmental programs on society, more complex and costly methods of program evaluation are required.

Systematic program evaluation involves *comparisons*—comparisons designed to estimate what changes in society can be attributed to the program rather than nonprogram factors. Ideally, this means comparing what "actually happened" to "what would have happened if the program had never been implemented." It is not difficult to measure what happened; unfortunately too much program evaluation stops here. The difficult but essential problem is to measure what would have happened without a program, and then compare the two conditions of society. The difference must be attributable to the program itself and not to other changes which are occurring in society at the same time.[6]

### Before versus After Comparisons

There are several common research designs in program evaluation. The most common is the "before and after" study which compares results in a jurisdiction at two points in time—one before the program was implemented and the other some time after implementation. Usually it is only target groups that are examined. These before and after comparisons are designed to show program impacts, but it is very difficult to know whether the changes observed, if any, came about as a result of the program or as a result of other changes which were occurring in society at the same time (see Design 1, Figure 15–1).

### Projected-Trend-Line versus Postprogram Comparisons

A better estimate of what would have happened without the program can be made by projecting past (preprogram) trends into the postprogram time period. Then these projections can be compared with what actually happened in society after the program was implemented. The difference between the projections based on preprogram trends and the actual postprogram data can be attributed to the program itself. Note that data on target groups or conditions must be obtained for several time periods before the program was initiated, so that a trend line can be established (see Design 2, Figure 15–1). This design is better than the before-and-after design, but it requires more effort on the part of program evaluators.

### Comparisons Between Jurisdictions With and Without Programs

Another common program evaluation design is to compare individuals who have participated in programs with those who have not; or to compare cities, states, or nations which have programs with those which do not. Comparisons are sometimes made in the postprogram period only; for example, comparisons of the job records of those who have participated in manpower training programs with those who have not, or comparisons of homicide rates in states which have the death penalty with the homicide rates in states without the death penalty. But there are so many other differences between individuals or jurisdictions, that it is difficult to attribute differences in their conditions to

[6]The following discussion relies upon Harry P. Hatry, Richard E. Winnie, and Donald M. Fisk, *Practical Program Evaluation* (Washington, D.C.: Urban Institute, 1973).

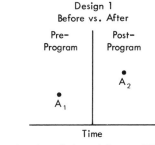

Design 1
Before vs. After

Pre-
Program | Post-
Program

$A_2$

$A_1$

Time

■ $A_2 - A_1$ = Estimated Program Effect.

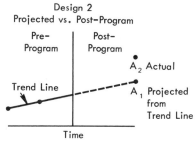

Design 2
Projected vs. Post–Program

Pre-
Program | Post-
Program

$A_2$ Actual

Trend Line

$A_1$ Projected
from
Trend Line

Time

■ $A_2 - A_1$ = Estimated Program Effect.

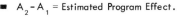

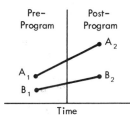

Design 3
With vs. Without Program

Pre-
Program | Post-
Program

$A_2$

$A_1$

$B_1$

$B_2$

Time

■ A has Program; B does not.
■ $(A_2 - A_1) - (B_2 - B_1)$ = Estimated
Program Effect.
■ Or difference between A
and B in rate of change
equals Estimated Program
Effect.

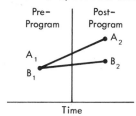

Design 4
The Classic Research Design:
Control vs. Experimental Groups

Pre-
Program | Post-
Program

$A_2$

$A_1$

$B_2$

$B_1$

Time

■ A has Program; B does not.
■ A and B identical in pre-program
period.
■ $A_2 - B_2$ = Estimated Program
Effect.

FIG. 15–1   Policy evaluation research designs

differences in government programs. For example, persons who voluntarily enter a manpower training program may have greater motivation to find a job or different personal characteristics from those who do not. States with the death penalty may tend to be rural states which have lower homicide rates than urban states regardless of whether they have the death penalty or not.

Some of the problems involved in comparing jurisdictions with and without programs can be resolved if we observe both kinds of jurisdictions before and after the introduction of the program. This enables us to estimate differences between jurisdictions before program efforts are considered. After the program is initiated, we can observe whether the differences between jurisdictions have widened or not (see

Design 3, Figure 15–1). This design provides some protection against attributing differences to a particular program when underlying socio-economic differences between jurisdictions are really responsible for different outcomes.

### Comparisons Between Control and Experimental Groups
### Before and After Program Implementation

The "classic" research design involves the careful selection of control and experimental groups which are identical in every way, the application of the policy to the experimental group only, and the comparison of changes in the experimental group with changes in the control group after the application of the policy. Initially, control and experimental groups must be identical, and the preprogram performance of each group must be measured and found to be the same. The program must be applied only to the experimental group. The post-program differences between the experimental and control groups must be carefully measured (see Design 4, Figure 15–1). This classic research design is preferred by scientists because it provides the best opportunity of estimating changes which can be from the effects of other forces affecting society.

## Time Series Policy Research:
## Gun Control

One interesting example of a "classic" before and after policy evaluation, with both experimental and control groups, was a study of the impact of handgun controls in New York and Boston. For many years these two large cities had the most restrictive handgun licensing laws in the United States. Despite these laws, handgun-related deaths in these cities were very high. "Experts" decided that this fact reflected the ease with which handguns could be brought into these cities from other areas with less restrictive laws. The policy solution, they said, was to limit the interstate transportation of handguns into states which restricted their sale. So, in the federal Gun Control Act of 1968, interstate traffic in firearms and ammunition to states which restricted or prohibited ownership of guns was prohibited by federal law.

Time series trends in handgun homicides are shown for New York and Boston (the experimental cities) and an average for fifty-seven other large cities (the control cities) both before and after the 1968 federal legislation (see Figure 15–2). Note that handgun homicides grew in *all* cities both before and after federal legislation. But handgun homicides grew faster in New York and Boston, the cities

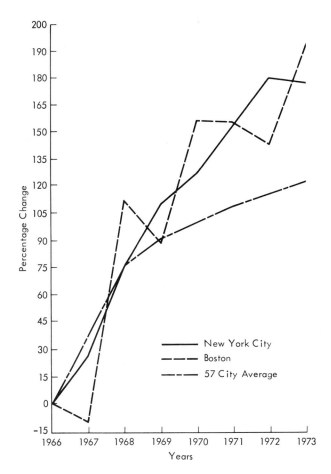

FIG. 15–2  Trends in handgun homicides, New York, Boston, and other cities
*Source:* Franklin E. Zimring, "Firearms and Federal Law: The Gun Control Act of 1968,"
*Journal of Legal Studies,* 4 (January 1975), 177, Fig. 6. Reprinted by permission.

with restrictive laws, than the average of the fifty-seven control cities.
These increases in handgun violence in the particular cities with the
most restrictive legislation clearly indicate that neither local nor federal
laws were working. If anything, the Gun Control Act of 1968 was having just the opposite effect intended. Based on these and other measures, the author of the study was forced to conclude:

> the data suggest that the Gun Control Act of 1968 did not result in a palpable dis-
> ruption of interstate handgun traffic.[7]

[7]Franklin E. Zimring, "Firearms and Federal Law," *Journal of Legal Studies,* 4 (January 1975), 133–98; also cited by David Nachmias, *Public Policy Evaluation.*

## Program Evaluation:
## Why Governments Do Not Know the Impact
## of Their Own Policies

Occasionally governments attempt their own policy evaluations. Government analysts and administrators report on the conditions of target groups before and after their participation in a new program and some effort is made to attribute observed changes to the new program itself. Policy experimentation is less frequent; seldom do governments systematically select experimental and control groups of the population, introduce a new program to the experimental group only, and then carefully compare changes in the conditions of the experimental group with a control group that has not benefited from the program. Let us turn first to some of the problems confronting policy evaluation studies; later we will describe policy experimentation.[8]

1. The first problem confronting anyone who wants to evaluate a public program is to determine what the goals of the program are. What are the target groups and what are the desired effects? But governments often pursue incompatible goals to satisfy very diverse groups. Overall policy planning and evaluation may reveal inconsistencies of public policy and force reconsideration of fundamental societal goals. Where there is little agreement on the goals of public program, evaluation studies may engender a great deal of political conflict. Government agencies generally prefer to avoid conflict, and hence to avoid studies that would raise such questions.

2. Many programs and policies have primarily symbolic value. They do not actually change the conditions of target groups but merely make these groups feel that government "cares." A government agency does not welcome a study that reveals that its efforts have no tangible effects; such a revelation itself might reduce the symbolic value of the program by informing target groups of its uselessness.

3. Government agencies have a strong vested interest in "proving" that their programs have a positive impact. Administrators frequently view attempts to evaluate the impact of their programs as attempts to limit or destroy their programs, or to question the competence of the administrators.

4. Government agencies usually have a heavy investment—organizational, financial, physical, psychological—in current programs and policies. They are predisposed against finding that these policies do not work.

5. Any serious study of policy impact undertaken by a government agency would involve some interference with ongoing program

[8]For an excellent discussion of policy evaluation, see Edward A. Suchman, *Evaluative Research* (New York: Russell Sage Foundation, 1967).

activities. The press of day-to-day business generally takes priority over study and evaluation in a governmental agency. More important, the conduct of an experiment may necessitate depriving individuals or groups (control groups) of services to which they are entitled under law; this may be difficult, if not impossible, to do.

6. Program evaluation requires funds, facilities, time, and personnel which government agencies do not like to sacrifice from ongoing programs. Policy impact studies, like any research, cost money. They cannot be done well as extracurricular or part-time activities. Devoting resources to study may mean a sacrifice in program resources that administrators are unwilling to make.

Government administrators and program supporters are ingenious in devising reasons why negative findings about policy impact should be rejected. Even in the face of clear evidence that their favorite programs are useless or even counterproductive, they will argue that

1. The effects of the program are long-range and cannot be measured at the present time.

2. The effects of the program are diffuse and general in nature; no single criterion or index adequately measures what is being accomplished.

3. The effects of the program are subtle and cannot be identified by crude measures or statistics.

4. Experimental research cannot be carried out effectively because to withhold services from some persons to observe the impact of such withholding would be unfair to them.

5. The fact that no difference was found between persons receiving the services and those not receiving them means that the program is not sufficiently intensive and indicates the need to spend *more* resources on the program.

6. The failure to identify any positive effects of a program is attributable to inadequacy or bias in the research itself, not in the program.

Recently Harvard Professor James Q. Wilson formulated two general laws to cover all cases of social science research on policy impact:

*Wilson's First Law:* All policy interventions in social problems produce the intended effect—if the research is carried out by those implementing the policy or their friends.

*Wilson's Second Law:* No policy intervention in social problems produces the intended effect—*if* the research is carried out by independent third parties, especially those skeptical of the policy.

Wilson denies that his laws are cynical. Instead he reasons that

Studies that conform to the First Law will accept an agency's own data about what it is doing and with what effect; adopt a time frame (long or short) that maximizes the probability of observing the desired effect; and minimize the search for other variables that might account for the effect observed. Studies that conform to the Second Law will gather data independently of the agency; adopt a short time frame that either minimizes the chance for the desired effect to appear or, if it does appear, permits one to argue that the results are "temporary" and probably due to the operation of the "Hawthorne Effect" (i.e., the reaction of the subjects to the fact that they are part of an experiment); and maximize the search for other variables that might explain the effects observed.[9]

## PPBS, Social Indicators, and Other Evaluative Tools

Despite these difficulties, however, there has been substantial progress in recent years in policy evaluation research. Increasingly, decision makers are turning to analysts to ask questions about the effectiveness of ongoing and proposed programs: What is it doing? Why do we need it? What does it cost? They do not always get good answers yet, but the need for systematic policy research is now recognized.

For example, variations of PPBS—Planning, Programming, Budgeting Systems—have been widely adopted by government agencies in recent years. Despite an elaborate terminology, PPBS is merely an attempt to rationalize decision making in a bureaucracy. It is part of the budgetary process—but the focus is on the *uses* of expenditures and the *output* provided for rather than on dollar amounts allocated by agency or department. The aim of PPBS is to specify, and hopefully to quantify, the output of a government program, and then to minimize the cost of achieving this output and to learn whether benefits exceed the cost. The first step in PPBS is to define program objectives. The next, and perhaps critical step, is to develop indices or measures of the level of accomplishment under each program—the "output." Then the costs of the program can be calculated *per unit of output*. Presumably this enables the decision maker to view the real cost-benefit ratio of a program (e.g., how much it costs to teach one pupil per year, or train one worker in a manpower program, or keep one child in a day-care center, etc.). This also provides a basis for more elaborate comparisons of the costs and benefits of alternative programs, or to analyze the "cost effectiveness" of alternative programs (to see which achieves a given goal at least cost).

[9]James Q. Wilson, "On Pettigrew and Armor," *The Public Interest,* 31 (Spring 1973), 132–34.

Some of the early enthusiasm for PPBS and related tools has cooled. PPBS was first introduced by Secretary Robert N. McNamara in the Defense Department in 1961 as a systematic method of determining the relative costs and benefits of alternative weapons systems. But establishing units of output and their costs and estimating the costs of alternative programs in *domestic* policy fields has proven more complex than similar tasks involving weapons systems.

First of all, it is difficult to establish prices for certain social outcomes, which are not usually sold and therefore have no price. How can we establish the value of finding a cure for cancer? How can we compare the value of finding a cure for cancer with the value of teaching poor children to read and write? A strict cost-benefit comparison would require that we add up the costs and benefits of each and choose the program with the higher excess of benefits over costs. But the benefits of certain programs may be of inestimable value. How do we set values on freedom from fear, good health, the pleasures of clean air, the joys of outdoor recreation, and so forth?

Second, different programs benefit different people. Public funds for higher education benefit middle-class groups more than public funds for literacy training. How do we calculate the benefits of college education for some groups in relation to the benefits of literacy training for other groups, even if costs were the same?

Finally, decision makers are constrained by the political process. They and their constituents have intuitive notions about the relative benefits of health, education, housing, or welfare programs, which are not likely to be changed by cost-benefit estimates.

A number of social scientists have advocated the development of a set of indicators to show social progress (or retrogression). They have urged the preparation of an annual "Social Report" similar to the President's Economic Report but designed to assess the social condition of the nation. Most Americans can agree on the values of a healthy, well-educated, adequately housed, and affluent population, even if they cannot agree on public policies designed to achieve these values. Perhaps a general assessment of the nation's progress toward these goals would be helpful in an overall evaluation of the effectiveness of public policy. At least that is the idea behind this "social indicator" movement. "Social indicators" are defined simply as quantitative data that serve as indices to socially important conditions of a society.

Presumably a set of social indicators and a social report would accomplish two things: first, it would focus attention on certain social conditions and thus make possible more informed judgments about national priorities, and second, by showing how different measures of social well-being change over time, it might help evaluate the success of public programs. In exploring the feasibility of social reporting, a team of social scientists working for the Department of Health, Education and Welfare suggested the development of a variety of measures similar to those shown in Table 15–2. Some of these social measures deal with health, education, and welfare; others with social trends such as women in the labor force, voter turnout, and vacations and leisure time. In 1976, the U.S. Department of Commerce collected some trend data on a wide variety of social indicators and published a report with a great many tables and figures similar to Figures 15–3 and 15–4. But more than anything else, the initial studies revealed great gaps in available information about the health and happiness of the American people.

**TABLE 15–2**  Suggested Social Indicators

| Indicator |
| --- |
| 1. Infant Mortality (per 1,000 live births) |
| 2. Maternal Mortality (per 100,000 live births) |
| 3. Family Planning Services (for Low-Income Women 15–44) |
| 4. Deaths from Accident (per 100,000 population) |
| 5. Number of Persons in State Mental Hospitals |
| 6. Expectancy of Healthy Life |
| 7. Three- to five-year-olds in School or Preschool |
| 8. Persons 25 and Older Who Graduate from High School |
| 9. Persons 25 and Older Who Graduate from College |
| 10. Persons in Learning Force |
| 11. Percent of Major Cities with Public Community Colleges |
| 12. Number of First-year Students in Medical Schools |
| 13. Handicapped Persons Rehabilitated |
| 14. Average Weekly Hours of Work—Manufacturing |
| 15. Labor Force Participation Rate for Women Aged 35–64 |
| 16. Average Annual Paid Vacation—Manufacturing |
| 17. Housing Units with Bathtub or Shower |
| 18. Percent of Population Illiterate |
| 19. Voters as a Percentage of Voting Age Population |
| 20. Private Philanthropy as a Percent of GNP |
| 21. Public and Private Expenditures for Health, Education and Welfare as a percent of GNP |
| 22. Percent of Population in Poverty |
| 23. Income of Lowest Fifth of Population |
| 24. Persons Who Work during the Year |
| 25. Life Expectancy |

*Source:* U.S. Department of Health, Education and Welfare, *Toward a Social Report* (Ann Arbor: University of Michigan Press, 1970).

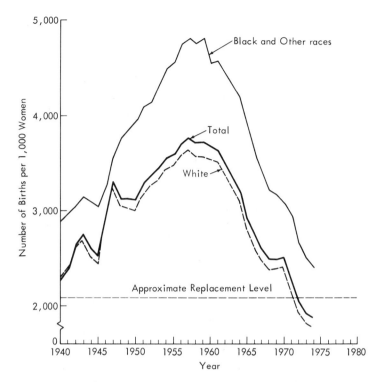

**FIG. 15–3** Fertility rates by race: 1940–1974

*Source:* U.S. Department of Commerce, *Social Indicators 1976* (Washington, D.C.: Government Printing Office, 1977).

But the task of choosing social indicators raises many *political* questions.[10] First of all, the choice of a particular indicator suggests a societal goal. Most people agree on the value of a longer life span and lower infant mortality rates. But should everyone graduate from college? Should every community have a community college? Should a large female labor force be a national goal? Should the government provide free family planning services to low-income families? And how do we set priorities among these goals?

There is a hidden political bias in the social indicators movement itself—a bias on behalf of liberal reform and social welfare. Proponents of social indicators and a Social Report are generally committed to

---

[10]For an excellent discussion of the political implications of social measurement, see Peter J. Henriot's "Political Questions About Social Indicators," *Western Political Quarterly,* 23 (June 1970), 235–55.

**FIG. 15–4**  Life expectancy at birth by sex and race: 1929–1974

*Source:* U.S. Department of Commerce, *Social Indicators 1976* (Washington, D.C.: Government Printing Office, 1977).

long-range government planning, bettering the lot of the poor and of minorities, and using government power to insure social welfare. Conservatives have reason to be suspicious of a movement which assumes that government can select society's goals and monitor progress toward these goals. Moreover, there is the assumption behind the social indicators idea that social measures can and should be affected by government policies. Government monitoring of social indicators *implies* government responsibility for social conditions. Finally, there is a concern that social accounting will lead to a totalitarian society in which every aspect of life is monitored and controlled by government. Even a supporter of social reporting writes:

> Any kind of Social Report would, in the eyes of many, entail a danger: it could involve government in making the kinds of judgments of value that, in our political order, are the prerogatives of the individual citizen or of the organizations of which

> he is a voluntary member. This danger is not imaginary. If—perhaps one should say when—we do have a Social Report, it will be necessary to subject it to rigorous and skeptical criticism.[11]

There is also an implicit political elitism in the notion of social indicators—the view that social scientists are the best judges of what is "good" for the people. In a democratic society, demands for public programs are supposed to originate in the political process from the felt needs of the people. But social accounting implies that social scientists will become "philosopher-kings" deciding what "problems" confront society and what are the "best" solutions for them.

Establishing a government agency to monitor social progress in the nation raises still other political questions: How will social indicators, and by implication social goals, be chosen? What influences will lobbying pressures have on the selection of indicators and the gathering of data? What safeguards are necessary in the "management" of data? To whom will the data used for social indicators be made available? What are the dangers to privacy that an extensive system of social records might involve?

## Experimental Policy Research:
## The Guaranteed Income Experiment

Many policy analysts argue that "policy experimentation" offers the best opportunity to determine the impact of public policies. This opportunity rests upon the main characteristics of experimental research: the systematic selection of experimental and control groups, the application of the policy under study to the experimental group only, and the careful comparison of differences between the experimental and the control group after the application of the policy.

Perhaps the best-known example of an attempt by the federal government to experiment with public policy is the New Jersey Graduated Work Incentive Experiment funded by the Office of Economic Opportunity. The experiment was designed to resolve some serious questions about the impact of welfare payments on the incentives for poor people to work.[12] In order to learn more about the effects of the present welfare system on human behavior, and more importantly, to learn more about the possible effects of proposed programs for guaranteed family incomes, the OEO funded a three-year social experi-

[11]Irving Kristol, "Social Indicators, Reports and Accounts," *The Annals* (March 1970), 11.

[12]See Harold M. Watts, "Graduated Work Incentives: An Experiment in Negative Taxation," *American Economic Review*, 59 (May 1969), 463–72.

ment involving 1,350 families in New Jersey and Pennsylvania. The research was conducted by the Institute for Research on Poverty of the University of Wisconsin.

Debates over welfare reform had generated certain questions which social science presumably could answer with careful, controlled experimentation. Would a guaranteed family income reduce the incentive to work? If payments were made to poor families with employable male heads, would the men drop out of the labor force? Would the level of the income guarantee or the steepness of the reductions of payments with increases in earnings make any difference in working behavior? Because current welfare programs do not provide a guaranteed minimum family income, make payments to families with employable males, or graduate payments in relation to earnings, these questions could only be answered through *policy experimentation*. But policy experimentation raised some serious initial problems for OEO. First of all, any experiment involving substantial payments to a fair sampling of families would be expensive. For example, if payments averaged $1,000 per year per family, and if each family had to be observed for three years, and if 1,000 families were to be involved, a minimum of $3 million would be spent even *before* any consideration of the costs of administration, data collection, analysis and study, and reporting. Ideally a *national* sample should have been used, but it would have been more expensive to monitor than a local sample, and differing employment conditions in different parts of the country would have made it difficult to sort out the effects of income payments from variations in local job availability. By concentrating the sample in one region, it was hoped that local conditions would be held constant. Ideally *all* types of low-income families should have been tested, but procedure would have necessitated a larger sample and greater expense. So only poor families with an able-bodied man age 18 to 58 were selected; the work behavior of these men in the face of a guaranteed income was of special interest.

To ascertain the effects of different levels of guaranteed income, four guarantee levels were established. Some families were chosen to receive 50 percent of the Social Security Administration's poverty level income, others 75 percent, others 100 percent, and still others 125 percent. In order to ascertain the effects of graduated payments in relation to earnings, some families had their payments reduced by 30 percent of their outside earnings, others 50 percent, and still others 70 percent. Finally, a control sample was observed—low-income families who received no payments at all.

The experiment was begun in August, 1968 and continued until September, 1972. But political events moved swiftly and soon engulfed the study. In 1969 President Nixon proposed the Family Assistance

Plan (FAP) to Congress, which, initially at least, guaranteed all families a minimum income of 50 percent of the poverty level and a payment reduction of 50 percent of outside earnings. The Nixon Administration had not waited to learn the results of the OEO experiment before introducing FAP. Nixon wanted welfare reform to be his priority domestic legislation and the bill was symbolically numbered HR 1 (House of Representatives Bill 1).

*After* the FAP bill had been introduced, the Nixon Administration pressured OEO to produce favorable supporting evidence in behalf of the guaranteed income—specifically, evidence that a guaranteed income at the levels and graduated sublevels proposed in FAP would *not* induce incentives to work among the poor. The OEO obliged by hastily publishing a short report, "Preliminary Results of the New Jersey Graduated Work Incentive Experiment," which purported to show that there were no differences in the outside earnings of families receiving guaranteed incomes (experimental group) and those who were not (control group).[13]

The director of the research, economics professor Harold Watts of the University of Wisconsin, warned that "the evidence from this preliminary and crude analysis of the earliest results is less than ideal." But he concluded that "no evidence has been found in the urban experiment to support the belief that negative-tax type income maintenance programs will produce large disincentives and consequent reductions in earnings." Moreover, the early results indicated that families in all the separate experimental groups, with different guaranteed minimums and different graduated payment schedules, behaved in a fashion similar to each other and to the control group receiving no payments at all. Predictably, later results confirmed the preliminary results, which were produced to assist the FAP bill in Congress.[14]

However, when the results of the Graduated Work Incentive Experiment later were *reanalyzed* by the Rand Corporation (which was not responsible for the design of the original study), markedly different results were produced.[15] The Rand Corporation reports that the Wisconsin researchers working for OEO originally chose New Jersey because it had no state welfare programs for "intact" families—families

[13]U.S. Office of Economic Opportunity, "Preliminary Results of the New Jersey Graduated Work Incentive Experiment," February 18, 1970. Also cited in Alice M. Rivlin, *Systematic Thinking for Social Action* (Washington, D.C.: Brookings Institution, 1971).

[14]*Final Report of the New Jersey Graduated Work Incentive Experiment*, David Kershaw and Jerelyn Fair (eds.). (University of Wisconsin, Institute for Research on Poverty, 1974).

[15]John F. Cogan, *Negative Income Taxation and Labor Supply: New Evidence From The New Jersey-Pennsylvania Experiment* (Santa Monica: Rand Corporation, 1978).

headed by an able-bodied, working age male. The guaranteed incomes were offered to these families to compare their work behavior with control group families. *But,* six months after the experiment began, New Jersey changed its state law and offered *all* families (experimental *and* control group families) very generous welfare benefits—benefits equal to those offered participants in the experiment. This meant that for most of the period of the experiment, the "control" group was being given benefits which were equivalent to the "experimental" group—an obvious violation of the experimental research design. The OEO-funded University of Wisconsin researchers failed to consider this factor in their research. Thus, they concluded that there were no significant differences between the work behaviors of experimental and control groups, and they implied that a national guaranteed income would not be a disincentive to work. The Rand Corporation researchers, on the other hand, considered the New Jersey state welfare program in their estimates of work behavior. Rand concluded that recipients of a guaranteed annual income will work 6.5 fewer hours per week than they otherwise would work in the absence of such a program. In short, the Rand study suggests that a guaranteed annual income will produce a very substantial disincentive to work.

The Rand study was published in 1978 after enthusiasm in Washington for a guaranteed annual income program—or "welfare reform"—had already cooled. The Rand study conflicted with the earlier OEO study and confirmed the intuition of many Congressmen that guaranteed annual income would reduce willingness to work. The Rand study also suggested that a *national* program might be very costly and involve some payments to nearly half the nation's families. Finally, the Rand study noted that its own estimates of high costs and work disincentives may "seriously understate the expected cost of an economy-wide . . . program."

## Problems in Policy Experimentation

The whole excursion into government-sponsored policy impact experimentation raises a series of important questions.[16] First of all, are government-sponsored research projects predisposed to produce results supportive of popular reform proposals? Are social scientists, whose personal political values are generally liberal and reformist, inclined to produce findings in support of liberal reform measures? Would the OEO have rushed to produce "preliminary findings" in the New Jersey

[16]For an excellent discussion of the problems and prospects of experimental policy research, see Frank P. Scioli and Thomas J. Cook, "Experimental Design in Policy Impact Analysis," *Social Science Quarterly,* 54 (September 1973), 271–91.

experiment *if* they had shown that the guarantees did in fact reduce the incentive to work? Or would such early results be set aside as "too preliminary" to publish? Because the participants in the experiment knew that they were singled out for experimentation, did they behave differently than they would have if the program had been applied universally? Would the work ethic be impaired if *all* American families were guaranteed a minimum income for life rather than a few selected families for a temporary period of time? Thus, the questions raised by this experiment affect not only the issues of welfare policy but also the validity of policy experimentation itself.

Experimental strategies in policy impact research raise still other problems. Do government researchers have the right to withhold public services from individuals simply to provide a control group for experimentation? In the medical area, where the giving or withholding of treatment can result in death or injury, the problem is obvious and many attempts have been made to formulate a code of ethics. But in the area of social experimentation, what are we to say to control groups who are chosen to be similar to experimental groups but denied benefits in order to serve as a base for comparison? Setting aside the legal and moral issue, it will be politically difficult to provide services for some people and not others. Perhaps only the fact that relatively few Americans knew about the New Jersey experiment kept it from becoming a controversial topic.

Another reservation about policy impact research centers on the bias of social scientists and their government sponsors. "Successful" experiments—where the proposed policy achieves positive results—will receive more acclaim and produce greater opportunities for advancement for social scientists and administrators than will "unsuccessful" experiments. Liberal, reform-oriented social scientists *expect* liberal reforms to produce positive results. When reforms appear to do so, the research results are immediately accepted and published; but when results are unsupportive or negative, social scientists may be inclined to go back and recode their data, or redesign their research, or reevaluate their results because they believe a "mistake" must have been made. The temptation to "fudge the data," "reinterpret" the results, coach participants on what to say or do, and so forth, will be very great. In the physical and biological sciences the temptation to "cheat" in research is reduced by the fact that research can be replicated and the danger of being caught and disgraced is very great. But social experiments can seldom be replicated perfectly, and replication seldom brings the same distinction to a social scientist as does the original research.

People behave differently when they know they are being watched. Students, for example, generally perform at a higher level when something—anything—new and different is introduced into the classroom routine. This "Hawthorne effect"[17] may cause a new program or reform to appear more successful than the old, but it is the newness itself that produces improvement rather than the program or reform.

Another problem in policy impact research is that results obtained with small-scale experiments may differ substantially from what would occur if a large-scale nationwide program were adopted. For example, a guaranteed annual income for a small number of families in New Jersey and Pennsylvania—a guarantee that lasted only three years—may not trigger as much change in attitudes toward work as a *nationwide* program guaranteed to last indefinitely. In the New Jersey experiments, its members may have continued to behave as their neighbors did. But if everyone had been guaranteed a minimum income, community standards might have changed and affected the behavior of all recipient families.

Finally, we must acknowledge that the political milieu shapes policy research. Politics helps decide what policies and policy alternatives will be studied. Certainly the decision to study the effects of a guaranteed annual income arose from the interest of reformers in proving that such a program would not reduce incentives to work, as charged by some opponents. Politics can also affect findings themselves, and certainly the interpretations and uses of policy research are politically motivated. Can it be merely coincidental that the guaranteed annual income was found to have no adverse effects when it was widely supported in the early 1970s, but it was later found to have major adverse effects on working behavior in the late 1970s after support for the program had declined?

Despite these problems, the advantages of policy experimentation are substantial. It is exceedingly costly for society to commit itself to large-scale programs and policies in education, welfare, housing, health, and so on, without any real idea about what works. Increasingly, we can expect the federal government to strive to test newly proposed policies and reforms before committing the nation to massive new programs.

## The Limits of Public Policy

Never have Americans expected so much of their government. Our confidence in what governments can do seems boundless. We have

---

[17]The term is taken from early experiments at the Hawthorne plant of Western Electric Company in Chicago in 1927. It was found that worker output increased with any change in routine, even decreasing the lighting in the plant. See David L. Sills, ed., *International Encyclopedia of the Social Sciences*, 7 (New York: Free Press, 1968), 241.

come to believe that governments can eliminate poverty, end racism, ensure peace, prevent crime, restore cities, provide energy, clean the air and water, and so on, if only they will adopt the right policies.

Perhaps confidence in the potential effectiveness of public policy is desirable, particularly if it inspires us to continue to search for ways to resolve societal problems. But any serious study of public policy must also recognize the limitations of policy in affecting societal conditions. Let us summarize these limitations:

1. Some societal problems are incapable of solution because of the way in which they are defined. If problems are defined in *relative* rather than *absolute* terms, they may never be resolved by public policy. For example, if the poverty line is defined as the line which places one-fifth of the population below it, then poverty will always be with us regardless of how well-off the "poor" may become. Relative disparities in society may never be eliminated. Even if income differences among classes were tiny, then tiny differences may come to have great symbolic importance, and the problem of inequality may remain.

2. Expectations may always outrace the capabilities of governments. Progress in any policy area may simply result in an upward movement in expectations about what policy should accomplish. Public education never faced a "dropout" problem until the 1960s when, for the first time, a majority of boys and girls were graduating from high school. At the turn of the century, when high school graduation was rare, there was no mention of a dropout problem. Graduate rates have been increasing every year, as has concern for the dropout problem.

3. Policies that solve the problems of one group in society may create problems for other groups. In a plural society one man's solution may be another man's problem. For example, solving the problem of inequality in society may mean redistributive tax and spending policies which take from persons of above-average wealth to give to persons with below-average wealth. The latter may view this as a solution, but the former may view this as creating serious problems. There are *no* policies which can simultaneously attain mutually exclusive ends.

4. It is quite possible that some societal forces cannot be harnessed by governments, even if it is desirable to do so. It may turn out that government cannot stop urban migration patterns of whites and blacks, even if it tries to do so. Whites and blacks may separate themselves regardless of government policies in support of integration. Some children may not be able to learn much in public schools no matter what is done. Governments may be unable to forcibly remove children from disadvantaged environments because of family objections even if this proves to be the only way to ensure equality of opportunity, and so on. Governments may not be *able* to bring about some societal changes.

5. Frequently people adapt themselves to public policies in ways

that render the policies useless. For example, we may solve the problem of poverty by government guarantees of a high annual income, but by so doing we may reduce incentives to work and thus swell the number of dependent families beyond the fiscal capacities of government to provide guarantees. Of course, we do not really *know* the impact of income guarantees on the work behavior of the poor, but the possibility exists that adaptive behavior may frustrate policy.

6. Societal problems may have multiple causes, and a specific policy may not be able to eradicate the problem. For example, job training may not affect the hard-core unemployed if their employability is also affected by chronic poor health.

7. The solution to some problems may require policies that are more costly than the problem. For example, it may turn out that certain levels of public disorder—including riots, civil disturbances, and occasional violence—cannot be eradicated without the adoption of very repressive policies—the forceable break-up of revolutionary parties, restrictions on the public appearances of demagogues, the suppression of hate literature, the addition of large numbers of security forces, and so on. But these repressive policies would prove too costly in terms of democratic values—freedom of speech and press, rights of assembly, freedom to form opposition parties. Thus, a certain level of disorder may be the price we pay for democracy. Doubtless there are other examples of societal problems that are simply too costly to solve.

8. The political system is not structured for completely rational decision making. The solution of societal problems generally implies a rational model, but government may not be capable of formulating policy in a rational fashion. Instead the political system may reflect group interests, elite preferences, environmental forces, or incremental change, more than rationalism. Presumably, a democratic system is structured to reflected mass influences, whether these are rational or not. Elected officials respond to the demands of their constituents, and this may inhibit completely rational approaches to public policy. Social science information does not exist to find policy solutions even if there are solutions. Moreover even where such information exists, it may not find its way into the political arena.

## Bibliography

HATRY, HARRY P., RICHARD E. WINNIE, and DONALD M. FISK, *Practical Program Evaluation.* Washington, D.C.: Urban Institute, 1973.

NACHMIAS, DAVID, *Public Policy Evaluation.* New York: St. Martin's, 1979.

RIVLIN, ALICE M., *Systematic Thinking for Social Action.* Washington, D.C.: Brookings Institution, 1971.

SUCHMAN, EDWARD A., *Evaluative Research*. New York: Russell Sage Foundation, 1967.

U.S. Department of Health, Education and Welfare, *Toward A Social Report*. Washington, D.C.: Government Printing Office, 1969.

WHOLEY, JOSEPH S., et al., *Federal Evaluation Policy*. Washington: Urban Institute, 1970.

# Index